[redacted]

F

PONS
Collins
Business English Dictionary

PONS

COLLINS

Business English Dictionary

von

P. J. Flynn und M. J. Wallace

Deutsche Berater

D. Förtsch, H. Pesch, U. Pesch-Itzstein

Klett

PONS Collins Business English Dictionary

Von: P. J. Flynn und M. J. Wallace
Deutsche Berater: D. Förtsch, H. Pesch, U. Pesch-Itzstein

CIP-Kurztitelaufnahme der Deutschen Bibliothek

Flynn, Patrick J.:
Pons Collins business English dictionary / von
P. J. Flynn u. M. J. Wallace. Dt. Berater
D. Förtsch ... – 1. Aufl. – Stuttgart :
Klett, 1986.
ISBN 3-12-517180-6
NE: Wallace, Michael J.:; HST

ISBN 3-12-517180-6

1. Auflage 1986

Druck: Collins Clear-Type Press
Printed in Great Britain

Contents

Vorwort

Das PONS Collins Business English Dictionary enthält die Bedeutungserklärungen zu den über 4.000 gebräuchlichsten Wörtern und Wendungen aus einer großen Vielfalt von Situationen des Wirtschafts- und Geschäftslebens. Neben den zentralen Begriffen aus den Bereichen *management, marketing, accountancy* und *production* u.a. werden dabei auch einige inzwischen weitverbreitete Begriffe aus der Datenverarbeitung abgehandelt. Das Schwergewicht in der Auswahl der wirtschaftssprachlichen Begriffe liegt auf dem britischen Englisch, doch werden auch wichtige und nützliche amerikanische Begriffe erklärt.

Beispiel:
Dow Jones Index
postcode (*US* zipcode)

Im Anschluß an die leicht verständliche englischsprachige Erklärung der Stichworteinträge steht der entsprechende deutsche Begriff.

In einem zweiten Teil des Wörterbuches sind die deutschen wirtschaftssprachlichen Entsprechungen noch einmal alphabetisch aufgeführt, so daß das Suchen und Nachschlagen eines Begriffes sowohl vom englischen als auch vom deutschen her erfolgen kann. Insofern vereinigt das PONS-Collins Business English Dictionary die Vorzüge eines einsprachigen Erklärungswörterbuches mit denen eines zweisprachigen Nachschlagewerkes.

Alphabetische Anordnung

Sämtliche Stichwörter erscheinen in streng alphabetischer Anordnung. Im Falle von Wendungen, wie z.B. **on record,** richtet sich die alphabetische Einordnung nach dem wichtigsten, funktionstragenden Bestandteil.

Beispiel:
on record steht unter **record.**

Klare Definitionen

Das Wörterbuch wurde unter der Zielsetzung verfaßt, daß insbesondere die Bedürfnisse von Nichtengländern bzw. Lernern von Englisch als Fremdsprache berücksichtigt wurden. So ist allergrößte Sorgfalt darauf verwandt worden, die Bedeutungserklärungen so klar und leicht verständlich wie irgend möglich abzufassen. Der Definitionswortschatz kommt weitgehend mit rund 2000 Wörtern aus. In der Regel sind Wörter, die in den Erklärungen benutzt werden und außerhalb des Definitionswortschatzes liegen, **halbfett** gedruckt. Somit ist angezeigt, daß diese Wörter im Wörterbuch definiert werden. Um Mißverständnissen vorzubeugen, sind halbfett gedruckte Wörter, die unmittelbar nach dem Hauptstichwort stehen, von diesem durch einen Doppelpunkt (:) getrennt.

Beispiel:
new issue : **shares** offered to the public for the first time.

Beispielsätze

Um die Bedeutungen sinnfällig und eindeutig zu machen und um aufzuzeigen, wie die Wörter und Wendungen im Kontext gebraucht werden, wurden zahlreiche Beispielsätze hinzugefügt.

Beispiel:
Market demand the total sales of a **product** in a period (usually a year). *The market demand for our brand of soup is 12,000,000 cans this year.*

Verweise

Gibt es zwei oder mehr gleichbedeutende Bezeichnungen für ein und dieselbe Sache, so wird aufeinander verwiesen.

Beispiel:
fixed expense *see* **fixed charge**

Außerdem wird auf solche Wörter verwiesen, die in einem wichtigen Bedeutungszusammenhang mit dem Stichwort stehen.

Beispiel:
macroeconomics the study of the whole **economy** of a country i. e. a country's production, demand, prices, **imports, exports** etc. and their effects on each other. *See also* **microeconomics.**

Wortarten

Wortarten sind in den Fällen angegeben, wo das gleiche Wort mehr als einer Wortart angehört.

Beispiel:
export *verb* und **export** *noun*

Stilangaben

Die Sprachgebrauchsebene eines Wortes ist bezeichnet, wenn sie vom umgangssprachlichen Standard abweicht.

Beispiel:
dole *(informal)*, **emolument** *(formal)* **Murphy's Law** *(informal and humorous)*

Fachgebietsangaben

Wo es nützlich schien, ist hinter dem Stichwort das Fachgebiet angezeigt, dem das Stichwort in seiner angegebenen Bedeutung zuzurechnen ist.

Beispiel:
attachment *(law,)*
lay days *(shipping)*

A

A1 (1) best quality. *Your goods must be in A1 condition.* (2) tested and found in excellent condition according to **Lloyd's Register of Shipping**

◆ (1) erstklassig (2) erstklassige Schiffsbeschaffenheit

ABC *see* **Audit Bureau of Circulation**

above-the-line advertising expenditure money paid for advertising in any of the following **media:** cinema, magazines, newspapers, posters, radio, television

◆ Kosten für klassische Anzeigenwerbung

absenteeism failure of workers to go to work, often without good reason

◆ (unentschuldigtes) Nichterscheinen bei der Arbeit

absentee landlord one who owns property but rarely visits it and who appoints an agent to collect the rent

◆ nicht ortsansässiger Haus-, Grundbesitzer

absolute address the exact position of a piece of information in the **memory** of a **computer**

◆ absolute Adresse

absolute monopoly the complete control by one company or organisation of the production of a **product** or the supply of a **service** for which there are no others offered. *British Rail have an absolute monopoly of intercity rail service*

◆ uneingeschränkte marktbeherrschende Stellung

absorption the taking over of a small company by a larger one; during this **process** the small company may lose its original name. *See also* **takeover, merger**

◆ Firmenübernahme

absorption costing a method of deciding how much it costs to produce something. The total costs are divided by the number of units produced so that each unit carries the same share of all the costs

◆ Produktionskostenaufteilung auf unfertige Erzeugnisse

abstract short form of a report or **document.** *An abstract of the report has been prepared so that you don't have to read the whole thing*

◆ Kurzfassung

accelerator a **theory** that the amounts of money which a company spends on new factories or machinery depends on the amount that people spend in the shops. Thus if people spend more money this extra spending will cause an increase in the amount that companies will spend on new factories or machines or materials for making goods. This in turn will make more jobs and more spending

◆ Akzelerationsprinzip

acceptable quality level the greatest amount of faulty units that will be allowed by a **production manager**

◆ höchstzulässige Produktionsausschußquote

acceptance a written promise to pay the amount shown on a **bill of exchange.** The person accepting the conditions on the bill of exchange (the **acceptor**) will do so by signing across the face of the bill

◆ Akzept

access a way in which something can be reached or entered

◆ Zugriff

access time the amount of time between asking for and getting information from a **computer**

◆ Zugriffszeit

accident insurance: insurance covering loss as a result of injury or death from an accident

◆ Unfallversicherung

accommodate to lend money over a period of time taken to arrange a formal loan

◆ eine Übergangsfinanzierung gewähren

accommodation money lent over a short period of time until the borrower can find other **funds.** *We are urgently looking for an accommodation from the bank to cover our expenses for the next few days*

◆ Übergangsfinanzierung

accommodation bill a type of **bill of exchange;** the person who signs it has received no goods or services in exchange but is only helping someone by means of the bill to raise money

◆ Gefälligkeitswechsel

accommodation party a **party** who accepts or signs an **accommodation bill**

◆ (Wechsel-) Begünstigter

account (1) a record or statement of money received and paid out. *See also* **account balance, current account.** (2) an arrangement for keeping money in a bank etc. (3) a regular customer of a company. *This firm bought £1,000 of our goods last week — it's becoming one of our best accounts* (4) **on account** as an advance payment for money that is owed. *Can you give me £6 on account now and the rest next week*

◆ (1) Aufzeichnung der Einnahmen und Ausgaben (2) Bankkonto (3) Kunde (4) (als) Anzahlung

accountancy the profession of an **accountant;** the management of the **financial** affairs of a company. *See also* **accounting**

◆ Buchführungswesen

accountant a person who is qualified to record and report on the movement of money into and out of a company and also to prepare a company's **annual accounts**

◆ Bilanzbuchhalter; Abschlußprüfer

account balance (1) the amount that is overpaid or is owing for goods or **services.** (2) the difference between the totals of all the **debit** entries and all the **credit** entries in an **account**

◆ (1) Saldo (2) Kontosaldo

account executive a person, especially in an **advertising agency,** who is responsible for all matters relating to one or more customers (**accounts**) of a company, and who tries to improve business relations between the accounts and the company. *See also* **account** (meaning 3)

◆ Verbindungsmann; Stammkundenbetreuer

accounting the activity of recording and reporting on the movement of money or goods into and out of a company. *See also* **accountancy**

◆ Buchführung

accounting machine a machine for preparing **invoices, payrolls** and other **accounting** records

◆ Buchungsmaschine

accounting period (1) the normal time between the date of one **balance sheet** of a company and the date of the next. (2) the period of time, e.g. a week or a month, at the end of which a company regularly examines its financial position

◆ (1) Abrechnungszeitraum (2) Rechnungsabschnitt

account payable the amount of money owed by a buyer to a seller for goods or **services** received

◆ Verbindlichkeiten

account payee only words written across the face of a cheque. They mean that the amount shown on the cheque will be paid only into the **bank account** of the person who is to receive the money

◆ nur zur Verrechnung

account receivable the amount of money owed to a company by a customer (or **debtor**)

◆ ausstehende Forderungen

account stated the **account** between two people or organisations who have been trading with each other showing a balance which they have agreed upon

◆ anerkannter Rechnungssaldo

accredited agent an agent who has **documents** from a company which prove that he has power to act on behalf of that company

◆ bevollmächtigter Vertreter

accrued charges expenses which have occurred and which are due to be paid at a date in the future. For example, if a company pays for electricity at the end of every three months then the cost of the first month's electricity is an accrued charge

◆ aufgelaufene Kosten

accrued interest the **interest** which is due but not yet paid. For example if a bank pays interest on savings only at the end of the year then the interest due on the first six months' savings is accrued interest

◆ aufgelaufene Zinsen

acid test *see* **liquidity ratio**

acknowledgement a notice to the sender of goods, money, or a letter informing him that they have been received

◆ Empfangsbestätigung

acquisition the act of one company buying another

◆ Firmenaufkauf

acquisitive society a society in which people always want to buy the very latest things on the market, sometimes used to describe the people of the rich places of the world

◆ Erwerbsgesellschaft; die Oberen Zehntausend

across-the-board applying to everyone, to all cases: *an across-the-board wage increase* i.e. the same amount of increase is given to each worker in the factory

◆ allgemein

action *(law)* a civil case in a court of law

◆ Zivilverfahren

action limit **(quality control)** the line on a chart which shows when action must be taken to reject or improve a **product**

◆ Aktionsschwelle

active partner one who shares in the ownership of a company and takes an active part in the running of the business. *See also* **sleeping partner**

◆ tätiger Teilhaber

activity chart a chart which shows each part of the work to be done and also the time for each part of the work to be finished

◆ Arbeitsgliederungsplan

activity sampling recording of the work that is being done by a worker or a machine at certain times so that total work done over the whole period can be **estimated**

◆ stichprobenartige Fertigungskontrolle

act of bankruptcy any action by which a **debtor** becomes liable to be judged by the court as unable to pay his debts (i.e. be judged **bankrupt**), e.g. the act of leaving the country to avoid paying bills, the informing of **creditors** that he cannot pay his debts

◆ Konkursvoraussetzung

act of God something unexpected which happens without human help, e.g. a flood which destroys a factory or a storm that sinks a ship

◆ höhere Gewalt

ad. *(informal) short for* **advertisement**

added value *see* **value added**

address the position of information in the **memory** of a **computer**

◆ Adresse

addressing machine an office machine for putting addresses on envelopes or letters, using metal plates each of which has a separate address on it

◆ Adressiermaschine

adjourn *(formal)* to end (a meeting) for a stated time

◆ vertagen

adjournment *(formal)* the act of **adjourning.** *The Chairman called for an adjournment until Tuesday*

◆ Vertagung

adjudication the decision of a court of law between two **parties,** e.g. between a company and a **trade union**

◆ gerichtliche Entscheidung

adjuster (insurance) a person who **assesses** losses for an **insurance company**

◆ Schadenssachverständiger

adjusting entry something written into a company's accounts, done so that the accounts will show the correct financial position at a certain date. For example, if an error is found then an adjusting entry would be made instead of the error itself being changed

◆ Berichtigungsbuchung

administration (*or, informal* **admin.**) (1) the controlling or managing of something, especially a public or private organisation. (2) paperwork in a company such as form-filling or letter-writing

◆ (1) Verwaltung (2) Geschäftsverkehr

administrative expenses money that a company pays which is separate from the costs of actually producing the goods in the factory, e.g. the salaries of office staff or the cost of telephone and postage

◆ Verwaltungskosten

administrator (1) a person who controls or directs the affairs of a company. (2) a person who is appointed by a court to take charge of the possessions of someone who has died without leaving a will

◆ (1) Verwalter (2) Nachlaßverwalter

ad valorem *(Latin)* according to value, usually used of a tax or duty put on certain goods by a country. The tax will vary according to the value of the goods

◆ nach dem Wert

advance (1) a loan or **overdraft** from a bank. (2) a loan by a company to a worker until his wages are paid. (3) a payment by a company of part of the cost of goods or **services** which it has still to receive

◆ (1) Überziehungskredit (2) Vorschuß (3) Vorauszahlung

advance factory *(UK)* a factory built in certain areas of the country before it is really needed in the hope that businessmen will rent or buy it and so attract work in that area

◆ Industriepark in Vorlage

adverse trade balance (*or* **adverse balance of trade**) a situation when the value of a country's **exported** goods is less than the value of its **imported** goods. *See also* **balance of trade**

◆ passive Handelsbilanz

advertise to make (something, usually goods or **services**) known to companies or the general public, e.g. by means of newspapers, magazines, posters, **point-of-sale,** cinema, television or radio

◆ werben

advertisement (1) a notice of something which is being **advertised.** (2) the act of **advertising**

◆ (1) Anzeige (2) Werbung

advertisement manager the person in charge of the selling of **advertising**

on behalf of a company owning one of the following: newspapers, magazines, cinemas, television stations, radio stations or poster sites. *Compare with* **advertising manager**

◆ Anzeigenleiter

advertising the planning or **publishing** of facts or opinions to arouse people's interest and persuade them, e.g. to buy something

◆ Anzeigenwesen

advertising agency a company which provides the **services** of designing and making **advertisements,** placing them in suitable **advertising media,** and carrying out research

◆ Werbeagentur

advertising manager a person in charge of planning and overseeing a company's advertising. *Compare with* **advertisement manager**

◆ Werbeleiter

advertising media the means by which a company informs people of its goods or services, e.g. newspapers, magazines, posters, cinemas, television and radio

◆ Werbeträger

advertising rates the basic charges made by the owners of the **advertising media** for the use of their **services.** *See also* **advertisement manager**

◆ Anzeigentarif

advertising strategy the overall plan of how, where, when and at what cost a company's **advertising** will be carried out

◆ Werbestrategie

advertising theme the subject matter which is repeated in all of a company's **advertising,** e.g. the goodness of the product *(Guinness is good for you)* or the low prices

◆ Werbethema

advice note a printed sheet sent by a supplier to a customer containing details (e.g. quantity, weight) of goods ordered but not yet delivered

◆ Versandanzeige

advocate *(in Scotland)* a **barrister**

◆ beim Supreme Court zugelassener Rechtsanwalt

affiliated company a company that is owned by another company, but usually managed separately

◆ Tochtergesellschaft

affluence the state of being affluent

◆ Wohlstand

affluent having plenty of money and or possessions: *the affluent society,* i.e. people in rich countries who have plenty of money to spend

◆ wohlhabend

after-sales service service provided by a seller to a buyer after the sale has been made, e.g. advice, repairs or **servicing** of goods. *Our garage gives free after-sales service*

◆ Kundendienst

agency (1) the business, or office of an agent. (2) a business or organisation which gives a certain **service**

◆ (1) Agentur (2) Dienstleistungsunternehmen

agenda a list of what is to be discussed at a meeting

◆ Tagesordnung

agent a person who represents another person, company, etc., with that person's or company's approval, often with a written **contract** stating this

◆ Vertreter

agent's commission the sum of money paid to an **agent** for selling something for someone else, usually an agreed percentage of the selling price

◆ Vertreterprovision

agreed procedure the steps which

should be taken in an agreed order, to help in the smooth running of a business, e.g. for the settling of any dispute between a company and its workers

◆ vereinbarte Verfahrensordnung

agreement (1) a **contract,** usually written, between one person or company and another. (2) the act or fact of agreeing

◆ (1) Vertrag (2) Einwilligung

AIDA the first letters of 'Attention, Interest, Desire, Action'. These are the **responses** of a buyer that some salesmen are trained to get so that a sale can be made

◆ AIDA-Formel

aided recall (**market research**) a method used to help a person remember a **product** or an advertisement by reminding the person of something connected with the product or advertisement. For example when used to test how good an advertisement has been the person might be shown part of the advertisement to see if he can remember the rest of it

◆ Erinnerungshilfe

air cargo (*or* **air freight**) goods which are sent by air

◆ Luftfracht

air terminal a place in a town where one can get transport to and from an airport. *See also* **terminal**

◆ Terminal

air waybill (*or* **air consignment note**) a **document** prepared by the carrier of the goods (or his **agent**) stating the nature of the goods, the name of the sender and the charges for carrying the goods. The conditions of the **contract** of carriage are usually included

◆ Luftfrachtbrief

ALGOL (*stands for* Alg(orithmic) O(riented) L(anguage)) a **computer language** used mainly for **programming** scientific problems

◆ ALGOL

all found of wages, with all the necessary things (e.g. accommodation, meals etc.) provided. *His army pay was fifty pounds a week all found*

◆ alles in allem

all-in-rate (*or* **all-in-price**) a rate or price that includes all the extras which are in addition to the basic rate or price. For example an **all-in-price** of a **product** to a buyer would include delivery charge, duty, tax, etc

◆ Inklusivpreis

allocation a part that is given; a share of something. For example, a buyer may want ten cases of some **product** which is in short supply but his allocation may only be five

◆ Zuteilung

allocation of overheads the charging of a part of a cost or overhead to a particular department of a company, e.g. a part of the total rent to each department of a large store

◆ Geschäftskostenaufteilung

allotment the number of **shares** which have been given to people who have applied to buy a new issue of shares

◆ Zuteilung

allowance (1) a sum of money given regularly, e.g. an allowance of £50 per week to a salesman for travelling expenses. (2) money taken off the cost or price of something, usually for a special reason. For example, a shop may make an allowance of £10 off the price of a new television set because the buyer has pointed out a slight mark on it. (3) the allowed difference of size in the manufacture of a **product.** For example, a company may decide to make steel bars 250 millimetres long with an allowance of 1 millimetre either way. In this case bars of 251 and 249 millimetres would be acceptable. (4) the amount of a person's **income** on which **income tax** is not charged

◆ (1) regelmäßiger Zuschuß (2) Preisnachlaß (3) Toleranz (4) Steuerfreibetrag

allowed time the time agreed between a company and a worker for certain activities, e.g. meals, or cleaning his/her machine

◆ Vorgabezeit

amalgamate to join together (two or more companies or groups). *In 1976 the trade unions for engineering workers and foundry workers joined to form the Amalgamated Union of Engineering and Foundry Workers*

◆ fusionieren

amalgamation the act of **amalgamating**

◆ Fusion

amortization the recovery of money, in parts, over a period of time, e.g. when payment is made by **instalment,** or, if a company buys a machine which it thinks will last five years it may decide to recover this money by charging its **profit and loss account** with one-fifth of the machine's value each year, for five years. *See also* **depreciation**

◆ Amortisation

analog computer a **computer** in which the **data** are represented by measurements (lengths, angles, voltages) rather than by numbers, used especially in science and industry. *See also* **digital computer**

◆ Analogrechner

analyse to make an **analysis** of

◆ analysieren

analysis the breaking down of something into parts so that a closer study can be made. *Total sales this year were above last year's total but an analysis has shown that sales to most European countries were less this year*

◆ Analyse

annual *adjective* yearly; appearing or happening once a year: *annual report*

◆ jährlich

annual *noun* a book or magazine produced once a year, with the same title but different information for each year

◆ Jahrbuch

annual abstract of statistics a book produced each year by the UK government giving details of all the main features of the **economy**

◆ ≃ Statistisches Jahrbuch

Annual General Meeting a company meeting which takes place once a year to which all its **shareholders** are invited, as requested by law. At this meeting the year's **profit and loss account** and **balance sheet** are discussed, and **directors** of the company are appointed

◆ Jahreshauptversammlung

annual report a report sent each year by a company to the members of the company, and to certain other persons. It usually contains the **profit and loss account, balance sheet** and details of the company's activities during the previous twelve months

◆ Jahresbericht

annuity a fixed sum of money which is paid yearly to a person for a number of years. Annuities can be bought from an **assurance company.** For example, a person could arrange with an assurance company to pay the company now an agreed sum of money in return for a yearly income, or annuity, of (say) £1,000 from his sixty-fifth birthday until his death

◆ jährliche Zahlung

anticipated profit a profit which is yet to be earned, e.g. the profit a company will earn on goods that are made but not yet sold

◆ erwarteter Gewinn

anti-dumping duty a tax on certain **imported** goods to prevent them being sold at prices lower than the home-produced goods

◆ Antidumpingzoll

anti-trust legislation *(US)* laws to encourage competition, usually price competition, by preventing **mergers** or **amalgamations** which could result in higher prices

◆ Kartellgesetzgebung

applicant a person who puts in an **application** for something

◆ Bewerber

application (1) a request for something, e.g. a job, a place in a college etc. *Applications must be in by Friday.* (2) a way in which something can be put to use. *The new invention has several applications in industry.* (3) (**computers**) a type of problem to which **data-processing** methods can be applied. (4) hard work: *to succeed by sheer application*

◆ (1) Bewerbung; Antrag (2) Anwendung(-smöglichkeit) (3) Anwendung (4) Fleiß

application form a **document** which is filled in and signed by a person who is applying for something, e.g. a job, a passport, a driving licence

◆ Bewerbungs-; Antragsformular

application package (**computers**) a **program** which has been designed to do a special job, e.g. list all the sales figures, or keep up to date all the wages to be paid

◆ Anwendersoftware

applied economics the part of **economics** which has to do with the study of practical problems, e.g. the study of the selling price and demand for UK oil

◆ angewandte Volkswirtschaft

apply (1) to use for a certain purpose. *They applied all their resources to the building up of new business.* (2) **apply for** to make a (formal) request for (something), usually in writing: *to apply for a job.* (3) to put onto. *Apply the glue with a knife.* (4) to be effective or fitting. *These rules do not apply here*

◆ (1) verwenden (2) sich bewerben um; beantragen (3) auftragen (4) zutreffen

appraisal interview a discussion to judge the value of a person using the **appraisal method**

◆ Beurteilungsgespräch

appraisal method a method of judging the ability of a person to do his work. This method requires the manager and the worker to agree on a certain plan of work, to train the worker to do that work and then after an agreed time to review what has been achieved by the worker. *See also* **appraisal interview**

◆ Methode zur Leistungsbeurteilung einer Person

appreciate to increase in value. *Because the company has been making large profits the market value of its shares has appreciated*

◆ Wertsteigerung erfahren

appreciation an increase in the value of something. *The appreciation in value of my house is due to the high demand for houses in this area*

◆ Wertsteigerung

apprentice a young person who works for a company for an agreed number of years to learn a trade

◆ Auszubildender

apprenticeship (the time of) being an **apprentice.** *I want to be an engineer but it requires a five-year apprenticeship*

◆ Lehre

appropriation the practice of setting aside a sum of money for a special purpose. *The company's advertising appropriation this year will be £100,000*

◆ Bereitstellung von Geldmitteln

appropriation account the part of the **profit and loss account** which shows how the **net profit** is divided between **tax, dividends** and **reserves**

◆ Aufstellung über die Verteilung des Bilanzgewinns

approval: on approval a method of selling goods by which they are sent, at the buyer's request, for examination. If he does not like them he will send them back within an agreed time. If he likes them (i.e. if they meet with his **approval**) he will keep them and pay within an agreed time

◆ zur Ansicht

aptitude test a type of examination used to judge if a person will be able to do a certain type of job

◆ Eignungsprüfung

arbitration the method used to settle a **dispute** between the people involved (e.g. **a trade union** and a **company**) by which they agree that the dispute will be decided by an independent person (the **arbitrator**)

◆ Schiedsverfahren

arbitration clause a condition in a **contract** which states that if there is a **dispute** between the **parties** to the contract the matter will be settled by a fair and independent person (the **arbitrator**)

◆ Schiedsklausel

arbitrator a person chosen by the **parties** in a **dispute** to settle any matter on which they cannot agree. The arbitrator is chosen in the belief that he/she will be fair and will suggest a method of agreement based on common sense rather than law

◆ Schiedsmann

archive (1) a place in which records of various kinds are stored for reference. (2) (**computers**) the place in which information is stored and to which the computer has not got direct **access**

◆ (1), (2) Archiv

area sample a method of **sampling** whereby a number of towns, or districts are first randomly selected (i.e. chosen by chance) and then within those chosen a **random sample** is taken. *See also* **stratified sampling, cluster sampling**

◆ Flächenstichprobe

arithmetic mean the result when all the quantities in a set of quantities are added together and the total is divided by the number of quantities in the set. For example, the arithmetic mean of 3, 1, 6, 2 and 8 is found by dividing the total (20) by the number of quantities (5) which is 4. Often shortened to **mean** or **average**

◆ arithmetisches Mittel

array (1) a series of numbers arranged in a specific order, e.g. from the highest to the lowest. (2) a set of numbers arranged in rows and columns

◆ (1) Zahlenfolge (2) Matrix

arrears money that is due but not yet paid. *See also* **fall into arrears**

◆ Zahlungsrückstände

articles of association the rules and conditions covering the relationship between a company, its **shareholders** and its directors

◆ Satzung einer Gesellschaft

artwork the original drawings or pictures for something, e.g. an **advertisement**

◆ Bildentwurf

'A' shares (*or* **non-voting shares**) **shares** in a company which have the same rights as **ordinary shares** but do not allow the owner to vote at a meeting of **shareholders** of the company

◆ stimmrechtslose Aktien

assembly line a method of manufacture by which a **product** passes along a line of workers or machines in a factory. At each stage along the line work is done on the product until it is completed

◆ Fließband

assess to judge the quality or worth of (a person or thing)

◆ einschätzen

assessment a judgement, e.g. of the ability of a person to do a certain task. *The company makes an assessment of the progress of all trainee managers every three months*

◆ Einschätzung

assessor (1) a person who decides the amount of tax to be paid by someone. (2) person who decides the value of damage done to property for **insurance** purposes

◆ (1) Steuerschätzer (2) Schadensabschätzer

asset something that is owned by a person or a company, such as money, a building, a car. *See also* **fixed assets** *and* **current assets**

◆ Vermögenswert

asset stripping the act of taking over a company and then selling off the **assets** to make a profit

◆ Aufkauf eines Unternehmens und anschließende Anlagenausschlachtung

assign (1) to **transfer** to others (the rights to money or property). This can be done legally by a deed of assignment. (2) to set aside for someone's use. *An office will be assigned you for the time you are working here*

◆ (1) übereignen (2) zuteilen

assignee the person to whom something has been **assigned**

◆ Zessionar

assignment (1) the **transfer** to another of rights to money or property. (2) a signed agreement about a transfer of rights to money or property. (3) a task that has been given to a person. *He is working abroad on a special assignment*

◆ (1) Übereignung (2) Übertragungsurkunde (3) Auftrag

assignor a person who **assigns**

◆ Zedent

associated company a company which is partly owned by another company (i.e. between 20% and 49% of its **shares** are owned by another company)

◆ Beteiligungsgesellschaft

associate director a person who acts as a director of a company with the company's approval, but who has not been formally appointed as a director

◆ Führungskraft, noch nicht offiziell zum Direktor ernannt

associated states non-member states of the **EEC** which have special trade agreements with the EEC

◆ Assoziierte Staaten

Association of Scientific, Technical, and Managerial Staffs (*or* **ASTMS**) a UK **trade union** for professional and clerical workers

◆ Gewerkschaft für wissenschaftliche, technische und leitende Mitarbeiter

assurance *see* **insurance**

assurance company *see* **insurance company**

assured a person who enters into an **assurance** contract

◆ Versicherter

ASTMS *see* **Association of Scientific, Technical, and Managerial Staffs**

ATM (*or* **Automatic Teller Machine**) a **computerised cash dispenser,** used mainly in banks

◆ Geldautomat

attachment *(law)* the stopping of the sale, or disposal, of a **debtor's** money or goods (which are in the hands of a third **party**) until the settlement of a **claim** against the debtor

◆ Pfändung

attitude survey (1) (**market research**) a method of finding out what people think of a **product,** by question-and-answer or by group discussion. (2) a method used to find out what workers think of their work, or workplace, or company, with a view to improving these

◆ (1) Meinungsumfrage (2) betriebliche Meinungsumfrage

attorney (1) a person who is appointed to act on behalf of someone else, especially in legal matters, or under the **power of attorney.** (2) (*US*) a lawyer

◆ (1) Bevollmächtigter (2) Anwalt

Attorney General the chief legal officer of the government in some countries

◆ Kronanwalt; Generalstaatsanwalt; ≃ Generalbundesanwalt

auction *noun* a method of selling goods in which the goods are sold to the highest bidder. These sales usually take place in auction rooms where buyers can see the goods to be auctioned

◆ Auktion

auction *verb* to sell goods in this way

◆ versteigern

auctioneer a person who sells goods at an **auction.** He is an agent of the owner of the goods offered for sale, and is paid a **commission** on the sale of the goods to the highest bidder

◆ Auktionär

audience (1) a group of people reading, listening, watching any of the **media,** but especially television, cinema or radio. (2) a group of people listening to or watching a performance such as a play, speech or film

◆ (1) Zuschauer; Zuhörer (2) Publikum

audience research the finding out of facts about what kind of people watch certain television programmes, read certain newspapers etc; such information is useful e.g. in deciding where to advertise

◆ Leserforschung; Hörerforschung

audio-visual aids teaching aids which can be both seen and heard such as films, television or slices with spoken explanations

◆ audiovisuelle Lehrmittel

audit *noun* an examination of a company's **books of account** to make sure they are a fair and true record of a company's trading

◆ Revision

audit *verb* to examine (**books of account**) in this way

◆ Revision durchführen

Audit Bureau of Circulation (**ABC**) *(UK)* an organisation which provides proof of the actual sales of newspapers and magazines

◆ freiwillige Auflagenselbstkontrolle

auditor a person appointed by a company to examine the **books of account.** He/she has to state if the accounts are a fair and true record and the resulting report becomes part of the company's **annual report**

◆ Revisor

authorised capital the amount of **capital** up to which a company may issue **shares.** A company's authorised capital will be stated in its **memorandum and articles of association** and is usually also shown in the company's **balance sheet.** *See also* **nominal capital**

◆ Grundkapital

authority the power to do something or to get others to do something. *Do you have authority to sign this cheque? The manager has the authority to employ or dismiss work-*

ers. (2) an organisation which has certain powers, especially from the government: *a local authority*

◆ (1) Befugnis (2) Behörde

automatic data processing any form of **processing** of information (data) by a machine

◆ automatisierte Datenverarbeitung

Automatic Teller Machine *see* **ATM**

automatic vending the sale of goods, such as cigarettes, from a machine where one pays by putting money into the machine. *There is an automatic vending machine on each floor*

◆ Automatenverkauf

automation the use of machines that need little or no human control to do work which used to be done by people

◆ Automatisierung

autonomous work groups a group of workers who decide their own output of work, when and how the work will be done and who will do it. Sometimes also they carry out their own trading. In a company with autonomous work groups, the management are advisors only and do not make decisions for the group

◆ autonome Arbeitsgruppen

average (1) *see* **arithmetic mean.** (2) (**marine insurance**) sharing of the loss of a ship's **cargo** amongst several **insurers**

◆ (2) Versicherungsschadensumwälzung

average cost the cost resulting from dividing the total **costs** (**fixed costs** plus **variable costs**) by the number of units produced

◆ Durchschnittskosten

average fixed cost the cost resulting from dividing the total **fixed costs** by the number of units produced

◆ durchschnittliche Fixkosten

average variable cost the cost resulting from dividing the total **variable costs** by the number of units produced

◆ durchschnittliche variable Kosten

award a decision reached by an **arbitrator** when a **dispute** between two **parties** has been sent to him for settlement

◆ Schiedsspruch

B

back cover (**advertising**) the outside of the back page of a magazine which carries an advertisement

◆ vierte Umschlagseite

backdate to put a date on (an agreement or **document**) which is earlier than the date on which it was drawn up. For example, on 30 June a **trade union** may reach an agreement with a company for a wage increase which is backdated to 1 June

◆ rückdatieren

back duty tax which should have been paid in the past and which is payable now

◆ Steuerrückstand

backer a person or organisation that supports a business idea with money

◆ Kapitalgeber

backlog (1) an amount of work which has gathered over some time and which still has to be done, e.g. when one has been on holiday, or away from work through illness. (2) an amount of goods which still have to be sold

◆ (1) Arbeitsrückstand (2) Warenrückstände

back pay wages which are due for work done but which were not paid at the proper time

◆ Nachzahlung von Lohnrückstand

back-to-back credit: credit given to a foreign buyer by a UK bank or **finance** house which is acting as a contact between a foreign seller and the foreign buyer. The seller gives the papers covering the sale to the UK bank (or finance house) which then issues them in its own name to the buyer, the seller's name being kept secret

◆ Gegenakkreditiv

back-up something ready to be used in place of another should it fail, e.g. a back-up power supply to be used if electricity should fail

◆ Reserve-

back-up storage (**computers**) tape or disk copies of informaton for use if the computer's original tapes or disks should be lost or damaged

◆ Reservespeicher

backward integration taking over by a company of another company which supplies it with **raw materials** or parts for manufacture, e.g. if a company which sells canned foods takes over the company which supplies the cans

◆ Geschäftsausweitung durch Aufkauf der Zulieferfirmen

bad debt money which is unlikely to be paid, and which is treated as a loss. *The company finally went bankrupt because it had so many bad debts*

◆ uneinbringliche Forderung

bad faith (in) a dishonest state of mind; (with) an intention to cheat. *You don't have to follow a contract if you can prove it was signed in bad faith*

◆ Unredlichkeit

bailee a person who has possession of the goods of another for a certain purpose with the agreement of that other, e.g. a shoe repairer, a garage, a dry-cleaner

◆ Treuhänder

bailor a person who gives his goods or property to a **bailee**

◆ Hinterleger

balance *noun* (1) the difference between the total **credit** entries and the total **debit** entries in an **account.** (2) what is left over; the remainder

◆ (1) Saldo (2) Rest

balance *verb* to make the total **credit** entries equal the total **debit** entries of (an **account**)

◆ saldieren

balance brought forward (*or* **balance b/fwd**) the net **balance** on an **account** brought forward from the previous **accounting period**

◆ Saldovortrag

balance carried forward (*or* **balance c/fwd**) the net **balance** on an **account** brought forward to the next **accounting period**

◆ Saldoübertrag

balance in hand money which can be used for payments

◆ Kassenbestand

balance of payments a country's **balance sheet** of total payments to other countries and the total received from them of goods and **services.** *See also* **balance of trade, invisible assets**

◆ Zahlungsbilanz

balance of trade the difference between a country's **exports** and **imports** of goods. The balance of trade is said to be favourable when the value of exported goods is more than the value of imported goods

◆ Handelsbilanz

balance sheet a statement showing the value of a company's **assets** and its **liabilities** at a certain date

◆ Bilanzaufstellung

balance-sheet ratios methods of using figures from a balance sheet to show how well or badly a company or its management are doing. Often figures from the **profit and loss account** are also used to give either a **ratio** or percentage measurement.

See also **current ratio, debtors to sales ratio, liquidity ratio, return on capital employed,** and Appendix 2

◆ Analyse der Bilanzverhältniszahlen

balanced budget a plan in which the expected **income** matches the expected payments

◆ ausgeglichener Haushalt

balancing item an entry of an amount of money in the **balance of payments** account to correct any errors made in the account during a particular period

◆ Ausgleichsposten

ballast heavy material which a ship carries to keep it steady at sea

◆ Ballast

banded pack a form of **sales promotion** in which two or more **products** are bound together, usually with tape with the details of the reduced-price offer

◆ Mehrfachpackung im Einführungsangebot

bank a company with which money is placed to be kept securely and where it can earn **interest,** and where loans and other **financial** business are carried out

◆ Bank

bank account an **account** (meaning 2) with a bank. *See also* **current account, deposit account**

◆ Bankkonto

bank-book a book in which a record of the money one puts into and takes out of a bank is kept, a **passbook**

◆ Sparbuch

bank charge an amount charged by a bank for its **services**

◆ Bankgebühr

bank cheque *see* **bank draft**

bank deposit any money paid into a **current account** or a **deposit account** in a bank

◆ Bankeinlage

bank draft (*or* **bank cheque** *or* **banker's draft**) a cheque drawn by a bank promising to pay a stated sum on demand at a named office of the bank

◆ Banktratte

banker's order instructions to a bank to pay a stated sum of money to a person or organisation at certain dates

◆ Dauerauftrag

Bank for International Settlements (*or* **BIS** *or* **BIZ**) an international bank established by agreement with the Swiss government in 1930 in order to encourage the co-operation of the central banks of twenty-nine countries. It also acts as an **agent** in the settlement of international **financial** matters. Membership: the central banks of twenty-five European countries plus Japan, South Africa, Turkey and the United States. Headquarters: Basel, Switzerland. Official languages: English, French, German, Italian

◆ Bank für Internationalen Zahlungsausgleich (BIZ)

bank giro a method by which payment of an **account,** or other payments, can be made using **giro** forms available in UK banks

◆ Überweisung

bank holiday *(UK)* any normal working day on which banks and certain public offices are closed by law

◆ öffentlicher Feiertag

bank hours the times when banks are open to the public to do business

◆ Geschäftszeiten

bank loan any loan of money by a bank for a certain period at an agreed **interest rate**

◆ Bankkredit

banknote a **document** from a bank which promises to pay the bearer on demand and which is used as money

◆ Banknote

bank overdraft the amount of cash which a bank allows a customer to draw out of his **account** and which is more than the amount that he or she has actually paid in. It is therefore a loan from the bank, and **interest** is charged on it

◆ Überziehungskredit

bank reserves the money held by a bank to meet demands by customers

◆ Liquiditätsreserven

bankrupt *adjective* unable to pay one's debts

◆ insolvent

bankrupt *noun* a person who has been legally judged to be unable to pay his/her debts

◆ Insolvent

bankrupt *verb* to make (a person) **bankrupt**

◆ in den Konkurs treiben

bankruptcy the state of being **bankrupt**

◆ Insolvenz

bank statement a list, sent by a bank to a customer showing the amount of money paid into and taken out of the customer's **account** with the bank, and the **balance** remaining

◆ Kontoauszug

bar chart information given in the form of broad lines or **columns** drawn on paper, e.g. showing a company's sales for each month of the year. The difference in the height of the columns shows the difference between sales each month

◆ Balkendiagramm

bargain *verb* to talk about an agreement or **contract** with the aim of changing or impoving some part of it. *The union bargained for hours with the management over the amount of the wage increase*

◆ verhandeln

bargain *noun* (1) an agreement. *They finally struck a bargain on the price.* (2) something that is being sold for less than its real value. *They are selling it for £10 off the usual price — it's a bargain*

◆ (1) Einigung (2) günstiges Angebot

barratry any unlawful act done by a captain or crew of a ship to harm the owner's rights, e.g. sinking the ship or stealing the ship

◆ Baratterie

barrister a lawyer who has the right to speak and argue in the higher courts of law in England

◆ Prozeßanwalt

barter *verb* to exchange goods for other goods by way of payment, instead of using money. *The two countries bartered wheat in exchange for oil*

◆ Tauschhandel treiben

barter *noun* this system of exchange: *to trade by barter*

◆ Tauschhandel

base rate the lowest rate of **interest** which **clearing banks** offer to **depositors** of money. The rate of interest charged to borrowers will vary from ½% to 5% above that for **deposits**, depending on the kind of loan. The clearing bank base rate changes from time to time depending on economic conditions

◆ Eckzins der Londoner Clearing-Banken

BASIC (*stands for* Beginner's All-purpose Symbolic Instruction Code) a **computer language** which uses ordinary English words

◆ BASIC

basic rate (1) (*also* **basic wage**) the lowest possible wage that can be paid for a job, not counting **overtime.** (2) the lowest rate of **income tax** which applies when **allowances** have been taken off **income**

◆ (1) Ecklohn (2) Eingangssteuersatz

batch an amount of materials or parts of a **product** which is ordered or produced at one time. *We will need to make a batch of 25-millimetre screws for today's orders*

◆ (Produktions-) Menge

batch processing (computers) groups of records which are **processed** by the computer, one group at a time, e.g. if a company first enters all its **invoices** on the computer, followed by information on (say) **stocks,** then wages

◆ Stapelverarbeitung

batch production manufacture of the same article in groups rather than singly, e.g. the manufacture of metal screws of the same size, or the manufacture of shoes of the same size. *See also* **batch, mass production**

◆ Serienproduktion

bear (stock market) a person who sells **shares** in the belief that their price is about to fall. He or she may then buy them back more cheaply. *See also* **bull, bear market**

◆ Baissier

bearer a person who is in possession of a **document,** e.g. of a **bill of exchange** which is 'payable to bearer' i.e. payable to the holder of the bill

◆ (Wechsel-) Inhaber

bearer bonds: documents of ownership to **stocks, shares, debentures** etc. Ownership can be **transferred** by simply handing the bonds over to someone else, as bearer bonds are made out to 'bearer' and not to a name person

◆ Inhaberobligation

bearish (stock market) having or expecting falling **share** prices

◆ baissetendenziös

bear market (stock market) a situation when the price of shares is falling. *See also* **bull market**

◆ Baisse

below-the-line promotion expenditure money spent to increase sales by means other than advertising in newspapers, magazines, television, radio, cinema or posters, e.g. by offering prizes with a **product,** or giving one free with every one bought or paying for a **sponsored** event. *See also* **sales promotion**

◆ Werbeaufwand durch Sachleistungen

bench mark anything by which something else can be measured. *We should aim for a profit of £1 on every £10 of sales — that's the bench mark for success in our business*

◆ Maßstab

beneficiary a person who receives some gain, especially money or property

◆ Begünstigter

benefit-in-kind a gain or advantage, other than the payment of money, e.g. the regular use of a company car given to a worker

◆ Sachleistung

Benelux Economic Union a group of three countries (Belgium, Luxembourg and Netherlands) formed to develop **economic** links and to have a common **policy** also in **financial** and social matters. The present organisation was created 1958. Headquarters: Brussels. Official languages: French, Dutch

◆ Benelux

bequest a gift of money or property left in a will. *See also* **legacy**

◆ Vermächtnis

b/f *see* **brought forward**

bias *noun* a tendency to favour one point of view although there is not enough proof, or the proof is faulty

◆ Voreingenommenheit

bias *verb* to cause to have a **bias.** *The sample was biased in favour of male tastes*

◆ jmd. in eine bestimmte Richtung lenken

bid (1) an offer to buy something at a certain price, especially at an **auction.** (2) an offer by one company to buy all the **shares** of another. *See also* **takeover bid**

◆ (1) Gebot (2) Übernahmeangebot

bilateral agreement an arrangement or **contract** between two sides, e.g. two companies

◆ bilaterales Abkommen

bilateral trade the exchange of goods and/or **services** between two countries

◆ bilateraler Handel

bill *noun* (1) *see* **bill of exchange.** (2) an **invoice.** (3) a statement of the amount that has to be paid for goods or **services,** especially in a restaurant or hotel (*US* **check**). (4) **take up a bill** (*or* **retire a bill**) to pay a **bill of exchange** on or before the date on which it is due

◆ (2), (3) Rechnung (4) Wechsel einlösen

bill *verb* to send or give (someone) an **invoice** or statement of the amount that has to be paid

◆ eine Rechnung ausstellen

bill-broker a person or company that buys **bills of exchange** and **promissory notes,** often at less than their **nominal value** in order to cash them or else to sell them again

◆ Wechselmakler

billing the total amount of business done by an **advertising agency** during a certain period

◆ Umsatz einer Werbeagentur

bill of entry *(UK)* a **document** required by **Customs** and Excise showing details of goods that are to be **imported**

◆ Zolldeklaration

bill of exchange a written order without any conditions addressed by one person to another, signed by the person giving it, requiring the person to whom it is addressed to pay immediately or at some stated time a certain amount of money to a named person, or to the bearer of the bill; often used for foreign trade

◆ Wechsel

bill of health a certificate which states whether or not the crew of a ship are known to be suffering from any disease which can be easily spread to other people. A statement that they are not suffering from such a disease is called a **clean bill of health**

◆ Hafengesundheitsbescheinigung

bill of lading (*or* **B/L**) **(exporting)** a **document** which states the **terms** and conditions under which goods are to be transported, giving the name and address of the customer receiving the goods and the details of the goods themselves

◆ Konnossement

bill of sale a written agreement which gives the legal ownership of goods to another person, but not the actual possession of the goods. A bill of sale is often used to raise money, the borrower taking back the legal ownership when he repays the money borrowed

◆ Sicherungsübereignungsurkunde

bills payable (accounting) bills of exchange held and due for payment by the holder at some time in the future

◆ Wechselverbindlichkeiten

bills receivable (accounting) bills of exchange held and due to be paid to the holder at some time in the future

◆ Wechselforderungen

binary code: computer data or computer instructions written using the **binary system**

◆ Binärcode

binary system (**computers**) a number system in which there are only two base numbers (0 and 1); thus in binary system 1 = 01 but 2 = 10, 3 = 11, 4 = 100

◆ binäres Zahlensystem

bin card (*or* **bin tag**) a card kept near a container showing the amount of goods in it and sometimes showing also the amount ordered, amount sold from the container etc

◆ Lagerfachkarte

BIS *or* **BIZ** *see* **Bank for International Settlements**

bit the smallest piece of information in a **computer**, i.e. either 1 or 0. *See also* **binary system**

◆ Bit

black *verb* of workers, to refuse to handle (certain goods) because they think that to handle them will be against either their own interest or the interest of some other workers. For example during a **strike**, goods normally handled by the **strikers** may be **blacked** by other workers

◆ bestreiken

black *noun:* **in the black** having money in one's bank account. *We're in the black again at last*

◆ in den schwarzen Zahlen

blackball to exclude (a person) from a club or society by means of a secret vote of the members

◆ durch Geheimwahl ausschließen

black economy that part of the **economic** activity of a country which is carried out in secret to avoid paying tax, or because the activity is illegal

◆ Schattenwirtschaft

blackleg (*or* **scab**) *noun* a person who continues to work during a **strike**, or who takes the place of someone else who is on strike

◆ Streikbrecher

blackleg (*or US* **scab**) *verb* to act in this way

◆ sich als Streikbrecher betätigen

blacklist *noun* a list of persons or organisations who are considered to be slow payers of **bills**, or non-payers of bills, often made up by **credit agencies**

◆ schwarze Liste

blacklist *verb* to put the name of (a person or organisation) on such a list

◆ auf die schwarze Liste setzen

black market a **system** involving the illegal buying or selling of goods or **currencies** when their sale is **rationed** or officially controlled

◆ Schwarzmarkt

blank cheque (1) a cheque which is fully completed except for the amount of money to be paid, which the person cashing the cheque can fill in. (2) **give someone a blank cheque** to allow someone an unlimited amount of money to spend

◆ (1) Blankoscheck (2) jmd. einen Blankoscheck ausstellen

blank endorsement the act of writing one's name on the back of a **bill of exchange** etc. so that it becomes payable to the person who possesses it (the **bearer**)

◆ Blankoindossament

blanket agreement an agreement on wages or conditions of work etc., reached between representatives of the employers and representatives of the workers. A blanket agreement applies throughout the whole industry and not just certain factories

◆ ≈ Manteltarifvertrag

blanket coverage advertising which is directed at the public generally and not a specified **target audience**

◆ Mengenumwerbung

blanket policy an **insurance policy** which covers many different types of risk, e.g. a house may be insured against fire, theft and other risks under one blanket policy

◆ Pauschalpolice

blending mixing together of different kinds or quantities of something (often tea, coffee, whisky or tobacco) in order to make it more attractive to a possible buyer

◆ mischen; verschneiden

blind test a method of finding out how popular a new **product** might be with possible customers; members of the public are asked to give their opinion of a product without being given any information about what **brand** it is

◆ anonymer Test

block *noun* (1) a metal, rubber or plastic plate used for printing photographs or drawings. (2) **(computers)** a group of **characters** (letters, numbers etc.) which is treated as a unit

◆ (1) Klischee (2) Block

block *verb* (1) to make or form into a block. (2) to prevent the use or transfer of (money or other assets), usually for a political or legal reason. *See* **blocked account**

◆ (1) Klischee herstellen (2) sperren

blocked account a **bank account** from which no cash may be withdrawn except (perhaps) under certain conditions. For example a government may block the accounts of all foreigners, either completely or by stating that the cash in the account must be spent in the country in which it has been banked

◆ Sperrkonto

blocked currency coins and notes used within a country which may not be taken out of the country, e.g. because the country has **balance of payments** problems

◆ nicht frei konvertierbare und transferierbare Währung

block release a system of training by which trainees are allowed to leave their jobs for blocks of time (e.g. several weeks) with full pay so that they can go to an institute of further or higher education. *See also* **day release, sandwich course**

◆ blockweise Freistellung von Auszubildenden zur Weiterbildung

block vote (*or* **card vote**) a form of voting often used in **trade union** conferences where the voting power is decided by the number of workers which each **delegation** is supposed to represent. Thus a delegation which represents three million members could outvote two delegations which represent only one million members each

◆ geschlossene Stimmabgabe

blow up *verb* to make (a photograph, or part of a photograph) much bigger

◆ vergrößern

blow-up *noun* a photograph, or part of a photograph that has been made much bigger

◆ Vergrößerung

blue book *(informal)* a yearly report by the UK Central Statistical Office called **National Income and Expenditure,** containing a great deal of information relating to **economic** trends in the UK

◆ Blaubuch; ≃ Statistisches Jahrbuch

blue-chip investment an **investment** which is thought to be very safe, often because the company involved is a very large one, has been operating for some time and is known for good management. *See also* **gilt-edged securities**

◆ erstklassige, sichere Wertpapieranlage

blue-collar workers people who work with their hands in industry, especially to distinguish them from office-workers or **white-collar workers**

◆ Fabrikarbeiter

blueprint (1) a special type of photographic print of a design or technical drawing in which the design or drawing appears in white on blue paper. (2) a plan or way of doing something which has been followed by others or which has been laid out in some detail

◆ (1) Blaupause (2) aufgezeigte Vorgehensweise

blurb a written description of something which is intended to persuade people to buy the thing described, especially the description put on the cover of a book by a publisher

◆ Klappentext

board of directors a group of senior **executives** of a company who are responsible for directing the **policy** of the company and who have the final powers of control within the company

◆ Verwaltungsrat (mit Funktionen des Vorstands und Aufsichtsrates)

body copy the main text of written matter in an advertisement, as opposed to the headlines or illustrations that go with the advertisement

◆ Haupttext einer Anzeige

bold face a printing type consisting of thick black letters which makes words more easily noticed, as with the headwords of this dictionary

◆ Fettdruck

bona fide *(Latin)* done in **good faith,** without trying to hide something which should be known. For example a **contract** may not be **valid** if it has not been made in good faith: *a bona fide agreement. See also* **bad faith, good faith**

◆ in gutem Glauben

bond *noun* (1) a legal written promise to pay a sum of money at a certain time, or under certain conditions. Government and public companies issue bonds in return for money lent to them. *See also* **debentures, bearer bonds.** (2) **in bond** of goods, kept in a special store called a **bonded warehouse,** until duty is paid or until the goods are cleared from bond for **exporting**

◆ (1) Obligation (2) unter Zollverschluß liegen

bond *verb* (1) to put (goods) into a **bonded warehouse.** (2) *(law)* to place (a person) under a bond

◆ (1) unter Zollverschluß legen (2) jmd. zu etwas verpflichten

bonded goods goods on which **duty** has to be paid and which are kept in a **bonded warehouse** until removed for sale. Such goods are said to be **in bond,** a **bond** being signed by the owners stating that the duty will be paid when the goods are removed for sale

◆ Waren unter Zollverschluß

bonded warehouse a place where goods on which **duty** is due may be kept until the duty is paid or until the goods are cleared (examined) by **customs** for **export**

◆ Zollgutlager

bonding of salesmen a system by which an employer **insures** himself against dishonesty or carelessness by salesmen that he employs

◆ Vertreterhaftungsvertrag

bonus an extra amount of money paid out which is above what has been agreed; thus an employee may get a Christmas bonus in addition to his usual wages, or extra pay for successful work, a **shareholder** may get a **bonus issue,** or a person who has **invested** in an **insurance policy** may get a bonus **dividend**

◆ Bonus

bonus issue (*or* **scrip issue**) the giving out of **shares** to **shareholders** in a company in proportion to the number of shares they already have

◆ Ausgabe von Gratisaktien

bonus pack a way of making a **product** more attractive to customers by giving more than the usual amount of the product but at the same price as would be charged for the usual amount

◆ Bonuspackung

bonus payment a method of rewarding successful workers, e.g. salesmen, by giving them a **bonus**

◆ Zahlung von Prämien

book debts amounts due from **debtors** in the **books of account**

◆ Außenstände

book-keeping the recording of the **accounts** of an organisation

◆ Buchführung

books of account the records in which the **financial** affairs (**transactions**) of a business are shown. They may be in book form, on cards, on **magnetic tape** or on **magnetic disks**

◆ Geschäftsbücher

book token a **voucher** (meaning 2) which can be exchanged for a book or books in a bookshop

◆ Büchergutschein

book value the worth of a company's **assets** as shown in its **accounts.** The **market value** of the assets may be much higher. For example, the value of a company's buildings will be reduced in the accounts each year by a certain amount (**depreciation**)

◆ Buchwert

boom *noun* (1) a time of very fast general **economic** growth, bringing with it an increase in wages, prices, profits, employment and business opportunities. *See also* **depression, recession, slump, trade cycle.** (2) a time of fast growth and/or increased profits in a company

◆ Hochkonjunktur

boom *verb* to experience a **boom.** *The country is booming. The oil business is booming*

◆ einen rapiden Aufschwung nehmen

boom *adjective* showing fast growth and/or increased profits: *a boom economy*

◆ aufblühend

boom market a market in which demand is greater than supply, causing an increase in prices

◆ Haussemarkt

bought-out parts parts of a company's **products** which are bought from other companies

◆ Zulieferteile

bounce *(informal)* of a cheque, to be returned by a bank to the person or company presenting it for payment because there is not enough cash in the **account** of the person who has signed it to cover the amount of the cheque

◆ platzen

bourse *(French)* term used in France and certain other countries for a **stock exchange**

◆ Börse

boycott *verb* to avoid social and/or business relations with (a person, a company or a country) in an effort to change their ways of thinking

◆ boykottieren

boycott *noun* the act of **boycotting.** *The country's business was suffering because of a trade boycott*

◆ Boykott

brainstorming a group **technique** used to produce new ideas; the main emphasis is on the quality of ideas produced even though some of them seem ridiculous; at a later stage the ideas are discussed and compared until some practical suggestions appear

◆ Brainstorming

branch *noun* (1) a division or section of a large business which is in a different area from the main division or section, e.g. a branch office. (2) (**computers**) a departure from the normal sequence (order) in a **program**

◆ (1) Zweigstelle (2) Verzweigung

branch *(verb)* (**computers**) to depart from the normal sequence (order) in a **program.** *See also* **branch out**

◆ verzweigen

branch manager a person in charge of a **branch** (meaning 1)

◆ Zweigstellenleiter

branch out to open another section of a business

◆ eine Zweigstelle eröffnen

brand a class of goods from a manufacturer with a name or mark which makes them different from other goods of the same kind. *This is my favourite brand of tea. See also* **trademark**

◆ Marke

brand awareness the extent to which those who are interested in buying a certain kind of goods are familiar with a certain **brand** name in connection with the goods they are interested in

◆ Markenbewußtsein

branded goods goods sold under the **brand** names of their manufacturers or suppliers

◆ Markenartikel

brand image a general idea of a **brand** in the minds of those who might be interested in buying a certain kind of goods

◆ Markenimage

brand leader the goods of a particular **brand** which have the largest share of the market for goods of that type

◆ Spitzenmarke

brand share *see* **market share**

break (*or* **commercial break**) a period of time on radio or television which is used for broadcasting advertisements

◆ Programmunterbrechung zwecks Werbung

breakage (1) the number or amount of goods that have been broken e.g. while being moved from one place to another. (2) payment to replace the value of goods that have been broken

◆ (1) Bruchschaden (2) Entschädigung für Bruchwaren

break even to reach the point where the amount of money that has gone out and the money that has come in are exactly **balanced** and no profit or loss is made. *See also* **break-even point**

◆ plus-minus-null abschließen

break-even analysis a **system** of working out the costs and the **incomes** for different levels of sales in order to find out the level of sales at which no loss (or profit) is made. Sales beyond this level should result in a profit

◆ Break-Even-Analyse

break-even chart a chart which shows the **fixed costs,** the **variable costs,** the total costs and the profit or loss at various levels of sales

◆ Gewinnschwellen-Diagramm

break-even point a point at which the total costs of a **product** or **project break even.** Sales beyond this point should result in a profit

◆ Break-Even-Punkt

breaking bulk the activity of buying goods in large quantities and selling them in smaller quantities, as done by a **wholesaler**

◆ Zerlegen einer Ware durch Großhändler in einzelhandelsfähige Mengen oder Abmessungen

break-up value (*or* **liquidating value**) what the **assets** of a company would be worth if it had to go out of business

◆ Liquidationswert

bribe *verb* to try to persuade (a person) to do something illegal or dishonest by offering something (e.g. a sum of money) in return

◆ bestechen

bribe *noun* what is offered in order to **bribe** a person

◆ Bestechungsgelder

bridging loan a short-term loan of money to allow one to buy one **asset,** e.g. a new house, while awaiting the sale of another asset, e.g. the buyer's present house, to pay for it

◆ Überbrückungsdarlehen

brief *noun* (1) a short list of the main points which must be kept in mind when a course of action is being taken. (2) a list of things which a person in a certain job may or may not do. *It is not within my brief to accept money from clients*

◆ (1), (2) Instruktionen

brief *verb* to tell (a person) the main points about something he/she has to do

◆ instruieren

British Standards Institution (*or* **BSI**) an independent organisation supported by the government, which lays down certain standards, e.g. for measurements of buildings etc

◆ Britischer Normenverband; ≃ Deutscher Normenausschuß

brochure a small thin book produced e.g. to advertise a **service**

◆ Prospekt

broken lot goods for sale in less than the usual quantity, or in a set that is not complete, perhaps because they have been damaged in some way

◆ Restposten

broker an agent who buys or sells goods, **shares, services,** etc. for someone else in return for a **commission** (usually a percentage of the value of the goods etc. sold). *See also* **insurance broker, stockbroker**

◆ Makler

brokerage payment made to a broker by his client for buying or selling goods, **shares, services** etc. for the **client**

◆ Maklergebühr

brought forward (*or* **b/f**) the total of figures at the top of a page which has been carried forward from the bottom of a previous page. *See also* **carry forward**

◆ Übertrag

budget (1) a **financial** plan of what money may be received either over a certain period of time or in connection with a certain project, and how the money will be spent. (2) a national financial plan covering a certain period (usually a year) for what the government expects to receive from taxes etc. and what the money will be spent on; in Britain this plan is usually referred to as **the Budget**

◆ (1) Haushaltsplan (2) Staatshaushalt

budgetary control a method of checking on the **financial** success or failure of a business activity by making detailed **estimates** of everything to do with it over a certain period of time and comparing these with what actually happens so that the right action can be taken. *See also* **master budget**

◆ Haushaltskontrolle

budget period a period of time covered by a **budget**

◆ Haushaltsperiode

buffer stock (*or* **minimum stock** *or* **reserve stock** *or* **safety stock**) the quantity of goods or materials kept in store for future use in case of difficulties in supply, or an unexpected demand for these goods

◆ Vorratslager

building society an organisation which encourages people to save by paying **interest** and then lends this money at a higher rate of interest to people who want to buy their own homes. The money lent to the home-buyers is secured by means of a **mortgage** on the house that has been bought

◆ = Bausparkasse

built-in obsolescence (*or* **planned obsolescence**) a method of increasing sales either by designing the goods sold in such a way that they will last only for a limited time and will have to be replaced, or by regularly introducing designs which will make the customer feel that his present model is out-of-date

◆ geplanter Verschleiß und/oder absichtlich herbeigeführtes Altmodischwerden

bulk buying the buying of goods in large quantities, usually to get them at a lower price

◆ Mengeneinkauf

bulk cargo goods carried in a ship which are all of the same kind, and not usually divided into separate containers, e.g. oil, wheat

◆ Massengutladung

bull (**stock market**) a person who buys **shares** with a view to selling them at a profit before he is due to pay for them. *See also* **bear, bull market**

◆ Haussier

bulletin (1) a newsletter or information sheet from a society, association or other group. (2) an official announcement. (3) a type of news broadcast giving only the main items of news. *See also* **bulletin board**

◆ (1) Bulletin (2) amtliche Bekanntmachung (3) Tagesbericht

bulletin board (1) *(US)* a notice-board on which announcements, advertisements etc. can be placed. (2) a very large painted outdoor advertisement, usually placed in a prominent position, and often lit up in some way

◆ (1) Anschlagtafel (2) Reklamewand

bullion gold or silver in the form of bars or dust, but not in the form of coins

◆ ungemünztes Edelmetall

bullish (**stock market**) having or expecting rising **shares**

◆ haussierend

bull market (**stock market**) a situation when the prices of **shares** are rising. *See also* **bull, bear market**

◆ Börsenhausse

bureau de change *(French)* a type of small bank or a section of a bank, where dealings are made in foreign currency, e.g. by cashing **traveller's cheques**

◆ Wechselstube

burst *noun* (1) the broadcasting of a number of television advertisements within a short period of time. (2) (**computers**) putting a number of **records** into a **store** but with gaps of time left for the computer to be used for other purposes

◆ (1) geballte Werbung (2) Stoßbetrieb

burst *verb* (**computers**) to divide (the continuous printed sheet coming from the computer) into separate sheets

◆ trennen

business *noun* (1) commercial activity: *to take up business as one's career.* (2) a particular organisation involved in commercial activity; a company. *The Government is encouraging small businesses.* (3) what one does to earn a living; duty or occupation. *What line of business are you in?*

◆ (1) Geschäftswesen (2) Firma (3) Berufssparte

business *adjective* connected with commercial activity: *a business career*

◆ Geschäfts-

business agent (1) *see* **agent.** (2) *(US)* a full-time official of a **trade union** who represents a local **branch** during **negotiations** with employers and also acts as its **treasurer**

◆ (2) Gewerkshaftsvertreter

business card a small card which can be used to introduce oneself or which can be left with a person who might want to contact one again; it usually has one's name, position in one's organisation, and the address and phone number of the organisation

◆ Visitenkarte

business cycle *see* **trade cycle**

business enterprise = **business** (meaning 2)

business forecasting judging what is likely to happen in the future to a company's sales, costs and profits. Forecasts are made usually after considering the trends of things which affect the company, e.g. the **economy,** the industry that it is in and the activities of **competitors**

◆ Geschäftsprognose

business game *see* **management game**

business indicators facts or information helpful for anyone who has to make decisions about a business activity. *In the petrol business, the number of new cars sold is a good business indicator*

◆ Geschäftsbarometer

buy to get in return for money or by paying a price. *They bought the company for £250,000*

◆ kaufen

buyer (1) a person who buys goods for a business. (2) a person in charge of a department concerned with buying goods. (3) a person in charge of a department in a **department store.** (4) anyone who buys something; a customer

◆ (1) Einkäufer (2) Einkaufsleiter (3) Abteilungsleiter (4) Käufer

buyer credit money allowed by a bank etc. to a person or company to buy goods or **services**

◆ Kundenkredit

buyer's market a situation in which a certain **product** is plentiful, resulting in a low price and low profit for the seller. *See also* **seller's market**

◆ Käufermarkt

buying behaviour (**marketing**) a way in which people behave when deciding whether or not to buy a certain **product** and the personal thoughts and feelings as well as other circumstances in the situation which will affect their behaviour

◆ Einkaufsverhalten

buying motives (**marketing**) the things which make a person or company willing to buy something, e.g. price, delivery times, brand loyalty

◆ Kaufmotive

buzz group a small group formed to discuss and share ideas on a certain matter. *See also* **brainstorming, syndicate**

◆ Diskussionsteam

bylaw (*also* **byelaw**) (1) *(UK)* a law which has not been passed by Parliament itself but by some organisation which has the backing of Parliament, e.g. a **local authority** or a **nationalised industry.** (2) *(US)* a regulation made by a **corporation** which states how the corporation should be organised and run. (*UK* **articles of association**)

◆ (1) Ortsvorschriften (2) Statuten

by-line a line which comes below the title of an article in a newspaper or a magazine, giving the name of the author

◆ Autorenzeile

by-product something produced as a result of the manufacture of something else. For example, sawdust is a by-product of the manufacture of tables, chairs etc

◆ Nebenprodukt

byte a group of **bits** (usually eight) which operate as one unit in a **computer**

◆ Byte

C

CA *see* **Chartered Accountant**

CAA *see* **Civil Aviation Authority**

cable *noun* (1) a thick bundle of wires usually laid underground or under the sea and used for sending messages. (2) a message sent in this way. *Send a cable to our agent in Germany*

◆ (1) Kabel (2) Telegramm

cable *verb* to send (a message) in this way: *to cable information overseas*

◆ kabeln

CACM *see* **Central American Common Market**

calculate to work out (a figure, cost etc.) by using numbers

◆ kalkulieren

calculated risk a decision to do something, where a risk is known, because the rewards (either **financial** or other) make the risk worth taking. *Even a shrewd businessman will occasionally take a calculated risk*

◆ kalkuliertes Risiko

calculation the act or result of **calculating**

◆ Kalkulation

calculator an **electronic** machine which can perform a limited number of mathematical operations. *See also* **computer**

◆ Rechner

calendar month (1) one of the twelve divisions of the year according to the calendar. (2) a period from a date to the same date in the next month, according to the calendar. *His contract runs for two calendar months, from 10 January to 10 March*

◆ (1) Monat (2) Kalendermonat

call (1) a demand by a company for payment of part or all of the money due on a **partly-paid share.** *See also* **called-up capital, option dealing.** (2) a visit by a salesman to one of his customers. *Our best salesman does twelve calls a day.* (3) **at call** especially of money in a bank, without delay. For example, a company that places money in a bank at call can have it back without delay, on request. (4) **on call** ready to go to work if called for. *There is always a doctor on call during the night*

◆ (1) Zahlungsaufforderung (2) Vertreterbesuch (3) auf Abruf (4) in Bereitschaft

call analysis a study of the pattern of visits by a salesman to his customers

◆ Vertreterbesuchsanalyse

call-back pay *see* **call-in pay**

called-up capital that part of the value of the **ordinary shares** which a company has asked its **shareholders** to pay. *See also* **call** (meaning 1)

◆ eingefordertes Kapital

call-frequency the number of visits that a salesman makes to his various customers in a given time. *See also* **calling cycle**

◆ Besuchshäufigkeit

calling card — business card

calling cycle the average time between calls by a salesman on any particular customer. *The calling cycle in our salesforce is four weeks. See also* **call frequency**

◆ Besuchsrhythmus

call-in pay (*or* **call-back pay**) a form of payment made to a worker who is actually called in to do a job for which he has kept himself ready on his employer's instructions

◆ Arbeitslohn für Erscheinen aufgrund einer Aufforderung

call report a short written account of a visit by a salesman to a customer, or a **prospect,** which he will send to his manager

◆ Vertreterbericht

campaign an organised series of actions intended to reach some result: *an advertising campaign*

◆ Kampagne

cancel (1) to make a mark on (something, e.g. a postage stamp) to prevent it being used (again). (2) to say that (something) should not be done or should not happen, even although it has already been agreed: *to cancel an order/an appointment*

◆ (1) entwerten (2) rückgängig machen

C and F (*or* **Cost and Freight**) in international trade, cost and **freight.** When an **exporter** quotes a C and F price, his price includes all costs up to loading the goods over the ship's rail and freight up to a named foreign port. *See also* **CIF, CIFC, FAS, FOB**

◆ bedingt frachtfrei

canvass (1) to call on (people) for some purpose, e.g. to try to get their support, to find out their opinions on something or to sell them some **product.** *See also* **cold canvassing.** (2) to call on (a selected **sample** of people, or a complete group of people) in order to find out their opinions, for research purposes

◆ (1) werben (2) Meinung erforschen

canvasser a person, especially a salesman or saleswoman, who **canvasses.** *See also* **cold cavassing**

◆ Werber

CAP *see* **Common Agricultural Policy**

capacity (1) the amount that something can hold or contain. *The tank has a capacity of fifty litres.* (2) a position, e.g. in an organisation: *to act in the capacity of a manager.* (3) an ability to pay a debt when it is due. *See also* **due date.** (4) ability to perform a task or to produce something. *This machine is working at maximum capacity,* i.e. it is not able to work harder or produce more. (5) (**computers**) the number of words or **characters** that can be **stored.** (6) (**computers**) the range of numbers (within certain limits) that can be **processed** in a **register**

◆ (1) Fassungsvermögen (2) Funktion (3) Zahlungsfähigkeit (4) Leistungsfähigkeit (5), (6) Kapazität

capital (1) the money belonging to people or companies which is available for **investment.** *The amount of capital needed to start a business is much greater than it was ten years ago.* (2) the amount of money made available to a company by its owners, banks or **investors.** *He started his business with a capital of £10,000, only £5,000 of which was his own money; the remainder was put up by his bank.* (3) the amount of **assets** left to a business after all of its current debts have been paid. (4) *short for* **nominal capital.** *See also* **capital employed**

◆ (1) Kapital (2) Geldmittel (3) Nettobetriebsvermögen (4) Grundkapital

capital account (1) a record of **transactions** which relate to the partners or owner of a business, showing the **capital invested** in the business and the amounts taken out of the business. (2) a section of a country's **balance of payments** statement, which records all payments not in the **current account**

◆ (1) Kapitalverkehrsbilanz (2) Kapitalkonto

capital allowance a **system** of allowing the amount of money spent by a company on **fixed assets** (e.g. machinery, buildings, etc.) to be taken off the profit before tax is charged

◆ Anlagenabschreibung

capital assets the possessions of a company, such as buildings, which are used in running the business

◆ Anlagevermögen

capital budget a **financial** plan covering a stated time, showing the expected **purchases** of **fixed assets** (e.g. buildings, machinery), the dates, and the sources of money for payment of the **assets.** It will also show the timing and **income** from the expected sale of any of the company's fixed assets during the same period

◆ Investitionsplan

capital charges the costs related to money used in the business, e.g. cost of **interest** on money borrowed for the **purchase** of **assets**

◆ Kapitalkosten

capital employed (1) all the money **invested** in a business or project less the money that is currently owed. (2) **fixed assets** plus **current assets** less **current liabilities.** *See also* **net assets** and Appendix 2

◆ (1) investiertes Kapital (2) Betriebskapital

capital expenditure money spent by a company to buy **fixed assets,** e.g. land, buildings, machinery, office furniture, vehicles, etc

◆ Kapitalaufwand

capital formation an increase of **fixed assets** in a company, e.g. by getting more factories, machinery, etc

◆ Kapitalbildung

capital gain a rise in the value of a **fixed asset,** e.g. a building

◆Kapitalzuwachs

capital-gains tax a tax on gains from the sale of a **fixed asset.** Some assets are exempt from this tax, e.g. privately-owned cars and household goods

◆ Kapitalertragssteuer

capital goods manufactured goods that are to produce, or help in the production of, other goods, e.g. factory buildings, machinery and tools

◆ Kapitalgüter

capital-intensive describes an industry, e.g. oil-refining, which uses a large amount of machinery in relation to the number of workers in producing the goods. *See also* **labour-intensive**

◆ kapitalintensiv

capital investment (1) the buying by a company of **assets** needed to carry on its business, e.g. land, buildings, machinery, etc. *See also* **capital expenditure.** (2) the buying of **stocks** and **shares** to make a gain. (3) putting money into a **deposit account** to gain **interest**

◆ (1) Kapitalanlage (2) Aktieninvestition (3) Spareinlage

capitalise (1) to change the **reserves** of a company into **capital** by issuing free **shares** to **shareholders** (usually called a **bonus issue**). (2) to provide capital for (a business). (3) **capitalise on** to turn (something) to one's advantage. *The firm capitalised on its out-of-town location by selling to rural markets*

◆ (1) kapitalisieren (2) Kapital zur Verfügung stellen (3) Kapital schlagen aus

capitalism an **economic system** that encourages the private ownership of industry and commerce

◆ Kapitalismus

capitalist *adjective* (1) owning or controlling a large amount of wealth. (2) supporting **capitalism**

◆ kapitalistisch

capitalist *noun* (1) a person or organisation owning or controlling a large amount of wealth. (2) a person or organisation supporting **capitalism**

◆ (1) Kapitalist (2) Anhänger des Kapitalismus

capital levy a tax on the total value of a person's money and possessions, a wealth tax

◆ Vermögenssteuer

capital movement the flow of money between countries, e.g. **investment** in **assets,** the sale of such assets, loans, the repayment of loans

◆ Kapitalverkehr

capital structure the way in which the **capital** of a company is made up, e.g. **shares** and long-term **loans.** *See also* **gearing**

◆ Kapitalstruktur

capital transfer tax a tax applied to the giving of **assets** as a gift, or in a will at death

◆ Erbschafts- und Schenkungssteuer

caption a short printed explanation of a photograph, drawing etc

◆ Bildtext

captive audience usually used in relation to advertising, a group of people who must watch or listen since they have no choice in the matter, e.g. a cinema audience. *The advertising spot during the TV news is quite costly — there's a large, captive audience*

◆ unfreiwilliges Publikum

captive market buyers who must buy a certain **product** from a certain supplier because they have no choice in the matter. *Owners of Polaroid cameras are a captive market for Polaroid films*

◆ Monopolmarkt

carbon (1) (*also* **carbon paper**) (a sheet of) specially-coated paper put between sheets of writing paper to make copies on the sheet(s) below. (2) (*also* **carbon copy**) a copy made using **carbon paper**

◆ (1) Durchschlagpapier (2) Durchschlag

card-carrying member an active member, especially of a **trade union** or political party

◆ eingetragenes Mitglied

card index a box or tray of cards arranged in a special order and on which is written information on some subject, e.g. a list of books in a library in alphabetical order of author

◆ Kartei

card punch a machine that puts information onto cards in such a way that a **computer** can read and understand it, used in the preparation of **punched cards**

◆ Lochkartenstanzer

card reader a **device** used to feed **punched cards** into a **computer**

◆ Lochkartenleser

card vote a vote taken by a count of cards (e.g. membership cards of a **trade union**) held up by members at a meeting or conference. One member may hold more than one card, depending on how many people he represents. *See also* **block vote**

◆ Abstimmung mit Delegiertenstimmen

career a job or profession for which one is trained and which one intends to follow. *A career in accountancy is very worthwhile*

◆ Laufbahn

car expenses costs related to owning and using a car, e.g. petrol, garage, rent, repairs, road tax

◆ Autounterhaltungskosten

cargo goods carried on an aircraft, ship or vehicle, usually in exchange for payment. *The ship carried a cargo of cotton. See also* **freight charge**

◆ Fracht

car hire (1) the temporary use of a car in return for payment. (2) the business of car hire. *Their charges for car hire are reasonable*

◆ (1) Automieten (2) Autovermietung

Caribbean Community and Common Market (*or* **CARICOM**) a group of 12 countries formed in 1973 for **economic** cooperation between members. Headquarters: Georgetown, Guyana. Official language: English

◆ Karibische Gemeinschaft und Gemeinsamer Markt (CARICOM)

CARICOM *see* **Caribbean Community and Common Market**

carriage (1) the carrying of goods for payment; the cost of this. *The goods were £100 but carriage cost another £10.* (2) the part of a typewriter which moves the paper along

◆ (1) Transport(-kosten) (2) Wagen

carriage forward the cost of delivery of the goods (**carriage**) to be paid by the receiver of the goods

◆ Fracht zahlt Empfänger

carriage free when goods are delivered by the seller at no cost for delivery. *This furniture is £150, carriage free*

◆ frachtfrei

carriage inwards the amount a buyer pays for delivery of goods received

◆ vom Käufer getragene Frachtkosten

carriage outwards the amount a seller charges to cover cost of delivering goods. *Our selling price for the machine is £200 plus carriage outwards £50: total cost to you £250*

◆ vom Verkäufer getragene Frachtkosten

carriage paid when a seller pays the delivery charges of goods sold to a stated place. *Carriage paid, London*

◆ frei Haus

carriage return the return of the **carriage** of a typewriter to the left-hand margin

◆ Wagenrückholtaste

carrier a person or business that carries goods (or people) from one place to another for payment

◆ Spediteur

carry forward (*or* **c/f**) in **accounts,** words written at the bottom of a page of figures to show that the total has to be carried over to the top of the next page. *See also* **brought forward, balance brought forward, balance carried forward**

◆ Vortrag

carte blanche full freedom of action, usually in a certain area. *The company gave the agent carte blanche on the matter of who to call on for orders*

◆ Carte blanche

cartel an informal group of companies which join together to carry out **policies** for the benefit of all members, e.g. on prices, **discounts, products** and markets

◆ Kartell

case history a written record of the past history of a company

◆ Firmengeschichte

case method teaching or training through the use of **case studies** (i.e. using records of real or fictional companies to provide the learning experience of business)

◆ Fallmethode

case study a description of a company, usually in printed form but sometimes on slides, tape or film which is used to train people, e.g. in how to solve business problems and make business decisions

◆ Fallstudie

cash *noun* (1) money in coin or notes. (2) in business, cash includes cheques or other **documents** that can be quickly changed into **cash in hand,** or in the bank

◆ (1) Bargeld (2) flüssige Mittel

cash *verb* (1) to receive money from a bank or a person in exchange for (a cheque). *He went to the bank and cashed a cheque for £10.* (2) to pay money to a person in exchange for (a cheque). *He was short of money, so I cashed his cheque for £20*

◆ (1) einlösen (2) zu Geld machen

cash account an **account** which records the payment and receipt of money in a business. *See also* **cash book**

◆ Kassenbuch

cash and carry a method of selling goods at lower prices, where the buyer not only pays cash at the time of sale (instead of receiving **credit**) and also carries the goods away himself, instead of the seller delivering

◆ Selbstabholung gegen Kasse

cash-and-carry warehouse a large store where goods are sold at low prices if paid for at once and taken away by the buyer

◆ (Verbraucher-) Abholmarkt

cash-and-carry wholesaler a business which buys goods from the manufacturers and other suppliers (usually on **credit**) and sells these goods to **retailers** at low prices providing the retailers pay for the goods at once and take the goods away themselves. *See* **cash and carry**

◆ Abholmarkt für Großhandel

cash bonus (life insurance) a share of the profits earned by a life insurance company paid to the insured in cash instead of being added to the amount of the **policy.** *See also* **bonus**

◆ Sonderausschüttung in bar

cash book a **book of account** in which is recorded the payment and receipt of money. *See also* **cash account**

◆ Kassenbuch

cash card a plastic card from a bank etc., specially numbered for each customer, which allows the customer to **withdraw** cash (in the form of **banknotes**) from his/her **account** at any time of the day or night. The card is fed into an **ATM** and, providing certain simple instructions are followed, the required amount of cash is issued by the machine

◆ Geldautomatenkarte

cash discount a **discount** allowed for prompt payment. For example, 2½% 10 days printed on an **invoice** means that 2½% may be taken off the amount shown on the invoice if payment is made within 10 days

◆ Skonto

cash dispenser a machine for giving out money. *See also* **ATM**

◆ Bargeldautomat

cash flow (1) a supply of cash which is needed by a company to meet its regular weekly or monthly expenses. (2) the flow of cash into a company (cash inflow) in the form of payment by customers or money from the sale of **assets,** and the flow of cash out of a company (cash outflow) in the form of payment of expenses and **purchase** of assets. *We often have a cash-flow problem.* (3) the difference of cash inflow and cash outflow of a company (or of a certain project). Sometimes called **net cash flow.** *See also* **cash-flow statement**

◆ (1) – (3) Cash-flow

cash-flow statement a weekly or monthly plan of the expected **cash flow** (meaning 2)

◆ Cash-flow Planung

cashier (1) a person in charge of all cash **transactions** in a company, i.e. the recording of the receipts and payment of cash, cheques and **bills of exchange.** (2) in a bank, a person who receives and gives out cash to the public. (3) a person who receives cash from customers in a shop etc

◆ (1) Kassenführer (2) Schalterbeamter (3) Kassierer(in)

cash-in-hand in business, money held to hand in the form of coin or **banknotes**

◆ Barbestand

cash on delivery (*or* **COD**) a condition of sale, made by the seller of the goods, that payment must be made at the actual time they are delivered, often used where goods are ordered and delivered by post. The post office will collect the cash at the time of delivery and pass the money back to the seller

◆ per Nachnahme

cash price the price the seller will sell at if the buyer pays immediately

◆ Barzahlungspreis

cash reserves money set aside in case of need. *The company has ample cash reserves should we decide to expand*

◆ Bargeldreserven

cash surrender value *see* **surrender value**

cash with order a condition made by a seller that payment must be received along with any order for goods

◆ Bezahlung bei Bestellung

cassette (1) a container of film that can be easily placed into a camera. (2) a container of **magnetic tape** that can be easily placed into a **tape recorder**

◆ (1), (2) Kassette

casting vote a vote used by the **chairman** of a meeting if the votes for and against something are equal

◆ ausschlaggebende Stimme

casual worker a worker not employed on a regular basis but only if and when there is work for him/her

◆ Gelegenheitsarbeiter

catalogue (1) a book containing a list of goods for sale with description, price and how to order, and sometimes also illustrations of the goods. *See also* **catalogue buying.** (2) a list of names, places, goods etc. in a certain order so that any item can be easily found. *In this library the catalogue is arranged by subject*

◆ (1) Warenverzeichnis (2) Katalog

catalogue buying buying goods by using a company's **catalogue** to choose and order them, rather than buying them in a shop

◆ Kauf per Katalog

caveat emptor (*Latin* let the buyer beware) a legal term meaning the buyer should use his common sense when buying goods, for if he suffers loss because he does not do so, the law will not help him

◆ Mängelprüfungspflicht des Käufers

CC *see* **column centimetres**

CCC *see* **Customs Cooperation Council**

CCTV *see* **closed-circuit television**

Ceefax a **viewdata system** run by the British Broadcasting Corporation

◆ Ceefax (Btx-System)

census the counting of the whole amount of something, e.g. all of the people in a country (**population**

census), the total number of cars that use a certain road (traffic census). Such information helps in the planning decisions of government, **local authorities** and companies. *The UK population census includes information on age, sex, occupation, number of children, etc*

◆ Zensus

Census of Production a yearly inquiry by the government's business **statistical** office to provide information about the country's manufacturing industries, e.g. size, location, output, etc

◆ statistische Erfassung der Produktion

Central American Common Market (*or* **CACM** *or* **MCCA**) a group of Central American countries formed in 1960 to set up a **common market** of member states and a customs union. Membership: Costa Rica, El Salvador, Guatemala, Nicaragua. Headquarters: Guatemala City. Official language: Spanish

◆ Zentralamerikanischer Gemeinsamer Markt (CACM)

central bank a bank set up by a government to carry out the government's **financial** business, e.g. raising loans for the government, controlling the issue of notes, and influencing the rate of interest; in the UK, the Bank of England

◆ Zentralbank; ≃ Deutsche Bundesbank

centralise to move control of (something) to the headquarters of an organisation. *All the buying is done at head office — it has all been centralised*

◆ zentralisieren

central processing unit (*or* **CPU**) the heart of the **computer.** It **coordinates** and controls the actions of all the other units, carries out all the arithmetic and the **processes** applied to **data**

◆ Zentraleinheit

Central Statistical Office an organisation set up by the UK government to collect and **process statistics** on **economic** aspects of UK life

◆ ≃ Statistisches Bundesamt

Centre for Interfirm Comparisons (*or* **CIFC**) an independent organisation set up to carry out comparisons of management **ratios** between companies on a confidential basis

◆ Zentrum für Betriebsvergleiche

centre-spread *see* **double-page spread**

certificate an official **document** showing proof of something, e.g. marriage (marriage certificate), birth (birth certificate), education (Higher National Certificate)

◆ Bescheinigung

certificate of health an official **document** giving details of the condition of foodstuffs, or animals, or the produce of animals, e.g. milk, beef

◆ Gesundheitszeugnis

certificate of incorporation a **document** from the **Registrar of Companies** as evidence that a company has met the various requirements of the Companies Act

◆ Gründungsurkunde

certificate of insurance an official **document** from an **insurance company** as proof that an insurance **contract** exists between the company and a named **party.** It is a shortened version of the insurance contract and states the main things covered by the insurance; it may be required by law, e.g. in motor insurance

◆ Versicherungsnachweis

certificate of origin a **document** stating that certain goods were produced or manufactured in a named country, used when **exporting** goods to a country which charges different **tariff** rates depending on the origin of the goods

◆ Ursprungszeugnis

certificate of value a written proof given by the supplier of goods that the value of goods as stated in the **export invoice** is the true value used, e.g. where the amount of tax on the goods depends on the value of the goods

◆ Warenwertbescheinigung

certified accountant a member of the Association of Certified and Corporate Accountants who is thus properly qualified to **audit accounts** of **limited companies**

◆ öffentlich zugelassener Wirtschaftsprüfer

c/f *see* **carry forward**

chain of command (*or* **line of command**) formal lines of **communication** in a company through which management instructions and information are passed

◆ Befehlskette

chain store a shop or store which is one of many owned by the same company, each in a different place

◆ Kettenladen

chair *verb* to be in charge of (a meeting); to be the **chairman** of (a meeting)

◆ Vorsitz führen

chairman (*or* **chairperson**) (1) a person in charge of a meeting. (2) the holder of the highest **office** (meaning 3) of a company, committee etc. *He has been made chairman of the board*

◆ (1) Vorsitzende(r) (2) Präsident(in) (3) Vorstandsvorsitzender

chamber of commerce an association of companies in an area which tries to help and protect the trade interests of member companies

◆ ≃ Handelskammer

Chancellor of the Exchequer the British government minister who is in charge of the **exchequer**

◆ Schatzkanzler

channel of distribution (*or* **distribution channel**) the way goods go from the producer to the user. For example, a company making chocolates may decide to reach **consumers** by way of **wholesalers** to small shops to consumers, or by way of supermarkets to consumers. Each route would be a different channel of distribution. See Appendix 7

◆ Absatzweg

channels of communication the ways in which information flows, e.g. within a company, between managers, between managers and workers, between directors and managers. *Compare with* **communications**

◆ Informationskanäle

character (**data-processing**) one of a set of symbols used to represent a letter, or a number, or a punctuation mark, etc., e.g. the letter 'a' is a character in the alphabet

◆ Zeichen

charge *verb* (1) to ask (a certain amount of money) for goods or services. *How much do you charge for delivery?* (2) to make a note of (money owed). *Please charge it to my account.* (3) *(law)* to accuse (a person) formally of having committed a certain crime. *He was charged with drunken driving.* (4) to cause (a battery etc.) to take or store electricity

◆ (1) berechnen (2) in Rechnung stellen (3) anklagen (4) aufladen

charge *noun* (1) an amount of money **charged** (meaning 1). *For a small extra charge you can have the goods delivered.* (2) *(law)* the act of **charging** (meaning 3). *He has been arrested on a drugs charge.* (3) an amount of electricity held in a battery etc. (4) control; responsibility. *Who is in charge of this department?*

◆ (1) Gebühr (2) Anklage (3) Ladung (4) Verantwortung

charge account an arrangement between companies and customers whereby goods or **services** can be bought and payment is made later

◆ Kundenkonto

chargehand the leader of a group of workers (usually under the level of **foreman**)

◆ Vorarbeiter

charges forward when the buyer of goods pays only when they are delivered, or after delivery when a **bill** is sent to the buyer

◆ Zahlung nach Warenerhalt

chart *see* **graph**

charter *noun* (1) a formal **document** from the king or queen or government to a city, bank, college, company, etc. stating its purposes and rights. *The university received its charter in 1963.* (2) the basic rights or principles of an organisation. *Charter of the United Nations.* (3) the act or practice of **chartering.** *See also* **charter party**

◆ (1) Gründungsurkunde (2) Charta (3) Chartern

charter *verb* to hire (a ship, plane, etc.) for a special purpose

◆ chartern

chartered accountant a member of the Institute of Chartered Accountants in England, Wales, Scotland or Ireland, the governing body with rules of conduct which the chartered accountant must keep to. Membership of the Institute is given after passing examinations and serving a period with a company of **accountants** who are members

◆ Wirtschaftsprüfer

charter party (*also* **charter party contract**) a **contract** between persons hiring a ship and the shipowner

◆ Chartervertrag

cheap (1) low-priced, not costing much money. *There are special cheap train tickets to London for students.* (2) good value for money. *This is a good quality camera going cheap.* (3) poor quality, worth little. *All she could find were cheap souvenirs*

◆ (1) billig (2) preiswert (3) minderwertig

cheap money money which can be borrowed at low **interest** rates. A cheap money policy is sometimes carried out by governments to encourage **investment** in new factories and so increase employment and demand for goods

◆ billiges Geld

cheat *verb* (1) to take money or property unfairly or dishonestly. *He cheated the customs — he didn't declare the goods.* (2) to take an unfair advantage. *He passed the examination by cheating — he copied the answers from the man in front*

◆ (1) betrügen (2) täuschen

cheat *noun* (1) a person who **cheats.** (2) something done by **cheating**

◆ (1) Betrüger (2) Betrug

check list a list used to help the memory. Each item is usually **checked off** with a tick (√) as it is referred to. *The engineer referred to his check list when servicing the car. Each researcher had a check list when she carried out the survey of house-owners*

◆ Checkliste

check off to mark (things on a list) to show that they have been dealt with

◆ abhaken

check-out an exit in a self-service or supermarket store where the value of the goods bought is recorded, totalled and payment is made

◆ Kasse

cheque (*US* **check**) a written order to a bank to pay a certain sum to the person named on the cheque from the **account** of the person who signed the cheque. A cheque is a **bill**

of **exchange drawn** on a banker, payable on demand and is a common way of settling debts. It can also be **endorsed** and passed to someone else to pay into his/her account. *See also* **crossed cheque**

◆ Scheck

cheque book a book of cheques given by banks to their **current account** customers

◆ Scheckheft

cheque card a card given by a bank to those who have an **account** with it. It **guarantees** payment by the bank of any cheque written by the owner of the card, up to a certain amount

◆ Scheckkarte

chicken feed *(informal)* a very small amount of money. *That is chicken feed compared with what people get paid in the oil business*

◆ Hungerlohn

chief executive the person who has overall responsibility for the day-to-day running of a business. In the case of a **limited company** the chief executive is usually the **managing director**

◆ Vorstandsvorsitzender; Generaldirektor

chip (*or* **microchip** *or* **silicon chip**) (**computers**) a very small piece of silicon (about 6mm square) on which have been etched hundreds, sometimes thousands, of tiny **devices** which store and use **data**

◆ Chip

CIF in international trade, **cost, insurance and freight.** A CIF price includes all costs up to loading the goods over the ship's rail, the cost of **marine insurance** for the goods and the cost of carrying the goods from a UK port to a named foreign port. *See also* **CIFC, FAS, FOB**

◆ cif

CIFC (1) international trade, cost, insurance, freight, commission. A CIFC price includes all charges given for CIF plus commission to an agent who helped to get the order and who may be an agent of the buyer or the seller. *See also* **CIF, FAS, FOB.** (2) *see* **Centre for Interfirm Comparisons**

◆ (1) frei Empfangshafen inkl. Provision

circular a printed announcement, advertisement, letter, of which many copies are made and sent to people who may be interested in the contents

◆ Rundschreiben; Wurfsendung

circulating capital *see* **working capital**

circulation (1) the total number of copies bought or given away free of a book, magazine, or newspaper. *Newspapers today are battling to build up circulation.* (2) a movement of something, e.g. money or news from person to person. *We hope the new manager will improve the circulation of information between departments*

◆ (1) Auflage(nziffer) (2) Umlauf; Verbreitung

city: The City (*short for* **the City of London**) (1) the financial centre of the UK. (2) a collective name for the financial institutions in the City of London. *Compare with* **Wall Street**

◆ die City

Civil Aviation Authority (*or* **CAA**) a UK **authority** set up in 1971 to develop and control civil air transport in the UK, e.g. by **promoting** the reasonable interests of users of civil air transport; by deciding which air routes should be given to which airlines; by issuing **certificates** of air-worthiness

◆ ≈ Zivile Luftfahrtbehörde

civil case a court case dealing with the rights of private citizens

◆ Zivilprozeß

CKD *see* **completely knocked down**

claim *verb* (1) (especially **insurance** and law) to ask for (something due, e.g. money). *The cargo was lost when the ship sank, so the company claimed under its marine insurance policy.* (2) to say that something is true. *This customer claims he has already paid his bill*

◆ (1) Ansprüche geltend machen (2) behaupten

claim *noun* the act of **claiming.** *She put in a claim to the insurance company*

◆ Anspruch

claimant *(law)* a person who makes a **claim**

◆ Kläger(in)

class (1) a group having qualities of the same kind. *Our customers fall into two classes: wholesalers and retailers.* (2) one of a series of grades into which certain types of **service** (especially travel) are divided: *a second-class rail ticket; fly first class; a third-class hotel.* (3) a special group. *In the UK you're in the upper class, the middle class or the working class.* (4) a group of pupils or students

◆ (1) Gruppe (2) Klasse (3) Gesellschaftsklasse (4) Klasse

classified (1) divided or arranged in a certain order or class. *In this library all books are classified by subject.* (2) put into a secret group. *The information on the new product for the army is classified* (i.e. the public is not allowed to know about it)

◆ (1) eingeteilt (2) für geheim erklärt

classified advertising small advertisements in a newspaper or magazine arranged in a certain order or class, e.g. advertisements under 'gardening', 'personal' or 'lost and found'

◆ Kleinanzeigen

clean bill of exchange a **bill of exchange** sent to the **importer's** bank, for **acceptance** by the importer, the other shipping **documents** having gone direct to the importer. *See also* **documentary bill of exchange**

◆ reiner Wechsel

clean bill of health *see* **bill of health**

clean bill of lading a receipt from the **carrier** (to the person sending the goods) when goods are going by sea, which states that 'the goods are in good order and condition'

◆ reines Konnossement

clearance certificate a customs **document** issued to a UK ship leaving for a foreign port which states that it has obeyed UK customs **regulations**

◆ Zollbescheinigung

clearance sale a special sale of goods at lower prices to clear a seller's **stock** of goods

◆ Ausverkauf

clearing bank (1) a bank that is a member of the **London Bankers' Clearing House.** (2) any UK **commercial bank** or **joint-stock bank**

◆ (1) Clearingbank (2) Geschäftsbank

clerical of the work or position of a **clerk.** *We all have to do some clerical work*

◆ Büro-

clerk (1) a person **employed** in an office or shop to do paperwork such as keeping records, filing, typing. (2) *(US)* a shop assistant

◆ (1) kaufmännischer Angestellter (2) Verkäufer

client a person or company that pays for the **services** of a professional person or organisation, e.g. a lawyer, an **insurance** agency. *I can recommend this advertising agency — our company has been a client of theirs for years. See also* **customer**

◆ Kunde

clip (1) a short-part of a film cut from a complete film. (2) a metal fastener for holding together papers or **documents**

◆ (1) Filmausschnitt (2) Heftklammer

clipping service an **agency** which will cut out and supply pieces of news or advertisements from the press about something in return for payment. *See* **press cuttings**

◆ Zeitungsausschnittdienst

clock card a card used by workers when **clocking-in** (or **clocking-on**)

◆ Stechkarte

clock in (*or* **on**) of workers of a company, to record the times at which they start and finish work. *The workers here clock in at 8.30 a.m. See also* **time card**

◆ stechen

close company a company controlled by five or fewer **shareholders** and in which the public has less than 35% of the **shares**

◆ Kapitalgesellschaft, die von fünf oder weniger Personen beherrscht wird; ≃ Familien-GmbH

closed-circuit television (*or* **CCTV**) a television system which sends pictures by wire to a limited number of television receivers, used in education, training and for security, e.g. for watching the public in a shop etc

◆ interne Fernsehanlage; Fernsehüberwachungsanlage

closed-shop describes an organisation which employs only those people who are members of a certain **trade union**

◆ Unternehmen, das nur Gewerkschaftmitglieder beschäftigt

closing entries entries in the **books of account** at the end of an **accounting period** to allow the **profit-and-loss account** to be made up for the period

◆ Abschlußbuchungen

closing prices the prices of **shares** at the end of a day's trading on the **stock market**

◆ Schlußkurs

closing the sale the point of a sales **interview** at which the seller asks the buyer for an order

◆ Geschäftsabschluß

cluster analysis (**market research**) a method in which a variety of information on people, **products,** etc. is sorted out into groups or clusters with each cluster having broadly the same characteristics. *See also* **cluster sampling**

◆ Klumpenauswahlverfahren

cluster sampling (**market research**) a method of **sampling** by which the people to be questioned are in areas grouped or clustered together. This lessens the time and cost of interviewing. Using this type of sampling, care must be taken that **bias** does not enter the results. *See also* **area sample, cluster analysis**

◆ Klumpenstichprobe

CMEA *see* **Council for Mutual Economic Assistance**

coaching teaching or training. *The sales manager insists on coaching his staff on selling at every sales meeting*

◆ Training

coaster a ship which sails round the coast from port to port

◆ Küstenschiff

COBOL (*stands for* Common Business Oriented Language) a **computer language** used especially in business

◆ COBOL

Cocoa Producers' Alliance (*or* **COPAL**) a group of countries formed in 1962 to discuss common problems of pricing, producing and marketing cocoa. Members include Brazil, Cameroon, Ecuador, Gabon,

Ghana, Ivory Coast, Nigeria, Trinidad and Tobago

◆ Vereinigung Kakaoproduzierender Staaten (COPAL)

COD *see* **cash on delivery**

code of practice the printed conditions under which members of certain professions agree to do their business. For example, the advertising profession publishes a code of practice advising members how to conduct the business of advertising: *The Code of Advertising Practice*

◆ Standesordnung

codicil a written or printed addition to a will altering, explaining or **cancelling** the will

◆ Testamentsnachtrag

coin metal currency as distinct from paper currency; a piece of this. *I can give you the £1 I owe you but it's all in coin. Can you give me a five-pence coin in the change?*

◆ Münze

cold call a sales call on a **potential** buyer (who is not yet a customer of the salesman's company) when no invitation to call has been arranged

◆ unangemeldeter Vertreterbesuch

cold canvassing calling on **potential** buyers (who are not customers of the salesman's company) uninvited, with the hope of selling goods to them

◆ unangemeldeter Werbebesuch

collate (1) to examine or compare (books, records, texts etc.) so that the differences can by noted. (2) to put together individual pages of (printed matter) in a certain order

◆ (1) vergleichen (2) zusammentragen

collateral (*also* **collateral security**) something promised as **security** for the repayment of a loan. *I asked the bank for a £5,000 loan and they asked me for the title deeds to my house as collateral*

◆ Sicherheit

collective bargaining: negotiation between the management of a company and the representatives of the workers (usually members of a **trade union**) where wages, working hours, complaints, etc. are discussed

◆ Tarifverhandlungen

collective ownership ownership and control of a company shared between all who work for it. *The workers and managers bought the firm so now it's under collective ownership*

◆ Gemeinschaftsbesitz

college (1) a school for higher education usually offering degree or **diploma** courses. (2) a part of a university

◆ (1) höhere Bildungsanstalt (2) College

collision clause (**marine insurance**) a clause which covers a shipowner against having to pay for damage to other ships in collisions

◆ Kollisionsklausel

collusion secret agreement between two or more people with the intention of cheating or making an unlawful gain. *The manager of the shop thought there was collusion between two of his staff because a lot of stock had gone missing*

◆ abgekartetes Spiel

column (1) a line of figures arranged one below the other. *Add up this column of figures.* (2) a section of printed material running from the top of the page to the bottom. *This page is divided into two columns*

◆ (1) Zahlenreihe (2) Spalte

column centimetre (*or* **CC**) a unit of measurement of advertising space in newspapers, e.g. 5 column centimetres is a space 5 centimetres deep and one column wide

◆ Maßeinheit für Anzeigenraum

combine *noun* a group of businesses joined together for a common purpose, e.g. to control prices

◆ Firmenzusammenschluß

COMECON *see* **Council for Mutual Economic Assistance**

commando selling aggressive (hard-hitting) selling into a new market, often with a new **product,** and usually with a special sales force

◆ Anwendung aggressiver Verkaufsmethoden

commerce all the activities to do with the buying and selling of goods. *Britain depends on commerce — it has trading links with every continent*

◆ Handel

commercial *adjective* (1) relating to **commerce** or trade between companies or countries. *He says that taxation is ruining the commercial life of the country.* (2) having a possibility of profit. *He's thinking of going into electronics; he says it's a commercial proposition*

◆ (1) Handels- (2) einträglich

commercial *noun* an advertisement on television or radio or in the cinema

◆ Werbespot

commercial agent *see* **agent**

commercial bank a bank operating through branches, dealing with private individuals, companies and other organizations and which is in business to make a profit. Examples are Lloyds, Barclays, Midland, NatWest, Royal Bank of Scotland

◆ Handelsbank

commercial break *see* **break**

commercial credit time allowed for payment between companies, e.g. **credit** given by a manufacturer when dealing with another manufacturer, or when selling goods to a **wholesaler** or **retailer**

◆ Handelskredit

commercial treaty an agreement between two or more countries stating the conditions of trade between them

◆ Handelsvertrag

commission (1) a payment to an agent for his part in the sale or **purchase** of goods and **services** for a **principal,** often a percentage of the value of the goods or services. (2) a payment to an employee, e.g. a salesman, over and above his salary (often a percentage of his sales) to encourage greater effort. (3) (the giving of) a task or power. *We have been given the commission for the setting up of a new committee.* (4) a committee with special (government) power: *the Forestry Commission. See also* **commission agent, auctioneer**

◆ (1), (2) Provision (3) Auftrag (4) Ausschuß

commission agent a person who buys or sells goods or **services** in return for an agreed rate of **commission** (meaning 2)

◆ Provisionsvertreter

committee a group of people appointed to attend to special business. *See Jones about your complaint on conditions; he's on the works committee*

◆ Komitee

committee of inspection a group appointed by **creditors** of a company to **supervise** a company which is in **liquidation**

◆ Gläubigerausschuß

commodity something sold for profit; often used to describe things which can be graded, e.g. coffee, cotton, sugar, wheat, wool, and which are bought and sold on a **commodity exchange**

◆ Ware

commodity exchange a market where buying and selling is recorded on a national or international scale.

London is the centre for many commodity exchanges where each day's price is decided for commodities such as wool, wheat, coffee, etc. *See also* **commodity**

◆ Warenbörse

Common Agricultural Policy (*or* **CAP**) a policy agreed to by all members of the **European Economic Community** to protect the European farming industry. Under this policy the EEC fixes minimum prices for various farm **products. Imports** from non-members of the EEC must not fall below these prices. When EEC producers have **surplus stocks** for sale then the EEC will buy these stocks at slightly below the minimum price. The policy also encourages greater efficiency among EEC farmers by making cash grants out of the EEC **budget**

◆ gemeinsame Agrarpolitik

common carrier a person or business offering to transport goods for payment. Within his own area and conditions, he has to carry goods when requested, without undue delay and at a reasonable price, and he must have a government **licence** for this type of business

◆ Transportunternehmer

common law unwritten law based on custom and court decisions rather than laws passed by Parliament

◆ Gewohnheitsrecht

common market a union of several countries for **economic** purposes. *See* **European Economic Community**

◆ Gemeinsamer Markt

common ownership the ownership of something, e.g. land or a business, jointly shared by all, e.g. a cooperative society is a business in common ownership

◆ Gemeinschaftseigentum

common stock *(US)* – **ordinary shares**

(The) Commonwealth an association of countries which were in the past part of the British Empire, its main purpose being to encourage trade and friendly relations among members. Membership: 41 countries. The Commonwealth Centre is at Marlborough House, London, and the working language at Commonwealth meetings is English

◆ Commonwealth

communicate (1) to make (information, news, ideas, attitudes) known to a person or group. (2) to share or exchange information etc

◆ (1) mitteilen (2) kommunizieren

communication (1) an act of making information, news, ideas, attitudes known to a person or group. (2) a piece of information, or something containing such, e.g. a letter. *You will receive a communication from us next week.* (3) *plural* means of making **contact** with a person, group or region: telephones, telegraphs, railways, roads, airports. *After the bombing there were no communications left between the towns*

◆ (1), (2) Mitteilung (3) Kommunikation

communications mix the variety of methods which a company uses to send information to its customers, e.g. advertisements in the cinema and on television, radio, in magazines and newspapers, calls by salesmen

◆ Palette von Werbemitteln

communications satellite a man-made **device** above the earth which receives and sends to earth radio and television signals

◆ Nachrichtensatellit

community transit form a special **document** required by the **EEC** customs for the movement of goods between member countries

◆ Transitpapiere der EG

Companies Acts laws which govern the activities of companies

◆ ≃ Aktiengesetz

company a group of people who come together for the purposes of producing goods or offering a **service** and whose **regulation** is governed by one of the **Companies Acts.** A company so organised is a separate body under the law. *See* **private company, public company, joint-stock company**

◆ Unternehmen

company agreement an agreement between a single company and a **trade union** in the company

◆ Betriebsvereinbarung

company bargaining talks between the managers of a company and **trade union** officials with the hope of reaching agreement on wages, hours of work, or conditions etc. within the company. *Compare with* **collective bargaining**

◆ Verhandlungen über Betriebsvereinbarungen

company director a person who is a member of the **board of directors** of a company

◆ Direktor; Verwaltungsratsmitglied

company man a man who is totally in agreement with all that his company is doing, and all that his company plans to do

◆ loyaler Mitarbeiter

company promoter a person who organises the forming of a new company

◆ Person, die bei der Gründung eines Unternehmens die Vorarbeiten leistet

company reserves *see* **general reserves**

company secretary the person responsible for the preparation of final **accounts,** for administering the board's affairs, and for making sure that the company's legal **obligations** are met

◆ Company Secretary

company shares *see* **shares**

company store *(US)* a shop owned and managed by the company which sells goods to company workers

◆ betriebseigenes Geschäft

company union a **trade union** which operates within one single company

◆ Betriebsgewerkschaft

comparison test comparing, e.g. the price, taste, design etc. (or 'value for money') of competing **products**

◆ Warenvergleichstest

compatibility (1) the ability of different persons or things to agree, work, or act together. (2) the ability of **software** or **hardware** to be used with more than one type of **computer**

◆ (1) Vereinbarkeit (2) Kompatibilität

compensate to give **compensation** for something

◆ entschädigen

compensating error (**book-keeping**) an error which happens to **cancel** the effect of another error. *By mistake we overpaid £2 to Smith but then we also underpaid £2 to Jones, and because of that compensating error our cash balance is correct*

◆ ausgleichungsfähiger Fehler

compensation suitable payment for some loss or injury. *He suffered an accident at work and the company paid him £10,000 compensation*

◆ Entschädigung

compensation for loss of office a sum of money given to a director on his leaving the company before his **contract** with the company ends, e.g. when the company is **taken over** by another company which does not need his services

◆ Abfindung

competent (1) having ability or skill to do the work required. (2) having the legal capacity. *This court is competent to deal with the case*

◆ (1) kompetent (2) zuständig

competition (1) (the act of) trying to do or get something better than one's rivals. *There was fierce competition for the new contract.* (2) companies selling the same or similar **products** or **services.** *The competition are taking our customers, and our sales are down.* (3) a contest of skill or knowledge. *This company is running a competition — complete a slogan and you might win a new house*

◆ (1) Konkurrenzkampf (2) Konkurrenz (3) Wettbewerb

competitive advantage (*or* **competitive edge**) some benefit possessed by a **product** or some ability possessed by a company that makes it better in the market. *We have a great competitive advantage in our sales force — they are all highly-trained men*

◆ Wettbewerbsvorteil

competitive claims benefits offered to buyers by the various companies selling similar **products**

◆ Konkurrenzangebote

competitive edge *see* **competitive advantage**

competitive price a price for a **product** or **service** which is low when compared to other similar products or services

◆ konkurrenzfähiger Preis

competitor a rival, in business usually offering similar **products** or **services** to buyers. *Our main competitor is Jones & Co. They've been in the same business as ours for many years*

◆ Konkurrent

compilation time (1) the time taken to **compile** a **computer program.** (2) the actual time at which a computer program is compiled

◆ (1), (2) Kompilierzeit

compile (1) to put facts etc. together in order to make up (e.g. a report, a dictionary). (2) to create (a **computer program**) by means of a **compiler** (meaning 2)

◆ (1) verfassen (2) kompilieren

compiler (1) a person who **compiles,** e.g. a dictionary. (2) a **computer program** that changes instructions given in a **high-level language** into a **binary code** (1's and 0's) which the computer can understand and act upon

◆ (1) Verfasser (2) Compiler

complementary goods goods which have a sales level linked to the sale of other goods because they are used together, e.g. bread and butter, cameras and films, engines and oil

◆ Komplementärgüter

completely knocked down (*or* **CKD**) (**exporting**) goods delivered in parts, to be put together by the buyer. This method reduces the cost of **freight** and is sometimes used by companies supplying goods such as furniture or cars

◆ vollständig zerlegt

compliments slip a small piece of paper with a company's name and address, often put in with something being sent, when no letter is needed

◆ Empfehlungszettel

component any part of a complete **product.** *The screws and the fuse are components of an electric plug*

◆ Bestandteil

composite demand the total purchase of a **product** which is used by a number of different industries, e.g. composite demand for steel will include the steel bought by the car, shipping and building industries

◆ Gesamtnachfrage

composite motion a **motion** put forward at a meeting which contains a number of separate motions on the same topic

◆ Sammelantrag

compound interest: interest due on the original sum of money plus any interest already earned. For example if a bank offers 10% interest on money **deposited** with it then £100 will in one year earn £10 interest. If the £100 and the £10 interest is left in the bank for a further year the compound interest on £110 will be £11

◆ Zinseszins

comprehensive insurance an **insurance** giving cover for many risks in one **policy,** e.g. a comprehensive car insurance will cover all known possible losses from accidents which happen while the car is in the owner's possession, or while it is being driven by someone else with the owner's permission

◆ kombinierte Haftpflicht- und Kaskoversicherung

compulsory purchase the buying of something by a government or **local authority,** using the power of the law. *Once the decision is made to build a new airport, there will be a compulsory purchase order on all these buildings*

◆ Zwangsverkauf

computer a calculating machine which can carry out complicated operations at very high speeds by **electronic** means

◆ Computer

computerise to cause (a machine, system etc.) to be operated by **computer;** to produce (information) by computer

◆ auf Datenverarbeitung umstellen

computer language a **system** of words and symbols by which information can be put into a **computer**

◆ Computersprache

computer peripheral a part of a **computer system** which is not part of the **central processing unit,** e.g. a **visual display unit, line printer**

◆ peripheres Gerät

con *see* **confidence trick**

concept an idea especially one connected with a certain thing, e.g. a **product** or **service.** *The product concept for this perfume is youthfulness and romance — advertising must stress these two things. The marketing concept is really a way of thinking about business, stressing the importance of the customer*

◆ Vorstellung

concession (1) something given up in a **negotiation.** *As a concession to your point about the price — we will reduce the price by £1.* (2) the right given by the owner of **premises** to another company allowing that company to trade on the premises. *Smith's have given us the concession to sell our jewellery in their department store in exchange for rent and a share of our profits from our sales*

◆ (1) Zugeständnis (2) Konzession

concessionaire a person operating a business or trade in **premises** owned by another. *See* **concession** (meaning 2)

◆ Konzessionär

conciliation the bringing together of the **parties** in a **dispute,** e.g. workers and management to try to reach a settlement between them. *See also* **arbitration**

◆ Schlichtung

conditional having a condition attached. *The lease is conditional on the building being used as a dwelling house only*

◆ vorbehaltlich

conditional sale agreement a **contract** for the sale of goods where it is agreed that the price may be paid in parts (or **instalments**) over an agreed period of time and where the ownership of the goods remains with the seller until the conditions of the contract are met

◆ Kaufvertrag unter Eigentumsvorbehalt

conditions of sale arrangements for the sale of his goods which a seller prints on his price lists and **invoices,** and which he expects buyers to keep to when ordering, e.g. payment in one month after receipt of goods

◆ Verkaufsbedingungen

conference a meeting or series of meetings for discussion and exchange of ideas. *The managers are in conference. She is going to a three-day conference on microcomputers*

◆ Konferenz

confidence trick (*also, informal* **con**) a piece of business in which a person is cheated, usually by someone pretending to be something different from what he/she actually is. *See also* **con man**

◆ Bauernfängerei

confidential (to be) kept secret, not (to be) told to others. *Please keep this matter confidential*

◆ vertraulich

confirm to say that (something) has actually happened or will definitely happen. *We are pleased to confirm your order of 19 May*

◆ bestätigen

confirmation the act of **confirming;** something which **confirms.** *Could you please give me confirmation of my flights by Friday?*

◆ Bestätigung

confirmed irrevocable letter of credit a **letter of credit** which cannot be changed in any way without the agreement of the **exporter** and **importer.** It is supported, or **guaranteed,** by two banks, one in the exporter's country and one in the importer's country. *See* **letter of credit**

◆ unwiderrufliches bestätigtes Akkreditiv

confirming house a business that acts for a foreign buyer, **confirming** orders placed in the UK, paying for these orders and overseeing the sending of the goods to the foreign buyer who pays a **fee** to the confirming house for these **services**

◆ Vertretung überseeischer Importfirmen

confiscate to take possession legally of (goods) against the owner's will

◆ beschlagnahmen

confiscation the act of **confiscating** *The goods entered the country illegally and so they were confiscated by the customs authority*

◆ Beschlagnahme

conglomerate a large group of companies which produce a variety of **products**

◆ Mischkonzern

con man *(informal)* a person who plays **confidence tricks**

◆ Schwindler

consensus of opinion commonly-held views within a group. *At the meeting the consensus of opinion was that the firm should go ahead with the new model*

◆ übereinstimmende Meinung

consideration (1) the act or process of thinking carefully about something. *Don't do that without due consideration.* (2) something of value passing between the **parties** to a **contract.** For example, the price paid for the goods, or delivery of the goods, may be seen as legal signs that a **contract** is in being. Other requirements for a contract are offer and acceptance. (3) any kind of payment. *He will help you for a small consideration*

◆ (1) Überlegung (2) Gegenwert (3) Gegenleistung

consign to send (goods) to someone. *We have received your order and have consigned your goods by ship*

◆ versenden

consignee a person to whom goods have been sent

◆ Empfänger

consignment (1) a quantity of goods which are being delivered. *Who is this consignment of cartons for?* (2) goods sent to an **agent** for sale where ownership remains with the sender until a sale takes place. *We have sent our agent some goods on consignment.* See **goods on consignment**

◆ (1) Warensendung (2) in Kommission

consignment note a printed paper describing goods which are being delivered from one **party** to another

◆ Frachtbrief

consignor a sender of goods

◆ Versender

consolidated united; combined into one

◆ konsolidiert

consolidated balance sheet a drawing together into one **balance sheet** of the balance sheets of other companies within a group. *The Ajax group of companies have just published their consolidated balance sheet*

◆ konsolidierte Bilanz

consortium a group of companies cooperating for a specific purpose. *A consortium is trying to get the contract not only to build the hospital but to supply all the equipment as well*

◆ Konsortium

constructive dismissal a legal term for the situation where a worker decides to leave his employment because of the unfair actions of his employers; he can still **claim** that it was the fault of the employer that he had to leave. *Compare with* **unfair dismissal**

◆ durch unzumutbares Arbeitgeberverhalten verursachte Arbeitnehmerkündigung

consul a person appointed by a government, living in a foreign country, whose duties include improving the business relations between that country and his own

◆ Konsul

consular fees charges made by a **consulate** for signing **export documents** and **invoices**

◆ Konsulargebühren

consular invoice a special form which an **exporter** must get from a **consulate** to prove the value and origin of the goods to be exported to the **consul's** country

◆ Konsulatsfaktura

consulate the office of a **consul**

◆ Konsulat

consult to discuss something with (someone else, usually an expert in some area). *We must consult a lawyer on this point*

◆ sich beraten lassen

consultant an expert in some part of medicine or business who gives his professional advice to a person or company. *They've called in a marketing consultant hoping his advice will improve their business*

◆ Berater

consultation a meeting to try to get advice, or to discuss a problem, so that a decision can be made

◆ Beratung

consultative management a style of management where managers seek the advice of those workers who may be affected by a decision, before the decision is taken

◆ Betriebsführung unter Ausdehnung des Mitspracherechts nach unten

consumer the actual user of a **product** or **service.** *Compare with* **customer.** For example, the consumer of baby-food is the baby but the customer for baby-food is the buyer

◆ Verbraucher

consumer advertising advertising directed at members of the public

◆ Verbraucherwerbung

consumer behaviour habits of people with regard to how and why they buy certain **products,** or shop in certain stores, or prefer certain newspapers or magazines. Suppliers of goods and **services** try to understand the buying habits of their **target markets** so that **products** and **services** can be improved to suit the market's needs

◆ Verbraucherverhalten

consumer credit loans by **retailers** or **finance** houses to customers to allow them to buy goods. The loans are paid back over a period of time. Such **credit** may be **hire-purchase, charge account,** or **interest-free loan**

◆ Verbraucherkredit

consumer durables: products used by the public for a relatively long life, e.g. refrigerators, televisions, cars

◆ langlebige Gebrauchsgüter

consumer goods goods bought by the general public (as opposed to those bought by companies), e.g. food, furniture, electrical equipment, cars

◆ Verbrauchsgüter

consumerism trying to protect the interests of the general public in their dealings with companies, especially in the purchase of goods and **services**

◆ Verbraucherschutz

consumer loyalty active support by customers, shown by their regular buying of a **service** or their regular use of a shop etc. *Even though there are several new shops near Benn's Store, it is still doing well — it has tremendous customer loyalty*

◆ Verbrauchertreue

consumer market all the people who buy to satisfy their own needs or those of their families. *Compare with* **industrial market**

◆ Verbrauchermarkt

consumer panel (marketing) a group of people who report on their use of a **product** or **service,** usually over a period of time. They are chosen so as to represent the market for the product or service

◆ Verbrauchertestgruppe

consumer sovereignty the power of the ordinary person as a buyer of goods in a free market; the choice of the ordinary buyer, e.g. the housewife, decides which **products** will survive and which will die out

◆ Verbrauchmarkt

consumption the act of buying or using up goods or **services.** *The consumption of men's shoes is higher than that of women's shoes*

◆ Verbrauch

contact *verb* to get in touch with. *You can contact her at her office*

◆ sich mit jmd. in Verbindung setzen

contact *noun* (1) the act of **contacting.** (2) the person one **contacts** or may **contact.** *Try to put me in contact with them. We have a contact in Paris*

◆ (1) Kontaktaufnahme (2) Kontaktperson

container something in which goods are held, especially a large case of standard size (the largest is 8 ft (2.4 m) × 8 ft (2.4 m) × 40 ft (12.2 m)) built to carry a large number of packages by lorry, rail, ship or air. Containers are packed at the sender's **premises** or at central **depots**

◆ Container

containerization the changing over to packing goods into **containers** away from docks (instead of into small packing cases and then onto ships). Containers can go by road, rail, air or in specially-built **container ships**

◆ Containerisierung

container ship a ship specially built to carry **containers**

◆ Containerschiff

continent one of the large areas into which the land of the world is divided

◆ Kontinent

the Continent *(informal)* the continent of Europe except for the British Isles

◆ Kontinentaleuropa

contingency something which may or may not happen. *We have a contingency fund of £5,000 to meet unexpected costs*

◆ Eventuellfall

contingency planning planning for events which may happen and which could disturb the main plan. *We plan to sell the new line to the shops in June and start the advertising in July but we have contingency plans if the new line is not ready by June*

◆ Ausweichplanung

continuous production *see* **flowline production**

continuous research research which is regular and part of a company's normal flow of information. *With regard to sales we believe in continuous research — every month we get reports from our research agency on the rate of sale of our product to consumers*

◆ fortlaufende Forschung

contraband goods which are illegally brought into or taken out of the country

◆ Schmuggelware

contract an agreement, which must be legally followed and obeyed, between persons or companies to do something, e.g. an offer of goods at a certain price which is accepted by a buyer

◆ Vertrag

contract of affreightment a **contract** made with a ship-owner for the carriage of goods by sea

◆ Chartervertrag

contract of employment a **contract** between a worker and a company on the wages, hours, etc. of the employment. In the UK a company must give everyone who works full-time for it such a contract of employment

◆ Arbeitsvertrag

contract of service a **contract** between a company and its director, or senior manager (or a **consultant**), usually stating the conditions of employment and the conditions under which the employment can end

◆ Dienstvertrag

contract in to sign a **contract** to take part in something, e.g. to join a **trade union**

◆ beitreten

contractor (1) a person or company that enters into an agreement. (2) a company that agrees to supply materials or **labour** for building jobs

◆ (1) vertragschließende Partei (2) Bauunternehmer

contract out to sign a **contract** not to take part in something, e.g. not to join a state **pension scheme**

◆ vertraglich ausschließen

contribute (1) to give a certain amount, especially along with others. *We all contributed to her retirement present.* (2) to write articles for a newspaper or magazine. *She contributes to the Economist*

◆ (1) beitragen (2) Beiträge liefern

contributed capital money paid to a company for its issue of **shares**

◆ eingebrachtes Kapital

contribution (1) something **contributed.** *My contribution towards Smith's leaving gift was £1.* (2) the difference between all the **variable costs** of a **product** and its selling price

◆ (1) Beitrag (2) Deckungsbeitrag

contribution analysis a method of checking on the costs of each **product** or **service** so that the **variable costs** are shown. When taken off the sales, these costs will show the **contribution** of each product or service towards the **fixed costs.** *See also* **break-even** and Appendix 3

◆ Vollkostenrechnungsanalyse

contribution pricing fixing a selling price for a **product** or **service** so that all **variable costs** are covered and some **contribution** helps to cover the **fixed costs.** *See also* **break even** and Appendix 3

◆ Preisbildung auf Basis von Deckungsbeiträgen

contributory pension a worker's **pension,** the cost of which is shared by the worker and his company

◆ beitragspflichtige Pension

control *verb* to measure, check or keep on course; to have power over. *We have a plan of sales for each month and we place the actual sales achieved against the plan. We note the difference then decide what to do — that way we control the plan. This office is controlled from headquarters*

◆ kontrollieren

control *noun* (1) the act of **controlling;** the power to **control.** *We are introducing new controls to prevent waste.* (2) *see* **control group**

◆ (1) Kontrolle

control account an **account** which checks a group of other accounts. This is done by entering in the control account the total of the **debits and credits** of the different accounts in the group. The **balance** of the control account should match the balance of the group of accounts

◆ Sammelkonto

control group a group which is the same in every way as a group which is being tested. For example, Group A, a test group (say, of housewives), may be tested to see whether they buy an existing **product** under a new label. Group B, the same in number, age, shopping habits, etc., would be offered the same product with the old label. Group B in this case is the control group, and the results of the test in Group A would be measured against the results in Group B

◆ Kontrollgruppe

controllable factors (marketing) things over which a company has some freedom of decision. For example, a company decides which **product** to make, at what selling price, through which customers, using what level of advertising. These controllable factors should be compared to the **uncontrollable** ones, e.g. the **economy,** the **competition,** new machines and methods

◆ beeinflußbare Faktoren

controlled economy an **economy** with a very high level of government direction over what is produced, when, and at what price. Examples are UK during World War II and present-day Russia. *See also* **control** *(verb)* and **planned economy**

◆ gelenkte Wirtschaft

controlling interest a person or group which has a majority of **voting shares** in a company. *See also* **control** *(verb)*

◆ Mehrheitsbeteiligung

control unit (**computers**) that part of the **central processing unit** which directs the order and timing of a computer's operations

◆ Steuereinheit

convene to call people together for (a meeting)

◆ einberufen

convenience foods food **products** which are wholly or partly prepared or cooked before they are offered for sale

◆ Fertiggerichte

convenience goods low-priced goods, bought regularly, which **consumers** want to buy with little effort and which are on sale in a large number of shops, e.g. canned soups, crisps, newspapers

◆ Güter des täglichen Bedarfs

convenor *or* **convener** a member of a **trade union** who arranges union meetings usually at his place of work and who is also in charge of such meetings. *See also* **chairman**

◆ Betriebsobmann

convertible loan stock (1) loan **stock** which is issued by a company and which carries the right to change it to **ordinary shares** or **preference shares** at some date stated on the **stock certificate.** (2) **stock** issued by the government which the holder can change into new stock (or exchange for cash)

◆ (1), (2) konvertierbarer Anleihestock

conveyancing the legal process of **transferring** ownership of property

◆ Eigentumsübertragung

cook the books *(informal)* to enter figures, or change figures, in **books of account,** dishonestly (usually for gain)

◆ Geschäftsbücher frisieren

cooling-off period a period of time in which both **parties** to a **dispute** agree to take no action. This gives both time to re-consider the position. *The threatened strike has been postponed. Both sides have agreed to a cooling-off period of four weeks*

◆ Abkühlungsfrist (gesetzlich festgelegter Zeitraum für Schlichtungsverhandlungen bei Arbeitskämpfen)

cooperate to work together

◆ zusammenarbeiten

cooperation the act of **cooperating**

◆ Zusammenarbeit

cooperative *adjective* working together; willing to act in this way. *You will find the staff most cooperative*

◆ kooperativ

cooperative *noun* a business which is jointly owned and run by the people who work in it

◆ Genossenschaft

cooperative advertising the sharing of advertising costs and effort by a manufacturer and a dealer

◆ Gemeinschaftswerbung

cooperative marketing: cooperation between a group of producers, **wholesalers** and **retailers** to produce, price and **promote** certain **products**

◆ genossenschaftliches Vertriebswesen

cooperative society a business owned by its members who **elect** a board to run the business and who share its profits

◆ Genossenschaft

Cooperative Wholesale Society (*or* **CWS**) a business, jointly owned by **cooperative societies,** which buys goods on their behalf from national manufacturers. It also owns factories where it produces certain **products** (e.g. bread, coffee), also on behalf of the co-operative societies

◆ genossenschaftliche Großhändlervereinigung

coordinate to organise (something) in such a way that the different parts happen together or in the right order. *A properly coordinated plan is much more likely to succeed*

◆ koordinieren

co-ownership shared ownership and often control of a business between its employees

◆ Miteigentum

COPAL *see* **Cocoa Producers' Alliance**

co-partnership a **profit-sharing** scheme in which workers have **shares** in the business in which they work

◆ Gewinnbeteiligung der Betriebsangehörigen

copy (1) the words printed in an advertisement. (2) words ready to be printed as a news item in a newspaper or magazine. *We need more copy for the sports page*

◆ (1) Werbetext (2) Stoff

copy date the date by which material to be printed should reach the publisher to ensure it is in time for publication

◆ Redaktionsschluß

copyright the legal right to ownership by a writer of his own written work. Under the Copyright laws the work of a writer is protected from being freely copied by others unless the writer's permission is given. (This protection in law extends to the original work of artists, film-makers, musicians etc.)

◆ Copyright

copy test (**marketing**) a test of the **copy** (meaning 1) of an advertisement to discover the interest, understanding, appreciation, etc. of the advertisement by the reader

◆ Copytest

copy typist a person whose job is to type the handwritten, typewritten or printed work of others

◆ Schreibkraft

copywriter a person who writes **copy** (meaning 1) for advertisements

◆ Werbetexter

corner the market to own enough of the manufacture of a **product** or **raw material** to have control over the selling price. *They tried to corner the market in silver so that they could increase the price*

◆ den Markt aufkaufen

corporate advertising advertising aimed at making a company better known and better respected

◆ Firmenwerbung

corporate identity (*or* **corporate image**) the picture in the public's mind of a company, usually coming from the style of the company's contact with the public, e.g. by letters, company reports, advertising, **sales promotion,** delivery vehicles

◆ Firmenimage

corporate objectives the long-term aims of a company, as planned by its directors (or the owner), e.g. aiming for a certain profit; aiming for a certain return on **capital employed**

◆ Geschäftsziele eines Unternehmens

corporate planning planning by a company to set up realistic aims (or **corporate objectives**) for the future of a company

◆ Unternehmensplanung

corporate strategy high-level decisions within a company which will help to reach the long-term aims (or

corporate objectives), e.g. for **products,** prices, markets, **market share,** costs of production

◆ Unternehmensstrategie

corporation an association of persons which, in law, is a separate legal body. Therefore a corporation can act on its own as if it were apart from its members

◆ juristische Person

corporation tax a tax on company profits. This has replaced **profits tax**

◆ Körperschaftssteuer

correlation a measure of the relationship between two variables (e.g. the sale of umbrellas and amount of rainfall), sometimes used to help in forecasting sales. *We have discovered a strong correlation between our monthly sales of sun-tan oil and the monthly hours of sunshine*

◆ Wechselbeziehung

cost *noun* a sum of money used to pay for labour, materials, rent, salaries, etc. to provide a **product** or **service.** *See also* **expense**

◆ Kosten

cost *verb* (1) to be sold for (a certain sum). *How much will that cost?* (2) to work out in advance how much (something) will cost

◆ (1) kosten (2) Preis kalkulieren

cost accountant a person who measures, **analyses** and reports on a company's costs in any part of its activities

◆ Kalkulator

cost allocation the charging of costs to certain **products,** or departments. *We allocate the advertising costs to the products on the basis of sales; so if a product has 50% of the total sales we charge it with 50% of the advertising costs*

◆ Kostenverteilung

cost and freight *see* **C and F**

cost-benefit analysis finding out the expected costs and the expected benefits of taking on a project so that a decision can be made to go ahead with it or not. *We did a cost-benefit analysis on opening another factory and as a result decided against it*

◆ Kostennutzenanalyse

cost centre a person, group, department, or piece of equipment, the cost of which is known and so can be used for **cost-control** purposes

◆ Kostenstelle

cost control the act of comparing actual costs with the planned (or expected) costs so that action will be taken to correct any difference in the two

◆ Kostenkontrolle

cost effective of a method etc., giving value for money, often in comparison with something else, e.g. spending money on advertising in newspapers instead of on television. *We decided to switch to television advertising. We found newspaper advertising wasn't cost effective*

◆ Kostenrentabilität

costing the act or **process** of **costing** (meaning 2)

◆ Kostenrechnung

cost, insurance and freight *see* **CIF**

cost, insurance, freight and commission *see* **CIFC**

cost of goods sold *see* **cost of sales**

cost of living the amount of money spent by a person or a family to keep up a certain standard of living

◆ Lebenshaltungskosten

cost-of-living index a measure of the **cost of living** using an **index of retail prices,** often expressed as a percentage. *The cost of living has gone up ten per cent this year*

◆ Lebenshaltungskostenindex

cost of sales (*or* **cost of goods sold**) the cost of materials, production wages, production overheads of goods sold

◆ Vertriebskosten

cost per inquiry (**advertising**) a measure of the average cost of receiving an inquiry as a result of an advertising **campaign**

◆ Kosten per Anfrage

cost per thousand the cost of reaching one thousand of the **target market** when advertising (in a newspaper, magazine, or on TV or radio). *We plan to use TV. The cost per thousand is much lower for us than if we use radio*

◆ Kosten pro Tausend

cost-plus a method of pricing whereby all costs are added to a profit figure to reach the selling price, often used in **contracts** for **products** that take a long time to complete (e.g. ships, aircraft, roads)

◆ Ermittlung des Verkaufspreises durch einen Gewinnzuschlag auf die Produktionskosten

cost-push inflation (*also* **wage-push inflation**) (**economics**) a **theory** that **inflation** is caused by workers demanding higher wages (without increasing **output**) followed by companies putting up prices (without an increase in demand following). *See* **demand-pull inflation**

◆ kostentreibende Inflation

cost variance the difference between the planned or expected cost of something and the actual cost

◆ Kostenabweichung

cost-volume profit analysis a method used to examine the relationships between the cost of a **product** or **service**, the amount sold at a certain price and the profit that results

◆ Kosten-Volumen-Gewinn-Analyse

council a group of persons appointed or **elected** to make rules or manage affairs on behalf of another body, e.g. a church, a town, a government. *The town council will decide the site for the new factories*

◆ Rat

Council for Mutual Economic Assistance (*or* **CMEA,** *or* **COMECON**) an organization formed in 1949 to encourage trade and friendly relations among its members. Membership: Albania, Bulgaria, Cuba, Czechoslovakia, German Democratic Republic, Hungary, Mongolia, Poland, Romania, Union of Soviet Socialist Republics, Vietnam. Headquarters: Moscow

◆ Rat für gegenseitige Wirtschaftshilfe (COMECON)

Council of Europe a group of European countries formed in London in 1949 to promote increased unity in Europe and to **cooperate** in the **economic,** social, cultural, scientific, legal and administrative areas. Membership: Austria, Belgium, Cyprus, Denmark, France, Federal Republic of Germany, Greece, Iceland, Ireland, Italy, Liechtenstein, Malta, Netherlands, Norway, Portugal, Spain, Sweden, Switzerland, Turkey, United Kingdom. Headquarters: Strasbourg, France. Official languages: English, French

◆ Europarat

counsel *noun* a legal adviser; in England, a **barrister;** in Scotland, an **advocate**

◆ Prozeßanwalt

counsel *verb (formal)* to give advice to. *He counselled him to study the contract well*

◆ jmd. etw. anraten

counterfeit *adjective* made in illegal imitation of something: *counterfeit money*

◆ gefälscht

counterfeit *noun* an illegal imitation. *This £50 note is a counterfeit*

◆ Fälschung

counterfoil the part of a ticket, cheque, etc. which is kept when the main part is taken off. *Keep the counterfoil as evidence of payment*

◆ Kontrollabschnitt

countermand to order that (something already ordered) should not be carried out

◆ aufheben

countersign to add a second signature to (a **document**) when this is needed for some purpose. *All cheques must be countersigned by a director*

◆ gegenzeichnen

counter trading a form of barter, usually between countries

◆ zwischenstaatlicher Tauschhandel

countervailing duty a tax on certain goods coming into a country because another country has put on a similar tax

◆ Ausgleichszoll

coupon (1) a piece of paper given to a customer by the manufacturer of a **product** or **service** which can be used, e.g. to lessen the price. *A 'three pence off' coupon for Ajax soap powder was delivered to all houses in the area.* (2) part of an advertisement, e.g. in a newspaper or magazine, inviting the reader to fill in his name and address and send it to the advertiser for more details of the product or service, or to place an order for the product or service

◆ (1) Gutschein (2) Einsendeabschnitt

coupon pack a **product** which contains a **coupon**

◆ Gutscheinpackung

cover *noun* (1) something which covers, a wrapping. *We are sending you the samples under separate cover.* (2) the outer pages of a magazine etc. (3) the **ratio** of the **dividends** of a company to its profits. (4) **security** for a loan. *What cover do you have for the loan?* (5) **insurance** against a risk. *Do you have cover in the event of a fire?*

◆ (1), (2) Umschlag (3) Deckungsverhältnis (4) Deckung (5) Versicherung

cover charge a charge made by a restaurant etc. which is in addition to the food and drink

◆ Kosten für ein Gedeck

covering letter a letter sent with a package etc. to explain its contents

◆ Begleitschreiben

cover note a printed notice from an **insurance company** stating that an insurance exists and giving brief details of it

◆ Deckungszusage

cover page front or back pages of a magazine, where higher rates are usually charged for advertisements

◆ Umschlagseite

cover price the selling price of a magazine or newspaper

◆ Einzelexemplarpreis

CPU *see* **central processing unit**

craft union a union of workers whose job requires **manual** skills and special knowledge of the trade (or craft), usually needing a lengthy training period to be served (an **apprenticeship**) before one is fully skilled in the craft

◆ Handwerkerinnung

crate a wooden box in which goods are packed for delivery

◆ Kiste

creative department part of an **advertising agency** where the creation of ideas and their design on paper is carried out

◆ Ideenabteilung

credit *noun* (1) time given, or time taken, to pay for goods which have been bought. *The price for this desk is £50. We can deliver to your address now and allow you four weeks' credit.* (2) an entry into an account which records money received. (*See also* **debit** *and* **letter of credit**). (3) **on credit** a method of paying for goods later than the time they are received. *You can have these books on credit and pay next month*

◆ (1) Kredit (2) Haben (3) auf Kredit

credit *verb* (1) to believe. *I wouldn't credit him with such skill.* (2) to mark (an account) to show that money has been paid. *We have credited your account with five pounds*

◆ (1) glauben (2) gutschreiben

credit account a customer's account in a shop, e.g. a **department store.** This allows the customer to buy goods and pay later, as the value of the goods will be charged to the customer's credit account

◆ Kreditkonto

credit agency a company which for a **fee** will find out and report on the **financial** strength or weakness of a person or a company, often employed by companies before delivering goods on **credit** to new customers

◆ Kreditauskunftei

credit balance the amount of money overpaid by a customer in an **account.** When the amount of money paid (**credited**) to an account is greater than the amount owed (**debited**) the difference will be a credit balance. *See also* **debit balance**

◆ Kreditsaldo

credit card a card from a bank, or **financial** company, or a store usually showing the signature and account number of the holder and allowing him/her to buy goods or **services** without paying at the time of sale. The amount is charged to his/her account and paid later

◆ Kreditkarte

credit control methods used by a company (which gives **credit**) to control the amount of credit, the time given to pay, how money is collected and its checks on new customers. *See* **credit agency**

◆ Kreditüberwachung

credit limit the point at which a company will refuse further **credit** to a customer. *I can't buy any more from Smith's department store. I've reached my credit limit*

◆ Kreditgrenze

credit note a notice sent to a customer showing the amount of money owing to a customer because of goods being returned, or because of some error on the company's part, e.g. sending the wrong order, overcharging. *See also* **credit balance**

◆ Gutschrift

creditor a person or company to whom something is owed as a result of a purchase of goods or **services** on **credit.** *He went out of business because he didn't have enough money to pay his creditors*

◆ Gläubiger

credit rating the amount of **credit** that should be allowed to a customer. Some companies use a **credit agency** to help them decide the credit rating of a new customer

◆ Einschätzung der Kreditwürdigkeit

credit squeeze a government decision to control the amount of loans from banks and the amount of **retail** sales on **credit**

◆ Kreditdrosselung

credit transfer *see* **Giro**

criterion (*plural* **criteria**) a standard against which something can be measured. *The sales manager has worked out various criteria by which the success of the sales campaign can be measured*

◆ Kriterium

crossed cheque a cheque with two line drawn over the face of it, within which are written '& Co.' (and company). This means that the cheque can only be paid through a bank

◆ Verrechnungsscheck

cubic measurement measurements of something by multiplying its length by its height by its breadth

◆ Raummaß

cum (*Latin, meaning* with) For example, (1) stock sold **cum rights** means the buyer has rights to new issue of **stock.** (2) **Shares** bought **cum dividend** means the buyer has the right to any dividend that may be about to be paid

◆ (1) einschließlich Bezugsrecht (2) mit Dividende

cumulative preference share a **preference share** which carries the right to a yearly **dividend** so that in any year when a dividend cannot be paid, it will be added to the following year's dividend and paid then

◆ kumulative Vorzugsaktie

currency coin and banknotes in use in a country for settling debts

◆ Währung

currency note a paper that is used as currency in a country

◆ Banknote

currency rate the rate at which foreign currency is exchanged. *The dollar stands at 1·5 to the pound*

◆ Wechselkurs

currency speculator a person or company that tries to make profits from changes in **exchange rates** by selling one currency for another

◆ Währungsspekulant

current account an account at a bank where a person or company puts money which can be **withdrawn** at any time, often done by cheque. Normally no interest is paid by the bank on money in a current account

◆ Kontokorrentkonto

current assets things owned by a company which are regularly used in the business and regularly replaced (as opposed to **fixed assets**). In a manufacturing firm current assets include: **raw material, work-in-progress, finished goods, debtors, cash.** *See* Appendix 2

◆ Umlaufvermögen

current liabilities a debt that must be paid by a company in the near future, usually within 12 months. In a manufacturing company these would include **creditors, bank overdraft, tax, dividends** due. *See* Appendix 2

◆ kurzfristige Verbindlichkeiten

current ratio a way of measuring a company's current debts (its **current liabilities**) in relation to what it currently owns (its **current assets**). For example, if current assets total £10,000 and current liabilities total £5,000, then the current ratio is 2:1

◆ Verhältnis von Umlaufvermögen zu kurzfristigen Verbindlichkeiten

current yield a measurement of the **dividend** received from a **share** in relation to the price paid for it. For example, price of share £200, dividend £20, current yield ($\frac{20}{200} \times \frac{100}{1}$ — 10%)

◆ Umlaufsrendite

curriculum vitae (*or* **CV**) a brief written account of a person's past history often used to support an **application** for a job. The CV will include such things as date of birth, education, work experience etc

◆ Lebenslauf

custom-built made to the special design of a person or company. *For this we need a special type of drilling machine — one that's custom-built for the job*

◆ spezialangefertigt

customer a person or company that actually buys something. *Compare with* **consumer. A wholesaler** of canned beans is a customer of the firm that makes the beans. The **retailer** is a customer of the wholesaler. The housewife who buys the canned beans is a customer of the retailer (and she may also be the **consumer**)

◆ Kunde

customer profile a description of the typical buyer of a **product** or **service,** usually drawn up after examining a **sample** of buyers. *The customer profile for our product is male, aged between 25 and 40, with an income of around £15,000 a year, married, and educated at university*

◆ Kundenprofil

customs an organisation under government control which collects taxes and duties, especially on goods coming into a country

◆ Zoll

Customs Cooperation Council (*or* **CCC**) an organisation formed in 1952 to agree on common customs methods and to aid international trade. Membership: 87 countries. Headquarters: Brussels. Official languages: English, French

◆ Rat für die Zusammenarbeit auf dem Gebiete des Zollwesens

customs duty duty or tax on goods entering or leaving a country. *See also* **excise duty**

◆ Zoll

customs entry *(UK)* a **document** completed by an **exporter** (or **importer**) of goods, giving details of goods, weight and value. Government **statistics** of UK **imports** and **exports** are made up from this

◆ Zolldeklaration

customs registered number a number, made up of five figures, given to an **exporter** by customs to help the export clearance of his goods. The number identifies the exporter's name and address. *See also* **clearance certificate**

◆ Zollregistriernummer

customs union a **free-trade** area in which all the countries apply the same **customs duties** (and other restrictions) on trade with countries which are outside the union. *See also* **common market**

◆ Zollunion

cut back *verb* to lower (costs) because of a fall in profit, or a fall in orders. *They're cutting back at the steel works so there's not much chance of getting a job there*

◆ kürzen

cutback *noun* the act of **cutting back**

◆ Kürzung

cut price a price below the normal or usual price

◆ Schleuderpreis

cut-throat competition very low prices offered by the sellers of a **product** with some sellers making their prices even lower than the others, so that little or no profit is made. *The traders in the fruit market are trying to sell off their stock of oranges before they go bad — it's real cut-throat competition as they try to get rid of them. See also* **price war**

◆ halsabschneiderische Konkurrenz

cutting *see* **press cutting**

CV *see* **curriculum vitae**

cybernetics the study of the way information moves and is controlled in business systems (e.g. a **computer**) and also in human systems (e.g. the nervous system)

◆ Kybernetik

D

D/A *see* **documents against acceptance**

damages the amount of money ordered by a court to be given to a person who has suffered harm. *She sued the company for damages*

◆ Schadenersatz

data facts, information. *Get me all the data you can on the Smith Company*

◆ Daten

data base a **store** of information especially in a form which a **computer** can handle

◆ Datenbasis

data-processing the handling of **data** by mechanical or **electronic** means

◆ Datenverarbeitung

date: to date until now. *He has kept a record of his sales to date*

◆ bis heute

day book a book used to enter the daily sales and **purchases** of a company

◆ Journal

day release a **system** of education whereby companies allow workers one day each week away from work, without loss of pay, to attend a course of study at a college. *He is on day release to improve his chances of promotion at work*

◆ tageweise Freistellung von Angestellten zur Weiterbildung

day shift in **shift-working,** a period of work during daylight hours, typically 8.30 a.m. to 5.30 p.m.

◆ Tagschicht

days of grace the number of days allowed for something, e.g. paying an **insurance premium,** after it has become due

◆ Respekttage

day-worker a worker who is regularly working during daylight hours in a company (as opposed to those working on **night-shift**). *We can tell the day-workers about the new rates of pay tomorrow morning, and the night-shift workers this evening*

◆ Tagschichtarbeiter

dead account a customer of a company that no longer buys. *Tell our representative he can stop calling on the Ajax company — they've closed down so they're a dead account*

◆ totes Konto

deadline a date, day or time by which something must be done. *We have to get our offer to buy into the post today if we want to meet their deadline*

◆ Stichtag

deadweight tonnage (*or* **dwt**) the maximum weight which a ship can carry

◆ Gesamtzuladungsgewicht

deal an agreement or **contract** between two or more people. *We've just signed a big deal with White Soap. We do all their advertising for twelve months*

◆ Geschäft

dealer a person who buys and sells goods either as a **wholesaler** or **retailer.** *Send out our new price list to all our dealers straight away*

◆ Händler

dear money money that can be borrowed only at high rates of **interest.** *See* **cheap money**

◆ teures Geld

death duty a tax on the property of a person who has died

◆ Nachlaßsteuer

debenture capital company **capital** from the sale of **debentures**

◆ Anleihekapital

debentures: securities given for money by a company which **guarantees** the holder's rights over the company's **assets**

◆ Obligationen

debit *noun* an entry in an **account** which records money that is owed.

See also **credit** (meaning 2)

◆ Soll

debit *verb* to charge (an account) with the cost of goods or **services** supplied. *Did you debit the Jones account with £50 for the desk which we delivered?*

◆ belasten

debit balance the amount of money still to be paid by an account. When the amount of money paid (**credited**) to an account is less than the amount owed (**debited**) the difference will be a debit balance. *See also* **credit balance**

◆ Debetsaldo

debit note a note sent to a customer showing that his **account** will be charged (**debited**) with a certain amount of money, usually sent to correct a mistake such as not charging enough for the goods when they were bought. *See also* **credit note**

◆ Lastschriftanzeige

debt (1) money, goods or services that are owed. *The amount of the Steel Company's debt is £5,000.* (2) **in debt** owing money. *They've been in debt for six months*

◆ (1) Schuld (2) verschuldet

debt collector a person employed to collect money that is owed to a **creditor.** *See also* **credit agency**

◆ Inkassomandatar

debtor a person or company that owes money to another

◆ Schuldner

debtors to sales ratio a measure of the relationship between a company's **debtors** (customers who owe money) and the sales. For example if the sales are £10,000 and the debtors are £1,000 the ratio is 10:1. Sometimes the ratio is shown as a percentage: Debtors/Sales × 100 = 10%

◆ Verhältnis von Warenforderungen zum Umsatz

debug to search for and correct errors in (a **computer program**)

◆ Fehler beseitigen

decentralization the **process** of moving some of the power to control a company from the head office to branches or departments of the company. *The company had grown so large that it became difficult for the directors to control it and so they introduced decentralisation*

◆ Dezentralisation

decision-making unit (*or* **DMU**) a group of people who influence a decision to buy something. For example if a company is planning to buy an expensive machine the people who will help to decide may include the company owner (or **managing director**), the factory manager, the buyer, and the **sales manager** (who will sell the **product** that the machine makes). *An important decision-making unit for the family car is made up of the husband, the wife, and the oldest child*

◆ für Entscheidungsfindungen zuständiges Team

decision tree a chart which shows the likely results (in branch form, hence the name) that stem from different decisions which could be taken to solve a problem

◆ Entscheidungsdiagramm

deck cargo: cargo carried on the deck of a ship (rather than in the hold and thus more at risk in a storm)

◆ Deckladung

declaration of solvency a statement made on oath by the directors of a company that it can pay all of its debts within twelve months, demanded by the Companies Acts when a company is closing down voluntarily

◆ Solvenzerklärung bei Geschäftsauflösung

deed a written agreement containing a promise by someone to do something (or not to do something) which is signed, may have a **seal** on it; a legal **contract**

◆ Vertragsurkunde

deed of covenant a written agreement to pay a fixed sum of money to a person or an organisation (usually a charity) for a stated number of years

◆ für wohltätige Zwecke eingegangene schriftliche Verpflichtung

default *verb* (1) to fail to pay a debt when it is due. *He defaulted on the payment of the loan.* (2) to fail to appear in court when ordered to by law

◆ (1) in Verzug geraten (2) nicht erscheinen

default *noun* (1) the act of **defaulting.** (2) an option in a **computer program** which the computer will choose if no other is chosen by the user

◆ (1) Verzug (2) Vorgabe-

defect a fault in a **product.** *The car had a defect in the steering*

◆ Defekt

defendant *(law)* the person against whom a **charge** (meaning 2) has been brought. *See* **plaintiff**

◆ Angeklagte(r)

deferred put off (until a later date)

◆ aufgeschoben

deferred annuity a type of **annuity** which begins at some time in the future

◆ Anwartschaftsrente

deferred creditor a person who is owed money by a **bankrupt** but who cannot be paid until others to whom the bankrupt owes money are fully paid, e.g. the wife of a **bankrupt**

◆ im Range nachstehender Gläubiger

deficit (1) the amount of something which is lacking or cannot be found. *There was a deficit of ten items in the goods which were delivered.* (2) the amount by which a person's expenses are greater than his/her **income.** *At the end of the week she had a deficit in her bank account of £20*

◆ (1) Defizit (2) Minus

deflate to bring about **deflation** in (the **economy** of a country). *The government plans to deflate the economy*

◆ eine Deflation herbeiführen

deflation lowering of the prices of goods and **services,** due to a fall in the level of work in the nation, the level of **incomes,** and the level of demand. *See also* **inflation**

◆ Deflation

defranchise *see* **disenfranchise**

del credere agent a special type of **agent** who gets orders for goods from a buyer and who also **guarantees** that the buyer will pay for them. The agent is usually paid a higher **commission** for this extra risk

◆ Handelsvertreter mit Delkredere

delegate *verb* (1) to give (a person) the power to act on one's behalf. (2) to give (some of one's duties and powers) to a **subordinate**

◆ (1) bevollmächtigen (2) delegieren

delegate *noun* a person who represents another person, or group of people at meetings. *The delegate from the trade union rose to speak. See also* **delegation**

◆ Delegierter

delegation (1) the act of **delegating.** (2) (**management**) the act of giving up some of one's duties and powers to a **subordinate,** perhaps because one has too much to do, or as a kind of training. (3) a group of **delegates.** *The Russian delegation arrived today*

◆ (1) Bevollmächtigung (2) Delegierung (3) Delegation

deliver to hand over (goods) to someone else

◆ liefern

delivery (1) the act of **delivering.** (2) part or all of an order on the way to a buyer or that has just arrived at a buyer's **premises.** *When the delivery arrived there were two cases short*

◆ (1), (2) Lieferung

delivery note a **document** which is handed over with goods as they are **delivered** to the customer, usually listing and describing the goods so that the customer can check it against what he has actually received

◆ Lieferschein

demand *noun* (**economics**) the amount of a **product** or **service** wanted by people who are prepared to pay the **going price** for that product or service. *There are times when gold is in very high demand. There is no demand for red shoes this year*

◆ Nachfrage

demand *verb* to **claim** as if by right. *The manager agreed to consider the improvements the union had demanded*

◆ fordern

demand analysis an examination of what affects the demand for a **product** or **service**

◆ Bedarfsanalyse

demand curve a **graph** which shows the **estimated** demands for a **product** at different prices. *See also* **demand schedule**

◆ Nachfragekurve

demand forecasting a method of finding out what the demand for **a product** or **service** is likely to be at different prices so that the price which might give the greatest profit can be shown

◆ Bedarfsprognose

demand-pull inflation (*or* **demand inflation**) (**economics**) a **theory** that **inflation** is caused by an increase in demand for goods which is greater than industry's ability to supply. *See also* **inflation, cost-push inflation**

◆ Nachfrageinflation

demand schedule a **table** or list of the **demand** for a **product** or **service** at various prices. See also **demand curve**

◆ Nachfragetabelle

demarcation dispute a disagreement between groups of workers belonging to different **trade unions** over which workers are allowed to do a certain job

◆ Kompetenzstreitigkeiten zwischen Mitgliedern unterschiedlicher Gewerkschaften

demography the study of human population, birth rates, death rates, marriage, employment, age groups etc

◆ Demographie

demonstrate (1) to show, especially how (something) works or how (something) is done. *We can demonstrate the new machine now.* (2) to gather in large numbers in a public place to show feelings about something. *Miners have been demonstrating about pit closures for about three days*

◆ (1) vorführen (2) demonstrieren

demonstration (1) a method of getting people to buy a **product** by showing it in action. *Our salesman will be happy to give you a demonstration of the new vacuum cleaner.* (2) a very large number of people who gather in a public place to show their feelings about something. *The workers held a big demonstration against the cut in pay*

◆ (1) Vorführung (2) Demonstration

demote to put into a lower rank or position. *He's so poor at his new job* *we may have to demote him. See also* **promote** (meaning 1)

◆ zurückstufen

demotion the act of **demoting**

◆ Zurückstufung

demurrage (1) the amount of money paid when goods have to be held at a port or airport because of a delay in having the goods cleared. (2) the amount of money paid to the owner of a ship when his ship is delayed from unloading **cargo**

◆ (1) Liegegeld (2) Überliegegeld

denationalisation the act of **denationalising**

◆ Reprivatisierung

denationalise to bring (a business or industry) out of public ownership and put it into private ownership. *See also* **nationalise, nationalised industry**

◆ reprivatisieren

denomination name for one of the grades into which certain things, especially money, are divided. *We have most denominations of banknotes*

◆ Nennbetrag

department a part of an organisation, usually responsible for a certain activity: *the sales department, the accounts department*

◆ Abteilung

Department of Trade and Industry (*or* **DTI**) *(UK)* a government department which gives advice and information to commercial and industrial organisations, e.g. on markets, buyers, **agents, EEC** rules, **statistics, imports, exports, tariffs**

◆ Handels- und Industrieministerium

department store a large **retail** store with a number of departments or sections, each selling a different kind of goods, e.g. a furniture department, a men's clothing department

◆ Warenhaus

deposit *noun* (1) an amount of money given to the seller of an article by the person buying it as a first payment, the buyer paying the rest of the money at a later time, either all at once or in equal amounts. *See also* **hire purchase.** (2) an amount of money left with a bank, usually to get **interest** on it, but perhaps also for safekeeping

◆ (1) Anzahlung (2) Bankeinlage

deposit *verb* (1) to leave in a bank (as in **deposit** meaning 2). *See also* **deposit account; depositor.** (2) to give (money) as a **deposit** (meaning 1)

◆ (1) einzahlen (2) anzahlen

deposit account a **bank account** in which money is kept with the aim of earning **interest.** *See also* **current account**

◆ Sparkonto

depositor a person who puts money into a **bank account.** *See also* **deposit**

◆ Deponent

depository a person with whom or a place where things of value are placed for safekeeping

◆ Hinterlegungsstelle

depot (1) a place where goods are stored, especially while waiting to be sent out. (2) a place where buses etc. are kept and **serviced.** (3) *(US)* a railway station

◆ (1) Lager (2) Depot (3) Bahnhof

depreciate to go down in value

◆ im Wert sinken

depreciation (1) a lowering in the value of a **fixed asset** (e.g. machinery) over a period of time. *See also* **amortisation.** (2) a lowering in the value of currency as compared to another currency. *See also* **appreciate**

◆ (1) Wertminderung (2) Kursrückgang

depression a long period of low business activity resulting in high unemployment. *See also* **boom; recession; slump; trade cycle**

◆ Wirtschaftskrise

depth interview (**market research**) a long conversation with a customer or **client** with the aim of getting information which might not be easy to get by other methods

◆ Tiefeninterview

derived demand (*or* **indirect demand**) demand for goods or materials which are used in making some other **product** (which is directly needed by customers). A demand for motor cars will lead to a derived demand for the steel used to make them

◆ mittelbar entstandener Bedarf

derv (*trademark: stands for* diesel-engined road vehicle) fuel used by heavy lorries etc

◆ Diesel

design *verb* to plan how (something) is to be made: *to design a new factory*

◆ entwerfen

design *noun* (1) a plan or drawing of something that is to be made: *a design for a new car.* (2) the way something has been put together considering either what it has to do, or its appearance: *a clever design; an attractive design.* (3) the art of planning how things are to be made, especially in terms of appearance: *a student of design*

◆ (1) Entwurf (2), (3) Design

designate appointed to a post but not yet actually in it: *the managing director designate*

◆ ernannt

desk research finding out about something, e.g. the sales of an industry, by using information which has been already published in some form. *See also* **field research**

◆ sekundärstatistische Auswertung

despatch *see* **dispatch**

destination the place to which a person or thing is going. *How long will the parcel take to reach its destination?*

◆ Bestimmungsort

devaluation a lowering of the value of a currency with regard to other currencies, especially when **fixed exchange rates** are in use, and the lowering is decided by the government. *See also* **revaluation**

◆ Abwertung

developing country (*or* **less developed country, under-developed country, emerging country**) a country which has begun to make some progress in using its **resources** in commerce and/or industry

◆ Entwicklungsland

development (1) the act of using the results of research to make a **product** more attractive, useful, profitable etc. *See also* **research and development.** (2) using the **resources** of an area to make it productive. (3) an area of land which has been made productive or profitable by e.g. planting of crops or building of houses

◆ (1) Entwicklung (2) Erschließung (3) Erschließungsgebiet

development area *(UK)* a part of the country which has been given special government help in order to attract business to it

◆ Fördergebiet

deviation a departure from what is normal, e.g. of a ship from its normal route; unless this is done for a good reason, it can make the ship's **insurance** cover **void**

◆ Abweichung

device a machine or tool which has been designed for a certain purpose

◆ Vorrichtung

diary method a **technique** used in **consumer** research by which a **sample** of consumers keep a record of the things they buy over a certain period of time. This shows changes in the level of sales of certain **products** and the effects of current advertising

◆ Methode zur Erforschung des Verbraucherverhaltens

dictate (1) to say (something) out loud so that someone else can write it down. *She dictates all her letters.* (2) to order or force other people to do something

◆ (1) diktieren (2) Vorschriften machen

dictation the act of **dictating;** what is **dictated** (meaning 1)

◆ Diktat

difference especially in banking, the difference between the amount of cash a **cashier** has at the end of a day and the amount stated in the records

◆ Differenz

differential a difference in pay which follows different levels of experience, responsibility etc. between workers

◆ Lohngefälle

differential advantage something about a **product** or **service** which to a user makes it preferable to another product or service. *See also* **competitive advantage**

◆ Wettbewerbsvorteil

digital computer a type of **computer** which can operate on **data** in number form. *See also* **analog computer**

◆ Digitalrechner

diploma a **certificate,** e.g. to show that one has passed the examinations of a college etc

◆ Diplom

direct access (*or* **random access**) (**computers**) a method of storing **data** which allows it to be retrieved from, or stored at a certain **location**

◆ direkter Zugriff

direct cost a cost directly connected with the production of a **product,** e.g. the cost of materials used or the wages paid to a worker who actually makes it

◆ direkte Kosten

direct debit an instruction from a customer telling his bank to **debit** his account with the bills of certain named **creditors.** This allows the customer to pay regular bills (such as the telephone or the gas bill), whose amount will not always be the same, without having to write cheques or pay postage, etc. *Compare with* **standing order**

◆ Direktabbuchung

direct expense a cost directly connected to some business activity, e.g. the wages of the people who make a **product**

◆ unmittelbarer Kostenaufwand

direct labour (*or* **direct wages**) (1) workers who actually make a **product.** *See* **direct cost.** (2) *(UK)* workers who are directly employed by a **local authority** on building houses and factories

◆ (1) Arbeiter in der Produktion (2) Bauarbeiter, die von der Kommunalverwaltung angestellt sind

direct mail selling goods by post, i.e. by sending advertisements directly to the address of the likely buyer, inviting him/her to order by mail (by post) using an order form provided

◆ Direktwerbung durch die Post

direct-mail shot a set of descriptions of a **product** with order forms sent to a number of different addresses at the same time. *See also* **direct mail**

◆ Postwurfsendung

direct materials cost any payment for materials which are directly linked to the making or selling of a **product,** e.g. the cost of boxes or cartons to protect the goods

◆ unmittelbarer Materialaufwand

director (1) a person chosen by the **shareholders** of a company to run the company on their behalf. (2) a person in charge of a unit or **project**

◆ (1) Direktor (2) Leiter

directors' report a yearly statement from the directors of a company to their **shareholders** explaining those events which affected the year's **financial** results and giving their opinion of the company's future

◆ Bericht der Geschäftsleitung

directory a book giving lists of information, often in alphabetical order: *telephone directory*

◆ Verzeichnis

direct selling a method of selling goods to the public without using a **retailer,** e.g. by **mail order, door-to-door selling**

◆ Direktverkauf

direct wages *see* **direct labour**

disablement benefits *(UK)* money paid by the government to a person who cannot work because of injury received at work

◆ ≈ Schwerbeschädigtenrente

disc *see* **disk**

discharge *verb* (1) to **dismiss** (a person) from employment. (2) to release (a person) from a **contract.** (3) to show formally that the conditions of a contract or agreement, **insurance policy** etc. have been met, and that one has no further claim. *He has discharged his debts*

◆ (1) kündigen (2) entlassen (3) begleichen

discharge *noun* the act of **discharging;** the evidence of this

◆ Kündigung

discharged bankrupt a person who has satisfied a court that he has done everything possible to pay his debts; this usually means that he is freed from any debts that have still not been paid. *See* **discharge** (meaning 3)

◆ entlasteter Konkursschuldner

discount *verb* (1) to lower the price of (something), often by a certain percentage to increase the sale. (2) to sell (a **bill of exchange**) to a third **party** (e.g. a bank) at a lower value than its **face value** in order to receive money immediately

◆ (1) nachlassen (2) diskontieren

discount *noun* (1) a lowering in the price of something: *to be sold at a discount.* (2) an amount by which a price has been lowered: *a discount of 20%.* (3) the difference between a **share's** face value and the lower value of its selling price

◆ (1) Preisnachlaß (2) Rabatt (3) Abschlag vom Emissionskurs

discounted cash flow (*or* **DCF**) a method of estimating the value of money that will come from an **investment,** e.g. a new factory or machine, over the coming years. Since money loses its value over time (£1 buys less now than 3 years ago) a company will want to find out the real value (i.e. today's value) of future flows of earnings from investments. This is worked out by **calculating** at today's value the estimated income of cash over the life of the investment

◆ Barwertrechnung (Berechnung der Rentabilität eines Investitionsprojektes)

discount house (1) an organisation which buys **bills of exchange** at lower than their **face value,** in this way providing immediate cash for the owners of the bills. (2) = **discount store**

◆ (1) Wechselbank

discount rate the **interest rate** which banks charge for providing immediate cash for **bills of exchange**

◆ Diskontsatz

discount store (*also* **discount house**) a large **retail** shop which sells goods at lowered prices. Profit is made by cutting down the usual range of goods and the **service,** e.g. delivery to customers

◆ Billigladen

discretionary income the amount of a person's salary or wages which is left over after he/she has met all necessary expenses (e.g. rent, heating) and which can therefore be spent on whatever he/she as a **consumer** wishes to buy

◆ frei verfügbares Einkommen

discriminate (against) to practise **discrimination** against a person, or group of people. *It is now illegal to discriminate against women in advertising of jobs*

◆ diskriminieren

discrimination the act of treating some people unfairly, especially because of their sex, race, nationality, religion or political beliefs

◆ Diskriminierung

disenfranchise (*or* **defranchise**) (1) to take away from (a person) the right to vote. (2) to take away a **franchise,** or any other special trading privilege from

◆ (1) Wahlrecht entziehen (2) Konzession entziehen

dishonour to refuse to accept or pay (something, e.g. a properly presented cheque or **bill of exchange**). *See* **notary public**

◆ nicht einlösen; Zahlung verweigern

disinflation a lesser kind of **deflation,** in which the amount that people have to spend is reduced but unemployment is not high. *See also* **deflation, inflation**

◆ Rückgang einer inflationären Entwicklung

disk (1) (**computers**) a thin flat circular plate on which data is stored. *See also* **floppy disk, hard disk, magnetic disk.** (2) a thin flat circular plate made of plastic onto which sounds, speech etc. are recorded. *See also* **record** (meaning 2)

◆ (1), (2) Platte

disk drive (**computers**) a machine which can record information onto a **floppy disk** or a **hard disk** and can play back such information

◆ Disk Drive

dismiss to send (a person) away, especially from a job

◆ entlassen

dismissal the act of **dismissing**

◆ Entlassung

dispatch (*or* **despatch**) *verb* (1) to send (goods, materials etc.) to the person who has ordered them. *I want all of today's orders dispatched by tomorrow.* (2) to do (a job or task) quickly

◆ (1) versenden (2) prompt erledigen

dispatch (*or* **despatch**) *noun* (1) the act of sending a person or thing to a certain place. *The dispatch of these goods is urgent.* (2) an official report: *a dispatch from the Home Office*

◆ (1) (Ver-)Senden (2) Depesche

dispatch department (*or* **despatch department**) the department of a business which is concerned with the sending of goods to customers

◆ Versandabteilung

display (1) the arrangement of things to be sold so as to attract the attention of possible customers. *See also* **display advertising.** (2) (**computers**) the **output** of information on a **visual display unit**

◆ (1) Warenauslage (2) Datensichtstation

display advertising a kind of advertising in newspapers and magazines which uses headlines, pictures, design and space to attract the reader's attention. *Compare with* **classified advertising**

◆ Großwerbung

disposable of goods, designed so that they can be thrown away after use: *disposable towels*

◆ Wegwerf-

disposable personal income the amount of a person's wage or salary which he/she can spend after **income tax, national insurance** etc. have been taken off

◆ verfügbares Einkommen

dispute a disagreement, e.g. between management and workers. *Industrial disputes often lead to strikes*

◆ Kontroverse

dissolution the act of **dissolving**

◆ Auflösung

dissolve to end (a company, partnership etc.) *See also* **liquidate, wind up**

◆ auflösen

distribute to cause (goods) to go from maker to user

◆ vertreiben

distribution (1) the actual movement of goods between companies. *See* **physical distribution.** (2) the way in which goods go from maker to user, e.g. from manufacturer to **wholesaler** to **retailer.** *See also* **channel of distribution** and Appendix 7

◆ (1) Verteilung (2) Vertrieb

distribution channel *see* **channel of distribution**

distribution cost a cost in getting goods from the producer to the user, e.g. of sending goods by rail

◆ Vertriebskosten

distributor a person who sells goods made by someone else, e.g. a **wholesaler** or **retailer.** *See also* **channel of distribution** and Appendix 7

◆ Wiederverkäufer

diversification the act or **process** of **diversifying**

◆ Programmausweitung

diversify (1) of a company, to go into new markets with new **products** or **services** (often done by taking over another company) so as to lessen the risks of only having a few products in a few markets. (2) to spread **investments,** e.g. **stocks** and **shares,** over different industries so as to lessen the risks if some investments should fail

◆ (1) Produktionsprogramm auffächern (2) Anlagen streuen

divestment a **process** by which a company sells its **assets** or **transfers** the ownership of part of its business to another company

◆ Abstoßen einer Beteiligung

dividend (1) the amount of money paid out of profits by a company to its **shareholders,** usually a percentage of the **nominal value** of the **shares** (e.g. a **dividend** of ten percent) or as so much to the pound, dollar, etc. (e.g. a dividend of 10p). (2) the amount of money paid out to the **creditors** of a **bankrupt,** expressed in the same way as (1)

◆ (1) Dividende (2) Konkursquote

dividend cover a method of expressing how much of the **net profit** of a company has been paid to the **shareholders** in the form of **dividends.** For example a dividend is 'three times covered' if one third of its net profits have been paid out in dividends

◆ Dividendendeckung

dividend warrant a cheque which is used to pay **dividends** to **shareholders** and can be cashed at a bank, and which also contains a **tax voucher,** which shows that tax has been paid on the dividend

◆ Dividendenanteilschein

dividend yield the amount paid in **dividend** as a percentage of the market price of the **share.** For example if the market price of the share is £1 a dividend of 25p would equal a dividend yield of 25%

◆ Dividendenrendite

division a part of something which is divided up, e.g. a company which is part of a larger group of companies: *Jones & Co., a division of the Waterman Group*

◆ Abteilung

division of labour a **system** of producing goods by splitting the **process** of manufacturing into different parts and arranging for each part to be carried out by a different set of workers. *See also* **assembly line**

◆ Arbeitsteilung

dock dues the **toll** paid by ships when they enter or leave a dock, used for the upkeep of the dock

◆ Dockgebühren

document a piece of paper which gives proof of something and/or information about it

◆ Dokument

document against acceptance (*or* **D/A**) describes the conditions under which the **documents** (e.g. **export invoice, bill of lading, insurance certificate** etc.) which are attached to a **bill of exchange** will be given to a foreign buyer, i.e. only when he accepts the accompanying bill of exchange. He can then collect the goods. *See also* **bill of exchange**

◆ Dokumente gegen Akzept

document against payment (*or* **D/P**) describes the conditions under which the **documents** (e.g. **export invoice, bill of lading, insurance certificate** etc.) attached to a **bill of exchange** will be given to a foreign buyer, i.e. only when he pays the bill of exchange immediately. He can then collect the goods

◆ Dokumente gegen Zahlung

documentary bill of exchange a **bill of exchange** to which **documents** (e.g. **export invoice, insurance certificate, bill of lading, certificate of origin**) are attached. An **exporter** will send it to a foreign customer as proof that he has sent off the goods agreed to in the **contract** of sale, or order, so that the foreign customer will **accept** the bill of exchange. *See also* **bill of exchange**

◆ Dokumententratte

documentary credit *see* **letter of credit, documentary**

do-it-yourself the making or repairing of things, e.g. in the home, normally done by tradesmen; the materials needed for this: *a do-it-yourself shop*

◆ Do-it-yourself

dole *(informal)* – **unemployment benefit:** *to be on the dole*

◆ Arbeitslosengeld

dollar a unit of money used by the US and many other countries. *See* Appendix 8

◆ Dollar

dollar area the area of the world where the US dollar is accepted as standard currency, e.g. Medway Islands, Panama Canal Zone, Puerto Rico

◆ Dollarblock

door-to-door selling a method of selling goods by calling on people in their own houses. *See also* **canvass**

◆ Haus-zu-Haus-Verkauf

dormant account a customer who used to buy goods regularly but no longer does so, though he might again in the future. *Compare with* **dead account**

◆ inaktives Konto

double crown a base unit of size for **posters** (20 inches by 30 inches, 508mm × 762mm)

◆ Posterformat

double indemnity *(US)* a provision in a **life insurance policy,** which allows for twice the amount insured to be paid if the person insured dies by accident, or under other specified conditions. *See also* **indemnity**

◆ Verdoppelung der Versicherungssumme bei Unfalltod

double-page spread (*or* **centre spread**) (**advertising**) a display of a single advertisement right across two pages of a newspaper or magazine

◆ doppelseitige Anzeige

double time wages at twice the normal rate for working at certain times (e.g. on Sundays) or under certain conditions

◆ Lohnverdoppelung

Dow Jones Index (*or* **Dow Jones Industrial Average**) the average price of thirty of the most important company **shares** in the New York **stock market,** published daily by the Dow Jones financial news service, and intended to give an idea of how well or badly the US stock market is doing. *See also* **Financial Times industrial ordinary share index**

◆ Aktienindex der New Yorker Börse

downgrade (1) to lower the importance of or payment for (a certain post). (2) to put (a person) in a lower post than the one he/she was in. *See also* **demotion**

◆ (1) niedriger einstufen (2) herabstufen

down market of goods or **services,** at the cheaper, lower-quality end of the market: *to go down market,* i.e. to start providing goods or services which are cheaper and of lower quality than before. *Compare with* **upmarket**

◆ Qualitätsverschlechterung

down payment the money which is paid at the signing of a **mortgage** or **hire-purchase** agreement

◆ Anzahlung

downtime (1) the time when machinery is not in use because of breakdown, routine repairs etc. (2) the time when a worker is being paid but cannot do his work for reasons that are not his fault, e.g. because a machine is being repaired

◆ (1) Ausfallzeit (2) betrieblich bedingte Verlustzeit

D/P *see* **documents against payment**

draft (1) a written order to a bank to pay a certain sum to a named person, or to the bearer of the order. (2) a **bill of exchange.** (3) a first, rough version of a letter or **document.** *This is just a first draft of the report*

◆ (1) Zahlungsanweisung (2) Tratte (3) Entwurf

draw (1) to pull; to attract. *The new window display should draw people in from the street.* (2) to take out. *He drew £100 out of his account.* (3) to write out (a cheque etc.) (4) of money, to earn (**interest**)

◆ (1) anlocken (2) abheben (3) ausstellen (4) erhalten

drawback a repayment of **duty** which has been paid on **imported** goods when these goods are later **exported**

◆ Zollrückvergütung

drawee a person, company, bank etc. that is ordered to make a payment in a **bill of exchange,** cheque or **draft.** *See also* **drawer**

◆ Bezogener

drawer a person, company, bank etc. that draws up (i.e. writes) a **bill of exchange,** cheque or **draft** ordering someone to pay money to a third person etc. (known as the **payee**)

◆ Aussteller

drill *verb* to bore into something, e.g. into the earth for oil

◆ bohren

drill *noun* a machine or tool for doing this

◆ Bohrer

drilling crew a group of workers who are employed to operate **drills** used for getting oil or other materials

◆ Bohrmannschaft

drill ship a ship used in **offshore** oil operations which carries the **rig** needed for **drilling** for oil and natural gases. *See also* **off-shore oilfield; oil rig**

◆ Bohrschiff

drop shipment an order from a manufacturer large enough to be delivered directly to a company's branch, or shop (instead of going to a company's central store then from there to the branch)

◆ Direktlieferung

dry goods soft goods, such as fabrics, cloths, textiles

◆ Kurzwaren

DTI *see* **Department of Trade and Industry**

due date the date on which a **bill** etc. has to be paid

◆ Fälligkeitsdatum

dues money which has to be paid, e.g. for the use of something: *dock dues*

◆ Gebühren

dummy (1) something which is made as a copy of the real thing, e.g. to show what it will be like when finished. (2) a model of a human figure, used to show clothes. (3) a person who allows his name to be used in someone else's business deal (so that the name of the person actually doing the deal does not become known)

◆ (1) Modell (2) Schaufensterpuppe (3) Strohmann

dump bin (*or* **dump display**) a container in a shop into which goods are piled for sale, usually in an untidy way so as to attract shoppers looking for a bargain

◆ Wühltisch

dumping an unfair trade practice of sending goods that cannot be sold in the home market into overseas markets at a price much lower than the manufacturer's home market, so as to keep up production at home or else to get a price advantage over competitors in the overseas market

◆ Warenausfuhr zu Schleuderpreisen

duplicate *noun* something exactly like something else, a copy

◆ Duplikat

duplicate *adjective* of which there is a **duplicate.** *This is a duplicate report*

◆ Zweit-

duplicate *verb* to make a copy of

◆ eine Zweitschrift anfertigen

durable goods goods which are supposed to remain in use for some time, e.g. televisions, washing machines. *See also* **consumer durables**

◆ langlebige Gebrauchsgüter

Dutch auction a type of **auction** where the **auctioneer** starts at a high price and gradually works his way down until there is a **bid** for the article sold

◆ Versteigerung mit laufend erniedrigtem Ausbietungspreis

duty (1) a government tax on goods, especially **imported** goods. (2) something which a person has to do as part of his/her job. *His first duty in the morning is to open all letters*

◆ (1) Verbrauchssteuer (2) Pflicht

duty-free of goods, on which no **duty** (meaning 1) has to be paid

◆ zollfrei

duty-free shop a shop, e.g. in an international airport, where goods are sold cheaply because they are free from certain kinds of **duty**

◆ Duty-free-Shop

E

E and OE *see* **errors and omissions excepted**

early closing the closing of shops etc. at lunch-time on a certain day of the week, varying from district to district. *Early closing here is on Wednesday*

◆ früher Ladenschluß

early shift in **shift working,** the period of work during the early part of the day, e.g. 8 a.m.–5 p.m.

◆ Frühschicht

early warning system a **technique** for finding out in good time if someone is going wrong with something in a business operation. *We have an early warning system which tells us when we are getting low on fuel*

◆ Frühwarnsystem

earned income *(UK)* money which is earned because of one's direct effort in work (as contrasted with money earned from **investments**), and therefore sometimes taxed less heavily. *See also* **unearned income**

◆ Arbeitseinkommen

earnest money money paid as a first payment, showing that one means to pay the full amount later

◆ Angeld

earnings everything that one earns. *You must declare all your earnings for income tax*

◆ Einkommen

earnings yield earnings per **ordinary share** (after tax) × 100 and divided by the market price of the

$$\text{share} = \frac{\text{earnings} \times 100}{\text{market price}}$$

◆ Ertragsergebnis

ease of prices on the **stock exchange,** to fall a little

◆ abbröckeln

easy money a situation when **interest** rates are low and banks and **building societies** have plenty of **funds** to lend

◆ billiges Geld

ECGD *see* **Exports Credits Guarantee Department**

econometrics the study of the relationships, if any, between **economic** variables (e.g. unemployment, wages) using mathematical and **statistical** methods

◆ Ökonometrie

economic (1) most efficient; most profitable; least wasteful. *They decided it was more economic to spend £10,000 on a new salesman than £10,000 on a new advertising campaign.* (2) connected with the **economy** or with the science of **economics:** *economic problems; an economic survey*

◆ (1) ökonomisch (2) wirtschaftlich

economical cheap to run etc., not wasteful: *an economical car. We try to use economical methods*

◆ sparsam

economic depression *see* **slump**

economic development the **process** of improvement of the wealth of a country or one of its regions, e.g. by increasing the production of food etc., building new roads, docks, railways, etc. *See also* **economic growth**

◆ Wirtschaftsentwicklung

economic geography the study of the earth with special reference to the **natural resources** and the development of trade and industry

◆ Wirtschaftsgeographie

economic goods things which are useful but not easy to get when one wants them and therefore the goods have a price

◆ knappe Güter

economic growth the rate at which the **national income** of a country increases, usually measured by the **gross national product** per head of population

◆ Wirtschaftswachstum

economic order quantity (*or* **EOQ**) the best amount of something to order, considering e.g. the cost of ordering (A); the cost of carrying it in **stock** (R); its annual sales or level of use (S); its unit cost (V)

◆ optimale Bestellmenge

economic planning a **system** of organising the **economy** (meaning 2) of a country following a plan worked out by the government. *See also* **controlled economy, planned economy**

◆ gesamtwirtschaftliche Planung

economics the study of the use of scarce **resources** in the production and marketing of goods and **services**

◆ Volkswirtschaft

economic system the way in which the industry, trade and commerce of a country is organised. *See also* **capitalism; mixed economy; socialism**

◆ Wirtschaftsordnung

economic trend the general direction in which the **economy** (meaning 2) of a country is developing

◆ Wirtschaftsentwicklung

economic warfare a situation in which countries struggle against each other, using trade and **financial** measures. *See also* **embargo**

◆ Wirtschaftskrieg

economics of scale ways of making goods more cheaply by making more of them, through the use of machinery, **automation** etc

◆ Kostenersparnisse durch Erhöhung der Produktion

economise to try to spend less money and to waste less

◆ einsparen

economist a person who writes and lectures on the subject of **economics**

◆ Volkswirtschaftler

economy (1) the **financial** state of a country. *The government says it is trying to improve the economy of the country.* (2) the operation of a country's business activities. *There is an article this week on recent changes in the British economy.* (3) not being wasteful. *We must use the utmost economy*

◆ (1) (Volks-) Wirtschaft (2) Wirtschaft (3) Sparsamkeit

edge up of prices on the **stock exchange,** to rise a little

◆ langsam anziehen

edit (1) to prepare (someone else's writing) for publication in a newspaper, magazine or book. *His job is to edit all new articles before they are sent to the printer.* (2) prepare (a film or tape recording) by cutting or by putting material into a different order

◆ (1) redigieren (2) schneiden

edition the total number of copies of a book, magazine or newspaper produced at any one time. *The book sold so well that it went into a second edition*

◆ Ausgabe

editor a person who **edits** a newspaper, magazine, book, film, or tape recording; the person in charge of the editing of a newspaper or magazine

◆ Herausgeber

editorial a **column** or columns of a newspaper or magazine giving the editor's opinion on some aspect of the news

◆ Leitartikel

EDP *see* **electronic data processing**

educational technology modern methods of giving knowledge or information (especially in schools, colleges and universities), using modern equipment, e.g. TV, **video**, film, slides, tapes, **word processors, computers**

◆ Unterrichtstechnologie

EEC *see* **European Economic Community**

effect (1) a result. *Our advertising had the desired effect — sales increased.* (2) *in plural* goods or belongings. *He took everything with him — all his personal effects.* (3) **to that effect** with that meaning. *I can't remember the exact words he used but he said we were all first-class workers, or words to that effect.* (4) **take effect** to come into being, to begin to operate. *The new law takes effect from Monday*

◆ (1) Wirkung (2) Inhalt (3) in diesem Sinne (4) in Kraft treten

effective able to bring about the planned result. *Our sales training was effective — all our salesmen reached their sales targets*

◆ wirksam

effective date the actual date of the start of a **contract** or agreement

◆ Zeitpunkt des Inkrafttretens

effective demand the total demand for a **product** or **service** at a certain price

◆ wirksame Gesamtnachfrage

efficiency the state of being **efficient**

◆ Leistungsfähigkeit

efficient able to work speedily, or well, without waste or with very little waste. *These new machines are highly efficient*

◆ leistungsfähig

EFTA *see* **European Free Trade Association**

Eight-twenty law *see* **Pareto's law**

elastic demand demand which changes greatly as a result of a small change in price, e.g. of sugar, tea, coffee, where a small price reduction can result in a very high sale

◆ elastische Nachfrage

elastic supply supply when a small change in price results in a large change in the supply of the **product**

◆ elastisches Angebot

elect to choose by voting. *She was elected chairman of the board*

◆ wählen

election the act or **process** of **electing**

◆ Wahl

electronic of or using **devices** in which electrons move in a vacuum, gas etc

◆ elektronisch

electronic data processing (*or* **EDP**) putting **data** (i.e. facts, numbers etc.) into a **computer** for the purpose of arranging the data into information which can be **analysed**

◆ elektronische Datenverarbeitung

embargo (1) an official order stopping the movement of goods, especially ships' **cargo.** *There is an embargo on certain goods going to Russia. See also* **sanction** (meaning 2). (2) the stopping of the publishing of news until a certain time or date. *There is an embargo on publishing the names of the people killed in the accident until their families have been informed*

◆ (1) Embargo (2) Nachrichtensperre

embassy the house and/or office of an ambassador; the ambassador and the people who work for him

◆ Botschaft

embezzle to use (money or property) that does not belong to one. *It turned out that the manager was embezzling the company's money*

◆ veruntreuen

emerging country *see* **developing country**

emolument *(formal)* a **fee,** pay, salary

◆ Vergütung

employ (1) to give paid work to. *When the business expands we shall employ more workers.* (2) *(formal)* to use. *Several different methods are employed in this process*

◆ (1) beschäftigen (2) anwenden

employee (*or* **employed person**) a person who is working for a company or other organisation (as opposed to a **self-employed person**)

◆ Arbeitnehmer

employee benefits things of value apart from wages or salary that an employee may receive, e.g. use of a company car, low-priced meals, or **luncheon vouchers**

◆ Sachbezüge für Angestellte

employee handbook a book given to new employees of a company which contains information about the company such as company history, **products, trade unions,** safety arrangements, **dispute** procedures

◆ Betriebshandbuch

employee participation workers sharing in the responsibility of making decisions about the company's future plans, usually with employees having seats on the **board of directors**

◆ Arbeitermitbestimmung

employer a person or company that pays people to do work

◆ Arbeitgeber

employers' association (*also* **employers' organisation**) a group of owners or directors of companies whose main purpose is to keep good relations between workers and the companies they work for. *Compare with* **trade association**

◆ ≃ Arbeitgeberverband

employment (1) the state of having a job. *I am in regular employment at last after weeks of being without a job.* (2) the kind of job one is employed in. *My present employment is teaching.* (3) relating to the number of people who have a job, or the number of jobs available in a certain area or industry. *The North Sea oil boom has boosted employment figures*

◆ (1) Anstellung (2) Tätigkeit (3) Beschäftigung

employment agency a company which supplies workers to other companies for payment

◆ Arbeitsvermittlungsbüro

employment exchange *see* **job centre**

encash to exchange (a cheque etc.) for cash

◆ einlösen

enclose to put (something) in an envelope, parcel etc., along with something else, especially a letter. *I enclose a cheque for £50*

◆ beifügen

enclosure (*or* **encl.,** *or* **enc.**) something **enclosed.** *The enclosures with his letter included a cheque for £50*

◆ Anlage

end-on course a college or university course made up of six months in college followed by six months in industry. Two new groups of students will thus join the course each year

◆ praxisbezogener Ausbildungsgang

endorse (1) to sign one's name on the back of (a **document**, e.g. a cheque). (2) to put a note or stamp on (a driving **licence**) showing that the holder has committed a motoring **offence.** *He had his licence endorsed three times for dangerous driving.* (3) to give one's support to (an action or point of view). *I endorse what you say.* (4) to lend one's name in support of (a **product**). *A well-known actress endorsed their product*

◆ (1) indossieren (2) eine Strafe vermerken (3) bestätigen (4) Namen für etwas hergeben

endorsee a person who is named on a cheque or **bill of exchange** as having rights to it

◆ Indossat

endorsement the act of **endorsing;** the signature or other sign that this has been done

◆ Vermerk; Indossament

endorser a person who puts an **endorsement** on a **document,** especially a **bill of exchange**

◆ Indossant

endowment a gift of regular sums of money to an organisation: *a hospital endowment*

◆ Stiftung

endowment assurance a **life assurance** where the benefit is payable at the end of an agreed time if the person buying the **policy** is still living, or at the time of death (if he/she dies earlier)

◆ Lebensversicherung

end product a completed **product** at the finish of a production **process.** *In the factory we mix chemicals but the end product is an expensive perfume*

◆ Endprodukt

end user the person who actually uses something. *The buyer of the baby food is usually the mother but the end user is the baby. See* **consumer**

◆ Endverbraucher

engaged of a telephone line, toilet etc., already being used. *I can't get through. The line's engaged*

◆ besetzt

enlargement a copy larger than the original, especially of a photograph. *Make an enlargement of this picture and we'll use it on the front page of the newspaper*

◆ Vergrößerung

enquire (*or* **inquire**) to ask (about something)

◆ sich erkundigen

enquiry (*or* **inquiry**) (1) the act of **enquiring.** *We have had many enquiries about our new product but so far very few sales.* (2) a careful examination of the facts about something. *There is to be a public enquiry about the spillage of waste into the river*

◆ (1) Anfrage (2) Untersuchung

enter (1) to go or come in(to). (2) to put (something) into a list, book or record, e.g. an amount of money into an account

◆ (1) eintreten (2) eintragen

enterprise (1) any type of business. *His firm is quite a small enterprise now though it used to be one of the biggest enterprises in town.* (2) courage or imagination in doing things. *The way he secured those export orders showed great enterprise. See also* **private enterprise**

◆ (1) Unternehmen (2) Unternehmergeist

entertainment (1) something amusing; something done for amusement. (2) the giving of food and drink, e.g. to business clients: *entertainment allowance*

◆ (1) Unterhaltung (2) Bewirtung

entrepreneur a person who owns a business and runs it, and takes the **financial** risks

◆ Entrepreneur

entry (1) the act of **entering.** (2) a record that has been **entered** (meaning 2)

◆ (1) Eintritt (2) Eintrag(-ung)

environment the outside conditions, especially those in which people work or live. *They claimed that the smoke from the company's factory was harming the environment.* See **external environment**

◆ Umwelt

environmental lobby a group of people who try to get others in authority (usually members of parliament) to take action to stop damage to the natural surroundings (e.g. trees, land, air, animals). *There is an environmental lobby trying to ban the use of chemicals on the land*

◆ Umwelt-Lobby

EOQ *see* **economic order quantity**

equal pay pay that is the same for men and women who are doing the same work

◆ gleicher Lohn

equilibrium price the price at which the quantity demanded equals the quantity supplied and where demand and supply are not likely to change

◆ Gleichgewichtspreis

equipment (1) things which are used in the carrying out of an activity. *The factory needs more equipment.* (2) the act of providing equipment

◆ (1) Ausstattung (2) Ausstatten

equities – equity (meaning 3)

equity (1) fairness, justice. (2) the rights of ordinary **shareholders** to a **share** in the profits of a company. (3) the **ordinary shares** in a company

◆ (1) Gerechtigkeit (2) Anspruch auf Gewinnbeteiligung (3) Stammaktien

equity capital that part of the total **capital** of a company which belongs to the owners of the business (the **ordinary shareholders**)

◆ Eigenkapital

eraser a piece of rubber etc. which can remove pencil, ink or typewriter writing or marks

◆ Radiergummi

ergonomics the study of the relationship between man and his work, his tools, machines, and surroundings, with the aim of improving **output** by improving the design of work **processes,** machines etc

◆ Ergonomie

errors and omissions excepted (*or* **E and OE**) sometimes used in letters, **invoices,** statements to state that the company is not liable for any clerical mistakes or omissions

◆ Irrtum vorbehalten

escalation clause the part of a **contract** which allows for price rises due to a rise in materials and wages

◆ Gleitklausel

escape clause the part of a **contract** which allows one of the **parties** under certain conditions to **withdraw** from the contract without paying any penalty

◆ Rücktrittsklausel

establish to set up, to bring into being. *The company was established in 1843*

◆ gründen

established brand a well-known **product** or **brand** which has a high level of sales

◆ gut eingeführte Marke

establishment (1) the act of **establishing.** (2) a large business. *Clark and Co. is a first class establishment.* (3) the people, buildings and machines within a large organisation

◆ (1) Gründung (2) Unternehmen (3) Betrieb

establishment charges the costs of people, machines, buildings within a large company. The **indirect costs** of a company. *See also* **establishment** (meaning 2)

◆ Generalunkosten

estate all the property or possessions of a person, especially someone who has died. (2) a large area of land used for a certain purpose; *an industrial estate. They own an estate in the north*

◆ (1) Nachlaß (2) (Industrie-) Gelände; Gut

estate agent a person whose business is to bring buyers and sellers of houses into contact with each other. *I've been to the estate agent to see if he will sell my house for me. See also* **agent**

◆ Immobilienmakler

estimate *verb* to judge how much something will cost, or to judge the length of time, or the size etc. *Can you estimate the cost of building the factory?*

◆ schätzen

estimate *noun* a judgement of the cost, time, etc. *I've received three estimates from three different firms. Compare with* **quotation**

◆ Schätzung; Kostenvoranschlag

estimator a person whose job it is to **estimate** costs etc

◆ Schätzer

estoppel *(law)* a rule whereby a person is prevented (or **stopped**) from denying something he has said or written. This rule of law for example could stop a company from denying the authority of its **agent** when it is obvious that such an agency is in existence

◆ Unzulässigkeit, eine eidliche Erklärung zu widerrufen

Euro-dollars: dollars in European banks which are used for trade in Europe, e.g. dollars in an English bank which are lent to a company in France

◆ Eurodollar

European Community see **European Economic Community**

European Court of Justice the law court of the **European Economic Community** responsible for putting into effect the rules of the **Treaty** of Rome. It meets in Luxembourg and has a judge from each member state

◆ Europäischer Gerichtshof

European Economic Community (*or* **EEC,** *or* **Common Market**) a group of countries set up by the **Treaty** of Rome in 1957. Its purposes are: to establish a **common market** within its member states; to encourage the development of **economic** activities and to raise the **standard of living** of the member states. Members: Belgium, Denmark, France, Federal Republic of Germany, Greece, Ireland, Italy, Luxembourg, Netherlands, United Kingdom. Headquarters: Brussels. Official languages: Danish, Dutch, English, French, German, Greek, Irish, Italian

◆ Europäische Wirtschaftsgemeinschaft (EG)

European Free Trade Association (*or* **EFTA**) a group of countries set up in 1960 for the purposes of increasing trade, employment, and the **standard of living** of its members. Membership: Austria, Iceland, Norway, Portugal, Sweden, Switzerland. Headquarters: Geneva. Working language: English

◆ Europäische Freihandelszone (EFTA)

evade to try to escape or avoid doing (something, e.g. paying tax)

◆ umgehen

evasion the act of **evading**

◆ Umgehen

evict to take (a person) away from a house or land by force of law

◆ Zwangsräumung betreiben

eviction order an order by a court of law that a person be **evicted**

◆ Räumungsbefehl

excess *adjective* above a certain limit, more than is necessary, spare: *excess capacity; excess demand*

◆ Über-

excess *noun* an amount which is above a certain limit or more than is necessary. *There is an excess of imports over exports this year*

◆ Übermaß, Überschuß

excess supply a situation when the supply of a **product** is greater than the demand for it

◆ Überangebot

exchange *verb* to give one thing for another. *He exchanged the faulty product for a new one*

◆ umtauschen

exchange *noun* (1) the act of **exchanging.** (2) the act of **exchanging** the money of one country for the money of another. (3) a building in which things are **exchanged,** bought or sold: *stock exchange.* (4) (*also* **telephone exchange**) a building in which telephone lines and calls are connected

◆ (1) Umtausch (2) Wechseln (3) Börse (4) Fernamt

exchange control a control put by a country on the buying and selling of other currencies and on the way its own currency is to be used to settle foreign debts

◆ Devisenkontrolle

exchange rate the rate (value) at which a currency may be exchanged for another currency, e.g. £1 = $1.40

◆ Wechselkurs

exchequer *(UK)* the government department in charge of the country's finances. *See also* **Chancellor of the Exchequer**

◆ Schatzamt; ≃ Finanzministerium

excise duty a tax put by a country on certain goods produced in that country, e.g. on tobacco and alcohol in the UK

◆ Verbrauchssteuer

exclusion clause a clause in a **contract** which states that something is not covered by the contract, e.g. what risks are not covered by an **insurance policy**

◆ Haftungsausschlußklausel

exclusive *adjective* limited to certain people or organisations only. *We have exclusive rights in this market. This is a very exclusive club*

◆ exklusiv

exclusive *noun* an important piece of news, photograph etc. which is given to one newspaper alone, or to one radio or television company. *I can see the Daily Star has an exclusive on the big fire in the city*

◆ Exklusivbericht

exclusive agency agreement a **contract** with an **agent** giving him alone the right to sell certain **products,** or to sell certain products into certain markets

◆ Alleinvertretungsvertrag

ex-directory of a telephone number, not in the telephone directory because the holder does not want the number to be publicly known

◆ Geheimnummer

ex dock (*or* **ex quay** *or* **ex wharf**) the price quoted includes all costs up to the point of delivery on land at the port and also includes unloading costs and customs duty

◆ ab Kai

execute to carry out, to put into effect. *Smith's the furniture company, were very quick in executing my order — I got my new office chair today*

◆ ausführen

executive a person having the power to plan and control certain activities within a company. *He is an executive in the sales department*

◆ Führungskraft

executive director a director who is a full-time member of the **board of directors** and who is in charge of a **department** within a company, such as *the sales director, the personnel director*

◆ hauptamtlich an der Geschäftsführung beteiligter Direktor; Vorstandsmitglied

executor a person appointed to see that the instructions in a will are properly carried out

◆ Testamentsvollstrecker

ex factory the quoted price includes all costs up to the point when the goods leave the factory. Any charges after that have to be paid by the buyer

◆ ab Werk

ex gratia payment money given in payment as a favour and not because one has to pay it. *Although the company felt it was not responsible for his accident at the factory nevertheless it decided to make an ex gratia payment of £100*

◆ freiwillige Zahlung

exhibit *verb* to show (**products** or **services**) to the public or trade for the purposes of increasing sales

◆ ausstellen

exhibit *noun (law)* something produced in a court of law as evidence

◆ Beweisstück

exhibition a show of something, e.g. of goods to try to increase sales; the place, usually a hall or public area, where this is held. *See* **trade fair**

◆ Ausstellung

exhibitor a person who or a company which rents space at an **exhibition** and puts goods or **services** on show

◆ Aussteller

ex officio *(Latin)* because of one's position. *As company director he is, ex officio, a member of the board of directors*

◆ von Amts wegen

expand to (cause to) grow larger. *We are trying to expand our business*

◆ erweitern

expansion the act of **expanding.** *The video market is growing — and this expansion will continue*

◆ Erweiterung

expenditure (1) the spending of money. *The company's expenditure on the new machinery ran into thousands of pounds. See* **capital expenditure.** (2) the spending of time or care or effort

◆ (1) Ausgaben (2) Aufwand

expense (1) money paid by a worker in connection with his job, e.g. money paid for petrol by a salesman for his car. *You will have £9000 a year plus expenses.* (2) cost which is related to marketing goods or **services** or related to the **administration** of a company: *selling expense, office expense*

◆ (1) Spesen (2) Kosten

expense account a statement of cash spent in connection with one's business, which the company will refund, e.g. a salesman's **expense** account

◆ Spesenabrechnung

expiry the ending (of an agreement etc.); the date on which this happens

◆ Verfalldatum

explore to examine carefully in order to find out more. *We have to explore all the possibilities of this company's offer*

◆ erforschen

exploration well an oil well sunk in order to find out if oil is actually there, and in what quantity

◆ Probebohrung

export *verb* to send (goods) out of the country for sale. *See also* **exports**

◆ exportieren

export *noun* (1) the act of **exporting.** (2) something **exported.** *Most of our exports go to the Third World*

◆ (1), (2) Export

export agent a person who agrees to sell goods by acting on behalf of a company in another country. *See also* **agent**

◆ Exportvertreter

Export Credits Guarantee Department (*or* **ECGD**) *(UK)* a government **insurance** service for UK **exporters** which can protect an exporter against certain risks, e.g. the failure of the buyer to pay

◆ Versicherungsbehörde für Ausfuhrbürgschaften

exporter a person who or organisation which **exports**

◆ Exporteur

export house (1) *(UK)* a company which buys goods from a UK manufacturer and then **exports** them at a profit. (2) *(UK)* a company which cooperates with a UK manufacturer in all matters to do with the manufacturer's exports, e.g. getting export orders, holding **stocks** delivery, advertising etc

◆ (1) Exporthaus (2) Exportmakler

export licence a government **document** which is needed before certain goods can be sent out of the country for sale, e.g. drugs, weapons

◆ Ausfuhrgenehmigung

ex quay *see* **ex dock**

ex-rights: shares or **securities** bought or sold with no rights to any **dividend** or new shares (which may be offered at less than the market price). *See also* **cum**

◆ ex Bezugsrecht

ex ship the price quoted includes all costs up to the point of delivery at the port but while the goods are still on board the ship. The buyer is responsible for all charges after that including unloading and customs duty

◆ frei ab Schiff

external of the outside; outside something; foreign; *the external walls of the building; external trade*

◆ Außen-

external environment all those forces outside of the company which a company cannot control but which affect its plans, e.g. politics, legal, social, cultural, **economic** forces

◆ äußeres Beziehungsfeld

extractive industry businesses which take materials from the land or sea, e.g. oil, coal, stone, fish

◆ Industrie der Steine und Erden

extraordinary general meeting a special meeting of a company, called by the directors or the **shareholders,** to discuss some urgent matter which cannot wait till the **annual general meeting**

◆ außerordentliche Hauptversammlung

extraordinary resolution a subject which a company discusses at an **extraordinary general meeting** in order to take a decision on it. For the **resolution** to be put into action the meeting must support it by more than three-quarters of the votes present at the meeting

◆ qualifizierter Mehrheitsbeschluß

extrapolation the act of making an **estimate** of the future (usually to do with figures) using facts already known. *He noted the sales for each of the past nine months and using these figures he extrapolated the sales for the next two months*

◆ Extrapolation

extrinsic value the value of something (e.g. gold) after it has been made into an object for selling (e.g. a gold ring). *See also* **intrinsic value**

◆ äußerer Wert

ex warehouse the quoted price includes all costs up to the point when the goods leave the warehouse. Any charges after that have to be paid by the buyer

◆ ab Lager

ex wharf *see* **ex dock**

ex works the price quoted includes all costs up to the point when the goods leave the seller's works. Any charges after that have to be paid by the buyer

◆ ab Werk

F

face-to-face selling selling to a buyer in the buyer's presence (as distinct from selling to a buyer by telephone or by letter, or by advertisements)

◆ vis-a-vis Verkauf

face value (1) the worth of a coin or banknote as shown on its face. (2) the worth of a **share, product** etc. as stated on it. *The face value of the shares is £1.00 each but they are selling for £1.50*

◆ (1) Nominalwert (2) Nennwert

facsimile an exact copy of something written (such as a letter or a **document**) or a copy of a photograph. *He took from his pocket the agreement — it was not the original but a facsimile*

◆ Faksimile

factor *noun* (1) a company which buys or takes over the debts of another company at a price less than the **face value** of the debts. By this means the selling company gets cash from the factor immediately and the factor earns profit by collecting the full value of the debts from the debtors. (2) a type of agent who not only receives orders for his **principal's** goods but who buys the goods from the principal and also stores them. (3) a fact, event, or thing which brings about a result. *The main factor in the firm's success was the big demand for its product*

◆ (1) Factoringgesellschaft (2) Kommissionär (3) Faktor

factor *verb* to carry out the business of a **factor** (meaning 1). *He factors company debts*

◆ Schulden aufkaufen

factors of production land, **labour, capital** and management. *For a country to make economic progress all the factors of production must be present*

◆ Produktionsfaktoren

factory a building where goods are made by the use of machines, usually in large quantities

◆ Fabrik

factory acts laws covering the health, safety and **welfare** of workers in factories. The UK Factories Act 1961 brought many of these separate laws together to cover many aspects of the welfare of workers

◆ Arbeiterschutzgesetzgebung

factory agreement an agreement reached between a company and all its workers in one of its factories (as distinct from an agreement with only a section of the workforce, or an agreement covering all of the company's factories)

◆ Betriebsvereinbarung

factory costs all the costs of production (materials, wages, power, and factory heating etc.)

◆ Produktionskosten

failure (1) a company which cannot pay its debts. *The company's c failure — it will close soon.* (2) lack of success; an unsuccessful person or thing. *He never took any risks because he was always afraid of* *failure. They tried out the new product but it was a failure*

◆ (1) Pleite (2) Mißerfolg; Versager

fair *adjective* (1) just. *This is a fair price we're offering you.* (2) honest. *To be fair, we admit you have never let us down before.* (3) reasonable. *He stands a fair chance of winning*

◆ (1) fair (2) ehrlich (3) recht gut

fair *noun* (1) a kind of **market** (meaning 2), usually one held in a certain place at a certain time. *The local cattle fair is in September.* (2) – **trade fair**

◆ (1) Markt (2) Messe

fair-trade agreements trade agreements between countries which allow for the **duty-free** exchange of goods between them

◆ Zolltarifabkommen

Fair Trading Act 1973 a UK law which gives protection to the public against unfair actions by **monopolies** and against **mergers** which may not be in the public interest. It also promotes greater competition in industry and amongst **retailers**

◆ Verbraucherschutz- und Kartellgesetz

fair wear and tear damage to goods brought about by normal use. *This car is guaranteed for one year except for parts which have to be replaced through fair wear and tear*

◆ allgemeine Abnutzung

fall-back pay a fixed sum of money paid as wages when the full wages cannot be paid due to reasons which are not the fault of the workers. *The building workers who were preparing the ground for new houses will not be able to work because of the flooding and will receive fall-back pay instead of their full wages*

◆ garantierter Mindestlohn

falling market a situation when the value of goods or **shares** is going down. *Since the decline in trade there is a falling market in oil shares*

◆ Baissemarkt

fall into arrears not to keep up one's payment of a debt or one's rent etc. *Could you lend me some money? – I've fallen into arrears with the rent*

◆ in Verzug geraten

false pretences words or actions intended to deceive. *He got money from customers under false pretences by claiming to be an agent of a well-known company*

◆ Vorspiegelung falscher Tatsachen

family allowance regular payments by the UK government to the parents of children, related to the number of children in the family below a certain age

◆ ≃ Kindergeld

family expenditure survey a yearly survey by the UK government of how families spend their **income**

◆ Indexvergleich der Familienlebensunterhaltskosten

family income supplement money paid by the UK government to those families whose **income** is below a certain level

◆ Unterstützungszahlung an einkommensschwache Familien

family life-cycle a theory that different stages of family life cause demand for certain types of **products.** Thus young married people buy a lot of such items as cookers, carpets, televisions, while married people with children of school age buy a lot of do-it-yourself products, games, books

◆ Nachfragezyklus in Abhängigkeit von den Stadien der Familienentwicklung

farm out to have (some work) done by someone else in order to complete a job. *We will do all the brickwork for the new houses but we will farm out* *all the woodwork — the doors, windows and so on*

◆ (Aufträge) weitervergeben

farm subsidies the **subsidies** given to farmers by the government when the market price of certain farm **products** is too low to provide a fair profit

◆ Subventionierung von Agrarerzeugnissen

FAS *see* **free alongside ship**

fast-moving consumer goods (*or* **FMCG**) low-priced goods in regular demand such as butter, milk, canned soups, coffee, tea, etc.

◆ Waren mit hoher Umschlagsgeschwindigkeit

father of the chapel (*or* **FOC**) name given to a male **shop steward** in the printing and publishing unions. *See also* **mother of the chapel**

◆ gewerkschaftliche Vertrauensperson im Druckgewerbe

favourable balance of trade *see* **balance of trade**

feasibility study a close examination of the costs and benefits of a project to decide if a company should undertake it. *We plan to do a feasibility study first before deciding whether or not to buy the £10,000 computer*

◆ Durchführbarkeitsuntersuchung

featherbedding employing more workers on a job than is necessary. *When the trade union insisted that three men and not one should operate the new machine the management thought that this was featherbedding*

◆ Anstellung nicht benötigter Arbeitskräfte

feature (1) something which makes one thing or person different from another. *A feature of all products is that they are guaranteed against defects for three years.* (2) a special study or article in a newspaper on some subject. *The Daily News has a feature on the Royal Family today.* (3) full-length film in a cinema. *The feature was about beasts from outer space*

◆ (1) Merkmal (2) Sonderbeitrag (3) Spielfilm

federation (1) the coming together of various groups which have certain interests in common but which wish also to keep a certain amount of independence; the union thus formed, e.g. the Federation of International Civil Servants' Associations. (2) a form of politics in which a certain amount of self-government is allowed to the states etc. making up the union; a country with this form of government. *The USA is a federation*

◆ (1) Verband (2) Bund

fee (1) money charged for work done by a professional person, such as a lawyer, doctor or accountant. *The dentist's fees are very high.* (2) a sum of money paid, e.g. for entrance to something, for instruction. *We can't afford the school fees any more.* (3) *(law)* a right or **claim** to property that can be inherited

◆ (1) Honorar (2) Gebühr (3) Lehen

feed *verb* (1) to cause **data** to be put into a **computer** for **processing.** (2) to give information to (a person). *I'll go to the managers' meeting and feed you with the information that I get there*

◆ (1) zuführen (2) mit Informationen versorgen

feed *noun* (1) the part of a machine etc. by means of which it is supplied with material, e.g. the **feed** of a **computer** puts **data** into it for **processing.** (2) food for animals. (3) a meal taken by animals or babies: *three feeds a day*

◆ (1) Zuführung (2) Futter (3) Fütterung; Mahlzeit

feedback any kind of **response** which will show whether something will have to be changed and in what way. For example a TV company may try out a new programme but the **feedback** (the viewing figures) may show that the public do not like it. *What's the feedback on the new model which we're trying out?*

◆ Feedback

felony serious crime

◆ schweres Verbrechen

fiche *see* **microfiche**

fidelity bond a type of **insurance** which protects an employer against loss through an employee who is dishonest or who neglects his/her duties

◆ Kaution gegen Veruntreuung

fiduciary *(law)* a person who acts for the benefit of someone else, e.g. a **trustee**

◆ Treuhänder

field force (marketing) a group of researchers who **interview** possible customers near where they live or work

◆ Außendienstkräfte

field organisation a **system** used for arranging the work of a **field force**

◆ Außendienstorganisation

field research a method of finding out about possible customers' attitudes to a **product** or **service** by going out and **interviewing** them. *See also* **desk research**

◆ Primärerhebung

field sales manager a person who is responsible for controlling and training a **sales force** (group of salesmen)

◆ Außendienstleiter

FIFO *see* **first in first out**

figures *see* **round figures**

file *noun* (1) a box or folder in which letters and similar **documents** on a certain subject are kept together for reference. (2) a collection of such documents. *We have the case on file.* (3) an organised set of **data stored** in a **computer**

◆ (1) Aktenordner (2) Akte (3) Datei

file *verb* (1) to put (a **document**) on **file.** (2) to record (something) officially. (3) (**computers**) to save and **store** (**data**)

◆ (1) zu den Akten nehmen (2) registrieren (3) Daten speichern

final demand a last written request for payment before legal action is taken. *I've received a final demand from the rates people*

◆ letzte Zahlungsaufforderung

final dividend the last **dividend** paid by a company in the **financial year**

◆ Schlußdividende

finance *noun* (1) the study of the **management** (meaning 3) of money. *A good manager must understand finance.* (2) money supplied to a company by **shareholders,** lenders etc. *I'm worried about the company's level of finance.* (3) the supply of money for a particular **project**

◆ (1) Finanzwesen (2) Finanzen (3) Finanzierung

finance *verb* to provide money for (something). *The new factory will be partly financed by the government*

◆ finanzieren

Finance Act a law passed by the UK government (usually each year) which allows the government to get through taxes (e.g. **income tax, corporation tax**) the money it needs for the **financial year**

◆ Finanzgesetz (Teil des Haushaltsgesetzes)

finance market a place where bankers and **financiers** arrange the borrowing and lending of money

◆ Finanzmarkt

financial accounting the **process** of presenting statements to the **shareholders** and/or management of a company to allow them to see what progress it is making

◆ Finanzbuchhaltung

financial management the **process** of finding money for a company, then planning and controlling the use of it for the benefit of the company

◆ Finanzverwaltung

financial ratios (*or* **accounting ratios** *or* **management ratios**) direct comparison of two quantities within a company to give a measurement or **ratio.** For example, the **current ratio** shows how well a firm's **current liabilities** are covered by its **current assets,** as follows:

$$\frac{\text{current assets}}{\text{current liabilities}} = \frac{£100{,}000}{50{,}000} = 2{:}1$$

This ratio shows that current liabilities are covered twice over. *See also* Appendix 4

◆ finanzwirtschaftliche Verhältniszahlen

financial risk a danger of loss of money in a business **project.** *To invest in the Brown Company just now is taking a big financial risk*

◆ finanzielles Risiko

financial statement a **document,** such as a **balance sheet,** which describes the **financial** situation and/or performance of an organisation

◆ Bilanz

Financial Times industrial ordinary share index the average price of thirty of the most important company **shares** in the UK **stock market,** published daily by the Financial Times newspaper, and intended to give an idea of how well or badly the UK stock market is doing. *See also* **Dow Jones Index**

◆ Aktienindex der Financial Times

financial year a period chosen by a company as the one on which it will base its **accounts:** this may or may not be the same as the calendar year (1 January to 31 December). *Our financial year ends on 31 March. See also* **fiscal year**

◆ Geschäftsjahr

financier a person or company that provides **funds** for companies and other organisations. *Three well-known financiers are backing the Bell Construction Company in the building of the new hotel*

◆ Financier

fine *noun* an amount of money which a person is made to pay because a law or rule has been broken

◆ Geldstrafe

fine *verb* to make (a person) pay a **fine**

◆ zu einer Geldstrafe verurteilen

finished goods completed **products,** ready for sale

◆ Fertigwaren

fire insurance one of the main kinds of **insurances** which protects against loss caused by fire and certain other **risks**

◆ Feuerversicherung

firm *noun* a company or partnership

◆ Firma

firm *adjective* (1) not going to be changed: *a firm offer.* (2) of prices of **stocks** and **shares** on the **stock exchange,** steady, likely to rise

◆ (1) verbindlich (2) fest

first in first out (*or* **FIFO**) a method of valuing **stocks** of goods which have been bought in over a period at different prices: by this method the value of goods in **stock** is based on the value of those which were bought most recently. *See also* **last in first out**

◆ zuerst eingekauft – zuerst verkauft

first-line management (*or* **front-line management**) people who are directly responsible for **supervising** workers on the **shop floor,** e.g. **foremen.** *The boss said we had to support the foremen; they were our frontline managers*

◆ Manager an der 'Front'

fiscal connected with public money or taxes: *fiscal year*

◆ Finanz-

fiscal measures steps taken by a government to control the **economy** of a country, for example by tax changes

◆ steuerliche Maßnahmen

fiscal year a period of twelve months regarded as a unit by the government for the collection of taxes, in the UK for personal tax from 6 April to 5 April the following year, and in the US from 1 July to 30 June. *See also* **calendar year, financial year**

◆ Steuerjahr

fixed assets: assets owned by a company which are meant to be used by it in the running of the business over a long period of time, e.g. land, buildings, machinery. *See* Appendix 2

◆ Anlagevermögen

fixed capital the part of the wealth of a company that is **invested** in **fixed assets.** *See* Appendix 2

◆ Anlagekapital

fixed charge (*or* **fixed expense**) (1) an amount of money which a company has to pay out which does not change no matter how much or how little business the company does, e.g. the repayments of a loan. (2) a **claim** which a person who or organisation which had lent money to a company has on a particular item of the company's **assets** if it cannot pay its debts. *See also* **floating charge**

◆ (1) feste Belastung (2) dingliche Pfändungssicherheit

fixed cost an amount of money which has to be paid in order to produce goods, and which does not change according to the amount of goods produced, e.g. the rent paid for a factory. *See* appendix 6

◆ feste Kosten

fixed exchange rate a fixed level at which a government tries to keep the value of its currency in relation to other currencies. *See also* **floating exchange rate**

◆ fester Wechselkurs

fixed expense *see* **fixed charge**

fixed-price contract a business agreement in which the person who has to provide the **service** is not allowed to change the agreed price for any reason

◆ Festpreisvertrag

fixtures and fittings things which are not part of a property (house, factory etc.) but which are attached to it, e.g. an electric light switch, a shelf, a table, chairs etc.

◆ Betriebs- und Geschäftsausstattung

flag of convenience the flag of a country where a ship can be **registered** so that it can be run cheaply without having to follow the regulations and tax-laws that are normal in other countries

◆ billige Handelsflagge

flash pack a type of package which displays information that the contents are being sold at a special low price, as part of a **promotion** to improve sales

◆ augenfällige Werbepackung

flat rate a payment which does not change, e.g. a worker may be paid at a flat rate of £4 per hour no matter how much he produces

◆ Pauschalsatz

flat yield *see* **current yield**

fleece *(informal)* to steal money from (a person) by cheating him. *He fleeced him over the years of £12,000*

◆ jmd. schröpfen

flexible working hours (*or* **flexitime**) an arrangement by which an employee has some control over his working time, e.g. by being able to start or finish at certain times that are convenient for him, as long as the agreed number of hours are worked

◆ gleitende Arbeitszeit

flip-chart a method of showing information, consisting of large sheets of paper which can be turned down or torn off to show the next sheet

◆ Flip-chart

float *verb* (1) to (cause to) rest on the surface of a liquid. (2) to start (a company), e.g. by offering **shares** in it for sale. *See also* **flotation.** (3) to allow (a currency) to be bought and sold freely, without a fixed **exchange rate**

◆ (1) schwimmen (2) gründen (3) floaten

float *noun* a small amount of money kept for change or to cover small expenses. *The shopkeeper always started the day with a float of £10. See also* **imprest system, petty cash**

◆ Wechselgeld

floating charge a **claim** which a person who has lent money to a company has on all of a company's **assets** (and not just on one asset). *See also* **fixed charge**

◆ schwebende Belastung

floating exchange rate an **exchange rate** not controlled by the government, but allowed to go up or down, according to demand. *See also* **fixed exchange rate, float** *(verb,* meaning 3)

◆ flexibler Wechselkurs

floating rig a **rig** (meaning 1) which floats and can be moved from one area to another, as it is needed

◆ schwimmende Ölbohrinsel

floor walker a person employed by a **store** to mix with the customers so as to be able to prevent theft from the store

◆ Ladenaufsicht

floppy disk (**computers**) a flexible **magnetic disk**

◆ Floppy disk

flotation the act of starting up a company, e.g. by selling **shares** in it. *See also* **float** (*verb,* meaning 2)

◆ Gründung

flotsam (1) parts of a ship or its **cargo** which have been thrown overboard and which are still afloat. (2) wreckage which is afloat from a sunken or damaged ship. *See also* **jetsam**

◆ (1) Treibgut (2) treibendes Wrackgut

flow-chart (*or* **flow-diagram**) a chart or diagram which shows how one stage in a **process** follows another, step by step

◆ Arbeitsablaufdiagramm

flow-line production a **technique** of producing goods in which the goods, as they are being manufactured, go in a line from one part of the factory to the next until they are complete. *See also* **assembly line, division of labour**

◆ Fließbandproduktion

fluctuate especially of prices, to rise and fall a lot. *Prices on the stock market are fluctuating because of rumours about a general election*

◆ schwanken

fluctuation the act of changing up and down: *the fluctuation of prices in the stock market*

◆ Schwankung

fly-by-night *adjective* (something which is) not to be relied on; not to be trusted, especially in **financial** matters. *Don't buy anything from him: he is a salesman from a fly-by-night company*

◆ zweifelhaft

FMCG *see* **fast-moving consumer goods**

FOB *see* **free on board**

folder (1) a cover made from stiff paper used for holding loose papers, notes etc. *He carried his documents in a folder.* (2) a piece of folded paper which advertises something. *They had designed an attractive folder to advertise their services.* (3) a machine that folds envelopes or paper

◆ (1) Aktenmappe (2) Prospekt (3) Falzmaschine

folio (1) a sheet of paper of a standard size which has been folded in the middle to give four pages. (2) a book made of such sheets. (3) a sheet of paper which has been numbered on one side only. (4) a printed page number. (5) (**book-keeping**) two facing pages in a **ledger** which both have the same number. (6) *(law)* a unit for measuring the length of a legal piece of writing (in UK, 72 or 90 words, in US, 100 words)

◆ (1) Folio (2) Foliant (3) einseitig numeriertes Blatt (4) Seitenzahl (5) Kontobuchseite (6) Einheitswortzahl

foot the bill *(informal)* to pay the money that is due for something. *Who is going to foot the bill for all this entertaining?*

◆ bezahlen

forecast *verb* to tell in advance what may happen in the future, often by examining what is happening at the present or has happened in the past

◆ voraussagen

forecast *noun* something told in advance in this way. *We need a forecast of sales for the next six months*

◆ Voraussage

foreclose to sell an **asset** (e.g. a building, machine) belonging to a person who has **mortgaged** it, because he can no longer pay the mortgage

◆ Zwangsvollstreckung betreiben

foreclosure an action taken against a person who has **mortgaged** his property, but who cannot repay his debt. By this action he is taken to court and (if he still cannot pay) he loses all claim to his property

◆ Zwangsvollstreckung

foreign bill *(UK)* any bill of exchange that is not drawn and payable in the UK, or drawn in the UK on a person normally living there. (*US* **external bill**)

◆ Fremdwährungswechsel

foreign exchange (1) a **system** by which the currency of a country is changed into the currency of another country. (2) the currency of a foreign country

◆ (1) Devisenkurs (2) Devisen

foreign exchange broker a person who arranges for the exchanging of the currencies of different countries

◆ Devisenmakler

foreign exchange market a group of people who deal with each other in exchanging foreign currencies

◆ Devisenmarkt

foreign investment (1) the act of putting money for profit into business in another country. (2) an amount of money that has been put into another country in this way

◆ (1), (2) Auslandsinvestition

foreign trade the exchange of goods and **services** for profit between different countries

◆ Außenhandel

foreman (1) a person who is in charge of a group of workers. *See also* **first-**

line management. (2) *(law)* the chief member of a jury

◆ (1) Vorarbeiter (2) Obmann

forge to imitate the appearance of (something) unlawfully: *to forge a signature/cheque/will*

◆ fälschen

forgery (1) the act of **forging** something. *He was arrested for forgery.* (2) something that has been **forged.** *This note looks like a forgery*

◆ (1), (2) Fälschung

FORTRAN (*stands for* *For*mula *Tran*slation) a widely-used **computer language,** used especially for scientific and technical purposes

◆ FORTRAN

forward contract a promise to buy or sell **commodities** or **securities** at a fixed price at a future date

◆ Terminabschluß

forward exchange the buying or selling of foreign currency at an agreed fixed rate but completing the **contract** (the actual purchase or sale) at a future date

◆ Devisentermingeschäft

forward integration a situation in which a company takes over the **retail outlets** for its goods so that it has a direct link with its customers. *See also* **backward integration; horizontal integration; vertical integration**

◆ vertikales Betriebswachstum

forward purchasing sales *see* **futures**

forward rate an **exchange rate** that is agreed for the buying and selling of currency at some future date. *See also* **forward exchange**

◆ Terminkurs

forward sales goods that have been sold with delivery fixed for some time in the future

◆ Terminverkauf

four p's *see* **marketing mix**

franchise (1) a method of selling **branded** goods or **services** by which the owner of the brand name (the **franchiser**) allows someone else (the **franchisee**) to sell the goods/services within a certain area in return for a payment (based e.g. on the amount of goods supplied or sold). (2) (**marine insurance**) part of a **policy** in which it is agreed that **claims** will only be made above a certain amount, but that successful claims above that amount will be paid in full (to save time and money being wasted on small claims)

◆ (1) Lizenz (2) Franchise

franchisee *see* **franchise** (meaning 1)

franchiser *see* **franchise** (meaning 1)

franco domicile free of delivery charges between the seller's warehouse and the buyer's place of business. (Commonly used in the **import/export** of goods). *See also* **Incoterms**

◆ frei Haus

frank (1) to put a mark on (a stamp) which shows that it has been used. (2) to put a mark on (an envelope) with a **franking machine**

◆ (1) freimachen (2) frankieren

franking machine a machine which can be used by offices which send out a lot of mail. The machine prints and records the proper amount of postage on the envelope, so that stamps do not have to be used, and at the same time can print an advertisement for the company that is sending the letter or parcel

◆ Frankiermaschine

fraud (1) the act of getting a person to believe something which is not true, usually in order to get something illegally. (2) *(informal)* a person who is not what he **claims** to be. *He is a fraud — he says he is a lawyer and it is* *clear he isn't.* (3) a **product** which does not live up to its **claims.** *It is a fraud – it went rusty in a couple of months yet it claimed to be stainless steel*

◆ (1) Irreführung (2) Schwindler (3) reiner Schwindel

fraudulent dishonest; intended to deceive others for **financial** gain etc.: *a fraudulent scheme*

◆ betrügerisch

free alongside ship (*or* **FAS**) (**exporting**) free of delivery charges to a point alongside a named ship. Any costs of loading the goods onto the ship will have to be paid for by the buyer. *See also* **Incoterms**

◆ frei Längsseite Schiff

free currency any currency which is allowed to move freely between countries without any rules to stop it. *You can take as much sterling out of the country as you want – it's a free currency*

◆ frei konvertierbare Währung

freedom of association the right of people to group themselves together for some joint advantage, e.g. the right of workers to group themselves into **trade unions**

◆ Vereinsfreiheit

free enterprise an **economic system** in which businesses can compete against one another with very little interference from the government

◆ freie Marktwirtschaft

free gift something given away without any charge with certain goods so as to improve the sales of those goods. The buyer may receive it with the goods, or he may have to send away for it with proof that he has bought the goods, or he may receive the gift if he agrees to buy or at least examine the goods

◆ Werbegeschenk

freelance *adjective* working independently without being employed by one organisation. *She is a freelance journalist and you will see her articles in several papers*

◆ freiberuflich

freelance *noun* a person who does **freelance** work. *This is the first time they have employed a freelance*

◆ Freiberufler

freelance *verb* to work as a **freelance**

◆ freiberuflich tätig sein

free movement of labour a situation in which workers are allowed to move from one country to another to work as in the **European Economic Community**

◆ Freizügigkeit der Arbeitnehmer

free of particular average (**marine insurance**) the **underwriters** are liable only for a total loss and not for a partial loss, except under certain circumstances, e.g. if goods are washed overboard

◆ frei von Teilschaden

free of tax of goods or **income** etc., on which a tax does not have to be paid

◆ steuerfrei

free on board (*or* **FOB**) in international trade, when the seller's price includes the cost of goods, packing, delivery to the port and all charges in placing the goods on board the ship (or to the airport if going by air). *See also* **Incoterms**

◆ frei Schiff

free on rail in international trade, when the seller's price includes any expense in delivery to a railway at a named place. *See also* **Incoterms**

◆ frei Waggon

freepost *(UK)* a **service** provided by the Post Office by which a person can reply to an advertisement etc. without paying any postage (which is paid by the company etc. using the service)

◆ portofrei

free trade an **economic system** in which the exchange of goods from one country to another is not limited by **tariffs** or by **quotas**

◆ Freihandel

freight *noun* (1) the transporting of goods by sea, air or (especially *US*) by road or rail. (2) money paid for this: *freight charges*

◆ (1) Frachtbeförderung (2) Frachtkosten

freight *verb* to send goods by **freight.** *He was going to freight the goods to major cities in France*

◆ als Frachtgut befördern

freight forward any charges for the transporting of the goods must be paid by the person receiving them

◆ Fracht gegen Nachnahme

freight inward the cost of **freight** paid on goods coming into a company

◆ Eingangsfracht

frequency the number of times something happens within a certain time. *The machine is breaking down with increasing frequency*

◆ Häufigkeit

frequency distribution (statistics) the number of times the units of a certain variable (e.g. salary, examination marks) happen. For example in a test marked from 0 to 10, it would show how many students scored 10, how many 9 etc.

◆ Streuung

friendly society (*US* **benefit association**) a group of people who make regular payments to a common **fund,** so that they have **financial** protection in case of sickness, death of a wage earner, etc.

◆ Unterstützungsverein auf Gegenseitigkeit

fringe benefit any kind of extra reward given to an employee in addition to his salary, e.g. cheap meals, use of a car etc. *See also* **employee benefits**

◆ freiwillige Sozialleistungen

front-line management *see* **first-line management**

frozen account money in a bank belonging to a person or company, which cannot be moved because of some legal (or government) rule

◆ Sperrkonto

frozen assets things belonging to a company (land, buildings, machinery, etc.) which cannot be sold because of some **claim** against them

◆ eingefrorene Guthaben

full cost the total cost involved in making something, including the **variable costs** and the current amount of the **fixed costs.** *See also* **absorption costing** and Appendix 7

◆ Vollkosten

full employment a situation where there are jobs available for all those who want them

◆ Vollbeschäftigung

fully-paid share a **share** of which the full **nominal** (or **par**) **value** has been paid

◆ voll eingezahlte Aktie

functional responsibilities the duties one has in a job. For example, the functional responsibilities of a **sales manager** includes **sales forecasting, sales training,** and reaching the planned level of sales and profits

◆ Dienstpflichten

fund *noun* an amount of money which has been set aside for a special purpose. *See also* **funds**

◆ Fonds

fund *verb* (1) to provide money for (a special purpose). (2) to change a short-term debt into a long-term debt

◆ (1) finanzieren (2) konsolidieren

funds (1) money available to be spent at any time. (2) all the **assets** of a company. (3) UK government **stocks** and **securities**

◆ (1) Geldmittel (2) Kapital (3) Staatspapiere

funds-flow analysis a careful examination of the movement of money into and out of a company

◆ Analyse des Finanzflusses

further education *(UK)* a section of the educational system which deals with the needs of students who are above school-leaving age but have not entered a university or **polytechnic.** *See also* **higher education**

◆ Weiterbildung

futures (*or* **forward purchasing sales**) **commodities** or **securities** which are bought or sold at a certain price now for delivery at some agreed time in the future

◆ Termingeschäfte

G

gain (1) an increase, a benefit. *We had a gain of 1% in our market share last month.* (2) a profit. *When costs were taken off the company had a gain of £1000*

◆ (1) Zuwachs (2) Gewinn

galloping inflation (*or* **hyperinflation**) very fast **inflation,** e.g. at a rate of about 5% per month

◆ galoppierende Inflation

gamble *verb* (1) to bet, to risk losing money in a game of chance. (2) to take a risk in something: *to gamble on the success of a product*

◆ (1) sich an Glücksspielen beteiligen (2) ein Risiko eingehen

gamble *noun* any action which carries a high risk of failure. *Putting a lot of money into something completely new is always a gamble*

◆ Risiko

gambler a person who **gambles**

◆ Spieler(in)

GATT *see* **General Agreement on Tariffs and Trade**

gazumping the act of selling a house at a higher price than that previously agreed

◆ entgegen mündlicher Zusage ein Haus an einen Höherbietenden verkaufen

GDP *see* **gross domestic product**

gearing the relationship between the value of a company's fixed-interest **loan capital** and its **ordinary shares.** If the amount of these loans is greater than the value of the ordinary shares the company is said to be **highly-geared.** If less, it is **low-geared**

◆ Verhältnis von bevorrechtigten Kapitalien zu den Stammaktien

General Agreement on Tariffs and Trade (*or* **GATT**) an international agreement, reached in Geneva in 1947, which tries to lower the **tariff barriers** between countries. Number of countries: 86. Headquarters: Geneva. Official languages: English, French

◆ Allgemeines Zoll- und Handelsabkommen

general audit a check of **accounts** in a company (usually done at the time of the preparation of the final accounts). *See* **audit**

◆ Jahresabschlußprüfung

general average loss (**insurance**) a deliberate loss of part of a **cargo** or parts of a ship at sea in order to save the ship and the rest of the cargo. When a captain orders goods to be thrown into the sea for this purpose, this loss is called a 'general average loss' and all those who have cargo on the ship or have an interest in the ship would have to pay into a special fund to recover the value of the goods thrown overboard, although they do not own the goods

◆ Schaden aus gemeinschaftlicher Havarie

general manager (1) a person who controls the work of other managers. (2) a person who decides on the aims of a company and who decides what amount of **personnel,** money and machinery are needed to reach the aims

◆ (1) Generaldirektor (2) Geschäftsführer

general meeting a meeting of all the members of a company such as an **annual general meeting** or an **extraordinary general meeting**

◆ Hauptversammlung

general reserves that section of the **balance sheet** which shows the profit kept for use within the company. Each year this retained profit goes to the general reserve. *See* Appendix 2

◆ allgemeine Rücklagen

general strike a situation when all the workers of the major **trade unions** stop working as a protest over something which is very important to them

◆ Generalstreik

gentleman's agreement a **contract** which does not have any force in law, but is based on the trust of each party that it will be carried out

◆ Vereinbarung auf Treu und Glauben

get down to brass tacks *(informal)* to discuss something (e.g. a business deal) seriously; to get down to the real point of discussion. *Let's get down to brass tacks: how much is this project going to cost?*

◆ zur Sache kommen

get the sack *(informal)* to lose one's job. *He got the sack for using company money for his own purposes*

◆ gefeuert werden

get-up-and-go *(informal)* great energy and willingness to do one's job. *Our company could use young men with your kind of get-up-and-go*

◆ Einsatzwille

ghost to write (an article, story or novel) on behalf of someone else. *The famous actor's autobiography was actually ghosted by a professional writer*

◆ Ghostwriter sein

gift (1) something, such as property or money, given without any payment to someone else. *Before his death the father gave his son the house as a gift.* (2) a natural ability or talent. *He seems to be able to make money from any business he tackles. It's a gift which he has*

◆ (1) Geschenk (2) Gabe

gift voucher (*or* **gift token**) a kind of ticket with the value clearly shown on it which can be bought in a shop then given to someone as a gift. The holder of the gift voucher can exchange it in a shop for something to the value of the voucher

◆ Geschenkgutschein

gilt-edged securities/stocks: securities/stocks issued by the government. There is little risk that the buying of government stocks will result in a loss and so the term 'gilt-edged' or 'gilts' usually means a safe **investment**

◆ Staatspapiere

gimmick something new or unusual which catches people's attention. *They've got a good gimmick for selling that new beer — they've sent up a thousand balloons with the beer's name*

◆ effekthaschender Gag

giro a system of sending money from an **account** in one branch of a bank to an account in another branch or bank. This method of settling debts is done by using the specially-printed giro forms available in the branch of any bank

◆ Giro

give-away something given away free with a **product** or **service** to keep increasing sales, e.g. a gardening magazine may have a give-away of a free packet of flower seeds. *See* **free gift**

◆ Probe(-packung)

glossary a list of unusual words or terms, usually at the end of a book. *This text book has a glossary of management terms*

◆ Glossar

glut more than is needed of something. *There is a glut of oranges on the market and prices are falling*

◆ Überangebot

gnomes of Zurich *(informal)* powerful Swiss bankers who are said to make large profits from changes in currency rates, and who are supposed to be so powerful as to cause changes in the **financial policies** of governments

◆ 'die Zürcher Gnome'

GNP *see* **gross national product**

go-ahead *noun (informal)* permission to do something. *We can't do anything until we get the go-ahead from our financial director*

◆ grünes Licht

go-ahead *adjective (informal)* willing to do new things. *It's a very exciting, go-ahead company to work for*

◆ fortschrittlich

goal an aim or desire. *Our long-term goal is an improvement in profits but the short-term goal is simply to survive*

◆ Ziel

going concern a business which is doing well. *He took over the business as a going concern*

◆ schwunghafter Betrieb

going price the amount that is being charged for something at the present time

◆ Marktpreis

going public the **process** of changing a **private company** into a **public company**. *I see the Crude-oil Company is going public — their shares are being offered for sale on the Stock Exchange*

◆ Umwandlung einer Personengesellschaft in eine Kapitalgesellschaft

going rate the rate that is being charged at present for wages, or for materials. *The going rate for crude oil is $30*

◆ üblicher (Lohn-) Tarif

golden handshake money given to a senior manager, or a director, of a large company at the end of his **contract of service** (or when his contract of service has been cut short). *He was with them for ten years and received a golden handshake of £5000 when he retired*

◆ 'goldener Händedruck' (Gratifikation bei der Verabschiedung eines leitenden Mitarbeiters)

gold reserves a country's **stock** of gold, held in reserve to settle international debts. *See also* **official reserves**

◆ Goldreserven

gold standard the use of gold to **guarantee** the issue of a country's paper money. The UK came off the gold standard in 1931, i.e. its paper money was no longer guaranteed by the full amount of gold

◆ Goldstandard

good faith honesty in dealing with other people in business, e.g. as supposed to exist between all those who have a **contract** between them

◆ Redlichkeit

goods things which are offered for sale (but not houses or land). *They have received our order and they say that our goods will be delivered tomorrow*

◆ Waren

goods and chattels *(law)* personal belongings

◆ Hab und Gut

goods on approval goods delivered to a person who may buy if he approves of the goods, i.e. if he finds them suitable

◆ Waren zur Ansicht

goods on consignment goods sent to an agent for sale

◆ Kommissionswaren

goods received note a note with the description and quantity of goods received by whoever has bought or ordered the goods. This can then be compared with the **advice note** or **delivery note,** or the **invoice** to check that the goods have all been received

◆ Liefereingangsbestätigung

goods returned note a note with the description and quantity of goods which have been returned by the person who has bought or ordered the goods. The selling company which receives these returned goods needs to record the details so that a **credit** can be given to the buyer

◆ Retourenquittung

goodwill (1) benefits that come to a company from being well-known to customers, or being well-placed (e.g. on a busy street) or from being known to be expert in some aspect of business (e.g. a maker of high-quality **products**). *There is a lot of goodwill for the Trent Shipping Company; they are just so reliable.* (2) a **financial** measurement of the worth of **goodwill** in a **balance sheet**

◆ (1) geschäftliches Ansehen (2) Firmenwert

go out of business to give up one's business, either willingly or by going **bankrupt.** *Many firms round here have gone out of business because of the recession*

◆ Geschäft aufgeben

go slow to do less work than normal so as to cause delays in **output.** Used sometimes by workers instead of a **strike** to bring attention to a disagreement with management. Also used as a noun: *There was a go-slow at the printing works last week*

◆ im Bummelstreik sein

government stock fixed-interest loans **issued** by the government. In the UK these offers of loans are called **gilt-edged stock** or **gilt-edged securities**

◆ Staatsanleihe

grading separating something (e.g. wool, grain) into different lots by quality or size etc.

◆ Güteklasseneinteilung

graduated pension a **pension** which is related to the earnings of the person before his/her **retirement**

◆ gestaffelte Sozialrente

graft *noun* (1) getting business, profits etc. by dishonest means, e.g. **bribery.** (2) *(informal)* work. *Coal-mining is hard graft*

◆ (1) Mauschelei (2) Plackerei

graft *verb* to get business etc. by **graft** (meaning 1)

◆ mauscheln

grant a gift of money, e.g. from the government, especially for education. *Some people say that the grants for students are too low*

◆ Stipendium

grapevine the way news spreads unofficially. *I heard on the grapevine we're getting a new manager*

◆ Gerücht

graph a drawing which shows the relationship between two sets of numbers. One set is marked off on an upright line, the other set of numbers is measured off on a line at right angles. The relationship between the two is shown by means of dots or lines etc. *See* **graph paper**

◆ Diagramm

graphics drawings, diagrams etc. in a newspaper, magazine or book

◆ graphische Darstellung

graph paper paper on which a **graph** is drawn. The paper is usually divided into small squares each of the same area to help make the graph clearer

◆ Millimeterpapier

gratuity (*or* **tip**) a gift of payment for good service

◆ Trinkgeld

graveyard shift *(informal)* a period of overnight work between midnight and eight in the morning

◆ Nachtschicht

green card an **insurance document** which a motorist must have when taking his car from the UK to drive in foreign countries. It shows that, if he has an accident, he has **third-party insurance**

◆ grüne Versicherungskarte

grievance a cause for complaint or protest usually by a **trade union** to a company. *The union leader wanted to see the management so that he could speak to them about the workers' grievances*

◆ Beschwerde

grievance procedure the methods agreed by a **union** and the management of a company for settling complaints

◆ Verfahren zur Regelung von Arbeitsstreitigkeiten

gross *noun (plural invariable)* a unit of 144

◆ Gros

gross *verb* to earn as a total amount before any **deductions** are made for tax or expenses etc. *He grosses £30,000 a year*

◆ brutto verdienen

gross circulation the total sales of a newspaper or magazine (before errors, or **returns** have been counted)

◆ Gesamtauflage

gross domestic product (*or* **GDP**) the value of all the goods and **services** produced by a country (usually in one year)

◆ Bruttoinlandsprodukt

gross income earnings before any **deductions** for tax etc.

◆ Bruttoeinkommen

gross margin a percentage added to the cost of goods: the amount left to cover all other expenses and provide a **net profit**

◆ Handelsspanne

gross national product (*or* **GNP**) the value of all the goods and **services** produced by a country including **income** from its **investments** in other countries

◆ Bruttosozialprodukt

gross profit sales less the cost of the goods sold, usually expressed in money terms (**gross margin** is usually expressed in percentage terms). *See* appendix 1

◆ Bruttogewinn

gross sales the total sales before taking off **discounts, returns,** breakages, mistakes in delivery etc. *See* appendix 1

◆ Bruttoumsatz

gross weight the total weight of a **product** including its wrapping, packaging, and the weight of the **outer** or **crate**

◆ Bruttogewicht

gross yield the profit from an **investment** before any deductions for expenses, tax etc.

◆ Bruttoertrag

ground rent the rent paid for land as opposed to rent paid for buildings on the land

◆ Erbbauzins

ground rules (unwritten) rules that apply in a special situation. *Be careful what you say at the managers' meetings; Jack will explain the ground rules to you*

◆ Grundregeln

groupage grouping together several different small orders into one load for delivery (usually in a **container**). Groupage is done to get lower delivery rates

◆ Sammellieferung

group discussion a research method by which a group of people are encouraged to speak freely on a subject. The subject might be a company's advertisement, **product,** price, label, etc. By giving their opinions the group show what people think and this may help a company to improve their **marketing mix**

◆ Gruppendiskussion

group dynamics the study of how groups of people behave and how persons within the group influence group decisions and actions

◆ Gruppendynamik

group incentives: incentives given as a result of a group of workers reaching a stated **target** for the group (as opposed to an incentive offered to each worker for reaching an individual target)

◆ Gruppenprämie

growth chart a chart used to plan and control work, e.g. in a **factory** or on a large **project.** The work is drawn on the chart on a plan of the time to be taken. The stages are then drawn in as they happen

◆ Arbeitsplanungs- und Kontrolldiagramm

growth rate an amount by which something has increased (usually stated as a percentage). Often used in relation to sales, **share value,** share of the market, production and other **factors** of business. *Over the past three years our profits have shown a growth rate of 10%*

◆ Wachstumsrate

guarantee *noun* (1) a firm promise in business (usually in writing or print) that certain agreements will be kept. *If our machine fails within two months of purchase we will replace it free of charge. That's our guarantee.* (2) a promise by one person to pay the loan of another should the latter fail to do so

◆ (1) Garantie (2) Bürgschaft

guarantee *verb* to give a **guarantee** for. *All our products are guaranteed for three years*

◆ Garantie leisten

guaranteed prices fixed prices which the government offers farmers for certain produce to encourage production. If the market price falls below this guaranteed price the farmers receive the difference from the government

◆ Garantiepreise

guaranteed wage an agreement between a company and its workers by which the company promises that the workers' wages will not fall below a certain figure each week

◆ garantierter Mindestlohn

guardian a person who has the legal right and duty to care for a young person and his/her property

◆ Vormund

guesstimate (made up from guess and **estimate**) a statement about the future which is not based on facts, or on very few facts. *They had done no market research so they had no real idea of what the sales would be but their guesstimate was £1 million*

◆ grobe Schätzung

guillotine (1) a method of stopping a debate in Parliament by fixing a time for taking a vote. (2) a paper-cutting instrument

◆ (1) Redezeitbeschränkung (2) Papierschneidemaschine

H

habeas corpus *(English law)* an order from a court requiring a person to come before the court or a judge as soon as possible, usually used to find out if a person has been lawfully or unlawfully kept in prison

◆ Habeaskorpusakte

haggle to argue over a price in a situation where a buyer and seller are each trying to get the best price; common in open street markets. *They haggled over the price for ten minutes and then agreed on £5*

◆ feilschen

hallmark a special mark put on an article of silver or gold after its quality has been tested. The mark indicates the quality, the maker and the city where the article's quality was tested. *He could see from the hallmark that the ring was 18 carat gold*

◆ Edelmetallprägezeichen

halo effect the result of noting some quality in another person which is greatly liked and has an effect on one's decisions. For example, a manager who interviewed a person for a job might be very impressed by the person's speech and clothing and might decide to employ that person even if these qualities were not necessary for the job

◆ Überdeckungseffekt

hammer *verb* to announce at the **Stock Exchange** that (a member) cannot pay his debts. *Smith is no longer a member of the Stock Exchange; he was hammered today*

◆ für zahlungsunfähig erklären (bei der Londoner Börse)

hammer *noun:* **under the hammer** offered for sale by **auction.** *He's selling all his furniture and it will be under the hammer next week*

◆ unter den Hammer kommen

handbill a small sheet of paper with a printed message or advertisement which is handed out to people

◆ Handzettel

handling charge (1) a charge made for moving goods (by hand or by machine) from one place to another, e.g. for moving goods from the dockside to a waiting lorry. (2) a charge made by a bank for operating a customer's **bank account**

◆ (1) Umladekosten (2) Kontoführungsgebühr

handout (1) a sheet of paper or leaflet giving information about something. *The salesman gave the customer a handout on the new product.* (2) something given away free, sometimes to advertise a **product**

◆ (1) Reklame (2) Werbegeschenk

hand over fist *(informal)* especially of making money, very quickly and without problems

◆ einen Reibach machen

harbour dues sums of money paid by ships for entering and for using a harbour

◆ Hafengebühren

harbour master the person in charge of a harbour and the position of the ships there

◆ Hafeninspektor

hard cash *(informal)* money that is available now, at once in payment (usually) for something. *He offered the garage £1000 hard cash for the car if he could drive it away at once*

◆ Bargeld

hard copy printed words or figures on a sheet of paper produced by a machine such as a **printer** (meaning 2) (and not the words or figures on a **disk** or tape). *Last month's sales figures are on the computer but we had better have them in hard copy for the sales meeting*

◆ Hardcopy

hard currency any currency that is readily accepted by many foreign countries in payment of debt (without changing it with another currency)

◆ harte Währung

hard disk a hard **magnetic disk**

◆ Hard disk

harden of a price of **shares** or goods, to rise, or to stop falling. *Shares fell slightly for most of the day until late afternoon when prices hardened*

◆ sich festigen

hard sell the selling of goods forcefully and with determination. *The manager told the sales force that the new product needed a hard sell to make it a success*

◆ aggressive Verkaufsmethoden

hardware (1) all the hard parts which make up a **computer** such as the machinery, the wires and so on, but not the **programs.** *See also* **software.** (2) goods (such as hammers, screws, nuts, bolts, etc.) which are sold in a **hardware store** or **ironmonger's** shop

◆ (1) Hardware (2) Eisenwaren

hatchet man *(informal)* a person who is employed to do things which will not be liked by other workers, such as getting rid of unwanted employees. *They say that he was appointed just as a hatchet man to get rid of some of the older staff*

◆ Rausekler, dafür angestellt, um mißliebige Angestellte loszuwerden

haulage (1) carriage of goods by road. *I want you to arrange for the haulage of 1000 cases of whisky to Dover.* (2) the charge for this. *Find out the haulage on a delivery of 1000 cases of whisky to Dover*

◆ (1) Straßentransport (2) Transportkosten

haulage contractor a company which **contracts** to carry goods by road. *See also* **haulage**

◆ Transportunternehmen

hazard a risk, danger. *The main hazard to Smith's new business was the low prices of the shop next door*

◆ Risiko

headhunter a company, or person, that tries to find suitable managers, or people for certain jobs, by approaching the managers direct (as opposed to advertising such jobs in the newspapers). Usually this contact is made without the manager's present company knowing about it. Often the offer of a job by a headhunter is accompanied by an offer of increased salary etc.

◆ Personalabwerber

heading the word or words which form the title to a section of writing, e.g. the chapter of a book

◆ Überschrift

head office (*or* **headquarters**) the part of the business where the top managers and (usually) the directors are. *We have branches all over the country but our head office is in Glasgow*

◆ Hauptgeschäftsstelle

health hazard any risk or damage to health, in business used to describe those caused by the type of work or the methods of work. *The fumes from the factory were considered to be a health hazard to the workers*

◆ Gesundheitsrisiko

heavy industry an industry which works with metals, e.g. iron or coal, or with heavy machinery, as in shipbuilding

◆ Schwerindustrie

heavy user a person or company that buys a lot of some **product** or **service.** *We have all bought brown bread at some time, but the heavy user buys it every day*

◆ Großverbraucher

hedging protecting oneself against loss due to price changes, especially by buying at a fixed price for future delivery. This dealing in **futures** can be in currency or **shares** or materials etc. For example, a bank might agree to a contract with a company to sell the company in three months' time a fixed amount of dollars for a fixed amount of pounds. To protect itself from changes in the value of the currencies the bank will hedge, i.e. it will try to buy now, for delivery in three months, at the same price or lower, the same amount of dollars

◆ Preisabsicherung

higher education education beyond the age of eighteen at a college of **further education** or at a **polytechnic** or university

◆ Hochschulbildung

high flier a very ambitious and/or very successful person

◆ Senkrechtstarter

high-level language a **computer language** which is used to write **programs** for a wide range of **computers.** Widely-used high-level languages are: **BASIC, FORTRAN, ALGOL, COBOL**

◆ höhere Programmiersprache

high-pressure selling forceful selling, when the salesman is only concerned with making the sale, without thought of the customer's real need. High-pressure selling is often accompanied by false **claims** about the **product,** or delivery, or price, all to make sure of the sale. *See also* **low-pressure selling**

◆ Verkauf um jeden Preis

hire to buy the use of (something) for an agreed period of time; to employ (a person). *He hired a van for a week*

◆ mieten

hire purchase a form of payment for goods where the buyer signs a **contract** called a **hire-purchase agreement.** The buyer agrees to pay a small part of the amount due at the time of buying and the remainder in equal parts over a fixed period of time. The buyer is not the legal owner of the goods until the last payment is made. *See also* **instalment purchase**

◆ Ratenkauf

histogram a picture, or chart, of how many in a group have a certain characteristic (such as age, height, examination mark) which is being studied. How often a certain age occurs for example will be shown by the length of the thick lines (or bars) on the chart

◆ Säulendiagramm

historic cost the actual cost of something which has been produced, not what it would cost now

◆ ursprüngliche Anschaffungskosten

HMSO (*or* **Her Majesty's Stationery Office**) *(UK)* the official supplier of government books and publications

◆ offizieller Lieferant von Regierungsberichten und Veröffentlichungen

hoard to save (money) with no intention of **investing** it or (goods) with no intention of using them. *It's no use hoarding your wealth when it could be put to good use*

◆ horten

hoarding a large easily-seen board, usually of wood, on which advertisements are placed. *Every hoarding had an advertisement for their new product*

◆ Plakatwand

holder in due course a person who accepts a **bill** in exchange for value he has given (e.g. goods or **services**), who believes that the bill is in every way a genuine bill, and has therefore the best legal right to the value of the bill

◆ rechtmäßiger Wechselinhaber

holder of value a person who possesses a **bill of exchange** for which some value has been given at some time (e.g. goods have been exchanged for it)

◆ Wechselinhaber, der das Papier entgeltlich erworben hat

holding company a company which controls one or more companies (by owning more than half the **ordinary shares** in them)

◆ Holdinggesellschaft

holiday pay wages or salary paid to a worker for the time he is on holiday

◆ Urlaubsgeld

home loan a loan of money from a bank or a **building society** when the value of the borrower's home is used to safeguard the loan

◆ Wohnungsbaudarlehen

home market trade done by a company in the country where it has its **head office,** and not abroad. *We're a British company but our home market takes only 10% of all the golf clubs we make; export markets take the rest*

◆ Binnenmarkt

homogeneous goods goods which have very little difference between them; goods of the same kind

◆ homogene Waren

honorary (*also* **hon.**) of an official of a company or society, unpaid. *He's the new hon. treasurer of the club*

◆ ehrenamtlich

honour *noun* (1) having honesty, and loyalty; good personal character. *He is a man of honour.* (2) a title of respect used when addressing judges. *Your honour, may I say . .*

◆ (1) Ehre (2) Hohes Gericht

honour *verb* (1) to have a high opinion of (a person). (2) to pay (something) when it is due: *to honour a debt/a cheque*

◆ (1) ehren (2) begleichen

horizontal integration the joining of two or more companies in the same industry. *See also* **vertical integration**

◆ horizontale Verflechtung

horse power (*or* **h.p.**) a unit for measuring the power of an engine. (In making measurement 1 h.p. = 0.7457 kW.)

◆ Pferdestärke

hot money money moved around quickly and/or regularly by its owners into countries, or **investments,** e.g. to get the highest **interest rates**

◆ heißes Geld

hot seat *(informal)* a difficult or dangerous position. *There were very few applicants for Mr Black's job: most people considered it too much of a hot seat*

◆ Schleudersitz

household all the people that live together in a house

◆ Haushalt

house magazine a magazine containing news and articles about a company and published by the company. House magazines are usually given free to company workers and sent also to large customers of the company

◆ Hausnachrichten

house-to-house selling calling direct on homes to try to sell goods. Some cosmetic companies and book companies sell their **products** in this way. *See also* **door-to-door selling**

◆ Tür-zu-Tür Verkauf

hull the body of a ship (as distinct from the masts, funnels etc.). *The ship's hull was rusted from its long sea voyage*

◆ Schiffskörper

hull insurance: insurance against damage to a ship (as distinct from its **cargo**)

◆ Seekaskoversicherung

human relations the study of social problems among people, e.g. those that arise in a company between and among its groups (or workers, **supervisors,** managers) and also between a company and its customers

◆ Human Relations

hyperinflation *see* **galloping inflation**

hypermarket a very large **self-service store,** usually over 3000 square metres, situated out of town, offering a wide range of household goods and groceries, and with plenty of parking space for cars. *See also* **superstore**

◆ Verbrauchergroßmarkt

I

IAEA *see* **International Atomic Energy Agency**

IBRD *see* **International Bank for Reconstruction and Development**

ICC *see* **International Chamber of Commerce**

ICJ *see* **International Court of Justice**

idle capacity machinery or workers not used to the full. *We don't have enough orders so for two days a week we have idle capacity*

◆ Leerlaufkapazität

idle money money that is not earning interest, that is not **invested**

◆ brachliegendes Kapital

idle time any time when machines or men are not working productively, e.g. due to a machine breakdown, materials not arriving

◆ Leerlaufzeit

IEA *see* **International Energy Agency**

IFAD *see* **International Fund for Agricultural Development**

IFC *see* **International Finance Corporation**

ILO *see* **International Labour Organization**

image a mental picture that people have of a company, person or product etc. This picture may be formed by the company advertising, or news of its activities in the press. *The company's image was harmed by the news of how badly it treated its workers and sales fell*

◆ Image

IMF *see* **International Monetary Fund**

impact the effect of something, e.g. an advertisement or a special **promotion** on the public. *The impact of the new advertisement was such that sales increased almost immediately*

◆ Auswirkung

imperfect competition a situation where a company or companies have such an influence over a market (usually because they are so large) that they can affect the price, the supply or the demand

◆ ungleiche Wettbewerbsbedingungen

impersonal accounts (bookkeeping) accounts which do not deal with people but with things such as goods, machines, cash, wages, rent etc. Impersonal accounts are divided into **real accounts** and **nominal accounts**

◆ Sachkonten

implied warranty a **guarantee** which is taken to exist although it may not be in writing, e.g. that goods should be fit for use or a new car should be safe to drive

◆ stillschweigende Garantie

import *verb* to bring (goods or **services**) into a country, especially for sale. *He was going to import wines from France*

◆ importieren

import *noun* (1) the act of **importing.** (2) something **imported.** *Britain has increased its imports this year*

◆ (1), (2) Import

import duty a tax on certain goods brought into a country

◆ Einfuhrzoll

importer a person who or organisation which **imports**

◆ Importeur

import licence a printed permission from the government which allows certain goods into the country

◆ Einfuhrgenehmigung

import quota a fixed number of a **product** allowed into the country by the government

◆ Einfuhrkontingent

import surcharge an extra tax on certain goods which is meant to discourage **importers** from bringing them into the country, usually aimed at protecting an industry, or helping the **balance of payments.**

◆ Importabgabe

imprest system a method of controlling **petty cash** in a business. The person in charge of the petty cash must have a **receipt** for each amount of cash given out. These are taken to the company's **cashier** who gives cash to the total of the receipts. By this means the petty cash is brought up to its original amount again

◆ Betriebskassenkontrollsystem

impulse goods goods which are bought when seen and not as a result of a plan to buy, i.e. bought on the spur of the moment. Impulse goods are usually cheap, and in high demand, e.g. matches, sweets, canned meats etc.

◆ spontan gekaufte Waren

Inc. *see* **incorporated**

incentive something offered to encourage greater effort. *We will offer extra payment to the salesman with the highest sales for the month — that should be a good incentive*

◆ Anreiz

incentive scheme a plan of more payment for more effort, e.g. a plan by which a salesman could earn more money if his sales are more than a certain amount. *Our incentive scheme is that each salesman will get £1 for every case which he sells above 100 cases each month*

◆ Prämiensystem

incidental expenses small payments or expenses which are in addition to the main expenses. *The business trip cost £1000 in travel expenses and about £50 for incidental expenses such as tips, taxis and so on*

◆ Nebenausgaben

income money coming in, e.g. from wages or salary (to a person), from sales (to a company), from **investments.** *He had a steady income of £15,000 a year, made up of £12,000 salary and £3000 interest from his savings*

◆ Einkommen

income and expenditure account a statement of a **non-profit-making organisation** (such as a **charity**) showing the money received during a period of time and all the money paid out in expenses. (It takes the place of the **profit and loss account** for a profit-making organisation.)

◆ Einkommen- und Ausgabenkonto einer gemeinnützigen Organisation

incomes policy rules which a government lays down in relation to increases in wages or salaries. *The government's incomes policy is based on no one getting a wage increase greater than 5%*

◆ Lohn- und Einkommenspolitik

income statement a written or printed list of money received and money paid out for a period, especially *(US)* a **profit and loss account**

◆ Erfolgsrechnung

income tax a tax on money received from salary, **investments,** rent, profits from business etc.

◆ Einkommenssteuer

in-company training training of workers which is done inside the company (and not by a business school or college). *I don't have to go away for training because the firm has an in-company training course*

◆ innerbetriebliche Weiterbildung

incompetent not able, not skilled, not qualified. *I don't know why they gave him a job, he's completely incompetent*

◆ unfähig

incorporate (1) to make (something) a part of something else. *I have incorporated your ideas in my speech.* (2) to form into a **corporation**

◆ (1) aufnehmen (2) (eine Gesellschaft) gründen

incorporated (*especially US, also* **Inc.**) formed into a **corporation**

◆ amtlich (als Aktiengesellschaft) eingetragen

Incoterms terms used in international trade whose meanings have been agreed by most of the trading countries of the world. These terms and their meanings have been drawn up by the **International Chamber of Commerce**

◆ Standardformeln für den internationalen Warenhandel

increasing returns to scale increasing efficiency by increasing **output**

◆ Steigerung der Wirtschaftlichkeit durch Mehrproduktion

increment something added to an existing amount, e.g. a salary increase. *I've had my yearly increment – another 5%*

◆ Erhöhung

incremental cost – marginal cost

indemnity (1) **security** against loss, or damage. *Your indemnity under this insurance will pay for all damage.* (2) **compensation** for a loss

◆ (1) Versicherungsschutz (2) Schadensersatz

indent *noun* an order from an overseas buyer to an **export house** to buy certain goods and send them to the buyer

◆ Auslandsauftrag

indent *verb* (1) to start a line of writing, e.g. on a letter, further into the page than the other lines. (2) **indent for** to put in an order for. *We'll have to indent for some more paper*

◆ (1) einrücken (2) bestellen

indenture a **contract** between a company and a young worker regarding the number of years he must work to become qualified in a certain trade

◆ Lehrvertrag

independent (shop) a shop owned by a single person or a single company (owning only this shop). See Appendix 7

◆ selbständiges Einzelhandelsgeschäft

index (1) a list of names, subjects etc., in alphabetical order, e.g. at the end of a book. *Look up the index and see what page deals with management.* (2) a similar listing but on separate cards and called a **card index.** *The library has all the books listed as a card index*

◆ (1) Register (2) Kartei

index-linked of increases in pay, salary or **pension** etc., related to the **cost-of-living index.** *The cost of living went up 5% this year and so did my pension – it is index-linked*

◆ der Inflationsrate angeglichen

index number a number which shows the relative change in prices, wages, **cost of living** etc. over a period of time. For example if a company is measuring its **export** sales it might give its total export sales for 1980 the value of 100. A ten-per-cent increase in sales in 1981 would be represented by the value 110. If in 1982 sales were five per cent up on 1980, then 1982 sales would be indexed 105

◆ Indexzahl

index of retail prices *see* **cost-of-living index**

indirect cost a cost not related to the making of a **product,** e.g. office costs, rates, rent, managers' salaries etc.

◆ Gemeinkosten

indirect labour costs wages paid to a factory worker who does not actually make the goods, e.g. to a person who keeps the factory clean

◆ Gemeinkostenlöhne

indirect material cost any cost of material which is not used in the making of the **product.** For example, the wood used in making a chair is a direct material cost but the materials used up in cleaning the machinery are an indirect material cost

◆ Materialgemeinkosten

indirect tax a tax which is not taken directly off **income** or profits, e.g. **value-added tax**

◆ indirekte Steuer

indorse *see* **endorse**

induction the act of introducing a person into a new position, in a company

◆ Einführung eines neuen Mitarbeiters am Arbeitsplatz

induction training teaching new workers the method etc. of a job

◆ Einführungsschulung für neue Mitarbeiter

industrial accident an injury which happens at work (at the factory or in the office). *See also* **occupational accident**

◆ Arbeitsunfall

industrial action action by workers which is intended to slow down, stop or interrupt the work of a company. It often follows on from an **industrial dispute**

◆ Streikmaßnahmen

industrial dispute an argument between management and workers over something, e.g. wages, hours of work, new machinery etc. The term is usually used when the disagreement could lead to a **strike**

◆ Arbeitskonflikt

industrial estate (*or* **trading estate**) an area in or around a city which has been set aside especially for offices and factories. Usually **sponsored** by the government, and usually the space is given for a low rent. *See also* **advanced factory**

◆ Industriegebiet

industrial goods goods that are bought by companies to help them in their own business, e.g. office desks and chairs, factory machinery, raw materials etc. *Compare with* **consumer goods**

◆ Investitionsgüter

industrialist a person who owns or controls a large factory or factories

◆ Industrieller

industrial market all the companies that buy goods or **services** to help them in their own business. For example the industrial market for cars is made up of all those companies which buy cars to help them carry on their own business. *See also* **industrial goods**

◆ Investitionsgütermarkt

industrial relations (*or* **labour relations**) attitudes between management and workers and how they relate to each other. *One thing about the Clyde Works Company, the industrial relations are very good — do you know they've never had a strike?*

◆ Verhältnis zwischen Arbeitgebern und Arbeitnehmern

industrial revolution *(UK)* the period from the 18th to the 19th century during which certain developments took place, e.g. the coming of power by water and steam, the move by people from farms to factories, the growth of cities, the inventions in spinning, weaving, in coal and steel making, the laying of the railway system

◆ industrielle Revolution

industrial tribunal a group of three people with the power to settle a **dispute,** if both sides agree to bring the dispute to the tribunal. It usually consists of a lawyer and two people to represent the interest of employers and workers respectively and is used to hear and settle **disputes** on such matters as pay due to a worker, meaning of certain terms in the **contract of employment** etc.

◆ Arbeitsgericht

industrious very hard-working

◆ fleißig

industry (1) work done in order to manufacture goods; the organisations concerned with this. (2) all companies. *Industry supports the new law on trade union strikes.* (3) work, especially hard work. *The industry of the working man can be seen in the high output figures*

◆ (1) Industriezweig (2) Industrie (3) Fleiß

industry-wide agreement an agreement between leaders of a **trade union** and representatives of all employers in a certain industry. *The print workers have a new industry-wide agreement on hours of work*

◆ Tarifvereinbarungen für einen gesamten Industriebereich

inelastic demand a situation where a large change in price has only a slight effect on people's willingness to buy something

◆ starre Nachfrage

inelastic supply a situation where the amount of something offered for sale changes very little when the price changes

◆ starres Warenangebot

inertia selling selling goods by delivering them although they have not been ordered, and then asking for payment. The seller depends on the receiver paying for the goods rather than going to the trouble of sending them back. In the UK, it is quite legal to refuse to send them back and to charge rent to the sender for storage space taken up by these goods

◆ Verkaufsaktion durch Zusenden unbestellter Waren

inflation continued increases in prices and wages which result in the value of money falling

◆ Inflation

inflationary spiral a situation when increases in wages causes costs to increase, which causes prices to increase, which causes demands for an increase in wages. *According to some politicians there's only one way to stop the inflationary spiral — no more wage increases*

◆ Inflationsspirale

information retrieval the **process** of getting information from a source of **data.** The data may be a paper in a filing cabinet or on tapes or **disks** in a **computer**

◆ Informationsabruf

infrastructure all the **systems** which support a country's industry and **economy,** e.g. road, rail, post and airway systems; factory, hospital, housing and education systems; radio, television and telephone systems; water, gas and electric systems. *You can tell a country's stage of* *economic growth from its infrastructure*

◆ Infrastruktur

ingot a bar of gold or silver

◆ Barren

inherent vice (**insurance**) a natural fault in the thing insured. For example, all food will go bad eventually, certain metal will rust easily under wet conditions. *Insurance companies will not pay out money for an inherent vice*

◆ Mangel infolge natürlicher Beschaffenheit

inherit to receive (something, e.g. property, money) which has been left by a person who has died. *He knows that when his father dies he will inherit the business*

◆ erben

inheritance something (e.g. property, money) which has been **inherited.** *His inheritance was a silver watch and £10,000*

◆ Erbe

initial sale the first sale of a **product.** *The initial sale of the new machine makes us hopeful for more sales in the future*

◆ Erstverkauf

injunction an order from a court ordering a person to do or not to do, a certain thing. *The customer got an injunction which stopped the company from selling the new baby food until it had further health tests*

◆ einstweilige Verfügung

injury benefit money paid to a worker because of an injury, or sickness, at his/her place of work. *He was off work for three weeks because of his injury and received injury benefit of £80 per week*

◆ Unfallgeld

Inland Revenue that part of the government in charge of collecting national taxes

◆ ≃ Finanzamt

innovate to do something in a new way, e.g. to make new **products** or **services.** *A company has to innovate or its products and its profits will die*

◆ neu einführen

innovation something which has been made or introduced for the first time. *Video is a wonderful innovation — but then so was the first photograph*

◆ Neueinführung

input something which is to be put into something else, e.g. information into a **computer**

◆ Eingabe

inquire *see* **enquire**

insert written or printed material which is placed inside something else, e.g. a magazine. *To help sales they are putting an insert in the form of an order card in every copy of the magazine*

◆ Beilage

insider dealings (*or* **insider trading**) buying or selling **stocks** and **shares** by people who have knowledge of some event which affects the value (when this information is not known to the general public). For example, knowledge is available to a director of the company which is about to make a **bid** for another company. If the director uses this knowledge to buy **shares** in the other company he is engaged in insider dealings

◆ Aktiengeschäfte durch Eingeweihte

insolvent of a person or company that is unable to pay debts when they fall due. *He has no money — he is insolvent*

◆ zahlungsunfähig

inst *see* **instant**

instalment a regular payment of a debt at certain intervals of time. *We are paying off the office furniture in* *instalments — £40 per week*

◆ Rate

instalment purchase buying by **instalments** where the buyer is already the owner. *Compare with* **hire-purchase**

◆ Ratenkauf

instant (*or* **inst**) this present month; sometimes used in business letters

◆ dieses Monats

in-store promotion advertising at the **point-of-sale,** i.e. inside the shop or the showroom, e.g. special price tickets, or a special **display** of the **products,** or the offer of free **samples**

◆ Werbung innerhalb des Ladens

instrument a legal **document,** e.g. a **contract**

◆ Dokument

insurable interest a legal relationship between the **insured** and the subject of the **insurance.** Before one can insure any property or insure against something happening, one must have an insurable interest in the matter; one can't insure against loss or damage of **cargo** unless one stands to lose **financially** from such loss or damage

◆ Versicherungsinteresse

insurance a **contract** with an **insurer** to make good any **financial** loss if a certain thing should happen. For example a businessman can protect himself against the financial loss of his factory being burned down or he can insure against loss of or damage to his **stocks,** or **cargo** etc. (The word **insurance** is generally used in connection with something that may happen, for example, a fire and the word **assurance** is used for something that must happen, for example, a death.)

◆ Versicherung

insurance broker a person who offers advice on and may arrange the best **insurance** for certain risks. A businessman sending goods by sea to Brazil may use an insurance broker to arrange the best **cover**

◆ Versicherungsmakler

insurance (*or* **assurance**) **company** a company that offers to make payments if a certain event should happen, e.g. a death, a fire, etc., in exchange for certain payments, called **premiums**

◆ Versicherungsgesellschaft

insurance policy a **document** laying out the terms of an **insurance contract**

◆ Versicherungspolice

insurance premium a payment which is made by the person who takes out an **insurance policy** or **contract**

◆ Versicherungsprämie

insured a person who or organisation which has taken out an **insurance policy** as protection against the **financial** loss of something happening, e.g. the loss of goods by fire

◆ Versicherungsnehmer

insurer an **insurance company** or **insurer at Lloyds** which **contracts** to pay the **financial** loss of something happening (e.g. the loss of a ship at sea) in exchange for the payment of a **premium.** *See also* **insurance, insurable interest**

◆ Versicherungsträger

intangible assets (*or* **invisible assets**) unseen **assets** which are of value to a company, e.g. having the **sole** rights to make a successful **product** (the **copyright**), or **patents,** or **goodwill**

◆ immaterielle Vermögenswerte

integrate to bring (parts) together to form a whole. *When forming the company plan he integrated all the sug-*

gestions of the managers

◆ integrieren

INTELSAT *see* **International Telecommunications Satellite Organisation**

intensive selling selling more to the company's existing customers by using more persuasion, e.g. more forceful selling, more advertising, more **sales promotion**

◆ Intensivverkauf

intercompany comparison (*or* **interfirm comparison**) a method of finding out if a company's performance is worse, as good or better than other companies in the same industry. This is done by matching a company's business results against the published results of other companies. These business results are in the form of **ratios** or percentages and will include for example: the percentage **gross profit,** expenses, **net profit** and **return** on **capital employed.** *See* **Centre for Interfirm Comparison**

◆ Betriebsvergleich

interest money paid to a lender of cash for the use of it

◆ Zinsen

interest-free loan money which is lent without the lender charging for its use. *Sometimes people help charities with interest-free loans*

◆ zinsloses Darlehen

interest rate a charge for the use of borrowed money. It is usually given as a certain percentage of every £100 borrowed for a year. *He borrowed money from the bank to buy a car and they are charging an interest rate of 20%; so for every £100 borrowed for a year he has to pay the bank £20*

◆ Zinssatz

interface (1) where different interests meet and affect each other, e.g. different jobs, different exports. *In our company we have improved the interface between management and workers.* (2) (**computers**) an **electronic device** for linking a **computer** to **peripheral equipment**

◆ (1) Interaktion (2) Schnittstelle

interfirm comparison *see* **intercompany comparison**

interim dividend an amount of money paid by a company to its **shareholders** before the end of its **financial year** with the intention of making another payment at the end of the year

◆ Zwischendividende

interim report a short statement given before the end of something, e.g. a report to **shareholders** issued by a **public company** before the end of its **financial year**

◆ Zwischenbericht

intermediary a person who passes proposals between two **parties** in a business deal, e.g. between a **trade union** and a company or between a buyer and a seller

◆ Vermittler

internal audit a check of one or more of the departments of a company, e.g. sales, production, **finance,** by expert employees of the company. The report which follows such an audit is usually made to the directors of a company

◆ betriebsinterne Revision

internal economies of scale savings in costs which a large company can make, e.g. by using up-to-date machinery, improving the training of its workers, cutting material costs by buying in bulk, spreading all costs over a greater **output** etc

◆ betriebsinterne Einsparungen

international having to do with more than one country. *If we want to sell more we have to export — we have to sell on the international market, not just the home market*

◆ international

International Atomic Energy Agency (*or* **IAEA**) an agency formed in 1957 which has a working relationship with the **United Nations.** Its purpose is to encourage the growth and use of atomic energy for the purposes of peace, health and prosperity throughout the world. Membership: 110 countries. Headquarters: Vienna. Official languages: Chinese, English, French, Russian, Spanish

◆ Internationale Atomenergiekommission (IAEA)

International Bank for Reconstruction and Development (*or* **IBRD,** *or* **World Bank**) **United Nations** bank, set up in 1944 to encourage the flow of **capital** between countries for **economic** purposes, to offer loans at fair **interest rates** to **developing countries.** Headquarters: Washington, DC. Membership: 139 countries. Official language: English

◆ Internationale Bank für Wiederaufbau und Entwicklung

International Chamber of Commerce an organisation with branches in many countries which aims to help companies with their general business and **economic** problems

◆ Internationale Handelskammer

international company = multinational company

International Court of Justice (*or* **ICJ**) the **United Nations** court formed in 1945 to settle **disputes** between members of the United Nations and to advise on legal matters raised by any of its official organisations. Headquarters: The Hague. Official languages: English, French

◆ Internationaler Gerichtshof

International Energy Agency (*or* **IEA**) a group formed by the **OECD** ministers in Paris in 1974 to agree on the sharing of oil between members in times of difficulties over oil supplies. Membership: twenty-one countries, including Australia, Belgium, Canada, Federal Republic of Germany, Italy, Japan, Netherlands, Sweden, United Kingdom, United States. Headquarters: Paris

◆ Internationale Energiekommission

International Finance Corporation (*or* **IFC**) a **United Nations agency** formed in 1957 mainly to encourage **private enterprise** in member states, especially the **less-developed countries.** Headquarters: Washington, DC. Membership: 118 countries. Official language: English

◆ Internationale Finanzierungsgesellschaft

International Fund for Agricultural Development (*or* **IFAD**) a **fund** formed by the **United Nations** in 1974 to help **developing countries financially** in all matters to do with food, including production, storage and distribution. Headquarters: Rome. Membership: 131 countries

◆ Internationaler Agrarentwicklungsfonds

International Labour Organisation (*or* **ILO**) an **agency** of the **United Nations** formed in 1946 to achieve **full employment** for its members, to raise their **standard of living** and to improve **working conditions.** Headquarters: Geneva. Membership: 144 countries. Official languages: English, French

◆ Internationales Arbeitsamt

International Monetary Fund (*or* **IMF**) an **agency** of the **United Nations** formed in 1974. Its purposes include: to promote world trade and the employment and **income** of its member states; to try to keep exchange rates steady; to loan money to member states for these purposes. Headquarters:

Washington, DC. Membership: 141 countries

◆ Internationaler Währungsfonds (IWF)

International Telecommunications Satellite Organisation (*or* **INTELSAT**) an international organisation of over a hundred countries formed in 1971 to develop, construct, operate and maintain the world-wide system of **communications satellites.** Membership includes: Argentina, Australia, Belgium, Canada, China, France, Japan, Saudi-Arabia, United Kingdom, United States, Vatican City, Yemen Arab Republic, Zaire, Zambia. Headquarters: Washington, DC. Offical languages: English, French, Spanish

◆ Internationale Organisation zur Entwicklung von Nachrichtensatelliten

interview *noun* a formal meeting between (usually) two people where one questions the other about something important, e.g. about a new job, or an increase in salary. *I am going for an interview for a job*

◆ Vorstellungsgespräch

interview *verb* (1) to hold an interview with. *They are interviewing six people for the job of sales manager. The Prime Minister was interviewed on TV last night.* (2) to try to get opinions from people, e.g. for a research survey. *The market research company planned to interview 100 housewives to find out what they thought about the new product*

◆ (1) interviewen (2) befragen

intestate *(law)* of a person who has died, without leaving a will. *He died intestate*

◆ nicht testamentarisch vermacht

intra vires (*Latin, meaning* within the powers) *(law)* of an action, e.g. by a representative of an organisation, which is **legally binding** on the organisation

◆ ermächtigt

in-tray a tray on a desk which contains letters, messages, **documents** which a manager has to attend to. (When attended to they will be placed in the **out-tray**.)

◆ Ablage für Eingänge

in-tray exercise a method of training a person in management by creating a business situation for him to handle. The in-tray exercise is a copy of a manager's busy day at the office. Urgent letters, **memos,** phone messages, **documents** all have to be attended to within a certain time. He has to consider each item in the 'in-tray' and come to a decision about it, then place it in the 'out-tray'

◆ Managementschulung, bei der der Kandidat in die Alltagssituation eines Managers versetzt wird

intrinsic value the worth of something in its natural state, e.g. the price of gold in its natural, unworked form is its intrinsic value. *See also* **extrinsic value, market value**

◆ intrinsischer Wert

introductory offer any special price, gift, etc. used by a company to get customers to try a **product** for the first time. *There's an introductory offer on this new toothpaste — you get two tubes for the price of one*

◆ Einführungsangebot

inventory (1) the value of the **stock** of something, e.g. the value of a company's **raw materials,** or **work-in-progress** or **finished goods.** (2) detailed list of **stock.** *We have to do an inventory of our entire stock of cigarettes and cigars.* (3) **stock**

◆ (1) Warenbestandswert (2) Bestandsaufnahme (3) Warenbestand

inventory control the act or **process** of keeping **stock** to a planned level. Methods of inventory control include **sales forecasts** etc.

◆ Bestandsüberwachung

invest (1) to use (money) so as to get a profit from it, e.g. by putting it into a bank or by buying **stocks** and **shares.** (2) to put (time, effort etc.) into something. *I have invested a lot of time on this project*

◆ (1), (2) investieren

investment (1) money used by a company to buy **assets,** e.g. land, buildings, machinery. *See* Appendix 2. (2) money used to buy **stocks, shares, securities** or placed on **deposit account** at a bank. *His investment gave him an additional income of £2000.* (3) the act of **investing**

◆ (1) Investition (2) Wertpapier (3) Investieren

investment grant money paid by the government to a company to help with its buying of new machinery, etc.

◆ Investitionszuschuß

investment income money in the form of **interest,** profit or **dividends** from an **investment**

◆ Erträge aus Anlagen

investment portfolio a list of where a person's or a company's money is **invested.** *His investment portfolio included £5000 invested in a steel company, and £10,000 invested in an engineering firm. See also* **investment**

◆ Wertpapierportfeuille

investment trust a company which offers its **shares** to the public and whose business is the buying and selling of **securities**

◆ Investmenttrust

investor a person who puts money into a company, or who buys **shares** to make a profit, or who paid money on **deposit** at a bank to earn **interest.** *As an investor in gold mines he took many risks. See also* **investment**

◆ Kapitalanleger

invisible assets *see* **intangible assets**

invisible exports/imports the **export/import** of **services** such as **insurance,** shipping, banking, tourism, which can earn money without any actual goods being sold

◆ unsichtbare Einfuhren/Ausfuhren

invoice a printed notice, sent to the buyer of goods which gives the details of the goods ordered (the number, size, price etc.) and of any **trade discounts**

◆ (Waren-) Rechnung

IOU (*short for* 'I owe you') a piece of paper with these letters on it, as well as the amount owed, the date and the signature of the person who owes the money; it can be used as a legal proof of debt. *I loaned him five pounds and he gave me an IOU made out for this amount*

◆ Schuldschein

ironmongers a **retail** shop which deals in goods made of metal such as locks, keys, spades etc. *See also* **hardware**

◆ Eisen- und Haushaltswarenhandlung

irrevocable letter of credit *see* **letter of credit**

issued capital the value of all the **shares** put out by a company to its **shareholders**

◆ ausgegebenes Kapital

issued price a price of **shares** etc. when first offered for sale to the public

◆ Emissionskurs

issuing house name given to the company or organisation which sells to the public a company's issue of new **shares.** Often the issuing house is a **merchant bank** and often the issue of new shares takes place when a **private company** becomes a **public company**

◆ Emissionshaus

J

jerry-built built using low-quality materials, poor workmanship, cheap methods. *You can tell the house was jerry-built, it has only been up a few months and the roof is leaking*

◆ schlampig gebaut

jetsam (1) goods which have been thrown overboard from a ship at sea in order to make a ship safer. (2) goods thrown over the side of a ship at sea which have been washed up on a shore. *See also* **flotsam**

◆ (1) über Bord geworfenes Gut (2) Strandgut

jettison to throw goods or part of a ship overboard (e.g. loose timber, torn sails etc.) in order to lighten the ship in a storm, to make the ship safer. *See also* **flotsam**

◆ über Bord werfen

jingle a short, repeated, song which advertises something while it is being shown in the cinema, or on television, or which advertises it on radio

◆ gesungener Werbespruch

job (1) an occupation, especially one by which one earns one's living. *I am the manager of the factory — that's my job.* (2) a piece of work. *I've been given the job of sorting out the letters this morning.* (3) an order which is being **processed** in a factory. *How is job number 146 getting on, is it finished?* (4) a crime, such as theft or burglary. *He is in prison for a job he did in London*

◆ (1) Beruf (2) Arbeit (3) Auftrag (4) krummes Ding

job analysis is a study of the detail of a piece of work to be done in a factory, e.g. cost of materials, time taken to complete it etc. *See also* **job** (meaning 3)

◆ Arbeitsanalyse

jobber a person who buys and sells on the **stock exchange**

◆ Wertpapierhändler

job card a card giving details of a **job** (meaning 3) in a factory, e.g. its number, the work to be done, time taken to do it

◆ Auftragskarte

job centre (*or formerly* **labour exchange**) a government office in the main part of a town or city which helps people to find jobs, e.g. by displaying cards with details of jobs which are vacant

◆ ≈ Arbeitsamt

job costing working out the cost of materials, wages etc. for a **job** (meaning 3) in a factory

◆ Auftragskostenrechnung

job description a list of the important factors of a **job** (meaning 1), e.g. the purpose, the duties and the responsibilities of the job. *The company sent him a job description and after reading it he thought he might have a chance of getting the job, so he applied for it*

◆ Arbeitsplatzbeschreibung

job enrichment the result of rearranging the methods of working, e.g. re-arranging how the parts of a car are fitted together in a factory, so that the workers are more in charge of how they work, have more responsibility for doing the work, and get more pleasure from the job

◆ Humanisierung des Arbeitsplatzes

job evaluation a method of judging the relative worth of **jobs** (meaning 1) within a company, deciding how much skill, responsibility, experience etc. they need

◆ Arbeitsplatzbewertung

job lot a group of different things bought or sold together usually at a low price. A job lot is usually made up of things left over from other ranges of goods. For example, if the contents of a house were being sold off, a job lot might be made up of unsold kitchen things offered at a low price

◆ Restposten

job mobility (*or* **labour mobility**) the extent to which people will move from one part of the country to another in search of **jobs** (meaning 1) or to change jobs. *The job mobility among managers in the UK is quite high*

◆ berufliche Beweglichkeit

job number a number given to each **job** (meaning 3), (or order, or **contract**) inside a company, so that its progress can be checked

◆ Auftragsnummer

job satisfaction the pleasure a worker gets from his/her work. It may come from the comradeship, the pay, the security, the chances of promotion, etc. in a job. *I know it's not well paid but I get job satisfaction from the job being a very responsible one*

◆ berufliche Zufriedenheit

job security the extent to which a worker feels that his **job** (meaning 1) will last. *Being a football team manager is a terrible job — there's no job security. If your team keeps losing, you are out!*

◆ Sicherheit des Arbeitsplatzes

job specification a detailed description of a **job** (meaning 1), including its responsibilities and the abilities and qualifications needed to do it

◆ Arbeitsplatzbeschreibung

joint account a **bank account** owned by two or more people. *My wife and I have a joint account at the bank*

◆ gemeinsames Konto

joint consultations talks between management and workers before decisions are made on matters which may affect the workers. *If we lay out the machinery in the way you suggest we will improve the output — but we must have joint consultations before we do anything like that*

◆ Besprechungen zwischen Unternehmungsleitung und Arbeitern

joint demand the sale of goods which are closely related, e.g. bread and butter, houses and cookers, cars and car radios

◆ Komplementärbedarf

joint owners two or more people who own the same property. *My wife and I are joint owners of the house*

◆ Miteigentümer

joint-stock bank a bank that is a **public company,** that is owned by **shareholders.** Their **financial** responsibility to the bank extends only to the **face value** of their **shares.** *See* **commercial bank**

◆ Aktienbank

joint-stock company a company whose **capital** is made up of **shares** held by a number of people

◆ Aktiengesellschaft

joint venture two or more companies or persons coming together for a special purpose (e.g. to get a **contract**). *Since the Jones Company were builders and the L & C Company were electricians they decided on a joint venture for the new hospital contract*

◆ Joint-venture

journal (*or* **day book**) (**bookkeeping**) the book in which all the **debit** and **credit** entries are written as they take place each day. These entries are then written into their appropriate **books of account**

◆ Journal

journey a day of business calls by a salesman. *I have five calls to make on today's journey. See also* **journey planning**

◆ Geschäftsbesuchstag

journeyman a workman who has trained over a period of years to become qualified in his trade. *See also* **apprentice**

◆ Geselle

journey planning planning a salesman's daily calls on customers. The plan for each day's calls will include the number of calls, the order in which the calls will be made, the route to be taken and the mileage to be covered

◆ Geschäftsbesuchsplanung

JP *see* **Justice of the Peace**

judgement creditor a person who has successfully brought an **action** against someone in a court of law and has 'obtained judgement' for the amount **claimed,** i.e. the law has ordered the debtor to pay a certain amount to the judgement creditor. *See also* **judgement debt, judgement debtor**

◆ Vollstreckungsgläubiger

judgement debt money which a court has ordered to be paid to a person (the **judgement creditor**)

◆ vollstreckbare Forderung

judgement debtor a person who has been ordered by the court to pay a sum of money to a **creditor.** *See also* **judgement creditor**

◆ Vollstreckungsschuldner

jumble sale a sale of used clothes, books etc. (usually to raise money for a good cause). *The old folk's club could do with a bus outing—let's have a jumble sale to raise the money*

◆ Flohmarkt

justice of the peace (*or* **JP**) a member of the public appointed to act as judge in a lower court of law

◆ Friedensrichter

K

K (1) short for one thousand. *The advertisement said the salary was £14K per year,* i.e. £14,000 per year. (2) **computer** term for the number 1024

◆ (1) K (2) Komputerbegriff für die Zahl 1024

KD (*or* **knocked down**) goods may be delivered KD, that is, knocked down into parts which can be put together again after delivery. For example, furniture, small sheds, some cars are **exported** on a KD basis, to be put together again when received

◆ (in Einzelteile) zerlegt

keelage money paid for the use of a port or harbour

◆ Hafengebühr

Kennedy round an agreement on **tariff** reductions (named after the US president John F Kennedy), reached in 1964 between the member states to the **General Agreement on Tariffs and Trade**

◆ Kennedy-Runde

keyboard the part of a typewriter, **computer** etc. with rows of letters and numbers, worked by pressing a special key for each letter or number

◆ Tastatur

keyed advertisement a method of measuring the response to an advertisement in a certain newspaper or magazine. For example an advertisement for jewellery might invite the reader to write to the company for more information. Included in the company's address might be the words: Dept. (L/T). Anyone answering this particular advertisement will be showing that he saw the advertisement in the London Times (which could be the meaning of the 'key': Dept. (L/T))

◆ Chiffrewerbung

key points (*or* **key factors**) the important points in a task, or a speech, or in a sales message. *The key points in this advertising campaign are* *three: the product is new, it does what we claim, and it is low-priced*

◆ zentrale Punkte

kickback (*or* **rake-off**) (*US: informal*) a secret (usually illegal) payment to a person to get an order or a **contract.** *There's a rumour they paid a kickback of 5% of the current price to someone in the company. See also* **bribe**

◆ Schmiergeld

kicked upstairs *(informal)* given a better-paid job inside a company but with less responsibility. A person is kicked upstairs to get rid of him usually from a post he cannot manage. *He was really no good at the job of marketing manager so they made him a director of one of our smaller companies: he was kicked upstairs*

◆ die Leiter hinaufgeschoben werden

kilometer 1000 metres (or about 0.6 of a mile, or about 1094 yards)

◆ Kilometer

kind: in kind (1) in goods, not money. *The workers on the farm are paid partly in kind; they get free eggs and milk.* (2) in the same way. *He insulted me and I replied in kind*

◆ (1) in Naturalien (2) auf die gleiche Weise

kite mark the symbol in the form of a kite which is the mark of the **British Standards Institution. A product** which carries this mark has passed the standard of quality set by the institution

◆ Qualitätszeichen des britischen Normenausschusses

knocked down *see* **KD**

knock-for-knock agreement (car **insurance**) an agreement between **insurance companies** that if two vehicles suffer damage in a crash each company will pay the insurance **claim** of its **client.** This saves the cost of many minor legal agreements

◆ Schadensteilungsvereinbarung

knocking copy advertisement which criticises another **product**

◆ herabsetzende Werbung

knocking-off time *(informal)* the time at which the working day ends. *I should be home by six o'clock because knocking-off time in our office is half-past five*

◆ Feierabend

know-how *(informal)* skill, knowledge, experience

◆ Know-how

L

lab *see* **laboratory**

label *noun* a piece of paper on a bottle or package which describes what is in it. *The label says it is safe for children. See also* **own brand**

◆ Etikett

label *verb* to fix or apply a label to (a **product,** a piece of luggage etc.). *In the labelling department the machines labelled the bottles at great speed*

◆ etikettieren

laboratory (*or* **lab**) a room or a building used for scientific work etc. *Our chemists have produced a new range of cosmetics in the lab. See also* **language laboratory**

◆ Labor

labour (*US* **labor**) (1) work. *Painting this fence is hard labour.* (2) people who do heavy work with their hands (usually) in a factory. *Management and labour are now in full agreement about the wage increase*

◆ (1) Arbeit (2) Arbeiter

labour agreement a **contract** between a company and its workers, e.g. on payment per hour. *They have reached a labour agreement on the number of holidays per year*

◆ Tarifvereinbarung

labour cost (1) wages and other expenses of workers in a company. *Our labour cost is higher now because of the last wage increase.* (2) wages and other expenses of workers on a particular job, or **product.** *The labour cost of this product — not counting the material — is £10*

◆ (1) Arbeitslöhne (2) Lohnkosten

labourer a worker who does heavy work with his hands. *He got a job at the factory as a labourer. He worked all day cleaning machines*

◆ Arbeiter

labour exchange *see* **job centre**

labour force (1) all the workers in a factory. *The labour force agreed to the wage increase.* (2) all the workers in a country. *It is a nation which attracts a lot of foreign firms because it has a well-educated labour force*

◆ (1) Belegschaft (2) Arbeiterschaft

labour-intensive industry a trade where a large amount of money is paid out in wages in relation to the money paid for **assets** (like buildings, machinery). *The retail trade is a labour-intensive industry. See also* **capital-intensive**

◆ lohnkostenintensive Industrie

labour market the number of workers in an area. *The high quality of the local labour market influenced the company's decision to relocate there*

◆ Arbeitsmarkt

labour mobility *see* **job mobility**

labour relations *see* **industrial relations**

labour turnover the rate at which people leave a company. Usually measured by:

$$\frac{\text{number of people who left during the year}}{\text{average number of people in the company during the year}}$$

◆ Fluktuation von Arbeitskräften

LAFTA (*or* **Latin American Free Trade Association**) *see* **Latin American Integration Association**

LAIA *see* **Latin American Integration Association**

laissez-faire the theory that governments should not interfere with how firms (or people) conduct their business

◆ freier Wettbewerb

lame duck a person or organisation that is weak and unable to manage his/her/its affairs. *The company is now a lame duck — its products are no longer selling*

◆ Versager

landed terms an export price which includes all charges up to the goods being unloaded at the port to which they have been sent

◆ Verkaufspreis inkl. Fracht und Entladungskosten

landing charges the cost of unloading goods from a ship plus the cost of moving the goods into storage plus **customs duties,** which have to be paid to the port authority where the goods arrive

◆ Landungskosten

landlady (1) a woman who owns property and rents it to others. (2) a woman who is in charge of a pub, inn, a small hotel etc.

◆ (1) Vermieterin (2) Wirtin

landlord (1) a man who owns property and who rents it to others. (2) a man who is in charge of a pub, inn etc.

◆ (1) Vermieter (2) Wirt

land registration the system of putting on record (i.e. registering) the ownership of land in England and Wales. These records help in the buying and selling of land and they are kept in the government department known as the **Land Registry**

◆ Eintragung im Grundbuch

language laboratory a room specially fitted out to allow a person to learn a foreign language by means of tape recordings. The person can learn the language at his/her own pace and can compare his/her speech with the voice on the tape. A teacher can help by listening to the student and giving advice

◆ Sprachlabor

larceny *(law)* theft

◆ Diebstahl

last in first out (*or* **LIFO**) a method of valuing **stock** at the earlier cost (rather than at current cost). *See also* **FIFO**

◆ zuletzt eingekauft – zuerst verbraucht

last will and testament a legal term for a person's final will which cancels any earlier will

◆ letzter Wille

latent defect a fault which is not seen. *The cars which left the factory in June were recalled because of a latent defect which was found in the steering*

◆ verborgener Mangel

Latin American Integration Association (*or* **LAIA**) a group of Latin American countries formed at Montevideo, Uruguay in 1980. It replaced the **Latin American Free Trade Association.** The aim is to lower **trade barriers** and thus increase trade between member states. Membership: Argentina, Bolivia, Brazil, Chile, Columbia, Ecuador, Mexico, Paraguay, Peru, Uruguay, Venezuela. Headquarters: Montevideo. Official languages: Spanish, Portuguese

◆ Lateinamerikanische Handelsgemeinschaft (LAIA)

launch (1) to begin something. *He launched into a story about business.* (2) to put (a plan) into action. *Next week we launch the new product onto the market*

◆ (1) anfangen (2) auf den Markt bringen

Law Society in England and Wales, the examining body for the profession of **solicitor.** It has authority over all solicitors whether they are working as solicitors or not with regard to conduct and discipline

◆ Anwaltskammer

lawsuit a non-criminal case in a court of law, i.e. a **civil case**

◆ Zivilprozeß

lawyer a person whose profession it is to give advice on the law and to speak in court on someone's behalf. *Compare with* **barrister, solicitor**

◆ Rechtsanwalt

lay days *(shipping)* the usual number of days allowed for the loading or unloading of **cargo** from a ship. If the work continues beyond these agreed lay days a **rental** (known as **demurrage**) will be charged

◆ Liegezeit

lay it/something on the line to give clear and strict instructions (about something). *The new manager laid it on the line to the workers: they either had to work harder or the company would go bankrupt*

◆ jmd. etwas einschärfen

lay off *verb* to stop employing (a person) (usually temporarily). *They had to lay men off at the steel works – there's no work for them*

◆ wegen Arbeitsmangel entlassen

lay-off *noun* the act of **laying off.** *There have been too many lay-offs in the coal industry lately*

◆ Entlassung wegen Arbeitsmangel

lay-off pay payment made to workers who have been sent home because there is no work for them, e.g. builders on a building site (because of the weather) or factory workers (because of a power cut)

◆ Entlassungsabfindung

layout the arrangement or design of a drawing, an advertisement, or printed material

◆ Layout

L/C *see* **letter of credit**

lead a person who writes in to a company for more information as a result of seeing an advertisement which offers something for sale. *They spent £10,000 advertising their washing machines and got 1000 leads for their salesmen to follow up*

◆ Verkaufskontakt

leader (1) a person in charge, who leads others. (2) a newspaper **column** which is the opinion of the editor on some piece of news. *Did you read this newspaper's leader on the election result? Compare with* **editorial**

◆ (1) Leiter (2) Leitartikel

lead time the length of time between ordering something and having it delivered. *When ordering supplies from the ABC company remember that their lead time is 2 weeks*

◆ Lieferzeit

leaflet a small sheet of printed paper, usually given free, which advertises a **product, service,** or event

◆ Reklamezettel

League of Arab States (*or* **Arab League**) a group of twenty-two Arab States formed in 1945 to strengthen the political, cultural, social and **economic** affairs of its members. Official language: Arabic

◆ Arabische Liga

leakage (**retailing**) loss of **stock** from wastage, e.g. bread, milk, vegetables which go bad; loss of stock from theft. *I expect £1000 of stock to be lost from leakage*

◆ einkalkulierter Warenverlust

leap-frogging the action of a group of workers when they try to get a pay rise which matches one given to another group in the same industry. *The engineers now want a pay rise to match the one given to the welders — it is another case of leap-frogging*

◆ Überspringen (von Gehaltsstufen)

lease *noun* a **contract** for the use of an **asset** (e.g. land, machinery) in return for a rent

◆ Pacht-; Mietvertrag

lease *verb* (1) to give a person the use of (something) through a **lease.** (2) to get the use of (something) through a **lease.** *They leased the property for ten years*

◆ (1) verpachten; vermieten (2) pachten; mieten

lease back *verb* to sell an **asset** (e.g. land, machinery) and then take a **lease** from the new owner to use the assets in return for rent

◆ verkaufen und gleichzeitig rückmieten

leaseback *noun* such an arrangement

◆ Verkauf mit gleichzeitiger Rückmiete

leasehold property which is held on a **lease**

◆ Pacht-; Mietbesitz

leasehold land land which is rented from the owner

◆ Pachtgrundstück

ledger a book in which all the **accounts** of a business are kept. Nowadays many businesses keep this information stored in **computers**

◆ Hauptbuch

legacy a gift made by a person in a will

◆ Vermächtnis

legal holiday a day when public banks are closed for business and when many companies are also closed, e.g. Christmas Day. *See also* **bank holiday**

◆ gesetzlicher Feiertag

legally binding having to be obeyed according to the law: *a legally-binding contract*

◆ rechtsverbindlich

legal reserve the part of a bank's **assets** which must be kept as cash in order to meet the **claims** of **depositors**

◆ gesetzliche Rücklagen

legal tender money which, if offered in payment for something, must be accepted by law

◆ gesetzliches Zahlungsmittel

legatee a person who receives something from a will

◆ Vermächtnisnehmer

legislation the making of laws by a parliament etc.; laws so made. *There is new legislation about drunken driving*

◆ Gesetzgebung

lender of last resort the source which can in the end create funds, in the UK, the Bank of England

◆ Kreditgeber letzter Instanz (Bank of England) ≈ Bundesnotenbank

less-developed country *see* **developing country**

lessee a person who **leases** someone else's property

◆ Pächter

lessor a person who gives his property on a **lease** to someone else

◆ Verpächter

letterhead a name, address, telephone number etc. printed at the top of a sheet of writing paper

◆ Briefkopf

letter of attorney *see* **power of attorney**

letter of credit (*also* **L/C**) (1) a letter from one bank to another which gives the receiving bank authority to pay a certain sum of money to the person named in the letter. This is also a method of payment used by foreign buyers. In this case the UK seller would have to present **documents** to show that the goods have been sent to the foreign buyer. There are various kinds of letter of credit, e.g.:

(2) **documentary letter of credit** a method of payment used by foreign buyers. The letter is issued by the buyer's bank to the seller's bank giving it **authority** to pay a certain sum of money to the seller. The seller will have to provide documentary proof (i.e. the shipping **documents**) that the goods have been **exported** to the buyer. It is important that every condition in the letter of credit is met by the seller or payment will be withheld. (For example, the documents have to be those named by the buyer, the goods, prices etc. have to be named).

(3) **irrevocable letter of credit** one that cannot be changed without the consent of the seller. The irrevocable letter of credit contains a promise that the **importer's** bank will pay the seller through the seller's own bank. If the seller is unsure that this promise to pay will be carried out (because, say, of political risks) then he will prefer to have this promise supported by a bank in his own country. This would be a **confirmed irrevocable letter of credit**

◆ (1) Akkreditiv (2) Dokumentarakkreditiv (3) unwiderrufliches Akkreditiv

letter of hypothecation a letter from a shipper of goods to a bank giving the bank the rights to these goods in return for a loan of money. In other words the letter of hypothecation acts as **security** for the loan

◆ Verpfändungsurkunde

letters of administration a **document** given by a court by which a person can be put in charge of the **estate** of a person who has died. *See also* **intestate**

◆ Testamentsvollstreckerzeugnis

letters patent an official **document** which gives the right to an inventor to make, use or sell his invention. This document is given by the **Patent Office.** *See also* **patent**

◆ Patenturkunde

leverage *see* **gearing**

levy *verb* to put a tax on (something). *Do you think the government will levy a tax on fires?*

◆ Steuer erheben

levy *noun* money collected by this means. *There is a training levy to be paid — and a capital levy*

◆ Abgabe

liabilities the amount of money that a company owes to others. *See* Appendix 2

◆ Verbindlichkeiten

liability (1) debt; sum of money that has to be paid. (2) the state of being legally responsible for loss, damage, a debt etc. (3) the amount of debt etc. that one is legally responsible for

◆ (1) Schuld (2) Haftung (3) Schuldposten

licence a printed permission, from a person in authority, to do something, e.g. a licence (from the government) to drive a car. *You need a special licence in Britain to sell tobacco*

◆ Lizenz

licenced trade a general description for companies which buy and sell beer, wines, spirits (for which a special **licence** is needed), e.g. hotels, public houses, restaurants etc.

◆ konzessionierter Alkoholhandel

licensee a person who holds a **licence,** e.g. to sell something such as tobacco, beer, wine, spirits (for which a licence is needed). *Mr Smith is the manager of the pub but the licensee is the owner, Mr Jones*

◆ Lizenzinhaber

lien a right to take goods in order to make the owner of the goods pay a debt

◆ Pfandrecht

lieu: in lieu (of) instead (of); as a substitute (for). *He was given a month's pay in lieu of notice,* i.e. he should have been told the month before that he was to lose his job, but instead he was given a month's salary to leave at once

◆ an Stelle von

life annuity a series of payments made by an **assurance company** to a person during his life but which stops on his death. *See also* **annuity**

◆ Leibrente

life assurance a **contract** by which an **assurance** (or **insurance**) **company** agrees to pay a certain sum of money when a named person (the **life assured**) dies or at the end of a certain period of time, if he/she is still alive. The person who enters into this contract with the assurance company will have to pay regular sums of money to the company in return for his benefit. *See also* **insurance company, insurance premium, insured, insurer**

◆ Lebensversicherung

life cycle *see* **family life cycle, product life cycle**

life expectancy the number of years a person is expected to live. *Life expectancy today is much longer than it was 100 years ago*

◆ Lebenserwartung

life style a way of living of a society or group of people. *Some say the life style of western countries uses up too many scarce resources*

◆ Lebensstil

LIFO *see* **last in first out**

lighter a low flat-bottomed boat used for carrying cargo between ship and shore

◆ Leichter

lighterage a charge made when goods have to be moved by a **lighter**

◆ Leichtergebühren

limitation period a period of time, fixed by law, after which legal **action** cannot be taken. *The court had to set him free because he had been held beyond the limitation period without a trial*

◆ Verjährungsfrist

limited (*or* **Ltd**) word which must come after the company name if it is a private **limited liability company.** *See also* **public limited company**

◆ mit beschränkter Haftung

limited liability company a company in which no **shareholder** can be asked to pay debts beyond the **face value** of his **shares. Liability** (meaning 3) is limited to this amount

◆ ≈ Gesellschaft mit beschränkter Haftung

limited partner a member of a partnership whose **liability** (meaning 3) is limited to the amount of **capital** he has **invested** in it

◆ beschränkt haftender Teilhaber

line manager a person in a company who is responsible for carrying out the orders of his superiors and who has authority over others

◆ Linienmanager

line of command a **system** in a company where each manager is responsible for carrying out the orders of the manager above him

◆ Instanzenweg

line of credit a loan made to a foreign firm or authority and supported by the **Export Credits Guarantee Department**

◆ Kreditlinie

line organisation a company structure where each manager reports directly to the person above him

◆ Linienorganisation

line printer a **device** which prints out information from a **computer** on wide sheets of paper, one full line at a time

◆ Zeilendrucker

liner a large ship which carries passengers

◆ Ozeandampfer

liquid asset an **asset** which can be quickly turned into cash, e.g. money owed by debtors

◆ flüssige Mittel

liquidate (1) to sell (an **asset,** e.g. land, buildings, vehicles, materials) for cash. *He will have to liquidate this old stock.* (2) to sell all the assets of (a company) for cash, and so close the company down

◆ (1) flüssigmachen (2) liquidieren

liquidated damages the amount of money, agreed to in a **contract,** which will be paid by one of the **parties** to the contract if he fails to keep his promise. For example, the contract may state that the Wine Shop Company promises to buy 1000 cases of wine each year from the French suppliers and if orders fall below that figure then £500 must be paid to the French supplier. The £500 is called liquidated damages

◆ Konventionalstrafe

liquidating value *see* **break-up value**

liquidation the act of **liquidating** (meaning 2). *I believe the newspaper shop has gone into liquidation*

◆ Liquidation

liquidator a person appointed to sell off a company's **assets** for cash, to share out this money to those owed money by the company, and then to divide up the rest between the owners

◆ Liquidator

liquidity the state of having cash (or **assets** which can be quickly turned into cash) to pay one's debts. *The company is in a state of liquidity — we can pay all our debts from our cash in the bank plus the amount owed to us by debtors*

◆ Liquidität

liquidity ratio (*or* **acid test**) this measures how well a company's **current liabilities** (what it owes just now) are covered by its cash (or by **assets** which can be turned into cash quickly, such as debtors)

◆ Liquiditätsgrad

listed company a company which is listed on a **stock exchange,** i.e. a **public company**

◆ börsennotierte Firma

listed securities: shares which can be bought and sold in a **stock exchange,** i.e. they are on the official list of shares which can be so traded

◆ börsennotierte Wertpapiere

list price a company's price, as printed in their list of prices. *The list price of this typewriter is £500 but we are selling it for £350*

◆ Listenpreis

litigation the **process** of asking a court to settle a **dispute**

◆ Rechtsstreit

litre a metric measure of liquid (1.7598 pints)

◆ Liter

live account a customer who is regularly buying. *This account, Jones & Co, is no longer a live account because the company has gone out of business*

◆ Stammkunde

living standards *see* **standard of living**

living wage pay for doing work which is just enough to buy the essentials of life, e.g. food, rent, heat. *The pay in this job is so low it is not even a living wage*

◆ Lohn, der gerade zum Leben ausreicht

Lloyd's a world-famous **insurance** centre in London which began in a coffee house run by Edward Lloyd in the seventeenth century. A wide range of insurances are arranged here. Members of Lloyd's are represented by **underwriting** managers, who deal only with **brokers**

◆ britische Versicherungsgesellschaft

Lloyd's agents people throughout the world appointed by **Lloyd's** to give information on shipping, aircraft etc., to Lloyd's. Lloyd's agents can also appoint experts to report on damage, or loss, of **cargo** or ships

◆ Agenten für Lloyd's

Lloyd's Certificate of Marine Insurance a **document** which proves that a **marine insurance** with Lloyd's is in existence. The certificate gives details of the insurance and the goods carried

◆ Lloyd's Seeversicherungsschein

Lloyd's List a daily newspaper giving details of arrival, departure and movements of ships, including losses and **claims**

◆ Lloyd's Schiffsnachrichtenblatt

Lloyd's Register of Shipping a detailed record of ships giving facts on **tonnage,** fittings etc.

◆ Lloyd's Schiffsregister

load *noun* (1) something being carried or to be carried. *A load of steel bars has just arrived at the factory. This load of goods has to go to a customer.* (2) the weight carried by a wall etc. *That is a load-bearing wall — if you knock it down the roof will fall in.* (3) the power of an electric charge

◆ (1) Ladung (2) Tragfähigkeit (3) Leistung; Spannung

load *verb* (1) to put (a **cargo**) onto a ship, truck etc. (2) to increase an **insurance premium** to cover certain expenses. (3) to put (a **program**) into a **computer memory**

◆ (1), (3) laden (2) Prämienzuschlag erheben

loading the amount by which an **insurance premium** is increased to cover expenses

◆ Prämienzuschlag

loan an amount of money given to a person, to be returned later. *How much of a loan were you looking for?*

◆ Darlehen

loan account an **account** opened by a bank when a person borrows money from it. In the account will be entered the amount of the loan and any payments made by the borrower

◆ Darlehenskonto

loan capital part of the **capital** of a company, given for a fixed period of time and entitled to **interest** for the loan. *See also* **share capital**

◆ Fremdkapital

loan shark *(informal)* a person who loans money at very high **interest** rates. *The man is a loan shark — he wants £30 interest on every £100 borrowed*

◆ Kredithai

lobby *noun* a person or group trying to influence someone in power (e.g. member of parliament, government minister) by argument or discussion. *A lobby met the minister and tried to talk to him on the matter*

◆ Lobby

lobby *verb* to try to get influence in this way

◆ Einfluß nehmen

local authority a form of government of local affairs whereby a group of people are elected by voters of the area to represent them. This group, called a corporation in England, has powers to spend money (given by the government) on such things as education, roads etc. and directs a permanent staff to organise these

◆ Gemeinde-; Stadtverwaltung

local press area or district newspapers published daily or weekly, giving all the local or area news (as distinct from the **national press**)

◆ Lokalpresse

location any place in a **computer** store which can contain one unit of information

◆ Speicherzelle

lock-out an action by a company to stop workers from going into its factory to work, e.g. closing the factory, or locking the gates; in other words, a **strike** by the company against the workers

◆ Aussperrung

lock, stock, and barrel everything, without exception. *He sold off everything in the shop, lock, stock, and barrel*

◆ mit allem Drum und Dran

logbook (1) a book kept by the master of a ship in which he writes all of the events during a ship's voyage, especially such things as the weather, ship's speed, etc. (2) (*formerly in UK*) a record of the ownership of a car

◆ (1) Logbuch (2) ≃ Kfz-Brief

London Bankers Clearing House a group of **commercial banks** which each day 'clear' the cheques which have been paid into each of the banks, i.e. they balance out the cheques which are payment to a bank and those that are payment by a bank. As a result, a cheque can be written by the banks concerned to settle any debt between them

◆ Abrechnungsstelle von Londoner Banken, die dem Clearing System angeschlossen sind

long-dated bill a **bill of exchange** due for payment a long time ahead

◆ langfristiger Wechsel

long-range plan one which plans the growth, e.g. of a company over the years ahead (usually five or more years). In making such a plan the company's strengths and weaknesses will be considered by the directors of the company, as well as the opportunities and threats in the market. *See also* **corporate planning**

◆ langfristiger Plan

long-term liability a debt or loan which has to be paid in a period greater than one year ahead, usually more than five years

◆ langfristige Verbindlichkeit

loose tools tools which are small enough to be moved easily within a factory, e.g. small power **drills,** spanners etc. *The value of our machinery is about £150,000 but there is another £20,000 in loose tools about the factory*

◆ bewegliche Werkzeuge

loss a failure to make a profit; a situation when money paid out on a **project** is greater than the money received. *We made a loss on that last contract — the costs were greater than our selling price*

◆ Verlust

loss leader a **product** or **service** sold at a very low price, i.e. without making a profit, so that customers will be attracted to other products (or services), which are profitable. *We sell the bags of sugar cheap as a loss leader to get the housewives into the shop to buy all the other lines*

◆ Lockvogelangebot

lost-business report a written explanation to a manager or a director as to why the company did not succeed in getting a **contract,** or why a regular customer is now buying from some other company

◆ Geschäftsverlustbericht

lot (1) a large quantity or number. *There were a lot of people working for the company.* (2) a number or group of similar things sold together at an **auction.** (3) (*mainly US*) an area of land set aside for a special purpose: *a parking lot*

◆ (1) viel (2) Posten (3) Gelände

low-level language (*also* **assembly language**) a **computer language** with simple features

◆ maschinenorientierte Programmiersprache

low-loader a specially-built vehicle with a low carrying area for carrying very heavy or tall loads by road or rail. *We will need a low-loader to get this machinery from London to York*

◆ Tieflader

low-pressure selling a method of selling where the salesman joins the buyer in solving the buyer's problem, rather than going after a quick sale. *See also* **high-pressure selling**

◆ Beratungsverkauf

lump sum an amount of money paid all together. *You can either get your pension at so much per week, or you can be paid one lump sum*

◆ Pauschalbetrag

lump system *(UK)* a method of employing workers in the building trade. The worker is not paid wages but is paid a lump sum of money when his work is done (i.e. he is treated as a separate company). This makes it easy for some workers to avoid paying tax on what they earn, and so attempts have been made to do away with this system

◆ Entlohnungssystem, bei dem Bauarbeitern am Ende des Bauvorhabens ein Pauschalbetrag gezahlt wird

luncheon voucher a slip of paper with an amount of money printed on it. These vouchers are given by some companies to their office staff and they are exchanged for meals in certain restaurants. *My pay is good and*

I also get luncheon vouchers

◆ Essensmarke

luxury a **product** or **service** which is over and above those needed for a normal **standard of living,** e.g. diamonds, furs, beauty treatments

◆ Luxus

luxury tax a tax put on **luxuries**

◆ Luxussteuer

M

M1, M3 *see* **money supply**

macadam a type of road surface made of a mixture of tar and small stones which is rolled onto a road to give a smooth hard surface

◆ Makadam

machine a man-made **device** driven by power (e.g. electricity) to do work. *With this drilling machine we can drill twenty holes in ten seconds*

◆ Maschine

machine code *see* **machine language**

machine downtime a time when a machine is not working because of a breakdown or because it is being repaired etc. *See also* **machine idle time**

◆ Maschinenausfallzeit

machine idle time a time when a machine is ready for work but is out of action because of lack of material, labour, or orders etc.

◆ Maschinenstillstandszeit

machine language (*or* **machine code**) information or **data** expressed in such a way that it can be directly understood by a **computer**

◆ Maschinensprache

machine loading planning the work to be done on a machine or machines in a factory so that the best use is made of time, men and machines for the work

◆ optimale Maschinenauslastung

machine shop a place (usually in a factory) where machines are operated

◆ Maschinensaal

machine tool a large machine for working on metal, wood, etc., e.g. a large **drilling** machine in a factory, a turning lathe, a grinding machine (all used to shape metal, wood, etc.)

◆ Werkzeugmaschine

machinist a person who works at a machine in a factory

◆ Maschinenführer

macro- *prefix* large, great, e.g. **macroeconomics.** *See also* **micro**

◆ Makro-

macroeconomics the study of the whole **economy** of a country, i.e. a country's production, demand, prices, **imports, exports,** etc. and their effects on each other. *See also* **microeconomics**

◆ Makroökonomie

magazine (1) a publication which appears regularly, usually every week or every month (sometimes called a weekly (magazine) or monthly (magazine)). It contains news, stories and items of special interest to the reader. Magazines are aimed at special groups of readers, e.g. young girls, golfers, older women, fishermen etc. (2) a room or store which hold bullets, rifles, gunpowder etc. *On the ship all the guns were stored in the magazine*

◆ (1) Zeitschrift (2) Magazin

magnate a very rich and powerful businessman, often one who owns a large number of companies: *an oil magnate*

◆ Magnat

magnet a material (usually metal) which can attract other pieces of metal to it

◆ Magnet

magnetic having the quality of a **magnet.** *He held everyone's atten-*

tion — he was a magnetic speaker

◆ magnetisch

magnetic board a board used for the display of figures, lines, etc. The board and the things on **display** have been specially treated so that they can be moved around the board without falling off. This is done by the use of **magnets**

◆ Magnettafel

magnetic disk (**computers**) a thin flat circular plate on which a large amount of **data** is stored. *See also* **floppy disk, hard disk**

◆ Magnetplatte

magnetic tape a long, narrow, thin film of plastic on which sound or other information is stored

◆ Magnetband

mail *noun* letters, parcels, etc. which are delivered by post. *Has the mail arrived yet?*

◆ Post

mail *verb (mainly US)* to send (letters, parcels etc.) by post

◆ mit der Post schicken

mailing list a list of names and addresses of people or companies with special interests, e.g. managers, fishermen, companies that make cars, home-owners, etc. Such mailing lists are often used by companies who want to contact likely buyers by post. *I must be on the Acme Insurance Company's mailing list — they keep sending me through the post details of their new insurance schemes*

◆ Anschriftenliste

mail order a form of buying and selling which uses the postal service instead of dealers. Mail-order companies advertise in newspapers and magazines and invite buyers to send off their orders by post. (Goods are often delivered by the same method but sometimes rail or road is used.) *See* **catalogue buying**

◆ Versand

mail-order house a company which sells goods by **mail order**

◆ Versandhaus

main frame name given to a large centrally-placed **computer**

◆ Mainframe

maintenance keeping something in a good condition, especially machinery. *With that sort of maintenance our machines rarely break down*

◆ Wartung und Instandhaltung

maintenance shift a special period of work, e.g. 6 p.m.-2 a.m., for the purpose of checking machines in a factory to make sure that they are in proper working order. *See also* **maintenance**

◆ Wartungsschicht

major shareholder a person who or organisation which owns more **shares** in a company than anyone else

◆ Hauptaktionär

make a killing *(informal)* to make a lot of **profit** in a business deal. *He bought oil shares when the price was low and when the price shot up he sold them and made a killing*

◆ ein Vermögen machen

make good (1) *(informal)* to be a success. *He started off a new business and this time he made good.* (2) to make up for (something that one has lost, damaged, etc.) by some kind of payment. *If any of this equipment is damaged, you must make good the loss*

◆ (1) erfolgreich sein (2) ersetzen

make or buy the act of working out the benefits and costs to a company of making a part which is needed (for a machine or a **product**) and of buying in the part from another company. From its examination of benefits and costs a company will decide whether to 'make or buy'

◆ Entscheidung über Eigenfertigung oder Fremdbezug

manage (1) to be in charge of certain activities (or a certain department) in a company. (2) to succeed in doing something which is difficult. *Will you help me to move this desk? I can't manage it by myself*

◆ (1) managen (2) schaffen

management (1) the act of **managing** (meaning 1). *The management of the office is a very important job.* (2) a group of managers, i.e. group of people inside a company who control and direct workers. *The management of the company met the workers to negotiate pay increases.* (3) deciding how **plant,** machinery, materials, men, money should all be used so that a company's **financial** aims can be reached. *The proper management of a firm's resources is the job of the board of directors*

◆ (1) Führung (2) Geschäftsleitung (3) Geschäftsführung

management accounting a special study of costs and profits by experts in **accountancy** inside a company, in order to give **financial** information to managers in a way which will help them to make better planning decisions on **products** and departments

◆ Rechnungswesen im Dienste der Unternehmensführung

management appraisal an examination of a manager's past work for the company so that his training needs and suitability for **promotion,** or increases in pay etc. can be seen. This appraisal is usually done by a superior (usually a director) on a regular basis

◆ Bewertung der Management-Leistung

management audit an examination of the ability of **management** in a company, their way of doing their work, their efficiency etc. This is done so that weaknesses in people's ability to do their job or weaknesses in the methods they use can be seen and corrected

◆ Prüfung der Management-Tätigkeit

management by crisis a manager's method — or style — of doing his job. This style of management allows the work done to get so bad (i.e. reach a crisis) that drastic, corrective action is necessary. The manager who manages by crisis does little planning since he waits for events to decide what he should do

◆ Management durch Krisen

management by exception a method of managing people by which a manager will set out a plan — or a **budget** — for the people who work for him. Only any extreme departure from the plan will be brought to his notice and he will thus have time to deal with other matters. For example, a sales manager sets out a plan of sales for a salesman as follows: Jan 40 units, Feb 50, Mar 45, Apr 60, May 50. If the actual sales were: Jan 40 units, Feb 30, Mar 45, Apr 40, May 50, then the salesman would report to his manager about the sales of February and April at the end of each of these months

◆ dezentralisierte Unternehmensführung

management by objectives (*or* **MBO**) a method of managing people by which a manager agrees with each worker a plan of work to be done in a stated time. These objectives all form part of a plan for the company. At the end of that time the manager and the worker will both decide whether the plan has been achieved. MBO is also used to plan the work of managers. *See also* **management appraisal**

◆ Unternehmensführung durch Zielvorgaben

management consultant a person who is an expert on management.

His business is to advise companies on management problems. *The steel company brought in a firm of management consultants to help them get back into profit*

◆ Unternehmensberater

management development planning the training needs of the managers of a company over the years ahead; especially training managers for future promotion

◆ Planung der Aus- und Weiterbildung von Führungskräften

management education training managers in the methods of management and in subjects related to managing people and **finance.** Such training can be in-house, or at college, university or a business school

◆ Weiterbildung von Führungskräften

management game (*or* **business game**) a method of training for management. The people being trained are put into teams, each team representing a company in an industry. Each team receives basic facts about **capital,** sales, **stocks,** cash, **products** etc., and has to solve its company's problems by making decisions, which affect each company in the industry. This changing pattern of results is meant to copy real life

◆ Management-Planspiel

management services those parts of a company's organisation which advise and help managers in making decisions, especially about **work study** and **organisation and methods**

◆ Management-Beratungsdienst

management style (*also* **managerial style**) the way in which a manager gets his workers to do their job, how he behaves towards them, his method of giving orders and of controlling them etc.

◆ Führungsstil

management training part of **management education;** improving a manager's ability to do work by giving him the chance to experience problems and to study how to resolve them

◆ Management-Schulung

manager (1) a person responsible for the control and training of a group of workers, for planning their work, setting their targets, and helping them in reaching those targets. (2) a person who **manages** (meaning 1) a department, a business, a shop etc. *See also* **manageress**

◆ (1) Manager (2) Geschäftsführer, Manager, Filialleiter, Abteilungsleiter

manageress a woman who is in charge of an office, a shop, a restaurant etc.

◆ Geschäftsführerin, Abteilungsleiterin, Filialleiterin

managerial style *see* **management style**

managing director the director of a company responsible for the day-to-day running of the business. (In the UK he is also known as the **chief executive;** in the US he is known as president.) In a small company the managing director is usually the person who set up the company and who is the major **shareholder.** In a large **public company** he is usually appointed to this position

◆ geschäftsführender Direktor; Vorstandsvorsitzender

mandate (1) an authority to act on someone's behalf. *He has a mandate to sign cheques on behalf of the owner of the firm.* (2) an authority to vote on someone's behalf. *The workers gave their shop steward a mandate to vote for them at the meeting*

◆ (1) Vollmacht (2) Mandat

manhole an opening in the road, usually covered with a heavy metal plate, down which a worker can go to repair gas and water pipes, etc.

◆ Kanalschacht

manifest an official list of the items loaded on to a ship, aircraft or vehicle. The manifest also lists the value, origin and **destination** of the goods and a copy is given to the customs

◆ Manifest

manpower planning planning the number and type of workers and managers a company will need in the future and planning also how to get them

◆ Personalplanung

Manpower Services Commission (*or* **MSC**) a body set up by the UK government in 1974 to run public employment and training services

◆ Behörde für Arbeitsbeschaffung, -vermittlung und Berufsausbildung

man-profile (*or* **man-specification**) a list of the skills needed in a person to do a particular job. *Before they advertised for a sales manager they drew up a man-profile for the job*

◆ Anforderungsprofil in einem bestimmten Beruf genügen muß

manual *adjective* done with the hands: *manual work*

◆ Hand-

manual *noun* a book of instruction about work or machines, or to help in training someone in a job. *For the first week in the firm he studied the training manual*

◆ Handbuch

manual worker a person who uses his/her hands, often without needing any particular skill

◆ Handarbeiter

manufacture to make something, especially using machinery in a factory. *Jim's firm manufactures nuts and bolts but his brother's company manufactures chocolates*

◆ herstellen

manufacturer a company which or person who manufactures something. *If the product is faulty send it back to the manufacturer*

◆ Hersteller

manufacturer's agent (*or* **manufacturer's representative**) a person or company that gets **contracts** for manufacturers. He works on **commission** in a certain area or region. *See also* **agent**

◆ Vertreter einer Herstellungsfirma

manuscript (*or* **MS,** *plural* **MSS**) the first copy of a book or article, handwritten (not typed) and not yet printed. *He sent the manuscript to the typist and when it was typed he sent it to the publishers*

◆ Manuskript

margin (1) the difference between the buying and selling price, i.e. the **gross profit.** *If I sell at £1.50 my margin is 50 pence because my buying price was £1.* (2) the edge of a page where there is no writing. *When you type the letter leave a good margin all round*

◆ (1) Spanne (2) Rand

marginal cost (*also* **incremental cost**) the cost of making one more unit. If the total cost of making 100 units is £200 and the total cost of one more (101 units) is £202, then the marginal cost of the last unit is £2. The marginal cost is also known as the **variable** or **direct cost**

◆ Grenzkosten

marginal land land which covers the cost of producing crops but which shows no profit

◆ an der Grenze der Rentabilität liegendes Land

marginal pricing fixing the selling price of a **product** at the **marginal cost** of making it

◆ Festlegung des Verkaufspreises in Höhe der Grenzkosten

marginal revenue the added **income** from the sale of one additional unit. *See also* **marginal cost**

◆ Grenzertrag

margin of safety the amount of sales which are made above the **break-even point.** For example, if total costs are £10,000 and total sales are £10,000 the break-even point is reached (no profit and no loss is made). If total costs are £10,000 and total sales are £15,000 the margin of safety is £5,000. The break-even point and the margin of safety can be shown as a **break-even chart.** *See* Appendix 3

◆ Sicherheitsspanne

marine insurance a **contract** between an **insurance company** and the owner of a ship, **cargo** or **freight** against loss at sea. The centre of marine insurance is **Lloyd's** of London

◆ Seeversicherung

marine survey an examination of a ship by a **Lloyd's agent** for the purposes of a **marine insurance**

◆ Schiffsprüfung

maritime law (*also* **the law of the sea**) a special area of law relating to ships ports, harbours etc.

◆ Seerecht

markdown lowering the price of something below its usual price; the amount by which it is lowered

◆ Preisnachlaß

market (1) people with money to buy a **product** and also the desire to buy it. *The market for our cigars is made up of males, smokers, earning over £20,000 a year who want a high-quality cigar.* (2) an area where things are sold. *We must develop in overseas markets.* (3) special place where buyers and sellers meet to do business: *the fish market, the stock market*

◆ (1) – (3) Markt

marketable which can be sold. *The new product seems to me to be a marketable item*

◆ marktfähig

market analysis examining a **market** (meaning 1) to find out facts about it, such as numbers, age, sex, etc.

◆ Marktanalyse

market channel *see* **channel of distribution**

market coverage the number of likely buyers reached by an advertisement. *I think we should advertise in the Daily News because it is read by most of our customers, so it gives us better market coverage*

◆ Marktdurchdringung

market demand the total sales of a **product** in a period (usually a year). *The market demand for our brand of soup is 12,000,000 cans this year*

◆ Marktbedarf

market forces things which affect the sale of a **product,** e.g. price, competition, state of the **economy**

◆ Marktkräfte

marketing (1) examining **products** and **markets** so that the right product reaches the right market at the right price and is supported by the right advertising and **sales promotion.** *See also* **marketing concept, marketing research, marketing plan.** (2) *(US)* shopping for goods. *I do the week's marketing on a Friday.* (3) the department of a company where the marketing staff work. *Take this sample up to marketing and find out what they think of it*

◆ (1) Marketing (2) Einkaufen (3) Marketing-Abteilung

marketing audit an examination of all the **marketing plans** and actions of a company to find out how well they are being carried out

◆ Vertriebs- und marktpolitische Unternehmensanalyse

marketing concept (*or* **marketing philosophy**) the belief in the following: since a company cannot live without customers it should find out what customers want first, then make **products** or **services** to satisfy them. A great deal of research is needed to find out the effect of any planned decision on the customer. *See also* **concept** (meaning 2)

◆ Absatzdenken

marketing manager a manager who plans, directs, controls the **marketing plan** of a company

◆ Marketing-Manager

marketing mix (*or* **the 4 p's**) **product,** price, place, **promotion.** Decisions on these four areas are the most important part of all **marketing plans.** The various decisions (the 'mix' of decisions) will differ for each product. For example, jewellery will have a different price and be sold through a different 'place' (shop) to chocolates

◆ Marketing-Mix

marketing philosophy *see* **marketing concept**

marketing plan the written aims of the company for the next period ahead (usually a year). It states which manager is responsible for each part of the plan, what he has to do, when he has to do it. Among the aims in the plan will be the **products** to be sold, total sales, prices, sales by **outlets, promotion,** the costs involved, the planned profit and **return on capital**

◆ Absatzplan

marketing planning the **process** of deciding, with the help of **research,** one or more parts of a **marketing plan.** *See also* **marketing research**

◆ Absatzplanung

marketing research gathering information from inside and outside the company about all aspects of the business, not just the market. By using this information managers should be able to make better decisions. *Compare with* **market research**

◆ Marktforschung

marketing strategy a method used to reach marketing aims. *Our marketing strategy this year is to advertise our new cooker in magazines read by the younger woman*

◆ Marketing-Strategie

market intelligence information from the market of interest to a company. *Compare with* **marketing research, market research**

◆ Marktinformation

market leader the company with the largest share of sales for a type of **product** or **service.** *They are the market leader in portable colour televisions*

◆ Marktführer

market-oriented company a company which allows the market to influence its major decisions, i.e. whose directors and managers believe in the **marketing concept**

◆ marktorientiertes Unternehmen

marketplace (1) a place where goods are bought and sold. *Our radio seems to be at the right price but in the marketplace it just doesn't sell.* (2) a special area, or square, for the sale of goods. *Every Saturday morning this whole street is turned into a marketplace*

◆ (1) Markt (2) Marktplatz

market potential all the likely buyers for a **product.** *Our new kind of room heater is not only for homes, but for offices, shops, stores — the market potential is very large*

◆ Marktpotential

market price the price at which most buyers buy — or the price at which most sellers sell. *We would like our* *shares to be selling at £2 each, but the market price is £1 only*

◆ Marktpreis

market report a report on the state of a market, giving information, e.g. on **stock exchange** prices, **interest rates** etc.

◆ Marktbericht

market research finding out all about the people who buy, or may buy, a company's **product** or **service.** This helps to answer such questions as: how many buyers in the market? what do they think of our product? what makes them buy? **Consumer** market research finds out about markets for **consumer goods** and **industrial** market research inquires into markets for **industrial goods.** *Compare with* **marketing research**

◆ Marktforschung

market research agency a company which carries out **market research** for other companies. It will help to identify and solve market problems

◆ Marktforschungsinstitut

market segmentation dividing a market into separate groups or segments each of which has something in common (which could influence the buying of a **product**). For example, a wine producer might divide the wine market by age, or sex, or area of the country, or **income** etc. New or existing wine products could then be aimed at these specific areas

◆ Marktaufteilung

market share the proportion of a market which prefers to buy a company's **product.** *Last year only 8% of the people who bought soup preferred ours but this year our market share has gone up to 10%*

◆ Marktanteil

market trend the way a market is changing. *The trend in this market over the past few years is steadily upward*

◆ Marktentwicklung

market value (1) the price buyers are prepared to pay. *He has had the car for over two years so the market value is much less than he paid for it.* (2) the value of the total market. *Each year the market value of canned meats is £100 million*

◆ (1), (2) Marktwert

mark-up the difference between the buying price and the selling price. If a shop buys in something for £1 and sells it for £1.50, the mark-up is 50 pence

◆ Handelsspanne

mass media ways of informing a very large number of people, e.g. television, radio, newspapers, cinema. *So many people wear jeans that if you want to advertise to them all you have to do is to use the mass media. See also* **media**

◆ Massenmedien

mass production making very large amounts of the same thing, by machinery. *There has been mass production of cars since the days of Henry Ford. See also* **batch production**

◆ Massenproduktion

master *noun* (1) the captain of a ship. (2) a male teacher in a school

◆ (1) Kapitän (2) Lehrer

master *verb* to become skilled in (something). *He's mastered the computer now*

◆ beherrschen

master budget a **budget** of **income,** spending, profit, **return on capital** employed etc. for a fixed period ahead, usually six months or a year. It is the main budget for the directors of the company as it is concerned only with the main **financial** areas, e.g. income, costs, profit, etc. *See* Appendix 4

◆ Gesamtetat

matched sample (**market research**) a **sample** (e.g. a group of people) which in all respects is the same as another sample. Matched samples therefore could be two groups of people of the same age, sex, income, etc. These two groups could be used to test two different **products.** Answers given about the products will be due to differences in the products because the groups (the samples) are matched

◆ abgestimmte Vergleichsstichprobe

mate (1) an officer on a merchant ship below the rank of captain. (2) a companion, especially at work. *He likes to have a drink with his mates now and then*

◆ (1) Maat (2) Kumpel

materials something to be used in the manufacture of goods. *I've ordered the materials for the new garage*

◆ Material

material(s) control the section of a company which makes sure that the right amount of materials at the right price is in **stock** when needed. *Materials control have found a new supplier of the brass rods which we need for our contract*

◆ Materialprüfung

materials handling the study of both the methods and the machines used in moving materials in and out of and around a company, so that more efficient methods and machines can be used

◆ Werkstoffbehandlung

maternity benefit *(UK)* money paid by the government to a woman while she is away from work just before and after the birth of a child

◆ Mutterschaftsgeld

mate's receipt a written statement given by a **mate** (meaning 1) to an **exporter** as proof that his goods have been put on board a ship

◆ Bordempfangsschein

matrix (1) an arrangement of numbers, letters or signs in rows and columns which make up a square. (2) a mould for casting metal

◆ (1) Matrix (2) Matrize

mature *adjective* (1) fully developed. (2) of a **bill of exchange, insurance policy** etc., due to be paid

◆ (1) reif (2) fällig

mature *verb* to become **mature.** *When this insurance matures, I will receive £10,000*

◆ fällig werden

maturity (1) the state of being **mature.** (2) (*also* **maturity date**) the date when a **bill of exchange, insurance policy** etc. **matures**

◆ (1) Reife (2) Fälligkeitsdatum

maximum *adjective* largest possible: *maximum load, maximum price*

◆ Höchst-; maximal

maximum *noun* the largest possible amount, or number etc.

◆ Maximum

MBO *see* **management by objectives**

MCCA *see* **Central American Common Market**

mean average. *The mean of 6 + 2 + 4 + 8 is 20 ÷ 4 = 5. See also* **arithmetic mean**

◆ Mittelwert

means test an official inquiry into the amount of money a person has, e.g. to see if he is in need of **financial** help from the government

◆ Überprüfung des finanziellen Status

measures of central tendency ways of finding out where most of the **values** are in a range of figures. *See* **mean, median** and **mode,** all of which are measures of central tendency

◆ Zentralwerte

mechanization the use of machines to help or to replace man at work

◆ Mechanisierung

media (*plural of* **medium**) the methods used to spread information, e.g. cinemas, magazines, newspapers, posters, radio, television etc. *They spent over £1 million advertising their new product — they used all the media. See also* **mass media**

◆ Medien

media analysis finding out the value of newspapers, radio, television etc. for advertising purposes. *See also* **media buyer, media planner**

◆ Werbeträgeranalyse

media buyer a person who buys advertising (in newspapers, magazines, television etc.). He/she works with the **media planner,** e.g. in deciding which **media** should be used

◆ Käufer von Werberaum, (-zeit)

median the middle value. The median is found by arranging the values from the lowest to the highest and taking the middle value. For example, in the following row of values: 7, 9, 11, 17, 21, 23, 25 the median is 17. *See* **measures of central tendency**

◆ Median

media owners companies which own the means of advertising to the public, e.g. cinemas, magazines, newspapers, **poster** sites, radio stations or TV stations

◆ Medienbesitzer

media planner a person who decides which advertising **media** (i.e. magazines, newspapers, television, etc.) are best for a particular **product.** A media planner will consider, e.g. the readers of a particular newspaper and the likely buyers of the product, and then decide if that newspaper should be included in the **advertising plan.** *See also* **media buyer, media research**

◆ Mediaplaner

media research the study of the people who read newspapers, magazines and posters, or who watch television and cinema, or who listen to the radio, in order to find out their number, sex, **income,** age, and what they think about the **products** and **services** advertised in the **media**

◆ Medienforschung

mediate to help to settle a **dispute** between two other people or organisations

◆ vermitteln

mediation the act of **mediating**

◆ Vermittlung

mediator a person who **mediates**

◆ Vermittler

medium *noun* a means by which information can be spread. *Television is a medium we can use to advertise our products. See also plural* **media**

◆ Werbeträger

medium *adjective* of middle amount, neither large nor small. *I take a medium size in suits*

◆ mittel-

medium-term liabilities debts which must be paid within the next two to five years. *See* **current liabilities, long-term liabilities**

◆ mittelfristige Verbindlichkeiten

memo (*or* **memorandum**) (1) a note of something from one person in a company to another. *I have a memo here from the works manager asking for a meeting.* (2) a note of something to be remembered. *Make a memo — we have to write to Jones before the end of the month*

◆ (1) Mitteilung (2) Notiz

Memorandum and Articles of Association a **document** drawn up when a company is formed which lists: its name, where the **head office** is, its aims, the amount of **capital,** the directors etc. This document is sent to the **Registrar of Companies**

◆ Gründungsurkunde und Satzung einer Gesellschaft

memory a **computer's store** of **data** which is ready for immediate use

◆ Speicher

merchandise *noun* – **consumer goods.** *Let's make sure all the merchandise can be seen by our customers*

◆ Ware

merchandise *verb* (1) to put goods on **display** to encourage sales. *If you don't merchandise the goods you won't sell them.* (2) to help **wholesalers** and **retailers** to sell goods which are made by a company, e.g. by **sales promotion, point-of-sale advertising**

◆ (1) Waren ausstellen (2) für Ware werben

merchandiser a person who **merchandises** (meaning 1). *After we deliver our goods to the shop we always send a merchandiser to put them on show to the customers*

◆ Fachmann für Warengestaltung

merchant a person who buys and sells goods. *He's a wine and spirits merchant*

◆ Kaufmann

merchant bank a company which lends money to other companies to help their trade or expansion. Merchant banks also give advice on **mergers, takeovers,** foreign currency, **hire purchase** etc.

◆ Handelsbank

merchantman a ship which carries **cargo** for trade

◆ Handelsschiff

merchant navy (1) all of a country's ships which are used to carry trade **cargo.** *Our merchant navy calls at ports all over the world.* (2) the men who work on such cargo ships

◆ (1) Handelsmarine (2) Matrose in der Handelsmarine

merger the joining of two or more companies to form one company. *Before the merger the two companies used to compete with each other but now they are the same company*

◆ Fusion

merit payment an additional payment made to an employee because of the use of special skill or because of special responsibility

◆ Leistungszulage

merit rating judging a worker's overall ability to do his job so that the amount of his regular pay can be decided

◆ Einstufung nach Leistung

meter a machine which shows the amount used of something: *parking meter, water meter*

◆ Zähler; -uhr

method study a close examination of the way people do certain tasks at work so that better, less costly methods can be planned and tried out

◆ Arbeitsmethodenanalyse

metric system a **system** of weights and measures based on the metre as a unit of length, the gramme for weight, and the litre for liquids

◆ metrisches System

metric ton (*or* **metric tonne**) 2204.6 pounds (lbs) in weight or equal to 1000 kilograms

◆ Metertonne

micro- *prefix* very small: *a microcomputer, microfilm, micro-processor. See also* **macro**

◆ Mikro-

microchip *see* **chip**

microeconomics that part of **economics** which studies individuals, companies, **products,** rather than the whole **economy.** *See also* **macroeconomics**

◆ Mikroökonomie

microfiche a small sheet of 8-millimetre film which has in it information equal to very many full-sized pages. This information can be read using a **microfiche reader.** *He checked the microfiche to see if the library had the book in stock*

◆ Mikrofiche

microfilm a roll of 8-millimetre film used for the storage of large amounts of information on a small area. *The last ten years' issue of the daily newspapers are now on microfilm at the library*

◆ Mikrofilm

micrometer an instrument used for exact measurement of short distances

◆ Mikrometer

middleman a person or company that links the maker of goods with the buyer or consumer, i.e. **wholesalers, retailers** and agents. *It's not true that middlemen simply increase the price and make big profits: they perform a useful task. See also* **channels of distribution** and Appendix 7

◆ Zwischenhändler

middle management managers in a company who carry out the orders of a **general manager** (or top management) and who report to him

◆ mittleres Management

mile a measure of length or distance equal to 1609 metres

◆ Meile

mileage (1) the distance travelled in miles. *What's the mileage between Edinburgh and London?* (2) *(informal)* the amount of use of something. *We got a lot of mileage out of the money spent on that sales contest last year — sales are still well up*

◆ (1) Entfernung in Meilen (2) viel von einer Sache haben

mileage allowance the amount of money given by a company to a person who uses his own car on company business. *The company sent me to London and I had to use my own car, but I was paid a very good mileage allowance*

◆ ≃ Kilometergeld

mineral natural, solid, non-living material from the earth, e.g. coal, oil

◆ Mineral

mineral rights permission to take from the earth in a certain area the **minerals** which lie there, e.g. coal, oil. *He claimed he had the mineral rights to a gold field in Australia*

◆ Abbaurechte

mini- *prefix* smaller than normal size: *mini-car, mini-skirt, mini-computer*

◆ Mini-

mini-computer a small to medium-sized low-priced **computer**

◆ Minicomputer

minimum *adjective* smallest possible: *minimum price, minimum quantity*

◆ Mindest-; minimal

minimum *noun* the smallest possible amount, or number

◆ Minimum

minimum stock the smallest amount of goods which a company normally keeps in **stock.** *Compare with* **buffer stock**

◆ Mindestbestand

minimum wage the lowest wage by law that can be paid to certain workers

◆ Mindestlohn

minor *(law)* a person under the age at which the law judges that he/she is responsible for his/her actions (in the UK, eighteen)

◆ Minderjährige(r)

minority interest a person or company that owns less than half the

shares in a company. *Although his family owned a lot of shares in the business they still held only a minority interest in the firm*

◆ Minderheitsbeteiligung

mint *noun* (1) the place where a country's money is made. (2) looking like new. *He had a 1936 Ford car which was in mint condition*

◆ (1) Münzanstalt (2) tadellos

mint *verb* (1) to make (coins). (2) *(informal)* to make a lot of (money). *His business is doing very well: he must be minting money*

◆ (1) prägen (2) ein Heidengeld verdienen

minute book a book which contains **minutes**

◆ Protokollbuch

minutes a record of what is discussed at a meeting. *He read the minutes of the last meeting*

◆ Protokoll

misrepresentation *(law)* telling a lie to get a **contract.** If a person signs a contract as a result of being told a lie about the **product** or **service** then he can take action in the courts for **damages**

◆ falsche Angaben

mixed economy the **economy** of a country where state-owned industries (e.g. coal, steel) exist alongside **private enterprise.** *France, Great Britain and America all have mixed economies*

◆ gemischte Wirtschaftsform

mobile shop a shop inside a van or other type of vehicle which can be driven from place to place

◆ Verkaufswagen

mobility of labour the extent to which workers will move to find new employment. *The mobility of labour is such that the jobs in the south cannot be filled although there are plenty of people idle in the north*

◆ Mobilität der Arbeitskräfte

mock auction (1) an **auction** in which certain people in the crowd are **bidding** not to own the thing offered for sale but to raise the price of it. (2) **— Dutch auction**

◆ (1) Scheinauktion

mock-up a full size copy of something, e.g. of a new car which a manufacturer intends to build next year. Meantime the mock-up can show the company experts all aspects of the new design

◆ Anschauungsmodell in Originalgröße

mode the value which is found most often in a range of figures etc., e.g. the commonest price in a range of prices, commonest age in a group of people. *See* **measures of central tendency, mean, average, median**

◆ häufigster Wert

model a copy of something, usually smaller than the real thing. *On his desk he had a model of a new factory*

◆ Modell

modification a small change made to something. *He showed the buyer the plans of the new machine with the slight modification which he had suggested*

◆ Modifikation

modify to make a small change or changes in. *Our first plan will cost too much; we shall have to modify it*

◆ modifizieren

monetarist a person who believes that the **economy** of a country can be managed by controlling the supply of money

◆ Monetarist

monetary to do with money. *The mark is the monetary unit of Germany*

◆ monetär

monetary policy what the government intends to do in matters related to money, e.g. taxes,

interest rates, borrowing etc. *The prime minister has made a long speech explaining the government's monetary policy*

◆ Währungspolitik

money an official way of paying for goods or **services,** i.e. coins, banknotes, cheques etc.

◆ Geld

money at call a debt or a loan which must be repaid as soon as the person who has given the money demands it

◆ Gelder auf Abruf

money for jam/old rope *(informal)* very easily-earned money. *It's a very easy job: money for jam, really*

◆ nachgeworfenes Geld

moneylender a person who lends money at **interest** for a living, or as a business

◆ Geldverleiher

money market the **process** by which companies deal in **short-term** loans and foreign exchange

◆ Geldmarkt

money-off pack a package with a printed message showing a special low price. *She bought the soap powder in the money-off pack because it was cheaper than the other brands*

◆ Sonderpreispackung

money supply the total amount of money and **near-money** in a country. This amount can be measured in various ways, including **M1** (a narrow measure) and **M3** (a much broader measure). *See also* **monetary policy, near money**

◆ Geldvolumen

monitor *noun* (1) a television set used to check and select programmes for broadcasting. (2) **— visual display unit**

◆ (1) Monitor (2) Bildschirm

monitor *verb* check, control. *We must monitor the actual sales figures so that we know when each salesman reaches his target*

◆ kontrollieren

Monopolies and Mergers Commission *(UK)* a government body which can inquire into the **merger** or **takeover** of any company where a **monopoly** may result. Monopoly here means where a company or group have control over one third of the market. After its inquiry, the Monopolies and Mergers Commission can advise the government about whether the merger or takeover should be allowed or not

◆ ≈ Kartellamt

monopolise to take or have control of a **product** or **service.** *The government have monopolised the large-scale production of coal*

◆ monopolisieren

monopolist a person or company with the sole right to make or sell a particular **product** or **service**

◆ Monopolist

monopoly a situation where a company or group of companies has control over a market. *At one time you could buy electricity from different companies but now it's a government monopoly*

◆ Monopolstellung

monopsony a situation where there is only one buyer in a market for a **product** or **service** (or for **labour**) although there may be many sellers

◆ Nachfragemonopol

monthly instalment a method of paying for goods or **services** by equal monthly payments for a fixed period. *See* **hire purchase**

◆ Monatsrate

moonlighting having two jobs, e.g. one during the day and another in the evening or during the night. *Yes. He's very rich and very tired; he's been moonlighting for the past year*

◆ Ausübung einer Nebenbeschäftigung

morale the degree of interest and confidence people have, e.g. in their job. *I believe the morale in this company is very high*

◆ Arbeitsmoral

moratorium a legal agreement between two persons or organisations to stop the payment of a debt, at least for a time

◆ Zahlungsaufschub

mortality rate *see* **death rate**

mortality table a list showing the expected life of people from the time they take out a **life insurance policy.** This list is used by insurance companies to help them decide the risk involved in any life insurance

◆ Sterblichkeitstabelle

mortgage *verb* to give rights to (property), e.g. to a **building society,** in return for a loan of money. Once the money has been repaid the rights to the property are also returned. *The company borrowed £120,000 from the bank but they had to mortgage the factory to get the loan*

◆ hypothekarisch belasten

mortgage *noun* an arrangement to hand over property as described above. *They had to take out a mortgage on the factory*

◆ Hypothek

mortgagee the person or organisation who lends money in a **mortgage contract**

◆ Hypothekengläubiger

mortgagor the person or organisation who borrows money in a **mortgage contract**

◆ Hypothekenschuldner

most-favoured-nation clause an agreement between countries that each country will give the others to the agreement the best possible **tariff** and **quota** terms

◆ Meistbegünstigungsklausel

mother of the chapel (*or* **MOC**) name given to a female **shop steward** in the printing and publishing unions. *See also* **father of the chapel**

◆ gewerkschaftliche Vertrauensperson im Druckgewerbe

motion a proposal put to a meeting or a **conference.** If a second person agrees with the motion (or **seconds** it) it is then discussed and voted on

◆ Antrag

motion study a detailed study of the movements of a worker doing a particular job. These movements are measured so that wasted movements can be cut down and the work improved

◆ Zeitstudie

motivate to give (a person) strong reasons for doing something. *He motivated his salesmen by telling them that the whole company was depending on them to get orders. See also* **motive**

◆ motivieren

motivation the state of being **motivated** to do something

◆ Motivation

motivational research inquiry into why people behave as they do. Often used in business to answer questions like: why do buyers prefer certain **products** to others?

◆ Motivationsforschung

motive an emotional cause or a reason for acting in a certain way. *His motive for working so hard was his desire to succeed at his job*

◆ Motiv

mover a person who makes a proposal, i.e. moves a **motion** — at a meeting or a **conference**

◆ Antragsteller

moving average the average as it changes over time. The moving average of a company's sales can be seen by taking the sales for each of the past twelve months and dividing by twelve. If this is done again when next month's sales are known it will be possible by comparing the two averages to see how the average is moving

◆ gleitender Durchschnitt

MS, MSS *see* **manuscript**

MSC *see* **Manpower Services Commission**

multilateral trade trade carried on between many countries

◆ multilateraler Handel

multinational *adjective* of many countries

◆ multinational

multinational *noun* a **multinational** company

◆ multinationaler Konzern

multiple a company which owns many **retail outlets** or branches. *The buyer at the multiple head office was offered the very best price if he would allow the salesman to supply all of the multiple's branches*

◆ Filialunternehmen

multiple bar chart information printed in the form of upright bars on a chart, each bar representing a different thing, e.g. to show the sales of **product** A over the past three years, compared to the sales of product B over the past three years. *See also* **bar chart**

◆ Mehrfachsäulendiagramm

multiple-choice question a question on a form with a choice of answers printed beneath it, one of which is the correct answer, used in **market research** and **surveys**

◆ Auswahlfrage

multiplier effect the result of e.g. a government **investing** in new roads, factories, machinery etc. This result is usually an increase in **income** (e.g. wages) greater than the amount of the original sum invested, with many people benefitting from a general increase in spending

◆ multiplikatorischer Effekt

municipal of a town or its **local authority**

◆ städtisch

Murphy's law *(informal and humorous)* a 'law' seen to operate in offices, factories and homes, on machinery and **projects** which says that if something can go wrong it will go wrong

◆ Murphy's Gesetz ('Was schiefgehen kann, wird auch schiefgehen')

mutual shared by more than one person, held in common: *mutual trust*

◆ gegenseitig; gemeinsam

mutual company a company owned by **policy-holders** etc. rather than by **shareholders**

◆ Versicherungsverein auf Gegenseitigkeit

N

nail: (pay) on the nail to pay money at the time of buying something. *He never gives his customers credit; it has to be cash on the nail*

◆ bar (pünktlich) bezahlen

name of the game *(informal)* the main part of something; what something is all about. *You can't succeed in business without taking some risks: it's the name of the game*

◆ das Wesentliche an einer Sache

national account a customer (or **account**) that has branches in many parts of the country

◆ landesweites Konto

national advertising making a **product** or **service** known all over the country by advertising in the **media**

◆ überregionale Werbung

national campaign a series of planned actions all over the country. *We are planning a national sales campaign followed by a national campaign for the new product*

◆ landesweite (Werbe-) Kampagne

national claim a demand for more pay or better conditions for all its members by a **trade union** in a particular industry. *The steel union's demand for more pay was on behalf of all its members in the industry, and the union said that its national claim was a fair one*

◆ überregionale gewerkschaftliche Forderung

National Coal Board (*or* **NCB**) a government body which organises the coal industry

◆ staatliche Kohlenbehörde

national debt money borrowed by the government to pay those expenses which are over and above the amount of taxes collected

◆ Staatsschuld

National Economic Development Office (*or* **'Neddy'**) a UK government unit which gives independent advice on the country's **economic** position and prospects

◆ Nationaler Wirtschaftsrat

National Enterprise Board *(also* **NEB**) *(UK)* a public body set up in 1975 to help the **economy,** e.g. by **investing** government money in industry and commerce

◆ staatliche Behörde für Unternehmensförderung

National Health Service (*or* **NHS**) *(UK)* the medical service for everyone in the country which provides treatment to cure and prevent illness. The service is paid for by companies, workers and the government. *See also* **national insurance**

◆ staatlicher Gesundheitsdienst

national income the value of all goods and **services** produced by a country over a period of time

◆ Sozialprodukt

national income and expenditure *see* **blue book**

national insurance payments made by workers and companies to help pay for the **National Health Service,** for **pensions** and unemployment pay

◆ ≃ Sozialversicherung

nationalisation the **process** of **nationalising.** *See also* **nationalised industries**

◆ Verstaatlichung

nationalise to bring under government control (a company or group of companies). *All of the railway companies were nationalised and they became known as British Rail*

◆ verstaatlichen

nationalised industry an industry owned by the general public, i.e. in the direct control of the state. There are no **shareholders** apart from the government. UK examples are: British Rail, British Gas Corporation

◆ verstaatlichter Industriezweig

national press newspapers which are sold in all parts of the country. *We can't afford to advertise in the national press. See also* **local press**

◆ überregionale Presse

NATO (*or* **North Atlantic Treaty Organisation**) a group of sixteen countries formed in 1949 for cooperation in defence, **economic** policies etc. Membership: Belgium, Canada, Denmark, France, Federal Republic of Germany, Greece, Iceland, Italy, Luxembourg, Netherlands, Norway, Portugal, Spain, Turkey, United Kingdom, United States. (In 1967 NATO military forces withdrew from France at France's request.) Headquarters: Brussels. Official languages: English, French

◆ NATO

naturalisation the act of making a person of foreign birth a citizen of a country. *He applied for naturalisation as a British citizen*

◆ Einbürgerung

natural resources the materials which are found in nature and can be used, e.g. oil, gold. *With its coal, gas and oil Britain is rich in natural resources*

◆ Bodenschätze

natural wastage a normal lessening in the number of people who are working in a company due to death, old age or leaving the job for another one. *Every year the company had to engage about ten more workers just to replace the natural wastage*

◆ natürliche Personalreduzierung

near-money (*or* **near-cash**) something which can be turned into cash very quickly, e.g. **bills of exchange**

◆ leicht liquidierbares Vermögen

NEB *see* **National Enterprise Board**

necessaries things which are needed. *He packed the necessaries for his journey: toothpaste, toothbrush, pyjamas, etc.*

◆ Bedarfsartikel

necessities things which one cannot do without, e.g. food, clothes, shelter. *He couldn't even afford the necessities of life*

◆ lebensnotwendige Güter

Neddy *see* **National Economic Development Office**

negative cash flow a situation when less cash is coming into a business than is going out of it. *He checked over the figures for the company's exports and discovered a negative cash flow for the first six months*

◆ Überhang der Zahlungsausgänge

negotiable instrument a **document** which can be given freely by one person to another, and which can be exchanged for cash, e.g. a cheque, **bill of exchange, promissory note**

◆ begebbares Wertpapier

negotiate to talk to one or more people with the aim of settling some matter; to reach (an agreement etc.) by discussion. *He wanted to negotiate an agreement with the buyer but he did not want to negotiate a low price*

◆ verhandeln über

negotiation the act of **negotiating.** *At last the contract was signed — it had taken two hours of negotiation with the buyer*

◆ Verhandlung

net (*or* **nett**) *adjective* with no further reductions or charges. *If she paid for the typewriter now she would get 5% off but if she didn't pay till the end of the month it would be net. See also* **net profit**

◆ netto, Netto-

net (*or* **nett**) *verb* to earn as a total amount after payment of all **expenses** and **tax.** *We netted £4000 on that deal*

◆ netto einnehmen, netto verdienen

net assets the value of all that a company owns, e.g. land, buildings, machines, **raw materials, finished goods** less what it owes, e.g. payment for raw materials, taxes due, **dividends** due, money owed to the bank

◆ Reinvermögen

net current assets the value of what a company owns which will be used up over the weeks ahead (i.e. the **current assets**), e.g. **raw materials, finished goods,** cash, less what a company has to pay over the coming weeks (i.e. the **current liabilities**), e.g. payment for raw materials, taxes due, money owed to the bank. *See* Appendix 4

◆ Umlaufvermögen

net income the amount left after payment of all expenses and taxes

◆ Nettoeinkommen

net loss the amount by which all the expenses are greater than the sales, e.g. total sales £100,000, total expenses £110,000, net loss £10,000

◆ Nettoverlust

net margin the **net profit** as a percentage of the sales. *Our profit was £100,000 from £1,000,000 of sales — a net margin of 10%*

◆ Nettogewinnspanne

net operating income (*or* **net operating profit**) the **profit** from a company's main business when all the expenses have been taken off the sales. It will not include profits from **investments** in other companies

◆ Nettobetriebseinnahmen

net profit the amount by which the **income** from sales is greater than all the expenses in a **profit and loss account.** *See* Appendix 4

◆ Nettogewinn

net sales total sales less any goods returned or damaged

◆ Nettoverkaufserlös

nett *see* **net**

net weight the weight of the goods less any wrapping or package

◆ Nettogewicht

network *noun* (1) any system of lines which cross each other at many places: *the railway network.* (2) a television or radio system where many stations are used to send out the same programme

◆ (1) Netz (Straßen-; Bahn-) (2) Sendenetz

network *verb* to broadcast (a television or radio programme) to many stations

◆ (Programme) im ganzen Netzbereich ausstrahlen

network analysis a method of planning a complicated job, e.g. building a factory, to find the best order of carrying out the work so that the job will be finished in the shortest possible time within the cost

◆ Netzplantechnik

net worth the total value of the **ordinary shares** of a company and the **reserves** as shown in the **balance sheet.** *See* Appendix 2

◆ Nettoanteil; Eigenkapital einer Gesellschaft

net yield the money from an **investment** less tax

◆ effektive Rendite

new issue: shares offered to the public for the first time

◆ Neuemission

new product development the **process** of bringing new **products** onto the market. *See also* **product development**

◆ Vermarktung neuer Produkte

newsagent a shopkeeper who or shop which sells newspapers and magazines as well as other goods, e.g. stationery, cigarettes, sweets

◆ Zeitungshändler

newsprint a kind of thin paper used in newspapers

◆ Zeitungspapier

news release *see* **press release**

new town development *(UK)* towns built since 1946, planned to contain a certain number of houses, factories, shops

◆ Planung und Aufbau von Trabantenstädten

NHS *see* **National Health Service**

night safe a place in a bank where money or other valuable things can be stored when the bank is closed. It is done by using a special opening in the outside wall of the bank

◆ Nachtsafe

night-shift overnight working hours, usually between 22.00 hours and 07.00 hours

◆ Nachtschicht

no-claims bonus a car **insurance** offered at a special low price because no **claim** has been made to the insurance company in the past year. *I've had two car accidents this year and made a claim each time — so that means I've lost my no-claims bonus*

◆ Schadensfreiheitsrabatt

nominal accounts: ledger accounts which record the **revenue** and **expenditure** of an **enterprise** (meaning 1)

◆ Sachkonten

nominal capital the total **face value** of all the **shares** that a company is allowed to issue. *See also* **authorized capital**

◆ Grundkapital

nominal value the **face value** of something, e.g. a **share** may have a nominal value of £1 but may be sold to someone for £1.25. *See also* **par** (meaning 2)

◆ Nominalwert

nominate to name (a person) for some special purpose. *I nominate John Smith to vote on my behalf at the next meeting*

◆ jmd. ernennen

nominee a person named by someone else to act for him/her in some matter. *See also* **nominate**

◆ Kandidat(in); Bevollmächtigte(r)

non-contributory pension scheme a **system** of paying for an employee's **pension** where the company pays the full cost of the pension scheme and the worker pays nothing towards the cost

◆ beitragsfreies Betriebsrentensystem

non-durable goods: products which do not last very long, e.g. shoes, food, drink, sweets, etc. *Compare with* **durable goods**

◆ Verbrauchsgüter

non-executive director a director of a company who is brought in to advise the other directors. He is not a full-time director and so is not an **executive** of the company. *Compare with* **executive director**

◆ Führungskraft ohne Entscheidungsgewalt bei der Geschäftsführung

non-price competition selling goods by means of some benefit other than a low price, e.g. selling canned soup on the basis of how quickly it can be cooked or on how good it tastes etc. *Their product was of high quality. The manufacturer believed in non-price competition*

◆ außerpreislicher Wettbewerb

non-profit-making organisation a group or company which has an aim other than making a profit, e.g. a charity, church, social service, school

◆ Organisation ohne Erwerbscharakter

non-taxable income money received on which tax need not be paid, e.g. **personal allowance, sickness benefit, unemployment** pay etc.

◆ nicht zu versteuerndes Einkommen

non-voting shares *see* **A shares**

Nordic Council a group of states formed in Copenhagen in 1952, for cooperation in matters of common interest. Headquarters: Stockholm. Membership: Denmark, Finland, Iceland, Norway, Sweden. Official languages: Danish, Norwegian, Swedish

◆ Nordischer Rat

norm the normal, average, usual. *Some salesmen make 20 calls a day in this firm but the norm is 14*

◆ Norm

normal curve a bell-shaped curve which shows the usual (or normal) distribution of the characteristics of a population: their intelligence, their **income,** their weight etc.

◆ Normalverteilungskurve

North Atlantic Treaty Organisation *see* **NATO**

notary public *(law)* a person, usually a **solicitor,** who has the special job of witnessing spoken and written statements and making them official

◆ Notar (in GB normalerweise ein in der niederen Gerichtsbarkeit zugelassener Rechtsanwalt, der mit Notarsaufgaben betraut ist)

note to fix a statement to (a **bill of exchange**) saying that the bill has been presented for payment and payment has been refused. This is usually done by a **notary public**

◆ einen Wechsel protestieren

notice (1) a statement (usually in writing) by one **party** to a **contract** that he will end the contract at a certain time. *I plan to leave the firm in two months' time so I've handed in my notice.* (2) the period of time before a contract ends. *I gave them two months' notice.* (3) a piece of written news about something. *Did you see the notice about the company dance? It is pinned up on the notice board*

◆ (1) Kündigung (2) Kündigungsfrist (3) Bekanntmachung

notice board a board on a wall to which notices may be fixed

◆ Anschlagbrett

not negotiable words written across the face of a cheque, meaning that it cannot be used by anyone who is not entitled to use it

◆ nicht übertragbar

null and void with no legal force. *The contract was null and void — a court wouldn't even consider it*

◆ null und nichtig

numbered account a **bank account** where the name of the person using the account is kept secret. Some countries, e.g. Switzerland, have laws which allow people to use such secret accounts

◆ Nummernkonto

numerical control control by a **computer** of a machine which makes things

◆ Computersteuerung

nuts and bolts *(informal)* the practical details. *I'll tell you about how the office is generally run: my assistant will explain the nuts and bolts*

◆ nähere Einzelheiten

O

O and M *see* **organisation and methods**

OAPEC *see* **Organisation of Arab Petroleum Exporting Countries**

OAS *see* **Organisation of American States**

OAU *see* **Organisation of African Unity**

objective *noun* the aim of something. *The manager explained the objective of the marketing plan*

◆ Ziel

objective *adjective* not influenced by personal feelings. *Let's be objective about this and just look at the facts*

◆ objektiv

objective test a list of questions to be answered where each question has only one correct answer. Thus the personal feelings of the person checking the answers will not influence the mark or score

◆ objektiver Test

obligation a duty, a state of having to do something, e.g. because one has signed a **contract** to do it

◆ Verpflichtung

obsolescence the state of being **obsolescent**

◆ Veralten

obsolescent going out of date; hardly ever used any more. *Things are changing so fast that some machines are obsolescent before they are out of guarantee*

◆ veraltet

obsolete no longer in use; out of date. *Let's not wait for our machinery to become obsolete — we will renew it now with up-to-date machinery*

◆ veraltet

occupancy the state or time of being an **occupant**

◆ Bewohnen

occupant a person who lives in or has the use of a room, building etc.

◆ Bewohner

occupation a person's trade; what he/she works at. *His occupation is a salesman*

◆ Beruf

occupational accident an injury at work caused by something to do with the job. *He injured his hand in a faulty machine, it was a typical occupational accident*

◆ Berufsunfall

occupational guidance advising a person on the sort of job he/she is best suited for

◆ Berufsberatung

occupational hazard a risk or danger to do with one's job. *Falling off ladders is an occupational hazard of window cleaners*

◆ Berufsrisiko

occupational pension scheme an arrangement whereby a worker receives a **pension** from his/her company after he/she retires from work

◆ betriebliche Altersversorgung

occupier an **occupant,** especially of a house

◆ Bewohner

occupy to live or be in (a house, office etc.); to take possession of

◆ bewohnen; in Besitz nehmen

OCDE *see* **Organisation for Economic Cooperation and Development**

OCR *see* **optical character reader**

odd-job man man who does various small jobs for payment

◆ Gelegenheitsarbeiter

OEA *see* **Organisation of American States**

OECD *see* **Organisation for Economic Cooperation and Development**

offence (1) a wrong action which is punishable by law, a crime. (2) something unpleasant or hurtful

◆ (1) Straftat (2) Beleidigung

offer *noun* (1) something offered. *I have a special offer on this video: £25 off the usual price.* (2) *(law)* the first step in a **contract.** *He made an offer to sell the goods for £10,000 which the buyer accepted*

◆ (1) Angebot (2) Vertragsangebot

offer *verb* to present (something) for taking or refusing. *They are offering potatoes at £3.00 a bag*

◆ anbieten

offer for sale the advertising of **shares** to the public. A company may sell through an **issuing house** which then offers them for sale

◆ zum Verkauf anbieten

offeror a person who makes an **offer** (*noun,* meaning 1)

◆ Anbieter

offer price the price at which a share or goods are offered for sale

◆ Angebotspreis

office (1) a place where a company does its paperwork, e.g. letters, orders, **invoices** etc. *Our head office is in Lincoln but we have branch offices at every factory.* (2) a room where a person does administration and paperwork. *Come into my office, I have the contract on my desk.* (3) a position of trust or **authority.** *He held high office in the government.* (4) a government department, e.g. the **Office of Fair Trading** or the Foreign and Commonwealth Office

◆ (1) Büro (2) Büro (3) Amt (4) Behörde; Ministerium

office-bearer a person in an organisation who holds an **office,** e.g. as **chairman, secretary, treasurer**

◆ Amtsträger

office hours hours when an **office** (meaning 1) is open to do business, usually 9 am to 5 pm

◆ Geschäftszeiten

office manager the person in charge of the people who work in an **office** (meaning 1)

◆ Geschäftsstellenleiter

Office of Fair Trading *(UK)* a government body set up to protect the public against unfair or illegal business activity

◆ Behörde gegen unlauteren Wettbewerb

officer a person with a position of **authority** or trust: *a customs officer*

◆ Beamter

official *adjective* said or done with the power of **authority.** *The news that we're closing the Glasgow factory is not official. If we decide to close it we will issue an official statement*

◆ amtlich

official *noun* a person who holds a position of responsibility in an organisation, especially a public organisation

◆ Beamter

official receiver a person appointed by the government to be in charge of the closing down of a company

◆ behördlich bestellter Konkursverwalter

official reserves a country's **stock** of gold and foreign money

◆ Währungsreserven

official strike a **strike** which has the support of the **trade union.** When a strike is **official,** the trade union may help its members on strike by making payments to them

◆ gewerkschaftlich genehmigter Streik

officiate to carry out the duties connected with a particular **office** (meaning 3). *Mr Jones will officiate as chairman*

◆ amtieren

off-licence a **licence** to sell alcoholic drinks for drinking elsewhere; a shop which sells alcohol in this way

◆ Lizenz zum Alkoholverkauf; Wein- und Spirituosenhandlung

off-line (computers) of a **peripheral,** not directly linked to a **central processing unit.** *See also* **on-line**

◆ offline

off-peak (1) of a time of day or of the year, less busy. *I prefer to fly during off-peak hours.* (2) existing during off-peak times: *off-peak prices; off-peak holiday*

◆ (1) außerhalb der Saison (2) verbilligt

off-shore (1) on the sea, at a distance from the land. (2) *(chiefly US)* from or in another country

◆ (1) küstennah (2) Auslands-

off-shore oilfield an area of ground under the sea, **off-shore,** in which there is oil

◆ küstennahes Erdölfeld

off-the-job training training at a college or training centre, away from one's place of work. *See also* **on-the-job training**

◆ außerbetriebliche Weiterbildung

off-trade the selling of alcoholic drinks to **off-licences, supermarkets** etc., rather than to **public houses**

◆ Verkauf von alkoholischen Getränken an Abnehmer ohne Ausschankerlaubnis

oil field an area where oil is found

◆ Erdölfeld

oil industry all the companies which have the main part of their business in the **processing** and sale of oil

◆ Erdölindustrie

oil rig a **rig** used for **drilling** for oil

◆ Bohrinsel

oil slick a quantity of oil which has leaked from a ship and covers a part of the sea

◆ Ölteppich

oil tanker a long, low ship used for carrying oil

◆ Öltanker

oil well a hole bored in the ground on land or under the sea to get oil

◆ Bohrloch

oligopoly a market where a small number of producers control a large amount of the supply of a **product** and so can influence the price

◆ Oligopol

oligopsony a market where a small number of buyers buy a large amount of a **product** and so can influence the price

◆ Oligopson

one-man business *see* **sole trader**

one-stop shopping a covered place containing many shops where one can buy many different types of goods without having to move one's car

◆ alles unter einem Dach

on-line (computers) of a **peripheral,** directly linked to the **central processing unit.** *See also* **off-line**

◆ online

on-the-job training any learning about a job which takes place at the usual place of work. *They were going to send me away on a course to learn the job but they decided to give me on-the-job training instead.* *See also* **off-the-job training**

◆ Ausbildung am Arbeitsplatz

OPEC *see* **Organisation of Petroleum Exporting Countries**

open account the most usual method of paying for any goods which are sold to a business. Goods are ordered, delivered and then payment is made at an agreed time, usually four weeks later. *See also* **credit**

◆ offene Rechnung

open an account to make an arrangement that one can leave or borrow money, or get **credit** from, a bank, shop etc.: *to open an account with one's local bank*

◆ ein Konto eröffnen

open cheque a cheque which is not crossed and therefore does not have to be paid into an **account.** Cash can be received by handing it across the counter at the appropriate bank

◆ Barscheck

open cover (*or* **open policy**) (**marine insurance**) a method of **insuring** goods when the value of the goods is not known at the time of the **insurance contract.** (A sum is agreed at the time of the contract and this is charged when the actual value of the goods is known). This method is used e.g. when many low-value orders are sent regularly by the same company to the same customer. At the end of the year the real value of all the goods sent can be added up and one payment made to the insurance company

◆ offene Police

open-door policy (1) of managers, being prepared to talk to workers in the office at any time. (2) of a country, allowing the goods from all other countries to be **imported** on the same terms

◆ (1) Politik der offenen Tür (2) freier Zugang für den Handel

open-ended question (market research) a question which does not invite one to answer from a given list of answers. For example: 'What did you like about the coffee?' is an open-ended question as one can answer it in any way one chooses

◆ offene Frage

opening (1) a job in a company which needs to be filled. *I hear there is an opening for a manager at Smith Brothers Company.* (2) the beginning of something: *the opening of the new factory*

◆ (1) freie Stelle (2) Eröffnung

open-plan offices offices with no (or very few) walls between one office and another

◆ Großraumbüros

open policy *see* **open cover**

open shop a factory or company where there is no **closed-shop** agreement

◆ Unternehmen, das die Beschäftigten nicht verpflichtet, einer Gewerkschaft beizutreten

Open University *(UK)* a university which is open to anyone and which teaches its students mainly at a distance, partly by means of television and radio programmes

◆ Fernuniversität

operate to (cause to) work or to be in action or to have effect. *That part of the factory is not operating yet*

◆ in Betrieb sein

operating assets: assets which are in regular use in a company, e.g. buildings, machines, materials, cash etc.

◆ Betriebsvermögen

operating budget a plan of **income** and **expenses** for a company covering a period of time, usually a year

◆ Budget der betrieblichen Aufwendungen und Erträge

operating costs the normal costs of running a business such as wages, salaries, rent, rates, etc., i.e. the expenses normally found in the **profit-and-loss account.** *See* Appendix 1

◆ Betriebskosten

operating profit a gain from a company's normal business over a period of time, usually a year. This profit does not include gains from **shares** or **investments**

◆ Betriebsgewinn

operating statement (1) a statement of the **income** and **expenses** of some part of a business, e.g. of one department of a **department store,** or the income and expenses of one **product** of a company. (2) *(especially US)* a **profit-and-loss account**

◆ (1) Betriebsergebnisrechnung (2) ausführliche Gewinn- und Verlustrechnung

operation (1) the way in which something works. *The operation of this machine is not easily explained.* (2) a piece of work to be done. *First you drill a hole in this part and the next operation is to drill a larger hole here.* (3) **in operation** in use. *There is a new rule in operation for getting time off work*

◆ (1) Arbeitsweise (2) Arbeitsgang (3) in Kraft; in Betrieb

operational research (*or* **operations research** *or* **OR**) using the methods of science on the problems of business so that productivity or profit will be improved, e.g. to get the best use of workers, materials, machines, money and time

◆ Unternehmensforschung

operative (1) coming into effect; coming into force. *The new rule is operative from next Monday.* (2) important, effective: *the operative word in this contract*

◆ (1) rechtswirksam werden (2) maßgeblich

operator (1) a person who operates something: *a machine operator.* (2) **the operator** a person who operates a telephone switchboard

◆ (1) Bedienungsperson (2) die Vermittlung

opinion leaders (*or* **opinion formers**) special groups of people whose opinions on new **products** or new ideas have a great effect on other people

◆ Meinungsbildner

opinion research finding out what people think of something by questioning some of them (a **sample**)

◆ Meinungsumfrage

opportunity cost the value of a certain course of action that one has decided not to follow. For example, the opportunity cost of using your savings to start up a business is the **interest** your money could have earned in a bank if you had not taken it out

◆ Alternativkosten

optical character reader a **device** which can read specially-printed information and pass it straight into a **computer**

◆ optischer Klarschriftleser

optimum best, most suitable. *Our optimum level of production is 10,000 units a week*

◆ Optimal-

optimum order quantity the amount which should be ordered of something which keeps the costs of ordering and holding such **stock** to the best level. *See also* **economic order quantity**

◆ optimale Auftragsgröße

option (1) a choice. *Have we any other option before we decide?* (2) a right to buy or sell something within a certain time usually at an agreed price. *He took up his option to buy, and bought 600 shares. We can give you a three-month option*

◆ (1) Wahl (2) Option

option dealing (stock exchange) the agreement to buy or sell **shares** at a certain price within a certain time. To enter this agreement one has to pay **option money.** If the option to buy (or sell) is not taken up within the agreed time, then one loses the option money

◆ Optionsgeschäft

OR *see* **operational research**

Oracle *(UK)* a **viewdata system** offered by independent television

◆ Oracle (Btx-System)

order *verb* (1) to tell (a person) to do something. *He was ordered to stay where he was.* (2) to ask for (something which one wants to buy). *They ordered ten more cases.* (3) to arrange in some special way. *The invoices are ordered according to the date they were received*

◆ (1) befehlen (2) bestellen (3) ordnen

order *noun* (1) the act of **ordering** (meanings (1) and (2)). *We have to obey the order. I've got six orders already this morning.* (2) a special arrangement of things. *The names are in alphabetical order.* (3) **on order** waiting to be delivered. *We have no shampoo in stock but it is on order*

◆ (1) Befehl; Bestellung (2) Ordnung; Reihenfolge (3) bestellt

order book a special book for writing in the details of any **order**

◆ Auftragsbuch

order/call ratio the relationship between the number of calls made on buyers and the number of **orders** received. *He called on 40 buyers and got 20 orders so his order/call ratio was 20 divided by 40 or 0.5:1*

◆ Verhältnis zwischen Kundenbesuchen und Aufträgen

ordinary share part-ownership of a company. Ordinary shares allow the **shareholder** to vote at company meetings and to receive a **dividend** (if the company says it will pay one). *See also* **ordinary shareholder, share,** Appendix 2

◆ Stammaktie

ordinary shareholder any person or business that owns **ordinary shares** in a company. They are considered to be the true owners of a company with the directors acting on their behalf in the day-to-day running of the business. Ordinary shareholders have no right to a **dividend** unless the company says that it will pay one to them

◆ Stammaktionär

organisation (1) an arrangement of parts of a group to form an effective whole; a business, company or other body. *Four units make up the firm's organisation. They are: production, marketing, finance and personnel, and over them all the managing director.* (2) the planning and arranging of something. *The organisation of the conference was very poor*

◆ (1) Unternehmen; Organisation (2) Organisation

organisation and methods (*or* **O and M**) the study of a company's **organisation,** the way it works, the **systems** it uses, so that these may be improved and the company made more profitable

◆ Organisationsanalyse

organisation chart a drawing of how a company is organised showing who is in charge of different parts of it, and how each part is related to the whole. *See also* **organisations, organisation structure**

◆ Organisationsplan

Organisation for Economic Cooperation and Development (*or* **OECD** *or* **OCDE**) an organisation founded in 1961 to help the **economic** growth and the **standard of living** of member states; to help the world **economy** and to improve the conditions of the poorest countries. Membership: Australia, Austria, Belgium, Canada, Denmark, Finland, France, Federal Republic of Germany, Greece, Iceland, Ireland, Italy, Japan, Luxembourg, Netherlands, New Zealand, Norway, Portugal, Spain, Sweden, Switzerland, Turkey, United Kingdom, United States. Headquarters: Paris. Official languages: English, French

◆ Organisation für wirtschaftliche Zusammenarbeit und Entwicklung (OECD)

organisation man a worker who is very interested in helping his company, even to the extent of harming his home life. *He worked late at the office all of last week — he's becoming an organisation man*

◆ ein der Firma verschriebener Mitarbeiter

Organisation of African Unity (*or* **OAU** *or* **OUA**) an organisation of fifty African states formed in 1963, to achieve a better life for the people of Africa, to defend their countries, and to promote cooperation between all nations of the world. Headquarters: Addis Ababa. Official languages: English, French, and when possible African languages

◆ Organisation für die Afrikanische Einheit

Organisation of American States (*or* **OAS** *or* **OEA**) a group of twenty-eight states formed in 1948, to achieve order, peace and justice among American states and to encourage the **economic,** social and cultural growth of its members. Headquarters: Washington, DC. Official languages: English, French, Portuguese, Spanish

◆ Organisation Amerikanischer Staaten

Organisation of Arab Petroleum Exporting Countries (*or* **OAPEC**) an organisation set up in 1968 for coordination of the petroleum policies of its members and other forms of cooperation. Members include Algeria, Bahrain, Iraq, Kuwait, Libya, Qatar, Saudi Arabia. Headquarters: Kuwait City, Kuwait

◆ Verband der Arabischen Erdölexportierenden Länder

Organisation of Petroleum Exporting Countries (*or* **OPEC**) a union of oil-producing countries formed in 1960 to agree on a basic policy for oil (including prices) and to help the economic growth of member states. Membership includes Algeria, Ecuador, Gabon, Indonesia, Iran, Iraq, Kuwait, Libya, Nigeria, Qatar, Saudi Arabia, United Arab Emirates, Venezuela. Headquarters: Vienna

◆ Verband der Erdölexportierenden Länder (OPEC)

organisation structure how a company has arranged its directors, managers and other workers, what their duties are, who they are in charge of, etc. *See also* **organisation chart**

◆ Organisationsstruktur

organise (1) to put (things or people) into order. *Let's get all those orders organised into wholesalers and retailers.* (2) to get (workers) to join a **trade union.** *The workers in the shipyard have been organised for years*

◆ (1) ordnen (2) gewerkschaftlich organisieren

outbid to offer a higher price than (anyone else), e.g. at an **auction**

◆ überbieten

outer a box or outside wrapping in which a number of products are sold. *There are ten packets of biscuits to the outer*

◆ Verpackungsmaterial

outgoings money that is being paid out. *If the outgoings are more than the money coming in, you're in trouble*

◆ Ausgaben

outlet a shop; a place where things can be sold. *We don't have enough outlets — we have to sell the new razor into more shops*

◆ Verkaufsstelle

out of order (1) not following one another properly. *These numbers are all out of order.* (2) of a machine etc., not working properly or needing repair

◆ (1) durcheinander sein (2) nicht funktionieren, außer Betrieb sein

out of stock (1) not having supplies of certain goods. (2) having sold all one's **stock.** *We can't supply this book at the moment, it's out of stock*

◆ (1) nicht vorrätig haben (2) nicht vorrätig sein

output (1) what is made, production. *Today's output was 40,000 shirts — well up on yesterday's output.* (2) information from a **computer,** often from a **line-printer**

◆ (1) Produktionsmenge (2) Ausgabe

output per man what is made divided by the number of men doing the work. For example, if 10,000 pairs of shoes were made by 100 workers, the output per man would be 100 pairs of shoes

◆ Produktionsleistung je Beschäftigter

outstanding (1) remarkable, excellent. *His ability as a manager is outstanding.* (2) of a debt etc., not yet paid. *There is still £5.00 outstanding on their account*

◆ (1) hervorragend (2) ausstehend

out-tray a tray on a desk containing letters, **documents** etc., that a manager has attended to. *See also* **in-tray**

◆ Ausgangsablage

overbook to book more (seats in a plane, rooms in a hotel etc.) than there is space for

◆ überbuchen

overcapitalise to put more money into (a company) than it can use, e.g. in the form of machines etc.

◆ überkapitalisieren

overdraft the amount of money owed to a bank by a person or organisation, usually an amount agreed by the bank and the customer. This agreement will also state when the money has to be repaid and how much **interest** is to be charged

◆ Überziehungskredit

overdraw to take out more money from (one's **account** in a bank) than the amount one has in it. *This month my account is £50.00 overdrawn*

◆ (Konto) überziehen

overdue late, having gone beyond the correct or agreed time. *Your account for £10,000 is now overdue. Please pay within seven days. They said our order would be here within a week and ten days have passed. It's three days overdue*

◆ überfällig

overhead an expense not directly related to producing a **product** or a **service**, e.g. selling expenses, **rates**, rent, managers' salaries etc.

◆ Gemeinkosten

overhead absorption a method of dividing parts of an **overhead** cost among certain **products** according to particular company rules. For example, a company may decide to allot the cost of advertising to products according to their total sales. Under this method a product that has 50% of the company sales would carry 50% of the total advertising expense

◆ Gemeinkostenverrechnung

overhead projector a machine which throws pictures of **graphs**, notes, etc. onto a screen from prepared sheets of clear film, used to illustrate a talk

◆ Overhead-Projektor

overmanning using more workers than are needed to do the work. *The real reason for the company's poor profits was its overmanning in the printing department*

◆ Überbesetzung mit Arbeitskräften

overproduction making more of something than there is a demand for

◆ Überproduktion

overriding commission a payment over and above the normal **discounts** and **commissions**, paid for some special reason. *If your company buys more than £50,000 of goods from us over the next twelve months, then we will pay an overriding commission of 1% on the value of all goods bought*

◆ zusätzliche Provision

overstock to hold more **stock** of something than is necessary at a given time

◆ Überbevorratung

oversubscribed of an issue of **shares** where the number issued is less than the number that could have been sold. *The shares were offered at £1 and were oversubscribed: three times the number offered could have been sold*

◆ überzeichnet

overtime hours worked beyond the normal working hours. *There's been a sudden increase in the number of orders — we'll have to ask the workers to work overtime*

◆ Überstunden

overtime ban a refusal to work **overtime,** sometimes called for by a **trade union** to strengthen the union's position in talks with the management on some matter

◆ Überstundenverbot

over-trading doing business beyond the limit of a company's **financial** strength, e.g. when it grows too quickly, or when more goods are being made than the company can pay for

◆ sich geschäftlich übernehmen

own brand (*or* **own label** *or* **private brand** *or* **private label**) goods which carry a **retailer's** or a **wholesaler's** name (or **brand**) on the label instead of a manufacturer's brand. Although they are so named, they are made under **contract** by manufacturers for retailers and wholesalers

◆ Hausmarke

P

PA see **particular average loss, personal assistant**

package the container in which goods are packed; a number of things packed; a number of things packed together. *Our Christmas cards are sold in packages of twenty-five*

◆ (Ver-) Packung

package deal a number of things offered or put forward for discussion together. *They offered them a package deal: they would build the hospital, put in all the equipment and plant the surrounding trees for a total price of £2 million*

◆ Verhandlungspaket

package tour a holiday with everything (travel, hotels etc.) arranged in advance by the travel agent and all sold at one fixed price

◆ Pauschalreise

packaging the covering around goods, sometimes used to advertise them (boxes of chocolates, perfume) and sometimes used to protect them (television, refrigerators). *I'm glad they sent the dishes in strong packaging, there isn't one broken*

◆ Verpackung

packing material such as straw, paper, etc. used to pack goods

◆ Verpackungsmaterial

packing case a strong box used to hold goods either for **storage** or for delivery

◆ Kiste

packing list a list of contents of a **packing case** with details of number, weight, etc. of the things in the case. *Look for the packing list. I want to check the contents*

◆ Versandliste

page rate the cost of a page of advertising in a magazine or newspaper

◆ Seitentarif

paid-up capital the actual amount of money paid to a company for its **shares**

◆ eingezahltes Kapital

pallet a square wooden frame on which goods are stored; it can be used, e.g. for quick carrying from a company's store to a company's delivery lorry

◆ Palette

palletisation changing to the common use of **pallets** to help with the delivery of goods

◆ Palettisierung

pamphlet a small book, containing a few pages, sometimes with charts, or photographs. *Have you a pamphlet on your latest cooker?*

◆ Prospekt

panel (1) a group of speakers at a meeting. *Among the panel of speakers was a well-known film actor.* (2) (**market research**) a group of shops or consumers that give information on **products** or **services.** *See* **consumer panel**

◆ (1) Gremium (2) Panel

paper currency money that is not in metal form like coins but in paper form like £1 notes, £10 notes, etc. *Compare with* **coin**

◆ Papiergeld

paper profit a gain made when something rises in value but is not actually sold. *My house is worth £30,000 now. Since I paid only £20,000 for it I've made a paper profit of £10,000*

◆ rechnerischer Gewinn

paperwork any work to do with letters, **memos, documents** etc. *I can't go to the pub tonight: I brought a lot of paperwork home which I must attend to*

◆ Schreibarbeit

par (1) average or normal. *Joe went round the golf course in 76 strokes. That's par for the course.* (2) of **shares,** the original price, the **face-value** price. If shares are sold at this price, they are sold **at par,** if at a higher price they are sold **above par,** if lower, **below par.** *See also* **parity.** (3) of a currency, equal value. *The US and Canadian dollars were at par at that time*

◆ (1) Durchschnitt; Par (2) Pariwert (3) Parität

paragraph one of the sections into which a piece of writing is divided (by beginning a new line for each section)

◆ Absatz

parallel import a **product** going into a country by a method not agreed to by the **exporter.** *We send all our goods to our agent in France: now we find that a French store is buying our goods from some other source — and we want to stop this parallel import*

◆ Paralleleinfuhr

parameter something fixed; a limit. *The new factory must not cost more than £250,000 and it must be built within nine months: these are the parameters laid down by the company*

◆ Rahmen

parent company a company which owns more than half the **shares** of another company. *See also* **subsidiary company**

◆ Muttergesellschaft

Pareto's law (*or* **Pareto effect**) the idea that a few important things or people have a great effect. For example, a small number of salesmen will make most of the sales; a small number of customers will create most of a company's profit; in a **retail** shop, a small amount of **stock** will take up most of the money **invested** in stock

◆ Pareto-Effekt

parity (1) equality, being equal. *We want parity of wages with the workers doing the same job in the drilling section.* (2) a situation when a currency's **forward rate** of exchange is the same as its **spot rate.** *See also* **par**

◆ (1) Gleichheit (2) Parität

Parkinson's law the idea that work will always increase to fill the time made available for it. For example, if you give a worker two hours to do a job he will take two hours and not less than this time

◆ Parkinson-Gesetz

partial loss (**insurance**) not a complete loss, but where damage or loss has occurred to only part of the property **insured.** (But for **marine insurance,** *see* **particular average loss.**)

◆ Teilschaden

particular average loss (*or* **PA**) (**marine insurance**) **partial loss** of the property **insured,** caused by something which it was insured against (e.g. a storm, collision) and not shared by the **insurers** of all the cargo (as happens for a **general average loss**)

◆ Schaden in besonderer Havarie

partly-paid share a **share** in a company. Only part of **the nominal value** of this share has been paid to the company that issued it

◆ noch nicht voll eingezahlte Aktie

partner (1) a person who takes part with others in a business. *The four of them set up as partners in a taxi business.* (2) a person who shares in some activity or venture. *Joe is my partner at golf*

◆ (1) Geschäftspartner (2) Partner

partnership an agreement between two or more people to share in a business together. Unless the agreement says otherwise, each partner shares equally the profits and losses of the business

◆ Personengesellschaft

part payment part of the full price of something paid to a seller as proof that one intends to buy it. *I'm buying a gas cooker; I paid £20 part payment on it today. I'll pay the rest at the end of the month and have it delivered*

◆ Teilzahlung

part-time worker (*or* **part-timer**) a person employed to work less than the usual number of hours in the working week. *They're taking on part-time workers at Clark's shoe factory: I wouldn't mind being a part-timer there*

◆ Teilzeitarbeiter

party (1) a person or group on one side of a legal **dispute.** (2) a person or group that agrees to a **contract.** *He refused to be a party to the agreement.* (3) a group of people who are together for some purpose, e.g. to go on holiday, to discuss business matters. *When Mr Heller arrives with the German party take them to the manager's office.* (4) a group of people who support a political cause: *the Conservative party; the Labour Party*

◆ (1) Partei (2) Vertragspartei (3) Gruppe (4) Partei

par value the **face value;** the value of a **share** at its issued price

◆ Pariwert

passbook a book given by a bank etc. to a customer with details of the customer's **account** with the bank. *He saw from his passbook that he had only £10 left in his deposit account*

◆ Sparbuch

pass off (1) to pretend that (something) is something else. *The company passed off their whisky as a real Scottish whisky when it was actually made in Japan.* (2) to pretend that one is someone else. *She passed herself off as a lawyer but they found she was only an office worker*

◆ (1) etwas ausgeben als (2) sich ausgeben als

patent (*or* **letters patent**) a legal right given by the **patent office** to a person or company to make use of or sell something new, usually for 16 years. *He took out a patent on his new type of camera*

◆ Patent

patent office a government office which gives **patents** and **trademarks**

◆ Patentamt

patent rights rights to a **patent.** UK patents apply only to the UK

◆ Patentrechte

patron (1) a person who gives help to something, e.g. a charity, by giving money to it or by allowing his/her name to be used in its support. (2) a person who goes often to a certain shop, theatre etc.

◆ (1) Förderer (2) Stammkunde

pawn *verb* to give (something of value) to a **pawnbroker** in return for a loan of money. *He decided he would pawn* *his best suit. Maybe the pawnbroker would give him the £10 he needed*

◆ verpfänden

pawn *noun* a place where things of value can be **pawned.** *He had to put his gold watch in pawn*

◆ Pfandhaus

pawnbroker a person or company that lends money in exchange for goods taken into the **pawn.** The goods may be taken out of pawn when the money is repaid (i.e. within six months). If the money is not repaid within six months the pawnbroker can sell them at an **auction**

◆ Pfandleiher

pay *verb* (1) to give money in exchange for something or for work done. (2) to give a profit or advantage. *It pays to make a detailed plan*

◆ (1) bezahlen (2) sich lohnen

pay *noun* money for work done. *He got his pay for the first week's work*

◆ Lohn

Pay as you earn (*or* **PAYE**) a **system** of **income tax** whereby tax is taken off wages or salaries at the time of payment

◆ Steuersystem, bei dem die Lohnsteuer direkt einbehalten wird

pay day the day wages or salaries are paid. *Pay day was on Friday every week for the factory workers and on the 28th of every month for the office workers*

◆ Zahltag

payee a person to whom money is paid

◆ Zahlungsempfänger

payload the total load or weight which a ship, lorry, plane can carry and get money for

◆ Nutzlast

payment the amount of money paid for something; the act of paying. *The firm liked its customers to make payments by cheque*

◆ Bezahlung

payment by results payment made for reaching agreed levels of work. *They had a payment-by-results system, so that the more you produced the more you earned*

◆ Bezahlung nach Arbeitsleistung

payment on account part payment of a sum of money owing

◆ Abschlagszahlung

pay off to dismiss (a person), i.e. to make up a worker's pay and pay him, and end the agreement to employ him

◆ auszahlen

pay packet a small envelope containing wages and usually also a piece of paper called a **pay-slip,** with details of how the wages have been made up

◆ Lohntüte

payroll a list of workers employed by a company and the weekly or monthly pay that they earn

◆ Lohnliste

pay-slip *see* **pay packet**

PDM *see* **physical distribution management**

peaceful picket a **picket** using non-violent methods, e.g. talking to the people at work, using **leaflets** and **posters** to explain their point of view

◆ friedfertiger Streikposten

peak the highest point of something. *Sales of our suntan oil reach a peak in August*

◆ Höchststand

peak demand a time when most people want a **service** or **product,** e.g. peak demand for gas is at breakfast time; for holidays, in the month of August. *See also* **off-peak**

◆ Spitzenbedarf

peddle (1) to go from place to place selling small things. (2) to sell illegal drugs

◆ (1) hausieren (2) mit Drogen handeln

pedlar, peddler a person who **peddles** (meanings (1) and (2)). *He was arrested for being a peddler of drugs*

◆ (1) Hausierer (2) Drogenhändler

peg *verb* to hold (prices or wages) at a certain level. *The firm planned to peg its price for the new camera at its present level*

◆ festsetzen

penalty clause a part of a **contract** by which one **party** has to pay a sum of money to the other party if the first party fails to carry out something in the contract, e.g. to deliver something by the agreed date

◆ Strafklausel

pending waiting to happen or to be attended to

◆ unerledigt

penetration pricing pricing a new **product** at a price well below other similar products so as to get a large share of the total sales quickly

◆ Preispolitik bei der Einführung neuer Produkte

pension a regular sum of money paid by the government or by a company to a person who has reached the age of retiring from work, or to a widow, or a person who is too ill to carry on working. *See also* **pension fund, pension plan, non-contributory pension scheme**

◆ Pension

pension fund a sum of money which has been collected from people in a **pension plan.** This **fund** is used to provide **pensions** for people who pay into the fund. Another source of money for the pension fund is from **interest** which the fund earns on its money in the bank, or in other forms of **investment.** A company's pension fund can be made up of money paid only by the company, the workers paying nothing towards the cost of their pension. *See* **non-contributory pension scheme, pension, pension plan**

◆ Pensionskasse

pension plan (*also* **pension scheme**) an arrangement by which people agree to pay a certain amount of their wages into a **pension fund** so that they can receive a **pension** when they retire (or when they are too ill to continue working). The UK government runs such a pension plan for workers but some companies prefer to have their own arrangements. *See also* **non-contributory pension scheme**

◆ Pensionsplan

pep talk *(informal)* a talk with a person that gives him/her encouragement, especially when he/she has not been successful so far. *The sales manager gave to his salesmen their weekly pep talk*

◆ aufmunternde Worte

per annum (*or* **pa**) each year. *A salary of £30,000 per annum*

◆ pro Jahr

P/E ratio *see* **price-earnings ratio**

per capita by (or for) each person in the population. *Germany has a very high income per capita*

◆ pro Kopf der Bevölkerung

per cent in one or for each hundred

◆ Prozent

percentage a rate worked out at so much in a hundred. *In only two weeks we have sold a high percentage of our stock — 87% to be exact*

◆ Prozentsatz

perfect competition (*or* **perfect market**) (**economic theory**) the perfect market, i.e. when the price of a **product** is the same to all buyers because buyers and sellers have full information about each other and the product, and there is nothing to prevent anyone becoming a trader in the market

◆ homogener Markt

performance appraisal judging how well a manager or other worker does his job, especially when this is part of a formal appraisal method, e.g. to find out his training needs, whether he should be promoted or have a pay increase. Records are kept of the worker's effort in reaching the aims and finally a discussion of his efforts (a performance appraisal) is carried out. *See also* **management appraisal**

◆ Leistungsbeurteilung

performance bond a legal promise (a **guarantee**) given by one **party** to another that the work of a third party will be carried out properly. For example, a company offering a **contract** to a builder may ask the builder to get a bank to give a guarantee that the builder will complete the work properly

◆ Gewährleistungsgarantie

performance review a meeting between a worker and the manager to discuss the worker's progress towards the aims set for the worker at their last meeting. *See also* **performance appraisal**

◆ Leistungsbesprechung

peril serious danger. *He was in peril of losing his job if they found out that he stole the money*

◆ Gefahr

periodical a magazine

◆ Zeitschrift

peripheral *adjective* not central. *The meeting decided not to discuss prices as this was peripheral to the main subject of the bank loan*

◆ peripher

peripheral *noun* (**computers**) a unit of **peripheral equipment**

◆ Peripheriegerät

peripheral equipment the parts of a **computer system** which are not part of the **central processing unit**, e.g. **visual display units, keyboards, line-printers**

◆ Peripheriegeräte

perishable goods goods which go bad quickly if not sold within a certain time, e.g. eggs, fish, fruit, milk

◆ leicht verderbliche Waren

perjury *(law)* the act of telling lies after swearing to tell the truth. *The judge asked the witness if he knew the punishment for perjury*

◆ Meineid

perks *see* **perquisites**

permanent lasting for a long time or for ever: *permanent staff. Compare with* **temporary**

◆ ständig

per procurationem (*or* **pp**) power given to sign or to act for another. *The letter was signed p.p. J. Jones & Co., S. Smith.* (S. Smith has the power to sign letters on behalf of the J. Jones Co.)

◆ im Auftrag

perquisites (*or* **perks**) benefits (apart from pay) that one gets in a job. *One of my perks is a company car which I can use as my own*

◆ Sondervergünstigungen

personal to do with one person. *These are my personal belongings. Compare with* **personnel**

◆ persönlich

personal accounts a company's record of payments to or from people, or companies. *See also* **account, nominal accounts**

◆ Kundenkonten

personal allowance an amount of one's **income** which is free of **income tax.** *The government said that it would raise the level of per* *sonal allowance so that workers would pay less income tax*

◆ persönlicher Steuerfreibetrag

personal assistant a person who helps a manager to do his job. *She got a job as a personal assistant to the sales manager*

◆ persönlicher Assistent

personal effects goods which one owns that can be moved around, e.g. books, clothes, paper

◆ bewegliche Habe

personal income tax payment made to the government from the earnings of a person, and not a company. *See also* **corporation tax, personal allowance**

◆ Einkommenssteuer

personal interview (1) a face-to-face talk with a person, especially someone in authority. *I have a personal interview with the boss of Brown Brothers Ltd for a job as manager.* (2) a talk with a person who is actually present. *The researcher had six interviews to carry out: three personal and three by telephone*

◆ (1) Unterredung (2) Interview

personality (1) a person who is well known in television, cinema, sport, etc.: *a personality of stage and screen.* (2) the qualities that make up a person's character. *He had a very strong personality*

◆ (1), (2) Persönlichkeit

personality promotion the selling of goods with the help of some well-known person from television, stage or sport. *See also* **personality** (meaning 1)

◆ Verkaufsförderung durch Anwesenheit berühmter Persönlichkeiten

personal loan a loan of money by a bank to a person to allow him/her to buy something, e.g. a car, clothes, a holiday

◆ Personaldarlehen

personal property all the goods which a person owns, e.g. house, clothes, papers, car etc.

◆ Privateigentum

personal selling selling done by a person who is face-to-face with the buyer (as opposed to selling, e.g. by post — *see* **mail order**)

◆ persönlicher Verkauf

personnel (1) all the people employed in a company etc.: the staff. (2) — **personnel department.** *Compare with* **personal**

◆ (1) Personal

personnel department the department in a company which deals with **personnel management**

◆ Personalabteilung

personnel management the selecting, employing and training of the workers and managers in a company. It is also concerned with the **motivation** of individuals and groups within a company, their well-being, and how they can be encouraged to help the success of the company

◆ Personalführung

personnel manager the person in charge of the **personnel department**

◆ Personalchef

person-to-person call a telephone call for which no charge is made unless a certain person is able to answer it, in which case there is an extra charge

◆ Telefongespräch mit Voranmeldung

PERT *see* **programme evaluation and review technique**

Peter Principle the **theory** that over a period of time people will be promoted to the level where, finally, they do not know how to do the job. This theory was put forward by L. J. Peter and R. Hall in the book *The*

Peter Principle, published in 1969
◆ Peter-Prinzip

petrodollars US dollars earned by oil-**exporting** countries that are then **invested** in the US and in European countries
◆ Petrodollar

petty cash a small amount of money kept by a company (in the form of coins and banknotes) to pay small expenses, e.g. postage stamps
◆ Bargeldkasse

petty cash book a book in which is recorded all of the small payments that have been made from the **petty cash**
◆ Bargeldkassenbuch

photocopier a machine which makes **photocopies.** *Go along to the photocopier and run off six copies of this letter*
◆ Fotokopierer

photocopy *noun* a photographic copy of a letter, **document,** drawing etc.
◆ Fotokopie

photocopy *verb* to make a **photocopy** of (a **document,** letter etc.)
◆ fotokopieren

physical distribution means used to move goods from the maker to the user. *Whether you use lorries or the railway the physical distribution costs of moving bricks are quite high*
◆ Warenverteilung

physical distribution management (*or* **PDM**) planning and controlling the movement and storage of all materials and goods into and out of a company
◆ Logistik

physical stocktaking the counting of the things in a shop, store, **warehouse** etc. by checking each one individually
◆ Warenbestandsaufnahme

picket *noun* a group of people on **strike** who form a group outside a place of work to try to make other workers join or support them; a member of such a group. *See also* **peaceful picket**
◆ Streikposten

picket *verb* to act as **a picket** at (a place of work)
◆ Streikposten stehen

pictogram a method of showing the differences between things (e.g. the number of cars sold each month) by using drawings
◆ Piktogramm

piece rate a certain payment for each piece of work done (instead of payment by the hour). *The piece rate in this factory is 10 pence for each box completed*
◆ Akkordlohnsatz

piecework a method of payment based on the work done (and not on payment by the hour). *They don't have payment by the hour in Smiths Ltd, they're all on piecework there*
◆ Akkordarbeit

pie chart a method of showing how the total of something (time, materials, **market share** etc.) is made up by using a circle which is sliced into various parts. The size of each slice shows the difference in the parts
◆ Kreisdiagramm

pile: make one's pile *(informal)* to make a lot of **profit,** become very rich
◆ einen Haufen Geld verdienen

pilfer to steal a small amount of something. *The wooden case was broken into and some of the goods had been pilfered*
◆ klauen

pilferage stealing in small amounts. *suppose we lose about £100 a year i pilferage*
◆ geringfügiger Diebstahl

pilot *noun* (1) person trained to take ships into or out of a harbour or through a canal. (2) a person trained to fly an aircraft

◆ (1) Lotse (2) Pilot

pilot *verb* (1) to act as a **pilot** for: *to pilot a ship safely into harbour.* (2) to try (something) out to see if it will be successful: *to pilot a new product*

◆ (1) lotsen (2) testen

pilot *adjective* used as a guide or trial to find out whether something will be successful. *They are going to build a pilot factory in Scotland. We are carrying out a pilot scheme for our new project*

◆ Versuchs-

pilotage a charge made by **pilots** (meaning 1) for their **services**

◆ Lotsengebühr

pioneer *noun* the first person to go into a country to develop it or to do something new. *As a salesman in this new region you should think of yourself as a pioneer*

◆ Pionier

pioneer *verb* (1) to show new methods, new ways, ideas to others. *He pioneered the use of the new product.* (2) to be a **pioneer** in something new

◆ (1) bahnbrechend sein (2) Bahnbrecher sein

pioneer selling selling a new **product** to buyers for the first time (or selling an old **product** to new buyers for the first time). *When you are out selling life insurance it is pioneer selling at every call. See also* **pioneer**

◆ Initialverkauf

piracy (1) robbery at sea. (2) the use of someone's written work, invention or **patent** without his agreement

◆ (1) Seeräuberei (2) Raubdruck

pirate *noun* a person who commits **piracy**

◆ Seeräuber; Raubdrucker

pirate *verb* to steal (**copyright** material). *Their new book has been pirated in several countries*

◆ Raubdruck herstellen

pitch *(informal)* the reasons for buying which a salesman gives to a buyer. *The buyer listened to the salesman's pitch but at the end he refused to buy*

◆ Überredungskünste

placement (1) the act of placing, e.g. workers in jobs. (2) work in a company, or work at a particular job. *They offered Jones a placement in their Kent branch and they offered Smith a placement as a salesman*

◆ (1) Einstellung (2) Stelle

plagiarise to use (someone else's work, e.g. a book, idea etc.) as if it were one's own. *He has plagiarised my book — he even has his name on it*

◆ plagiieren

plagiarism the act of **plagiarising**

◆ Plagiat

plagiarist a person who **plagiarises**

◆ Plagiator

plaintiff a person who brings another to court in a case dealing with the rights of private citizens. *See* **defendant**

◆ Kläger(in)

plan *noun* a carefully-thought-out course of action. *See also* **marketing plan**

◆ Plan

plan *verb* to prepare a plan (for). *We shall have to plan our sales campaign very carefully*

◆ planen

planned economy money, goods and other **resources** of a company planned and controlled by the government

◆ Planwirtschaft

planned maintenance (*or* **preventive maintenance**) checking machines, buildings etc. in a regular manner so that they remain free of trouble

◆ vorbeugende Wartung und Instandhaltung

planning permission *(UK)* permission from a **local authority** for the way land is used and the types of building built on it

◆ Baugenehmigung

plant (1) the machinery and other equipment in a factory, office, stores etc. *They are going to sell off the plant.* (2) a factory or building or group of these where work is done. *He has a plant outside the town*

◆ (1) Anlagen (2) Werk

plant bargaining talks at a factory between workers and managers about wage increases and/or working conditions. *Compare with* **collective bargaining**

◆ innerbetriebliche Tarifverhandlungen

platen the part of a typewriter which holds and moves the paper

◆ Walze

play the market to buy and sell **stocks and shares,** hoping for profit (but risking a loss) through a change in prices. *He played the market for a long time but in the end he lost all his money*

◆ an der Börse spekulieren

PLC *see* **public limited company**

pledge *noun* (1) something left with a **pawnbroker.** (2) something given as a sign of love, affection: *a pledge of friendship.* (3) a promise

◆ (1), (2) Pfand (3) Versprechen

pledge *verb* (1) to leave (something) with a **pawnbroker** as a **pledge.** (2) to promise. *He pledged his support for the project*

◆ (1) verpfänden (2) versprechen

plenary session a meeting attended by everyone with the right to be there. *In the afternoon there was a plenary session for the whole conference*

◆ Plenarsitzung

plough back profits to use profits to buy new machinery, factories etc. instead of paying out the profits to **shareholders.** *We've got the most up-to-date factory in the country because we've been ploughing back the profits*

◆ Reinvestierung von Gewinn

plug *(informal)* to advertise (something, e.g. a book, film) by saying its name often in public

◆ Schleichwerbung machen

point of order a question at a meeting about how the meeting is being run. *Point of order, should Mr Smith be present at this meeting?*

◆ Geschäftsordnungspunkt

point of sale (*or* **point of purchase**) the place where goods are bought, especially the shop or shelf from which they are sold. *The point of sale is important because that's where the customer decides to buy or not*

◆ Verkaufsort

point-of-sale advertising placing printed cards, pictures etc. near the goods in a **retail** shop to help sell them

◆ Werbung am Verkaufsort

policy (1) a plan of action. (2) a statement of aims. *The company's policy is to keep prices steady.* (3) a **document** which contains a **contract** of **insurance**

◆ (1) Taktik (2) Politik (3) Versicherungspolice

policy-holder a person **insured** under an **insurance policy**

◆ Versicherungsnehmer

political to do with a government and how it should govern

◆ politisch

political levy that part of a worker's payment to his **trade union** which goes to support the union's **political** views

◆ Anteil des Gewerkschaftsbeitrages eines Arbeitnehmers, der zur Öffentlichkeitsarbeit der Gewerkschaft verwendet wird

poll *verb* (1) to find out the opinions of a large group by asking questions of a **sample.** *They polled a sample of the users of the product.* (2) to receive votes at an election. *He polled 12,000 votes*

◆ (1) Meinungsumfrage veranstalten (2) Wählerstimmen erhalten

poll *noun* (1) the act of **polling** (meaning (1)); the result of this. *Opinion polls are not always to be trusted.* (2) the number of votes given. *There was a very heavy poll*

◆ (1) Befragung (2) Wahlbeteiligung

polytechnic a place of higher education which gives **diplomas** and often degrees in science, management, arts etc.

◆ Technische Hochschule

pool *verb* to join (a number of **resources,** e.g. money, **investments**) together

◆ zusammenlegen

pool *noun* (1) a joining together, sometimes by several companies etc., in this way. (2) the money etc. joined together in this way. (3) *see* **typing pool**

◆ (1) (Unternehmens-) Zusammenschluß (2) gemeinsamer Fonds

population (1) the total number of people who live in an area, city, country etc. *London has a very large population.* (2) the total number of anything (people, objects, fish etc.) from which a **sample** will be taken. This total number is also known as the **universe.** *There are 20,000 buyers of our product — that's our population and we will sample 200 of them*

◆ (1) Bevölkerung (2) statistische Masse

port (1) a place for ships to tie up; a harbour. (2) a town or city with a harbour. (3) the left hand side of a ship. *He turned the ship hard to port*

◆ (1) Hafen (2) Hafenstadt (3) Backbord

portable *adjective* able to be carried about: *a portable computer*

◆ tragbar

portable *noun* something **portable.** *I can bring my typewriter: it's a portable*

◆ Reise-; Koffer-

porterage the payment made at a port for the work of moving cargo

◆ Trägergebühren

portfolio (1) a large flat container for drawings etc. (2) a list of **shares** which a person owns in companies. *His portfolio was made up of oil shares and retail store shares*

◆ (1) Mappe (2) Portefeuille

positive cash flow a situation where more cash is coming into a business than is going out. *I expect we will have a positive cash flow by the end of the year from the new product*

◆ Überhang der Zahlungseingänge

post *noun* (1) a job, position. *He has a very good post in a car company.* (2) the **system** of delivery of letters, parcels etc. through the **Post Office.** *Has the morning post come yet?*

◆ (1) Posten (2) Post

post *verb* (1) to send (a letter, parcel etc.) through the **Post Office.** (2) to make an entry in a **book of account**

◆ (1) aufgeben (2) verbuchen

postage (1) the charge for sending a letter, parcel etc. (2) the value of the stamps on something to be sent by post. *The postage for the parcel was £2*

◆ (1), (2) Porto

postcode (*US* **zipcode**) the letters and numbers which form part of an address on an envelope to make delivery quicker and easier

◆ Postleitzahl

postdate to put a date later than the actual date of writing on (a cheque etc.)

◆ vordatieren

poster a large sheet of paper or cardboard on show to the public. *The poster advertised French perfume*

◆ Plakat

poste restante used along with the name of a certain **post office** as an address on a letter etc. to show that it should be kept at that post office until collected by the person to whom it is addressed; the department in a post office which deals with such letters etc.

◆ postlagernd

post free (*or* **post paid**) when the cost of postage is included in the price of goods

◆ portofrei

post office (1) **Post Office** a government department which deals with the collecting and delivery of letters, parcels, money etc. (2) **post office** an office which carries this out in a certain area. *There is a post office in every district*

◆ (1) die Post (2) Postamt

Post Office Box (*or* **POB**) a numbered place in a **post office** where mail is kept until it is collected by the holder of the number

◆ Postfach

post-test *verb* to test how well something was done. For example, after a company has put on a number of TV advertisements it may post-test buyers to see if the advertisements made them more likely to buy the company's **product.** *See also* **pre-test**

◆ den Werbewert prüfen

post-test *noun* the act of **post-testing**

◆ Werbewertprüfung

potential *adjective* (something) that can or may come into being. *The potential sales of the new product could be as high as £1,000,000*

◆ möglich

potential *noun* a possibility; what someone or something is capable of. *Their new product has great sales potential*

◆ Möglichkeit

pound (1) a unit of weight equal to 0.454 kilograms. *I lost three pounds in weight last month.* (2) the UK standard of money (**pound sterling**) equal to 100 pence

◆ (1), (2) Pfund

pound sterling the basic currency unit of the UK

◆ Pfund Sterling

power of attorney a legal **document** which gives one person the power to act and sign papers for another

◆ Vollmacht

PP *see* **per procurationem**

PR *see* **public relations**

practice *noun* (1) the act of doing something (as compared to thinking about it). *He put the plan into practice,* i.e. he puts it into action. (2) the usual way of doing something. *The practice in this firm is for the head cashier to open all the letters each morning.* (3) the work of a doctor, lawyer etc. *He's in practice as a doctor*

◆ (1) Praxis (2) Verfahrensweise (3) Praxis

practise *verb* (1) to do (something) over and over to become better at it.

You must practise your typing every day. (2) to do or work at: *to practise accountancy*

◆ (1) üben (2) ausüben

précis a shortened form of a speech or a piece of writing which keeps all the main points. *Write me a précis of the manager's report. Compare with* **precise**

◆ Auszug

precise (1) exact, correct. *These are the precise costs.* (2) taking care to be exact. *He spoke in a very precise manner. Compare with* **précis**

◆ (1) genau (2) präzise

pre-entry closed shop a company or factory where workers will not be employed unless they are already members of a **trade union.** *There is no hope of me getting a job at Whites. It is a pre-entry closed shop and I'm not in a union. See also* **closed shop, open shop**

◆ Unternehmen, das nur Gewerkschaftsmitglieder beschäftigt

preference shareholder a person who holds **preference shares** in a company

◆ Vorzugsaktionär

preference shares: shares which have a right to a **dividend** before anything is paid to the **ordinary shares.** Should a company sell off all its **assets** and close down, preference shares often have the right to be paid at their **face value** before payment is made to ordinary shares. The **voting rights** which come with preference shares are usually less than those of ordinary shares. Such details are given in a company's **articles of association**

◆ Vorzugsaktien

preferred position (advertising) a place in a newspaper or magazine where one wants one's advertisement to appear. The advertiser will have to pay extra (a **premium**) for this preferred position

◆ Sonderplazierung

preliminary expenses the costs of forming a company such as legal costs, cost of issuing **shares** etc.

◆ Gründungskosten

premises a building or buildings and the land on which it/they are built

◆ Grundstück und Gebäude

premium (1) an addition to the usual cost of something because that thing is now of greater value. For example, **shares** are sold **at a premium** when they are sold at a price above their **face value.** Also a banker may offer dollars for sale in four weeks' time **at a premium** if he thinks that the value of the dollar will have risen by then. (2) an amount payable to an **insurer**

◆ (1) Aufgeld (2) Versicherungsprämie

premium bond *see* **premium savings bond**

premium offer something extra which is offered to a buyer to make him/her buy more of a **product,** e.g. a silver spoon offered by a sugar manufacturer to buyers who send in a certain number of empty sugar bags

◆ Zugabeangebot

premium savings bond (*or* **premium bond**) a **bond,** issued by the UK government (sold in blocks of £5). Each bond is numbered and these numbers are put into a total pool of numbers. From this pool at regular intervals numbers are drawn. These numbers are given prizes of £25 up to £100,000. At any time the bonds can be exchanged for their **face value**

◆ Prämienschein

prepaid expenses costs which are paid although the goods and **services** are not yet used. For example, a company may pay its rent or rates for the period July to December in June of the same year

◆ vorausgezahlte Kosten

presentation (1) the act of putting before a meeting a carefully thought-out course of action or proposal, usually with the help of charts, film etc. *The advertising agency were asked to make a presentation of their planned campaign.* (2) the act of offering a **bill of exchange** for payment. (3) the act of offering a gift to someone. *Are you going to Bill's presentation? — He's retiring today*

◆ (1) Präsentation (2) Vorlage (3) Überreichung (-szeremonie)

present value today's value of money which is due to be paid at a certain date in the future

◆ Tageswert

press newspapers and other news **media** (television, radio) in general. *When the company announced it was going to close down, the press was at the door for more news*

◆ Presse

press conference a meeting at which the news **media** (newspapers, radio, television etc.) have been invited to hear some special news from a person or organisation and where the media can ask questions. *The company held a press conference to explain the reasons for the air crash*

◆ Pressekonferenz

press cuttings pieces of news about something cut from newspapers and magazines. *See also* **clipping service**

◆ Zeitungsausschnitte

press release (*also* **news release**) a special item of news about something written and sent to the **press** in the hope that it will be used by them. *The company issued a press release about the takeover*

◆ Presseverlautbarung

Prestel a **viewdata** system offered by British Telecom

◆ Prestel (Btx-System)

prestige advertising (*or* **corporate advertising**) putting information into newspapers, radio, television etc. which will improve the **image** of a company in the mind of the public

◆ Prestigewerbung

pre-tax before the amount of tax to be paid is taken off: *pre-tax profits*

◆ vor Steuern

pre-test *verb* to test (something) before it is carried out in full. For example, a newspaper advertisement may be pre-tested, so that its effect on likely customers will be checked before it is put into the newspaper

◆ im voraus testen

pre-test *noun* the act of **pre-testing**

◆ (Anzeigen-) Vortest

preventive maintenance *see* **planned maintenance**

price a sum of money asked for something which is offered for sale. *What's the price of that dress? See also* **cost, value**

◆ Preis

price control action by the government to stop prices rising so that the **cost of living** will not increase

◆ Preiskontrolle

price-cutting offering something for less than its usual price, usually in order to increase sales. *I see Macy's have started price-cutting again*

◆ Preissenkung

price discrimination setting different prices for the same **product** in different markets. *British cars are cheaper in France — do the British car companies use price discrimination?*

◆ Preisdiskriminierung

price earnings ratio (*or* **P/E ratio**) the current price of one **share** in a company related to the part of the profits (i.e. the **earnings**) that it gets. This **ratio** is worked out by first dividing the total profit by the number of **ordinary shares.** This will give the earnings per share which is then divided into the **market price** of one share to give the price earnings ratio

◆ Ertragsverhältnis

price fixing an agreement between companies which are selling the same type of **product** or **service** on the price which should be charged. (Such an agreement is often against the law unless it can be proved that the public gains by it.)

◆ Preisbindung

price index a method of measuring the rise or fall in prices by giving to the first year a value of £100. The following years are then shown as a percentage increase or decrease of this first (or base) year. For example:

Year:	1981	1982	1983
Price:	£1000	£1200	£1400
Index:	100	120	140

◆ Preisindex

price leader a major company in an industry whose price sets the price level for all the companies. An increase or decrease in price by the price leader is usually followed by the other companies in the industry moving their price up or down by the same amount

◆ Preisführer

priceless so valuable it cannot be priced. *The ancient Greek vase was priceless*

◆ unbezahlbar

price list a printed sheet showing the selling prices of various **products** of a company. *We bring out a new price list every month*

◆ Preisliste

price range the variety of prices for a **product** from the lowest to the highest. *The price range for these goods is quite large this year*

◆ Preisspanne

price-sensitive used to describe a **product** or **service** for which the demand falls when the price is increased

◆ preisempfindlich

price ticket a piece of paper etc. on which is printed the price of a **product**

◆ Preisschild

price war a situation when two or more companies continue to cut the price of a **product** or **service** in an attempt to increase their sales. *There is a price war in air fares to the USA*

◆ Preiskrieg

primary data information from an original source. For example, if a company makes a list of its own customers this is primary data, or if it questions its own customers the answers are primary data; but if it uses information which is published by others it is using **secondary data**

◆ Primärdaten

primary products: products from natural sources, e.g. of agriculture (wheat etc.), forestry (trees etc.), fishing, mining (coal etc.)

◆ Grundstoffe

prime cost *see* **direct cost**

prime time on television and radio, the time which attracts the biggest audience. *Television companies charge more for advertisements at prime time because there are more people watching*

◆ Hauptsendezeit

principal *adjective* chief, main, most important. *Our principal customers are car owners*

◆ hauptsächlich; Haupt-

principal *noun* (1) the sum of money on which interest is paid. *I pay back £20 interest each month and another £20 to repay the principal.* (2) the company, or person that an agent works for. *I'm an agent for Scotch whisky and my principal is S. McNab Limited, of Glasgow.* (3) the head of a college, school or university. *Compare with* **principle**

◆ (1) Darlehenssumme (2) Auftraggeber (3) Rektor

principle (1) a basic rule of personal conduct. *He is a man of very high principles.* (2) a basic rule which applies to something. *A basic principle of democracy is free speech. Compare with* **principal**

◆ (1) Prinzip (2) Grundsatz

printer (1) a person employed in the trade of printing (e.g. the printing of books, newspapers, etc.). (2) (**computers**) a machine which changes computer information into printed form on paper sheets

◆ (1), (2) Drucker

print-out (**computers**) printed information on paper sheets which comes from a **printer** (meaning 2)

◆ Ausdruck

prior charge the **security** for a loan to a company made with the condition that the money must be repaid before other loans

◆ vorrangige Belastung

private brand *see* **own brand**

private company *see* **private limited company**

private enterprise the owning and controlling of companies by private individuals and not by the state. *See also* **public ownership**

◆ Privatwirtschaft

private label *see* **own brand**

private limited company a company whose **shares** cannot be bought on the **stock exchange.** Private companies are often small, two-people or one-family firms. A UK private limited company is a **registered company** with a **Memorandum and Articles of Association** which state the rules and conditions under which it carries out its business. It must not have more than 50 **shareholders.** The letters Ltd after a business name mean that it is a private limited company

◆ ≈ Gesellschaft mit beschränkter Haftung

private property land or buildings owned by ordinary people or companies, i.e. not owned by the state

◆ Privatbesitz

private sector of the economy all the property and business activity in a country which is controlled by ordinary people and companies and which is not owned by the state or local government. *See also* **public sector of the economy**

◆ privatwirtschaftlicher Sektor

probability the likelihood of something happening. *If you toss up a penny one hundred times the probability is it will come down heads about fifty times*

◆ Wahrscheinlichkeit

probate *(law)* the **process** of proving that a will is **valid**

◆ gerichtliche Testamentsbestätigung

probationary period a short time at the start of a person's employment during which his/her ability to do the job will be tested. *My probationary period finishes next week; then I'll know if I'm still in a job or not*

◆ Probezeit

procedure a way of doing something. *We always try to follow the correct procedures*

◆ Verfahrensweise

proceed (1) to go on (with whatever one is doing). *Please proceed with your talk.* (2) to take legal action (against a person). *See also* **proceedings** *and compare with* **proceeds**

◆ (1) fortfahren (2) gerichtlich vorgehen

proceedings (1) how something is done: *the proceedings of the meeting* i.e. the way the meeting was carried out. (2) taking legal action. *I have started proceedings against the canned meats company.* (3) the reports of the meeting(s) of a society, conference etc.: *Proceedings of the Marketing Group. See also* **proceed** *and compare with* **proceeds**

◆ (1) Vorgehensweise (2) Prozeß anstrengen (3) Protokoll

proceeds money gained from the sale of something. *The proceeds from the new line helped the finances of the company*

◆ Einnahmen

process *noun* (1) a number of actions to get something done: *the manufacturing process.* (2) a special method of doing something. *We're using the silk-screen process.* (3) the whole action in a legal case: *the process of the law*

◆ (1) Prozeß (2) Verfahrenstechnik (3) Prozeß

process *verb* (1) to deal with (something) in some organised way: *to process an order.* (2) to treat or prepare (something, especially food) in a special way: *processed peas.* (3) (**computers**) to carry out some operation on (**data**) in order to get certain information etc.

◆ (1) bearbeiten (2) konservieren (3) verarbeiten

process chart a drawing which shows the order of events of a piece of work to be done, i.e. making, moving, storing etc. Since the process chart is a picture of the way the work is done, it can lead to better methods of doing it. *See* **process** (*noun:* meaning 1)

◆ Arbeitsablaufdiagramm

process industry a group of companies in the business of changing liquids, powder, grains etc. into finished or partly-finished form, e.g. the oil industry, the sugar industry, the wheat industry

◆ verarbeitende Industrie

procurement the act of buying; purchasing. *His job was the procurement of the best materials for the product*

◆ Beschaffung

produce *verb* (1) to make, manufacture, bring into being. *We produce steel plates.* (2) to show something for examination. *He produced his visiting card.* (3) to prepare (a play, film etc.) for showing on the stage, television, radio etc. *He will produce Macbeth in London*

◆ (1) herstellen (2) vorlegen (3) inszenieren; produzieren

produce *noun* what is made

◆ Produkt

producer (1) a person or company that makes or grows something. (2) a person who **produces** (meaning 3) a play or film

◆ (1) Hersteller (2) Produzent

product anything made by man or nature

◆ Produkt

product acceptance how much buyers prefer a certain **product.** *It has 15% of the market — that shows some product acceptance*

◆ Warenakzeptanz

product development making present **products** better in some way, e.g. in design, colour, more uses etc. *See also* **new product development**

◆ Fortentwicklung von Produkten

product differentiation making a **product** which might have many

competitors, e.g. toothpaste, soup etc., different in some way, e.g. by the **package,** the advertising, the price, the colour, the name etc.

◆ Produktdifferenzierung

product feature (*or* **sales feature**) a benefit which a company tries to point out to its buyers to make them buy. For example, benefits of a new soap may include: clear skin, attractive smell, freshness all day etc.

◆ besondere Eigenschaften eines Produkts

production (1) the act of making a **product.** (2) the quantity produced. *Production of coal has greatly increased.* (3) the way a play, film etc. has been produced: *a new production of Hamlet*

◆ (1) Herstellung (2) Produktion (3) Inszenierung; Produktion

production control managing materials, people, machines and methods so as to provide the planned **output** in the most profitable way

◆ Überwachung des Produktionsablaufs

production line a method of producing goods in a factory where the various stages of making the **product** follow each other in order. *See also* **assembly line**

◆ Fertigungsstraße

production manager a person who is in charge of the **process** of making goods in a factory

◆ Produktionsmanager

production-oriented company a company which thinks more of how it makes its **products** than its customers' needs. *See also* **marketing concept**

◆ fertigungsorientiertes Unternehmen

production overheads the **indirect costs** of running a factory area compared to the **direct costs** of actually making the **products,** e.g. heating costs, rates, cleaning costs, manager's salary etc.

◆ Fertigungsgemeinkosten

production planning that part of **production control** to do with **estimating** the materials, men and machines needed to satisfy future sales

◆ Produktionsplanung

production platform a raised metal or concrete floor through which oil can be pumped. It can be positioned on long metal legs resting on the sea bed or it can float above an **offshore oilfield**

◆ Förderplattform

productivity the relation between **input** and **output** within a company. Input is measured in the amount of people, machines, material and money put in, and output is measured in the amount of products or **services** produced. *We can increase our productivity by producing more with the same inputs*

◆ Produktivität

product liability insurance having a **policy** (meaning 3) which will protect a company from claims in the event of any harm to a customer caused by a fault in its **product** or the **packaging**

◆ Mängelhaftungsversicherung

product life cycle the **theory** that **products,** like people, are born, some die soon afterwards, others grow, get old and then die. If this is so, then new products must be made ready to provide the profits as the old products fail

◆ Entwicklungskurve eines Produkts

product mix all the different **products** which a company offers for sale. *Our product mix has too many slow sellers*

◆ Produktionsprogramm

product-plus *(informal)* something about a **product** which in the buyer's opinion makes it better than others of the same type. *This new golf ball is made to go further — that's a great product-plus. See also* **product feature**

◆ Produktvorteil

product test a way of finding out what users think of a **product.** One method is to ask a section of all buyers (a **sample**) what their views are on the various **product features** and compare this with their views on other products of the same type

◆ Warentest

profession a job which needs study for several years in a special branch of knowledge such as law or medicine. *The teaching profession requires a lot of commitment*

◆ (akademischer) Beruf

professional *adjective* (1) working in one of the **professions.** *He guessed that the other was a professional man: a doctor or a lawyer.* (2) showing or having skill in something which needs a long period of training to reach. *The way he handled the men showed that he was a very professional manager.* (3) doing or working at something for money (which others do for pleasure alone): *professional football player*

◆ (1) gehoben (2) fachmännisch (3) Berufs-

professional *noun* a person who is **professional,** especially someone who takes part in sport for his/her living and not just for pleasure

◆ Profi

proficiency test a test of how well a person can do a certain job

◆ Leistungstest

profit *noun* the result of more money coming in from the sale of a **product** or **service** than all the costs related to it. *See also* **earnings, income, margin, profit margin**

◆ Gewinn

profit *verb* to get profit or advantage (from something)

◆ profitieren

profitability the measure of the **profit** of a **product** or **service** in relation to the money **invested** in it. For example, it may take £100,000 to buy a factory, machines, materials, etc. to make something and the profit at the end of the year may be only £1000. The product will have made a profit but its profitability will be seen to be very poor. Profitability is the measure of the **return on capital** employed

◆ Rentabilität

profitable of a **product** or **service,** having an **income** greater than its costs. *Selling crisps is a very profitable business*

◆ gewinnbringend

profit and loss account (*or* **operating statement**) a record, which usually covers a year, of a company's total sales, total expenses, and showing either a **net profit** or a **net loss.** *See also* **gross profit, net profit** *and* Appendix 1

◆ Gewinn- und Verlustrechnung

profit centre a unit or department of a company which has to be responsible for its costs and its profits. *We run all our hotels on a profit-centre basis*

◆ Bilanzeinheit

profit margin the difference between a maker's selling price for a **product** and the cost of making it or between a **retailer's** or **wholesaler's** selling price and what he paid for it, e.g. buying price £1, selling price £2, profit margin £1 (i.e. the profit margin is 50% of the selling price)

◆ Gewinnspanne

profit sharing an agreement by which workers in a company each year get a certain part of its profit in addition to their normal wages or salaries

◆ Gewinnbeteiligung der Arbeitnehmer

profits tax *see* **corporation tax**

profit-volume chart a drawing showing: the number of a certain **product** sold, the total value of these sales, the **fixed costs,** the **variable costs** and the total profit reached. The chart shows how variable costs increase with each product sold and at what level of sales all costs are covered (the **break-even point**). *See also* **break-even chart** and Appendix 3

◆ Deckungsbetragsübersicht

pro-forma invoice a copy of an **invoice** sent to a buyer who may buy the goods; it gives all the details and the cost of the goods and is issued before an order is placed

◆ Proforma-Rechnung

program *noun* a set of instructions for solving a particular problem by a **computer**

◆ Programm

program *verb* (1) to write **programs** for a **computer.** (2) to prepare (**data**) to be handled by a computer. (3) to put a program into (a computer)

◆ (1)-(3) programmieren

programme (US program) (1) a list of names of actors and actresses (and the parts they have) in a play, or of singers or musicians taking part in an opera or a concert. (2) a list of items or pieces of music in a concert; a (complete) show in a hall, theatre etc., or on radio or television. *We waited till we had seen the complete programme.* (3) a list of duties or activities. *This is today's programme for our visitors*

◆ (1) Programmheft (2), (3) Programm

programmed instruction (*or* **programmed learning**) learning by small amounts (from a special book or **computer program**) with the student's knowledge of each stage being checked before he moves on to the next part of the program

◆ programmierter Unterricht

programme evaluation and review technique (*or* **PERT**) a method of checking the times taken to finish important parts of large, complex jobs such as making aircraft, ships, bridges etc. It helps the planning and control of such large **projects** and is closely related to **critical path analysis**

◆ Netzplantechnik

programmer a person who plans, writes and tests complete **programs** for a **computer**

◆ Programmierer

progress chaser a person in a company whose work is to see that orders get through their various stages in the factory, get finished and delivered on time

◆ Arbeitsflußüberwacher

progress payments payments made to a manufacturer (e.g. a builder) as each stage of a **contract** is finished, common in the cases of very large **contracts** such as ships, planes, etc.

◆ Zahlung nach Leistungsabschnitten

project *noun* (1) something carried out according to a plan. *How is the new factory project coming along?* (2) something which is put forward as a plan but on which no work has begun. *Let's have a look at this project of yours for a new product*

◆ (1) Projekt (2) Vorhaben

project *verb* (1) to stick out. *The window projects over the street.* (2) to plan; to say that something will happen. *We are projecting a large expansion next year*

◆ (1) vorspringen (2) vorhaben

projected planned, proposed, expected. *These are the projected costs of the new model*

◆ geplant

project group a small number of people who come together to solve a particular set of problems. For example, the head of a company might tell three of his managers to form a project group to solve the problems arising from moving to a new factory

◆ Projektgruppe

projection (1) the act of **projecting.** (2) something which **projects.** (3) a guess of future sales, future **output,** future profits etc., based on present and past figures. *My projection for next year is total sales of 10,000 units*

◆ (1) Planung (2) Vorsprung (3) Vorausberechnung

project manager a person in charge of solving the problems of one particular **project** (noun: meaning 1)

◆ Projektleiter

promissory note a promise in writing to pay, without any conditions, a certain sum of money to the holder of the note or to some other named person, either when the money is asked for or at some other named date

◆ Schuldschein

promote (1) to bring (goods or **services**) to the notice of buyers to increase sales. *It is a brand new product so we will have to promote it strongly.* (2) to help in the setting up of a company or some public event, e.g. a play, concert, boxing match. *Who is promoting the new company?* (3) to advance (a person) in a job, give (him/her) a better job with more pay; to advance (a person) in rank. *I think he is doing so well we could promote him to manager*

◆ (1) werben (2) fördern (3) befördern

promoter a person who **promotes** (meanings 1 and 2). *He is the main promoter of our sales in France*

◆ Promoter

promotion (1) action to help the sales of a **product** or **service,** e.g. a salesman making a sale; advertising a product in the press or television, radio, posters, cinema etc.; showing special tickets and displays at the **point-of-sale** to sell the goods. *We must make certain that all our promotion activities take place in the order that we planned.* (2) advancement in a job (or rank). *I'm doing so well I feel I'm due for promotion in this job*

◆ (1) Werbung (2) Beförderung

promotional mix methods used by a company to help the sale of its **products** or **services.** It includes advertising, personal selling, **sales promotion, publicity**

◆ Verkaufsförderungsmethoden

proof (1) showing that something is true. *Have you proof that our profits are falling?* (2) a first copy made of a piece of printed matter so that any mistakes can be put right before printing takes place. *I'm checking the proofs of my new novel.* (3) a measure of alcoholic content in a drink (e.g. gin, whisky). *It's 70 per cent proof*

◆ (1) Beweis (2) Korrekturfahne (3) Alkoholgehalt

proof of delivery usually a signature on a **delivery note** which is asked for by the firm sending the goods. Having such a signature is considered proof that the goods actually have been delivered and received

◆ Lieferungsnachweis

property (1) something which is owned. *That suit is my property.* (2) land, buildings which are or can be owned. *This looks like a very valuable piece of property*

◆ (1) Eigentum (2) Grundbesitz

property tax money asked for by the national or local government from a person because of the value of the land, buildings etc. which he/she owns. *See also* **rates**

◆ Vermögenssteuer

proposal something **proposed;** the act of **proposing**

◆ Vorschlag

propose to put forward (a plan, suggestion etc.) for consideration

◆ vorschlagen

proprietary goods: products owned by a company (i.e. only they have the right to make them)

◆ Markenartikel

proprietor an owner, especially of a business. *Who is the proprietor of this hotel?*

◆ Eigentümer

pro rata in proportion; at a certain rate. *Those who sell £100 of goods will get £1 bonus, those who sell £200 will get £2 bonus, and the rest pro rata*

◆ anteilmäßig

prospect *noun* (1) a person who may become a customer. *I want you to list all the prospects in your area.* (2) a hope (of something). *No, there's no prospect of that happening*

◆ (1) potentieller Käufer (2) Aussicht

prospect *verb* to search for gold, silver or other valuable things: *to prospect for oil*

◆ nach Bodenschätzen suchen

prospectus a printed notice which gives details about something, e.g. a college (what course can be studied there), a company (its aims, the amount of money it needs, and which asks the public to buy **shares** in the company)

◆ Prospekt

protectionism a **system** of helping trade inside a country by stopping goods entering the country which may harm that trade

◆ Protektionismus

protective practice *see* **restrictive practice**

protest *noun* a **certificate** (which is proof) that a **bill of exchange** has not been paid as ordered (has been **dishonoured**)

◆ Wechselprotest

protest *verb* to make a **certificate** that a person has refused to pay a **bill of exchange** (has **dishonoured** it). The certificate is usually written by a **notary public**

◆ Wechsel protestieren

protocol a **system** of rules of speech and behaviour which should be followed on certain important occasions such as when heads of state meet each other or when royalty is meeting someone

◆ Protokoll

prototype a first example of a **product** or machine from which other improved ones will be made. *Well, this is just the prototype, but it proves we can make a new computer at less cost than our present one*

◆ Prototyp

provident fund a source of **finance** for sickness, **insurance** and **pension schemes** etc.

◆ Unterstützungskasse

province (1) a division of a country, often for the purposes of government. *Canada is divided into provinces.* (2) **the provinces** the areas of a country away from the capital and other large cities

◆ (1), (2) Provinz

provincial of a **province** or **the provinces**

◆ Provinz-; provinziell

provision (1) **(accounting)** an amount of money set aside for renewing an **asset** (such as a building, machinery etc.) (2) an amount of money set aside for some known need: *provision for bad debts.* (3) *in plural* **provisions** food or food supplies. *We will need to get some provisions for our trip.* (4) a condition in some legal **document,** e.g. a clause in a **contract**

◆ (1), (2) Rücklage (3) Lebensmittel (4) Klausel

proxy an authority to act or sign for another person, e.g. to vote for him/her at a meeting or at an election

◆ Bevollmächtigter

PSV *see* **public service vehicle**

public *noun* (1) people in general. *The great British public.* (2) a particular group of people: *the cinema-going public*

◆ (1) Öffentlichkeit (2) Publikum

public *adjective* connected with people in general or with the government; open to people in general: *a public park; a public library; public ownership of the mines*

◆ öffentlich

public authority a public body employed to do work of benefit to the public and not for private profit. *The town council is a public authority. See also* **local authority**

◆ Behörde

public company a company whose **shares** can be bought or sold on the **stock exchange.** *See also* **public limited company**

◆ ≃ Aktiengesellschaft

public house (*or informal* **pub**) a building where alcoholic drinks can be bought and drunk

◆ Gaststätte

publicise to make widely known

◆ bekanntmachen

publicity any action to attract the public's notice to something, especially by reporting in the **media.** *They had a lot of publicity for the launch of their new product*

◆ Publicity

public limited company (*or* **PLC**) a **limited liability company** whose **shares** can be bought by the public

◆ ≃ Aktiengesellschaft

public ownership ownership of a business or property by the state. *The whole railway is in public ownership. See also* **private enterprise**

◆ Staatseigentum

public relations (*or* **PR**) any actions by an organisation which will improve relations between it and people who are important to it, including the general public. *I think we should improve our Report to our Shareholders — it would be good PR*

◆ Public Relations

public relations officer a person employed by a company to help its **public relations**

◆ PR-Chef

public sector of the economy the property and business activity in the country which is controlled by the state or local government. *See also* **private sector of the economy**

◆ öffentlicher Wirtschaftssektor

public service vehicle (*or* **PSV**) a vehicle which has a **licence** to carry passengers in return for payment, e.g. a bus, taxi

◆ öffentliches Verkehrsmittel

public utility a **service** (e.g. British Gas) or supply **system** (e.g. gas, water) which is used by the general public. In the UK such services are controlled either by the state or local government

◆ öffentlicher Versorgungsbetrieb

public works work paid for by the government to give **services** of use to the general public, e.g. building motorways, hospitals, schools etc.

◆ öffentliche Arbeiten

publish to print and offer (a book, magazine, newspaper etc.) (for sale) to the public (or to some special group). *We will have to publish a new price list for our customers*

◆ veröffentlichen

publisher a person whose business is the **publishing** of books. *He's in the publishing business — he's a publisher of children's books*

◆ Verleger

punch *noun* a tool or machine for making holes in something

◆ Locher

punch *verb* to make (holes) with or as with a **punch**

◆ lochen

punched card a card on which there is information in the form of holes which can be read by a variety of machines

◆ Lochkarte

purchase *verb* to buy. *We have to purchase a new machine*

◆ kaufen

purchase *noun* something bought. *He carried in all his purchases*

◆ Kauf

purchase officer (*or* **purchasing officer**) a person in a company in charge of buying the things the company needs, e.g. materials, oils, paint, machines etc.

◆ Einkaufsleiter

purchase order a form used by a buyer (see **purchase officer**) to detail the goods which a buyer wants from a seller and which is then given to the seller as an order

◆ Bestellformular

purchaser a person who buys

◆ Käufer

purchasing agent a person who buys goods on behalf of someone else for a payment (called a **commission**)

◆ Einkäufer

purchasing office an office in a company where all the buying for the company is carried out

◆ Einkaufsbüro

purchasing officer *see* **purchase officer**

purchasing power the value of money measured by the goods or **services** it can buy. *The purchasing power of the £1 is much less today than ten years ago*

◆ Kaufkraft

Q

qualified acceptance a **bill of exchange** which has conditions attached to it, e.g. as to where it is to be paid or the amount to be paid

◆ bedingtes Akzept

qualified accounts *or* **qualified report** a report by an **auditor** stating that he/she is not satisfied with something in the **accounts** which he/she has **audited**

◆ mit eingeschränktem Bestätigungsvermerk versehener Jahresabschluß

quality control a method of making sure that goods being produced are of the planned standard, usually done by taking **samples** of the goods (and possibly the materials they are made from) and examining them very carefully

◆ Qualitätskontrolle

quango a group of people set up by the government, but not directly controlled by it, with a special responsibility to advise on such matters as the countryside, prices, wages

◆ Gutachterkommission

quantity (1) an amount. *They ordered a quantity of wool from the suppliers.* (2) a large amount or a large number of something. *It is often cheaper to buy in quantity*

◆ (1) Menge (2) große Menge

quantity discount (*or* **quantity rebate**) an amount by which a price is lowered when a large amount of goods is ordered. *If you buy 600 we can offer you a quantity discount*

◆ Mengenrabatt

quantity surveyor a person whose job is to find out how much **labour** and materials will be required to build something

◆ Bausachverständiger

quarantine *verb* to force (a person, animal or thing) to remain separated from others to prevent the spread of disease. *The ship was quarantined*

◆ unter Quarantäne stellen

quarantine *noun* the state of being **quarantined.** *The ship spent ten days in quarantine*

◆ Quarantäne

quarter days *(UK)* the days which come at the end of the four quarters of the year when certain rents or **interests** may become due. In England, Wales and Ireland the days are: 25 March (Lady Day), 24 June (Midsummer Day), 29 September (Michaelmas), 25 December (Christmas Day); in Scotland: 2 February (Candlemas), 15 May (Whitsunday), 1 August (Lammas), 11 November (Martinmas)

◆ Quartalstage

quarterly *adjective* happening every 13 weeks: *quarterly payments*

◆ vierteljährlich

quarterly *noun* a magazine which is published four times a year

◆ Vierteljahresschrift

quartile (**statistics**) the value that lies midway between the lowest value and the middle value in a series of values, e.g. in a list of **accounts** arranged by value; or the value that lies midway between the highest value and the middle value. In other words the quartiles will divide a list of values into four equal parts

◆ Quartil

quarto (1) a size of paper 10 in. × 8 in. (254 mm × 203 mm). (2) a size of paper obtained when a sheet is folded twice, giving eight pages

◆ (1) Quartformat (2) Quart

questionnaire a list of questions used to find out information from people, especially about their likes and dislikes, their opinions and ideas etc.

◆ Fragebogen

queuing theory a **technique** which is used to find out about and thus lessen the amount of time that customers have to queue, e.g. in a **bank, supermarket**

◆ Warteschlangentheorie

quick ratio *see* **liquidity ratio**

quid *(informal)* a **pound (sterling)**

◆ ein Pfund Sterling

quid pro quo (*Latin, meaning* something for something) especially with reference to **negotiations,** something that is given in exchange for something else

◆ Gegenleistung

quire formerly 24, now more usually 25 sheets of paper or one-twentieth of a **ream**

◆ 25 Bogen Papier

quorum a number of people who have to be present at a meeting for its decisions to be effective according to the rules of the meeting

◆ beschlußfähige Versammlung

quota (1) an amount or share of something which someone is allowed to have. *The goods are in short supply and no one can be allowed to receive more than the quota.* (2) a limited amount (of people, goods etc.) allowed into a country by government regulations

◆ (1) Quantum (2) Quote; Kontingent

quota sampling a method of **sampling** in which the **population** is divided into certain groups (e.g. according to age, sex, income etc.). The number of people in each group is decided and then people are chosen for interview on the basis of convenience. *Compare with* **stratified sampling**

◆ Quotenauswahlverfahren

quotation (*or* **quote**) (1) a statement of how much certain goods or a certain **service** will cost, made by the person who will provide the goods or service in response to an inquiry by a possible customer. (2) a statement by a person trading in a certain market (e.g. the **stock market**) of how much something (e.g. **shares**) will cost either to buy or to sell

◆ (1) Preisangebot (2) Kursnotierung

quoted company *see* **listed company**

R

racket a dishonest way of making money in business. *They force the hotels to pay protection money or else they complain loudly about the food in the hotel's restaurant: it's a racket*

◆ Schiebung

rack jobber a **wholesaler** or manufacturer who puts a selection of his goods on show in a shop or store, calling from time to time to replace things that have been sold and collecting his share of the money from the sales

◆ Regalgroßhändler

railhead (the place at) the end of a railway line

◆ Endbahnhof

raise (1) to move to a higher position. (2) to arrange to get (money, a loan etc.). *They were not able to raise enough capital for the new project*

◆ (1) aufsteigen (2) beschaffen

rake-off *(informal)* a share of the profit from a deal, especially a deal which is illegal or when the share is in the form of a **bribe**

◆ (betrügerischer) Gewinnanteil

rally *noun* a recovery in the price of **stocks, shares** or **commodities**

◆ Aufschwung

rally *verb* to make a **rally**

◆ sich erholen

R and D *see* **research and development**

random done by chance without making a deliberate choice. *He tested the goods by selecting a few random examples for close examination. See* **random sampling**

◆ Zufall

random access *see* **direct access**

random sample a group of people or things which have been selected by **random sampling**

◆ Zufalls-Stichprobe

random sampling a **sampling procedure** in which every individual member of the group being **sampled** has an equal chance of being chosen. *See also* **quota sampling**

◆ Zufalls-Stichprobenerhebung

range *noun* (1) the amount by which things vary from the smallest to the largest. *We are looking for suits in the £100 to £150 price range.* (2) a number of different articles that are for sale. *He sells a very wide range of goods*

◆ (1) Spanne (2) Sortiment

range *verb* (1) to vary in price, quantity etc. between certain limits. *Their tyre prices range from £25 to £40.* (2)

to go freely from one place or subject to another. *The discussions ranged over a variety of problems*

◆ (1) sich bewegen (2) kreisen

rank *noun* the position which a person has in an organisation, especially a military or similar organisation. *He holds the rank of general*

◆ Rang

rank *verb* (1) to arrange (people or things) in order according to some principle (usually so that one can choose among them more easily). *The applicants for the job were ranked according to their exam results.* (2) to come into a certain class, above or below other classes. *He ranks as one of the best salesmen we've got*

◆ (1) einstufen (2) zählen zu

ranking the act of **ranking** (meaning 1)

◆ rangmäßige Einordnung

rate *noun* (1) an amount that is paid in exchange for some fixed amount of goods or **services.** *We pay our engineers at a rate of £10 per hour.* (2) a speed; an amount within a certain period of time. *His rate of travel was 50 miles per hour. We make machines at a rate of six per day.* (3) the amount of tax one pays as a percentage of one's **income.** *The tax rate has been lowered from 33⅓% to 30%.* *See also* **basic rate.** (4) the amount of tax one pays for certain public services: *the water rate. See also* **rates.** (5) the amount of **premium** paid or charged for **insurance** as a proportion of the total amount insured

◆ (1) Satz (2) Tempo (3) Steuersatz (4) Abgabe (5) Prämiensatz

rate *verb* (1) to place at a certain level when compared to others. *This is rated to be one of the most successful businesses in the country. He is not highly rated as a businessman.* (2) *(UK)* to give a certain value to (a property) for the purpose of paying local taxes. *See also* **rates**

◆ (1) (ein-) schätzen (2) für die Steuer einschätzen

rateable value *(UK)* the amount which might reasonably be charged for the yearly rent of a property: used as the basis for fixing the amount of **rates** (local taxes) which a property owner has to pay

◆ Steuerwert

rate card a **document** which shows how much it will cost to advertise (depending on size of advertisement, time of advertisement etc.) in newspapers, radio, television, posters etc.

◆ Anzeigenpreisliste

rate of exchange *see* **exchange rate**

rate of return an amount of money (**income,** profit) that is gained from an **investment,** usually expressed as a percentage of the total investment. For example, if a person invests £200 in a bank for a year and gains £20 at the end of that time his rate of return is

$$\frac{20}{200} \times \frac{100}{1} = 10\%$$

◆ Rendite

rates *(UK)* local taxes paid on both private and commercial property. *See also* **rate, rateable value**

◆ Kommunalabgaben

ratification the act of **ratifying** a **contract**

◆ Ratifizierung

ratify to agree to, and take responsibility for, the conditions of (e.g. a **contract** that has been **negotiated** on one's behalf). *The new contract will have to be ratified by the Board of Directors*

◆ ratifizieren

rating a number value which a person or thing has been given in a **rating scale.** *See also* **ratings**

◆ Bewertung

rating scale a method of comparing things, usually by giving each thing a number value. *On this rating scale each employee is given a number from 1 to 5 for the various aspects of his work. See also* **rating**

◆ Bewertungsskala

ratings the **estimate** of the audience of a television or radio broadcast, of special interest to advertisers who buy time on television or radio. *The comedy series has not been doing very well in the ratings. See also* **rating**

◆ Einschaltquote

ratio an amount of one class of people or things, when compared to another. *They produce cars and lorries in a ratio of three to one. See also* **current ratio**

◆ Verhältnis

ratio analysis using the **ratio** method to make various **financial** measurements of a company. *See* Appendix 6

◆ Analyse der Bilanzverhältniszahlen

ration *noun* an amount of something which a person is allowed to have in a time of shortage

◆ Ration

ration *verb* to limit the supply (of goods etc.) by **rationing**

◆ rationieren

rationalisation the act of **rationalising**

◆ Rationalisierung

rationalise to make (something, e.g. a company) more efficient by organising it in a less costly way. *We are rationalising production by having it all done in one larger factory*

◆ rationalisieren

rationing a **system** of making sure that there is a fair distribution of goods which are in short supply by limiting the amount that can be got by any one person, usually done by governments in time of crisis, e.g. war. *See also* **ration**

◆ Rationieren

rat race an organisation, group or society where everyone is in fierce **competition** with everyone else. *Jack is very unhappy with his present firm: he feels he's in the rat race*

◆ ständiger Konkurrenzkampf

raw materials materials which have not yet been manufactured or **processed** in any way. *Industry needs a constant supply of steel, coal and other raw materials*

◆ Rohstoffe

readership the number of people who actually read a publication as distinct from those who get a copy of it. *It has been found that an average three people read every copy of our magazine and so our readership is three times our circulation. See also* **circulation**

◆ Leserschaft

real accounts: ledger accounts which record **assets, capital,** equipment etc.

◆ Bestandskonten

real estate *(mainly US)* things which are owned but which cannot be taken away by the owner, e.g. houses, land

◆ unbewegliches Vermögen

real income the amount of **income** which a person has available to buy goods and **services**

◆ Realeinkommen

realisation of assets the act of selling the **assets** of a company for cash. *See also* **realise** (meaning 2)

◆ Flüssigmachung von Vermögenswerten

realise (1) to be sold for (a certain price). *His property realised several thousand pounds.* (2) to sell (property, **assets** etc.) for cash. *When he* *died, the other partners realised the company's assets*

◆ (1) einbringen (2) flüssigmachen

real time a period of time in which a **computer** is actually **processing data** as it is received. *The airline booking system uses a real-time system to make sure the flights are not overbooked*

◆ Echtzeit

ream a number of sheets of paper, formerly 480, now more usually 500, equal to twenty **quires**

◆ (altes) Ries

rebate a return of part of a sum of money which one has paid. *I've just had an unexpected income tax rebate. See also* **discount**

◆ Rückvergütung

receipt *noun* (1) a piece of paper which states that something has been paid for. *I'll pay you now but I must have a receipt.* (2) the act of receiving (something). *We are in receipt of your letter of 30th May*

◆ (1) Quittung (2) Empfang

receipt *verb* to give proof that (something) has been paid, e.g. by giving one's signature. *Could you receipt this bill?*

◆ quittieren

receivable (1) acceptable for payment. (2) owed, but not yet paid: *accounts receivable*

◆ (1) zulässig (2) ausstehend

receiver (1) a person who is officially appointed to take over the property of a debtor until as much as possible of his debts has been paid. *A receiver has been appointed in the Brook Shipbuilding Company. See also* **official receiver.** (2) a person who accepts stolen goods. *See also* **fence**

◆ (1) Konkursverwalter (2) Hehler

receiving order an instruction from a court appointing an official receiver to take over the property of a person or company that cannot pay his/her/its debts and to call a meeting of the **creditors.** *See also* **bankruptcy**

◆ Konkurseröffnungsbeschluß

reception (1) the act of receiving. (2) the place in a hotel, office etc. where visitors are received. (3) a formal party

◆ (1) Annahme (2) Rezeption (3) Empfang

recession a fall in business activity causing unemployment and other hardships, but not so serious as a **depression.** *See also* **boom, depression, slump, trade cycle**

◆ Rezession

recipient a person who receives something

◆ Empfänger

reciprocal trading a situation where a person who supplies certain goods or **services** to a company promises to buy from it other goods and services in return

◆ Gegenseitigkeitsabkommen

reclaim to make (an area that is not productive, e.g. a desert) into an area that can grow crops etc. *In the Netherlands, a lot of land has been reclaimed from the sea*

◆ urbarmachen

reclamation the act of **reclaiming**

◆ Urbarmachung

recommended retail price (*or* **RRP**) the amount which a manufacturer of **consumer goods** suggests that the goods should be sold for to the consumer. *Compare with* **resale price maintenance**

◆ empfohlener Einzelhandelspreis

record *adjective* the best or greatest ever. *Our factory has achieved record output this year*

◆ Rekord-

record *noun* (1) written account: *a record of these events.* (2) a **disk** (meaning 2) for playing music etc. on a record player. (3) a list of things which someone has done. *He had a good record while he was working for us.* (4) the best or greatest amount. *Our sales have reached a new record. Sales have broken all previous records*

◆ (1) Bericht (2) Schallplatte (3) Leistungen (4) Rekord

for the record so that something can be recorded as having been done. *Just for the record, we should not forget the wonderful job the staff have done*

◆ für die Akten

off the record not for publication, to be kept secret. *I don't think much of his management style, but that's off the record*

◆ inoffiziell

on record publicly known or stated. *He's on record as having actually admitted the results were down*

◆ belegt

record *verb* (1) to put down in writing for future use. *All his decisions have been recorded in these notebooks.* (2) to put (sound) onto a **disk** (meaning 2) or tape. *The managing director recorded his notes for his secretary to type up.* (3) to show on a scale. *The thermometer recorded 30° centigrade*

◆ (1) aufzeichnen (2) aufnehmen (3) verzeichnen

recorded delivery *(UK)* a **Post Office** service by which, for an extra charge, an official record is made of the sending and delivery of a letter or package

◆ eingeschriebene Sendung

recourse (1) the right of a person holding a **bill of exchange** to ask for payment for the bill from the **drawer** or **endorser** if the person who has accepted the bill cannot pay. This right does not exist if the drawer or endorser has written **without recourse** or **sans recours** *(French)* beside his signature. (2) a source of help in time of difficulty. *As a last recourse to get money we had to sell some assets,* i.e. there was no other source of help available. *They eventually had recourse to the stock market*

◆ (1) Regreßanspruch (2) Rückgreifen

recruit *verb* to take on (new soldiers in an army, new workers in a company etc.). *We have started to recruit for our new London store*

◆ rekrutieren

recruit *noun* a soldier who has just joined the army; a new worker in a company etc.

◆ Rekrut

recruitment the act of **recruiting**

◆ Rekrutierung

rectify to put (something) right

◆ berichtigen

red: in the red *(informal)* owing money, in debt. *In spite of all the economies we've made, we're still in the red*

◆ in den roten Zahlen

redeem (1) to become the owner of (something) by paying off money owed on it. (2) to pay off (a loan etc.): *to redeem a mortgage.* (3) to sell (**shares** etc.) for cash. (4) to keep (a promise). (5) to make up for (something one has done wrong or badly)

◆ (1), (2) tilgen (3) verkaufen (4) einhalten (5) wettmachen

redeemable (*or* **callable**) (1) with reference to **bonds, shares** etc., able to be bought back by the person who issued them, usually within certain time limits. (2) of bonds, able to be exchanged for cash

◆ (1) rückkaufbar (2) einlösbar

redeemable preference share a type of **preference share** which can be exchanged for cash or for another share by the issuer at some time in the future

◆ rückkaufbare Vorzugsaktie

redeploy to give (workers) new tasks to do which may sometimes involve **retraining** them. *There is no longer enough work in the department and so some people will have to be redeployed*

◆ anders einsetzen

redeployment the act of **redeploying** workers

◆ Einsatz an einem anderen Arbeitsplatz

redevelop to rebuild, replan (a building, an area)

◆ sanieren

redevelopment the act of **redeveloping**

◆ Sanierung

redraft *verb* to make a second draft or to write something again. *I shall have to redraft this letter*

◆ umformulieren

redraft *noun* (1) a foreign **bill of exchange** which is drawn by the holder of a **dishonoured** bill on the person who issued or **endorsed** the dishonoured bill. The new bill is for the amount of the dishonoured bill plus any expenses that have been involved in **protesting** it. (2) a letter, report etc. which has been written again with some changes

◆ (1) Rikambiowechsel (2) Neufassung

red tape time-wasting rules or **procedures** (especially with reference to government departments). *We've lost two weeks on this delivery because of government red tape*

◆ Bürokratismus

reduce to make smaller; to make less: *to reduce prices*

◆ reduzieren

reduction (1) the act of **reducing.** *We are trying to achieve a reduction in the rate of inflation.* (2) the amount by which something is less or smaller. *I could offer you a slight reduction in price if you pay cash*

◆ (1) Reduzierung (2) Ermäßigung

redundancy (1) the state of being **redundant.** (2) (**computers**) *see* **redundancy check.** (3) (**computers**) the unnecessary keeping of copies of **data**

◆ (1) betriebsbedingte Entlassung von Arbeitskräften (3) Redundanz

redundancy check (**computers**) the use of extra **characters** or **bits** to find mistakes

◆ Redundanzprüfung

redundancy payment the money given to workers who have been made **redundant**

◆ Entlassungsabfindung

redundant (1) unnecessary; not needed, especially with reference to a worker or workers whose labour is no longer needed. *The factory closed down and hundreds were made redundant,* i.e. they were unemployed because their labour was no longer needed. *See also* **redundancy payments.** (2) (**computers, communications**) not strictly necessary but useful when checking for errors. *See also* **redundancy check**

◆ (1) überflüssig; arbeitslos (2) redundant

re-export *verb* to send abroad again (goods which have been **imported**)

◆ wieder ausführen

re-export *noun* (1) something which has been **re-exported.** (2) the act of **re-exporting**

◆ (1) wieder ausgeführte Ware (2) Wiederausfuhr

referee *noun* (1) a person who is given the power to decide in a **dispute.** (2) a person who is named by someone applying for a job, loan etc. as one who can give opinions on the **applicant's** ability, honesty etc. *See also* **reference** (meaning 2). (3) in sport, a person who decides whether a game is being played according to the rules

◆ (1) Schiedsrichter (2) Referenz (3) Schiedsrichter

referee *verb* to act as a **referee**

◆ schiedsrichtern

reference (1) a (usually) written opinion on a person's character, ability, honesty etc. in support of someone's application for a job or a loan etc. *I sent a copy of the reference from my last employer when I wrote my application for the job at the bank.* (2) a person named by the **applicant** as one who will provide such support. *I named my last boss Mr Ford as a reference. See also* **referee** (meaning 2). (3) the act of referring to a book or an article, or part of a book, or article. (4) numbers and/or letters put at the top of a business letter so that it can be filed or found in a file. *The reference for this letter is JWB/757/4*

◆ (1) Empfehlungsschreiben (2) Referenz (3) Verweis (4) Aktenzeichen

refer to drawer a note stamped or written on a cheque by a bank which is refusing to **honour** the cheque for a certain reason (e.g. there is not enough money in the **account** of the person who signed the cheque); the person wishing to cash the cheque must refer to the person who has signed it to find out what the reason is

◆ zurück an den Aussteller

refinancing a method of repaying a loan by taking out another loan

◆ Umschuldung

reflate to **stimulate** (the economy) by increasing the money supply and so increasing employment and business opportunities. *See also* **inflate**

◆ die Konjunktur ankurbeln

reflation the act of **reflating.** *See also* **inflation**

◆ Ankurbelung der Konjunktur

regional development grant *(UK)* an amount of money given by the government to encourage business development in poorer areas of the country

◆ Staatszuschuß zur regionalen Förderung der Wirtschaft

regional employment premium *(UK)* an amount of money given by the government to employers to lessen the cost of employing workers in certain areas of high **unemployment**

◆ regionale Arbeitsplatzprämie

regional planning courses of action by the government to improve jobs, housing, education in certain parts of the country

◆ Regionalplanung

register *noun* (1) an official list: *register of shareholders.* (2) a special kind of **memory location** in a **computer** where information can be stored for a time and/or **processed**

◆ (1), (2) Register

register *verb* (1) to put in a **register** (meaning 1). *His name has been registered on our list of members.* (2) to send by **registered post.** *We had better register this parcel*

◆ (1) eintragen (2) per Einschreiben schicken

registered company a company which is on the official list of the **Registrar of Companies**

◆ eingetragene Gesellschaft

registered mail *see* **registered post**

registered office the official head office of a company as given to the **Registrar of Companies**

◆ eingetragener Gesellschaftssitz

registered post (*or* **registered mail**) *(UK)* a **Post Office** service by which, for an extra charge, letters and parcels are specially delivered and signed for on delivery; **compensation** is paid for loss. *See also* **recorded delivery**

◆ Einschreiben

registered trademark the official **trademark** of a company which has been listed so that no one else can use it

◆ eingetragenes Warenzeichen

register of directors a list which must be kept by every company, giving the directors' names, addresses, nationalities and other information

◆ Vorstands-; Direktorenverzeichnis

register of members a list of those who belong to an organisation

◆ Mitgliederverzeichnis

registrar (1) a person who is in charge of official lists and records. *The Registrar of Companies.* (2) an official who keeps the list of births, marriages and deaths in a particular area. (3) *(mainly US)* an employee of a company who keeps a record of the ownership of the company **shares.** (4) a hospital doctor who is next in **rank** to a **consultant**

◆ (1) Leiter einer Registerbehörde (2) Standesbeamter (3) Registerführer (4) Krankenhausarzt

Registrar of Companies the official who is in charge of recording details of companies **registered** in Britain

◆ Gesellschafts-, Handelsregister

registry (1) a place where records are kept. (2) *(shipping) the* **registering** of a ship's country of origin etc.

◆ (1) Registratur (2) Eintragung ins Schiffsregister

regression analysis (**statistics**) a **technique** by which one kind of change (or changes) can be used to predict another kind of change (or changes). For example, using this technique it might be possible to predict from the increase in **incomes,** the likely increase in video sales

◆ Regressionsanalyse

regressive taxation a method of raising taxes which results in lower-paid workers paying a higher proportion of their wages in tax than higher-paid workers

◆ regressive Besteuerung

regulate to control, to make or keep correct

◆ regulieren

regulation (1) the act of **regulating.** (2) a rule as to how something should be done. *That is against the regulations*

◆ (1) Regulierung (2) Vorschriften

reimburse to repay (a person) for money already spent. *You will be reimbursed for all expenses*

◆ zurückerstatten

reinstate to employ (a person) again in a position after he has been **sacked** or **suspended** from it

◆ wiedereinstellen

reinstatement the act of **reinstating**

◆ Wiedereinstellung

re-insurance an arrangement by which an **insurance company** will lessen its own risk in an insurance by sharing the risk with another insurance company or companies. A common arrangement, for example, when extremely costly things are insured, e.g. large aeroplanes, ships, oil wells, where one insurance company might judge that the risk is too great to take on its own

◆ Rückversicherung

reliability the state of being **reliable.** *These engines are well known for their reliability: they hardly ever break down*

◆ Zuverlässigkeit

reliable able to be trusted; able to be depended on with confidence: *a reliable company; a reliable machine; a reliable worker*

◆ zuverlässig

relief *see* **tax relief**

remit *verb* (1) to send (money etc.) to a person by post. *He used to remit £50 to his parents every month.* (2) *(law)* to send (a case) to another court. *His case was remitted to the local court for a decision.* (3) to send (something) to a person for the necessary action. *This problem has been remitted to Mr Smith and he is working on it.* (4) to free a person from a debt or punishment. *His sentence to life imprisonment has been remitted*

◆ (1) überweisen (2) verweisen (3) weiterleiten (4) erlassen

remit *noun* (1) *(law)* the act of sending a case to another court. (2) *(mainly Scottish)* a matter on which a person is expected to act. *This problem is not within my remit*

◆ (1) Verweisung (2) Aufgabenbereich

remittance (1) the act of sending money etc. by post. (2) the amount of money sent by post, often on a regular basis. *Your remittance should be sent to the address below. See also* **remit** (*verb:* meaning 1)

◆ (1) Überweisung (2) überwiesene Summe

remunerate to pay (a person) for something he has done. *He has been well remunerated for his services*

◆ bezahlen

remuneration (1) the act of **remunerating.** *Does he expect remuneration for these services?* (2) the amount of money paid to a person for something he has done: *very good remuneration*

◆ (1), (2) Bezahlung

rent *noun* the amount paid, usually regularly, for the use of a person's property, especially land and buildings. *I've let my house to a student for a very low rent*

◆ Miete

rent *verb* (1) to pay a person for the use of (property). *He rented the house for £100 per month.* (2) **rent (out)** to let a person use one's property in return for payment. *We rent out these flats for a very reasonable amount. See also* **hire**

◆ (1) mieten (2) vermieten

rental (1) the amount of money paid in rent: *a rental of £100 per month.* (2) the amount of **income** which is received from a property. *These flats have an annual rental value of £10,000.* (3) the amount of money paid for the **hire** of goods: *TV/telephone rental*

◆ (1) Miete (2) Mieteinnahmen (3) Leihgebühr

reorder level the level at which a fresh supply of a particular kind of **product** held in **stock** must be ordered

◆ Nachbestellungspunkt

rep *see* **sales representative**

repeal *verb* to **cancel** (a law). *This Act of Parliament will probably be repealed if the Opposition ever gets into power*

◆ aufheben

repeal *noun* the act of **repealing**

◆ Aufhebung

repeat purchasing the act of buying goods which are in frequent daily or weekly use (e.g. newspapers, bread, cigarettes etc.) and which therefore have to be bought often

◆ Nachkauf

replace to put a new or different thing or person in place of (an old one)

◆ ersetzen

replacement cost the present-day cost of **replacing** an **asset** such as building, machine, car etc.

◆ Wiederbeschaffungskosten

replacement demand the level of sales of a **product** to replace old or worn-out products. For example, the present-day sales of videos are to first-time buyers. When most homes have videos the demand will be mainly for replacement models. *Sales of radios are to satisfy a replacement demand*

◆ Ersatzbedarf

replacement value (**insurance**) the amount it would cost at current prices to buy the thing insured

◆ Wiederbeschaffungswert

reply-paid postcard a type of card which can be posted without having to put a stamp on it, used by companies to make it easy for customers to reply to advertisements etc.

◆ Rückantwortkarte

repossess to take back (property, especially property given under a **hire purchase** agreement), when the conditions of the agreement have not been met. *If you don't pay the rest of the money within a week, the television set will be repossessed*

◆ wieder in Besitz nehmen

representative *adjective* being an example of a group or class. *This is representative of the quality of product which we can deliver*

◆ repräsentativ

representative *noun* a person appointed to act for others. *We will send a representative of the company to the creditors' meeting. See also* **sales representative**

◆ Repräsentant

repudiate (1) to refuse to accept the conditions of (e.g. a **contract**). *The Board of Directors repudiated the contract which their negotiators had agreed.* (2) to refuse to pay (a debt)

◆ (1) (Vertrag) nicht anerkennen (2) (Schuld) nicht anerkennen

repudiation the act of **repudiating**

◆ Nichtanerkennung

reputed ownership a situation which can happen in case of **bankruptcy,** where someone (A) has been allowed to keep goods belonging to someone else in his possession, with the result that A's **creditors** think that the goods really belong to A: if A then becomes bankrupt, his creditors are allowed to have those goods considered as among A's possessions, and so they may be used to help pay his debts

◆ vermutetes Eigentum

requisition *verb* (1) to make an official demand for the use of (something that is needed) with or without payment. *During the war many cars were requisitioned by the military.* (2) to make a request for (the supply of materials etc.). *We shall have to requisition some more typing paper*

◆ (1) beschlagnahmen (2) anfordern

requisition *noun* (1) the act of **requisitioning.** (2) a **document** which requisitions something

◆ (1) Beschlagnahme; Anforderung (2) Anforderungsschein

resale price maintenance (*or* **RPM**) a system by which the minimum price for a class of goods is decided by the manufacturers (perhaps in agreement with **retailers**), and no **retailer**/shopowner or dealer is allowed to sell below that price. *In Britain, resale price maintenance is illegal as far as most goods are concerned*

◆ Einhaltung von Wiederverkaufspreisen

rescind *(formal)* to make no longer effective, **cancel** (a law, **contract**)

◆ annullieren

research and development (*or* **R and D**) the part of a company's activities concerned with discovering new **products** for the company and for making **technical** improvements in existing products. *See also* **new product development, product development**

◆ Forschung und Entwicklung

reserve currency a currency which can easily be changed into other currencies without loss and therefore can be used as a part of a country's **official reserves.** *The US dollar, the British pound, the German deutschmark and the Japanese yen have all been used as reserve currencies at some time*

◆ Reservewährung

reserve for bad debts an amount of money set aside to cover debts which are expected not to be paid. *The reserve for bad debts in the profit and loss account of most companies has increased because of the poor economic situation*

◆ Wertberichtigung auf Forderungen

reserve price *(UK)* the lowest price which a person who has put something up for **auction** is willing to accept. (*US and Scottish* **upset price**)

◆ Mindestpreis

reserves that part of the profit of a company which is not paid out to the **shareholders** but which is kept by the company for use for its **fixed** or **current assets.** *See also* **reserve currency, official reserves** and Appendix 2

◆ Rücklagen

reserve stock *see* **buffer stock**

residue (1) what is left of something. (2) what is left of a dead person's **estate** after all debts, expenses and special **bequests** have been paid. *The residue of his estate was divided equally among his children*

◆ (1) Rest (2) reiner Nachlaß

resolution a formal decision taken at a meeting. *A resolution was passed that all fees would be doubled. See also* **motion**

◆ Resolution

resources *plural* (1) the source of wealth in an area, e.g. agriculture, materials etc. *South America has vast natural resources.* (2) anything which belongs to an area, a company or a person and which can be used to advantage. *We shall have to make full use of our financial resources in the development plan*

◆ (1) Bodenschätze (2) Ressourcen

respondent (1) a person who has to answer to a **charge** that has been brought against him in law. *He was named as the respondent by someone who is suing him for £100,000.* (2) a person who answers questions in **market research**

◆ (1) Antragsgegner (2) Befragter

response (1) the act of replying. *I called but there was no response.* (2) a showing of interest (in buying a **product** etc.). *We advertised our product on television but so far there has been very little response*

◆ (1) Antwort (2) Resonanz

responsibility (1) the state of being **responsible.** (2) something that one is **responsible** for. *His new job carries heavy responsibilities*

◆ (1) Verantwortung (2) Pflichten

responsible (1) in charge (of). *You will be responsible for the conduct of the new sales campaign.* (2) capable of being blamed. *If anything goes wrong, you'll be held responsible.* (3) reliable: *a responsible worker.* (4) needing the ability to make decisions for which one will be held responsible: *a responsible position*

◆ (1), (2) verantwortlich (3) zuverlässig (4) verantwortungsvoll

restraint of trade a situation in which an employee is forbidden by **contract** to use knowledge got in his present employment for the benefit of another competing firm that he might work for in the future

◆ Wettbewerbsbeschränkung

restrictive endorsement a special kind of **endorsement** written on a cheque, **bill of exchange** etc. which restricts the rights of the person being given the cheque etc. (the **endorsee**)

◆ Rektaindossament

restrictive trade practice (*or* **restrictive practice**) an arrangement among companies about prices, production, shares, shares of the market etc. which means that there is less **competition** between them in these areas and (usually) more profit. *See also* **ring**

◆ wettbewerbsbeschränkende Geschäftspraktiken

retail *noun* the sale of goods direct to the general public, especially in shops, stores and by **mail order.** *See also* **wholesale** *(noun)*

◆ Einzelhandel

retail *adverb* (to sell) directly to the public. *You can buy it retail. See also* **wholesale** *(adverb)*

◆ im Einzelhandel

retail *verb* (1) to sell goods directly to the public. *He retails cigarettes and cigars.* (2) to be sold to the public (at a certain price). *These chairs retail at £50 each. See also* **wholesale** *(verb)*

◆ (1) im Einzelhandel verkaufen (2) im Einzelhandel kosten

retail *adjective* connected with the sale of goods directly to the general public: *the retail trade, retail prices. See also* **wholesale** *(adjective)*

◆ Einzelhandels-

retail audit (*or* **shop audit**) an examination of a **sample** of **retail** shops to give information on sales, **market shares,** prices, **distribution** etc.

◆ Einzelhändlerbefragung

retailer a person who sells goods directly to the public, e.g. a shopowner. *See also* **wholesaler**

◆ Einzelhändler

retailers' cooperative a number of **retailers** who group themselves together in order to keep costs down, e.g. by buying goods in **bulk,** by advertising together

◆ Einzelhändlereinkaufsgenossenschaft

retail outlet a place where goods are sold direct to the public, e.g. a shop or **supermarket.** *We are trying to increase the number of retail outlets for this new brand*

◆ Einzelhandelsgeschäft

retail price the price at which a **product** is sold by a **retailer**

◆ Einzelhandelspreis

retail price index a measure of changes in the price of goods from a certain point in time: if the average price of a range of goods at that point = 100, then changes in prices can be stated above or below that figure (usually above, because of **inflation**). *The retail price index has gone up from 100 to 174 in the past ten years*

◆ Einzelhandelspreisindex

retained earnings (*or* **retained income** *or* **undistributed profits**) profits which are not paid out to **shareholders** but are kept within a company so that they can be used if they are needed. *See also* **reserves**

◆ einbehaltene Gewinne

retainer (1) money paid for **services** to be used when needed. (2) money paid to a **barrister** for his **services**

◆ (1) Honorarvorschuß (2) Anwaltshonorar

retire (1) to (cause to) stop working, usually because a person has reached a certain age. *In Britain, most men retire at the age of 65.* (2) to leave a position one has been elected to, either by choice or because one has to. *The chairman and secretary have to retire at the end of this year, as they are only allowed to serve for two years.* (3) to pay (a **bill of exchange**) on the due date or earlier

◆ (1) in den Ruhestand treten (2) Amt niederlegen (3) einlösen

retirement the state of being **retired** from work. *His colleagues wish him many happy years of retirement*

◆ Ruhestand

retrain to train (a person) to do a new job, use new skills, or enter a new profession. *It is thought that in the future people may have to be retrained for new jobs two or three times in their working life*

◆ umschulen

return (1) the amount of money which is gained on an **investment,** often expressed as a percentage. *These bonds guarantee a return of 10%. See also* **return on investment.** (2) a report, especially one with facts and figures. *I want the sales returns for the last six months,* i.e. details of what we have sold in that period. *Have you sent in your tax return?* (3) *in plural* **returns** goods which haven't been sold and which are sent back to the **manufacturer** or **wholesaler**

◆ (1) Ertrag (2) Aufstellung (3) Retouren

return on investment (*or* **ROI** *or* **return on capital**) profit expressed as a percentage of the amount of money that has been **invested** in a company; often used as a method of judging how successful a company has been. *We are not expecting a very good return on investment this year*

◆ Anlageverzinsung

revaluation an increase in the value of a currency with regard to other currencies. The term is used when **fixed exchange rates** are in use, and the increase in value is decided by the government. *See also* **devaluation**

◆ Aufwertung

revenue (1) **income** from the sale of a company's **products** or **services,** from the sale of **assets,** or from **investments.** *Our revenue this year is up 10%. See also* **sales revenue.** (2) the amount of money a government raises by taxes. *See also* **Inland Revenue**

◆ (1) Einnahmen (2) Steueraufkommen

revenue account (**book-keeping**) a statement showing the **income** (**revenue**) and expenses of a business

◆ Ertragskonto

revenue expenditure money spent on running a business (compared with money spent on buying **assets**). *See also* **capital expenditure**

◆ Betriebsausgaben

reverse takeover a situation in which a smaller company makes a **takeover bid** for a larger company

◆ Übernahme einer größeren durch eine kleinere Gesellschaft

revoke *(formal)* to **cancel.** *This regulation has now been revoked*

◆ widerrufen

revolving credit (*or* **continuous credit**) a **system** by which the borrower borrows money up to a certain limit, and while the loan is being paid back, may borrow up to that limit again without **negotiating** a new loan

◆ Revolving-Kredit

rig *noun* a special large platform and **drill** used for getting oil and natural gas out of the earth or from the sea bed

◆ Förderturm; Bohrinsel

rig *verb (informal)* (1) to control prices, **shares** etc. in a **fraudulent**

way. *It is said that the prices of some of these commodities have been rigged, so don't buy them.* (2) **rig the market** to cause the prices of **shares** etc. to go up or down so as to make an unfair profit. *He rigged the market by buying so many shares that their value went up to far more than they were worth*

◆ (1) manipulieren (2) Kursniveau künstlich beeinflussen

rights issue the act of allowing **shareholders** to buy extra **shares** in a company at a cheaper price, usually according to the number of shares they already hold, e.g. one share for every two shares held. *The shares of that company have risen in value because a rights issue is expected*

◆ Bezugsrechtsemission

ring a group of businessmen who agree not to compete with one another but to keep prices at a level which allows them to make a large profit. *See also* **restrictive practice**

◆ Ring

risk *noun* (1) a danger. *If you invest your money in that company there is a risk that you might lose it all. See also* **calculated risk.** (2) a type of loss that can be **insured** against: *fire, injury and other risks.* (3) a thing or person considered in terms of a possible **insurance claim.** *He is a good risk,* i.e. it's not likely that a **claim** will be made because of him

◆ (1) – (3) Risiko

risk *verb* to take a chance with. *He risked his whole fortune to save the company*

◆ riskieren

risk analysis a **technique** of judging the likely good and harmful results of management decisions, especially in terms of how the various harmful possibilities might affect the company

◆ Risikoanalyse

risk capital (*or* **venture capital**) (1) the money **invested** by the **ordinary shareholders** of a company. *See also* **equity capital.** (2) the money invested in a **project** with a high risk of failure but with very high profits if successful, e.g. mining shares, oil shares

◆ (1) Eigenkapital (2) Risikokapital

risk manager (**insurance**) a person who examines various risks which his company is engaged in (**insuring** against fire, death, accident etc.)

◆ für Geschäftsrisiken verantwortliche Führungskraft

rival brand a competing make of goods. *We have to sell these beans cheaply because there are several rival brands*

◆ Konkurrenzmarke

robot a machine used to do work usually done by a person and which acts like a person, e.g. in its range of activities. *See also* **automation**

◆ Roboter

robotics the making and using of **robots**

◆ Robotertechnik

ROI *see* **return on investment**

role conflict a situation when a person, e.g. a manager, is expected to carry out two different kinds of activity which interfere with one another. *You may find that being a foreman and also being the trade union representative will give rise to some role conflict*

◆ Rollenkonflikt

role-play exercise a method of training in which the **trainees** take the parts of various people involved in a business situation, e.g. customer and salesman

◆ Rollenspiel

rolling plan a plan for a certain period of time (e.g. five years) which is examined and brought up to date at regular intervals, e.g. every year

◆ rollierende Planung

rolling stock the engines, carriages, vans etc. used by a railway

◆ rollendes Material

ROP advertisement *see* **run-of-paper advertisement**

round: in round figures (*or* **in round numbers**) to the nearest 10, 50, 100 etc.; roughly correct(ly). *Could you give me the year's trading results, in round figures?*

◆ in runden Zahlen

route card (*or* **route sheet**) a **document** which goes with something that is being manufactured and shows the different **processes** which it has to go through and where it has to be taken to for these processes to be done

◆ Arbeitsablaufkarte

royalty an amount of money paid to an author etc. for the use of his **copyright,** to the owner of an invention for the use of his **patent,** usually a certain amount for each thing sold. *The author gets a royalty of 10% of the selling price of each book sold*

◆ Tantieme

run: (1) **run on a bank** a situation where a bank's customers lose confidence in a bank and therefore all try to take out their money at the same time. (2) **run on the pound** a situation where people want to change the pound into other currencies as quickly as possible

◆ (1) Ansturm auf eine Bank (2) Ansturm auf das Pfund

runaway inflation *see* **galloping inflation**

running costs (1) money that is needed to keep a business going from day to day, e.g. wages, heating etc. *Highly automated factories are usually expensive to buy but have low running costs.* (2) money needed to keep machinery of any kind in use. *This car uses very little petrol so the running costs are low*

◆ (1) laufende Kosten (2) Unterhaltungskosten

run-of-paper advertisement (*or* **ROP advertisement**) advertisement that can be put anywhere in a magazine or newspaper and therefore should cost less

◆ Anzeige, deren Plazierung vom Verleger bestimmt wird

S

sack *noun* (1) a large bag made of coarse cloth, plastic etc., especially one used for holding grain etc. (2) **the sack** the act of **sacking:** *to get the sack*

◆ (1) Sack (2) Entlassung

sack *verb* to dismiss (a person) from a job. *When the theft was discovered he got sacked from his job as a manager*

◆ entlassen

safe deposit (*or* **safety deposit**) a place (often a bank) where valuable things may be left and kept safe for the person leaving them (the **depositor**)

◆ Tresorraum

safe deposit box (*or* **safety deposit box**) a box in a **safe deposit** in which things are kept for the **depositor:** he is usually given a key to open the box

◆ Banksafe

safety officer an employee in an organisation who is responsible for making sure that the health and safety of the workers are protected as far as possible

◆ für Fragen des betrieblichen Gesundheits- und Unfallschutzes zuständiger Mitarbeiter

safety stock *see* **buffer stock**

salaried paid by means of a **salary** (rather than **wages**)

◆ Gehalts-

salary a fixed regular payment for work done, usually paid monthly but often expressed as so much per year. *Her salary was £20,000 per year. See also* **wages**

◆ Gehalt

salary review an examination of the amount of money which an employee earns in terms of his work, the rate of **inflation** etc., to see whether he should be paid more and, if so, how much. *Many workers have an annual salary review*

◆ Gehaltsüberprüfung

sale (1) the act of giving goods in exchange for money. *There are laws which apply to the sale of food within certain times. He made a sale every five minutes, on average.* (2) the selling of goods at lowered prices. *This store holds a sale in January.* (3) an **auction.** *Some goods have been damaged by fire so we are holding a sale to see how much we get for them.* (4) the amount of goods sold. *The sale of television sets has been falling over the last few years*

◆ (1) Verkauf (2) Ausverkauf (3) Auktion (4) Absatz

sale and leaseback to get **capital** (cash) for one's business by selling one's business property and then renting it from the new owner for a certain period

◆ Rückvermietung durch die Leasinggesellschaft an den Verkäufer

sale or return a method of selling where a **retailer** or a **wholesaler** receives goods for sale on the basis that he will pay only for goods that are sold, the unsold goods being returned within a certain agreed time

◆ Kauf mit zeitlich begrenztem Rückgaberecht

sales aid any material which a **sales representative** can use to persuade customers to buy his goods, e.g. **leaflets, display advertising**

◆ Verkaufshilfe

sales analysis (1) the act of carefully examining all the details about the sale of goods. *A careful sales analysis will show us which markets to concentrate on.* (2) a table or diagram showing the main facts about the sale of goods within a certain period. *The sales analysis indicates that sales have been steadily improving since January*

◆ (1) Verkaufsanalyse (2) Analyse der Verkaufsergebnisse

sales audit an **analysis** of sales according to type of goods sold, areas where the sales have been made, type of **distribution channel** etc.

◆ Absatzprüfung

sales budget an **estimate** of the amount of goods which will be sold over a certain period of time, and also an estimate of the cost of reaching this level of sales; actual sales and costs will be measured against the **budget** at regular intervals

◆ Absatzplan

sales campaign planned activity to increase sales, usually for a certain **product,** area or type of customer. *Our customer is going to be mounting a big sales campaign in the London area next August. See also* **sales drive**

◆ Verkaufskampagne

sales conference a formal meeting of all the employees of a company connected with the selling of the company's **products,** in order to discuss past achievements, future **targets,** new sales **techniques** etc. *See also* **sales meeting**

◆ Versammlung des Verkaufsstabs

sales control the **process** by which the success of **sales representatives** is measured (e.g. the average value of sales, new **accounts** opened etc.)

◆ Absatzkontrolle

sales costs expenses which come directly from the attempt to sell goods to customers. *We are trying to cut down on sales costs by making fewer sales calls, but selecting our possible customers more carefully*

◆ Absatzkosten

sales drive a greater-than-usual effort to increase sales over a certain period. *Sales have been falling recently, so we shall be mounting a big sales drive soon. See also* **sales campaign**

◆ Verkaufskampagne

sales engineer a person with specialised **technical** knowledge of machinery etc. which helps him to sell **products** of that type

◆ Verkaufsingenieur

sales feature *see* **product feature**

sales figures a list of numbers of sales along with their totals, averages etc.

◆ Absatzziffern

sales folder a file or similar container which contains a collection of sales material

◆ Vertretermappe

sales force the **sales representatives** of a company

◆ Vertreterstab

sales forecast an **estimate** in advance of the amount of likely sales of a company's **products**

◆ Absatzprognose

sales incentive something which will encourage a **sales representative** or a **wholesaler** or a **retailer** to sell more. *As a special sales incentive, all retailers who increase their sales by 10% will be given special discounts*

◆ Verkaufsanreiz

sales inquiry a request for further information about a **product** from a possible customer

◆ Anfrage

saleslady *see* **salesman**

sales literature anything printed which helps to sell a **product.** *I always carry some pamphlets and similar sales literature*

◆ Verkaufsliteratur

salesman / saleslady / saleswoman/salesperson (1) a person who sells goods direct to customers in a shop or store. *Ask the salesman at that counter over there: I'm sure he'll be able to help you.* (2) **— sales representative**

◆ (1) Verkäufer/Verkäuferin

sales manager a person in charge of a group of **sales representatives** and responsible for all aspects of selling a company's **products**

◆ Verkaufsleiter

salesmanship the **technique** of persuading possible customers to buy something; the ability to do so. *His salesmanship has been the main reason for our increased success*

◆ Verkaufstüchtigkeit

sales manual a book or booklet given to a **sales representative** which contains information that will be useful to him in performing his duties

◆ Vertriebshandbuch

sales meeting a regular coming together of a group of **sales representatives** in order to review past sales and discuss plans for the future. *We hold our sales meetings usually every month. See also* **sales conference**

◆ Handelsvertreterversammlung

salesperson *see* **salesman**

sales planning the **process** of deciding on the details necessary to achieve sales **targets**

◆ Absatzplanung

sales promotion methods of encouraging sales, e.g. by using **com-**

petitions, free gifts etc.

◆ Absatzförderung

sales prospect a person or company that is likely to buy a certain product. *The sales manager gave his representatives a list of sales prospects*

◆ potentieller Kunde

sales quota the amount of goods that should be sold within a given period of time by a **sales representative,** or within a certain area, or with regard to a certain **product** etc. *All the salesmen exceeded their sales quotas last month*

◆ Absatzquote

sales representative (*or* **representative** *or* **rep**) a person whose job it is to sell a company's **products** to possible customers

◆ Handelsvertreter

sales revenue money received for goods sold over a certain period of time. *Compare with* **sales volume**

◆ Umsatzerträge

sales tax a type of tax which is collected on behalf of a government by the person selling the goods: the tax is added to the price of the goods. *See* **value-added tax**

◆ Umsatzsteuer

sales territory the area of the country or part of the market within which a **sales representative** has to work. *We have divided the country into eight sales territories, with a sales representative in each*

◆ Absatzgebiet

sales volume (*or* **volume of sales**) amount of goods sold. *Our sales volume has doubled since last year. Compare with* **sales revenue**

◆ Verkaufsvolumen

saleswoman *see* **salesman**

salvage *noun* (1) the act of saving ships and/or their **cargoes** from destruction at sea. (2) the act of saving any goods from destruction, e.g. by fire. (3) money paid to a person who rescues a ship and/or its **cargo** from destruction. (4) goods rescued from destruction at sea or from fire, flooding etc. *There is a sale of fire salvage lines being held tomorrow*

◆ (1) Bergung (2) Rettung (3) Bergelohn (4) Bergungsgut

salvage *adjective* connected with saving goods etc. in this way: *a salvage operation; salvage money*

◆ Bergungs-

salvage *verb* (1) to save (ships, their **cargoes** or other goods) from destruction. *The ship was salvaged even while the storm was still raging.* (2) to save from any kind of danger; to make good any kind of loss. *The failed businessman tried to salvage something of his reputation by repaying some of his debts*

◆ (1) bergen (2) retten

sample *verb* (1) to take (a small part of something) in order to judge the whole thing. *Would you care to sample this fruit?* (2) to test a small number of people who are typical of the whole group being examined

◆ (1) probieren (2) Stichprobe machen

sample *noun* (1) a small part of something which can be taken as typical of the whole thing. *Sales representatives often take samples of products to their customers. A chemist analysed a sample of the goods to see if the customer's complaint was true.* (2) a (usually small) amount of a **product** given free to possible customers to encourage them to buy. (3) (**statistics**) a number of people who are typical of the whole group being investigated

◆ (1) Warenmuster (2) Warenprobe (3) Sample

sample survey a type of investigation in which only a typical part of the total group to be examined is investigated. *See also* **random**

sampling, quota sampling, stratified sampling

◆ Stichprobenerhebung

sampling frame information about a group (i.e. **universe**) that is to be **sampled,** which will make it easier to identify which members of the group will be **surveyed**

◆ Stichprobenplanung

sampling procedure a method of finding out information about a large group of people by actually questioning only a small number of them. *See also* **quota sampling, random sampling**

◆ Stichprobenverfahren

sanction *noun* (1) permission (to do something). *You can only export these goods with the special sanction of the government.* (2) *in plural* **sanctions** actions taken against a country, usually by a group of other countries, in order to force the country concerned to do something. *The country was subjected to economic sanctions because it was encouraging terrorism*

◆ (1) Genehmigung (2) Sanktionen

sanction *verb* to allow, permit. *The committee has sanctioned our use of the building until midnight*

◆ genehmigen

sandwich course a method of organising studies so that the students spend part of their time at a college or university and part of their time in a place of work (office, factory etc.). *My son is doing a sandwich course in accountancy at the local polytechnic*

◆ Ausbildungsgang, bei dem sich Theorie und Praxis verbinden

sans recours *see* **recourse**

save (1) to avoid wasting; to avoid using up. *Save fuel! Save time by using the phone.* (2) to put (money) into a bank etc. instead of spending it. *I try to save 10% of my salary.* (3) (**computers**) to **store** (**data**) in such a way that it can be used again later

◆ (1), (2) sparen (3) speichern

savings money which has been saved. *His savings amounted to over £50,000*

◆ Ersparnisse

savings account an **account** for personal savings, sometimes with a slightly higher **interest rate** than a **deposit account**

◆ Sparkonto

savings bank a type of bank which is intended to help ordinary people to save. *See also* **trustee savings bank**

◆ Sparkasse

scab *see* **blackleg**

scarcity value a situation where something is valuable or expensive simply becuase it cannot be easily got. *Sometimes useless things are sold for high prices simply because of their scarcity value*

◆ Seltenheitswert

scatter diagram a chart on which the frequency of the occurrence of **data** is recorded as points or dots (small round marks): it can be seen at a glance what sort of pattern is formed by the data

◆ Streudiagramm

scenario (1) a short description of a play, film etc. giving the main details about what happens, where the action takes place, and so on. (2) an imaginary description of what might be the situation if certain possible things happened. *Let's try a scenario of what would happen if our sales doubled*

◆ (1) Szenarium (2) Szenario

schedule *noun* (1) a list, especially one showing when certain things should be done or should happen; a timetable: *an airline schedule. You must follow this schedule exactly*

Our visitor is behind schedule/ahead of schedule/on schedule (i.e. late/early/exactly on time). (2) a list, added to a legal **document** listing things which are mentioned in the document but which may be changed from time to time

◆ (1) (Zeit-) Plan (2) Anhang

schedule *verb* to arrange for something to happen at a certain time. *You are scheduled to speak at the Town Hall tonight*

◆ planen

scheduled flight a flight which is on the regular timetable of an airline

◆ Linienflug

scientific management a **system** of applying scientific rules to management. *See also* **operations research**

◆ wissenschaftliche Betriebsführung

scrap *noun* (1) a small piece of something: *a scrap of paper.* (2) used metal etc. which is available to be used again. *These old cars are only fit for scrap*

◆ (1) Stückchen (2) Altmaterial

scrap *verb* (1) to destroy; to do away with. *We are going to scrap all these old ways of doing things and try some new techniques.* (2) to make into **scrap** metal. *Just scrap these machines and see what you can sell them for*

◆ (1) zum alten Eisen legen (2) verschrotten

screen (1) to decide which people who have applied for a post should be **interviewed.** *After we've finished screening, we'll draw up the interview timetable.* (2) to check on (employees or possible employees) in defence or similar occupations where security is important to make sure that they are loyal (faithful to their country) and dependable. (3) to check (a new **product** or idea) against certain **criteria** at an early stage so as to check whether it is worth spending time and money on developing it

◆ (1) aussieben (2) überprüfen (3) prüfen

scrip issue *see* **bonus issue**

script *noun* (1) handwriting: *a very clear script.* (2) a method of writing or printing: *Roman script, Arabic script.* (3) the words of a play, speech etc. to be spoken by actors, politicians etc. *He writes scripts for television.* (4) an answer paper written by someone in an examination

◆ (1) Handschrift (2) Schrift (3) Text (4) schriftliche Arbeit

script *verb* to write a **script** for: *to script what someone will say*

◆ den Text schreiben zu

seal *verb* (1) to put one's **seal** on (something) to show that it has one's approval. (2) to close up (an envelope etc.) to make it impossible to get at the contents without tearing or breaking

◆ (1) besiegeln (2) versiegeln

seal *noun* (1) a mark on material (usually red wax) to show that the **document** it is attached to has been written with the approval of the person making the mark. *The King's seal was attached to the letter.* (2) a special mark made on certain **documents** from a company to show that they have been **issued** by the company: it is known as the common seal or company seal and a record of all such documents must be kept. (3) a solid thing such as a ring or stamp which makes such a mark. *He kept the company seal in a safe.* (4) something which keeps a letter or parcel etc. closed until it reaches its destination. *This glue will make a good seal.* (5) **under seal** kept in a locked place

◆ (1), (3) Siegel (2) Firmensiegel (4) Versiegelung (5) unter Verschluß

sealed-bid tender a method of offering to perform a **contract** by which each offer is put in a **sealed** envelope; at a certain fixed time all the offers are opened together and the best offer can be accepted

◆ Submissionsangebot im versiegelten Umschlag

seasonal adjustment the act of allowing for **seasonality,** e.g. in **sales figures.** *Sales have remained very steady this year, after seasonal adjustment*

◆ Saisonberichtigung

seasonal discount a lowering of the price of **products** to **retailers** at times when sales are usually low in order to encourage business. *We are trying to even out our sales over the year by offering seasonal discounts*

◆ Saisonabschlag

seasonality changes in sales for a **product** which happen at the same time every year. *Seasonality is a major factor in the tourist industry*

◆ Saisonbedingtheit

second *verb* to support (a **proposal** put forward by someone else) at a meeting. *Will you second the motion?*

◆ befürworten

secondary data: data taken from published sources of information and not gathered specially for the purpose. *See also* **primary data**

◆ Sekundärdaten

secondary picket a group of **strikers** who try to stop other workers from going into a factory, office etc. which is not directly involved in the **dispute.** *The coal miners decided to set up some secondary pickets outside the electricity generating stations*

◆ Streikposten bei einem nur mittelbar beteiligten Betrieb

secondary picketing act of setting up **secondary pickets**

◆ Bestreikung eines nur mittelbar beteiligten Betriebs

seconder a person who **seconds** a **proposal** at a meeting

◆ Befürworter

second-hand owned or used already

◆ aus zweiter Hand

second mortgage an agreement by which a person borrowing money gives his property as **security** for a second time, on the condition that the holder of the first **mortgage** has first claim if the borrower cannot pay his debts

◆ zweite Hypothek

secretary (1) a person who handles the paperwork for a person or company by typing letters, filing correspondence etc. (2) a person who does similar work for a club or society. (3) the minister at the head of some government departments: *the Home Secretary.* (4) a high-ranking civil servant. (5) *see* **company secretary**

◆ (1) Sekretär(in) (2) Schriftführer(in) (3) Minister(in) (4) Staatssekretär(in)

sector a division of something. *See also* **private sector, public sector of the economy**

◆ Sektor

secured creditor a person who is owed money but has a legal right to an amount of the borrower's property which is equal to (or more than) the amount of money he is owed

◆ abgesicherter Gläubiger

security (1) the state of being safe from danger or loss: *to be in the security of one's own home.* (2) protection against criminal acts, e.g. theft. *My firm has to spend thousands of pounds on security every year.* (3) property which is promised to a person lending money if the borrower cannot pay. *He put up his house and car as security for the loan.* (4) a **certificate** of ownership of **stocks, bonds** etc. for which repayment is **guaranteed:** *government securities*

◆ (1) Sicherheit (2) Sicherheitsvorkehrungen (3) Sicherheit (4) Wertpapiere

security of tenure the right to keep one's job or property provided certain conditions are met. *Any lecturer in this college who is employed for more than two years has automatic security of tenure*

◆ Kündigungsschutz

segmentation (*or* **market segmentation**) the dividing of a market into various groups (or **segments**), which will make it easier to direct a **product** at that section of the market, e.g. the age of the customers, their leisure interests, their occupations. *After putting segmentation into effect, we decided on two entirely different advertising campaigns to sell our product to different parts of the world*

◆ Marktaufteilung

selection board a group of people who have been given the duty of choosing the best person (or persons) for a job. *I have been given an interview for that job I wanted: I come up before the selection board on Monday*

◆ Bewerbungsausschuß

selection interview a meeting between the person (or persons) applying for a job and the person (or persons) who have to decide on who is the most suitable

◆ Einstellungsgespräch

self-assessment questions a type of question used in some learning situations, in which the student can check on his own progress by testing his knowledge against certain questions which he corrects himself

◆ Selbsteinschätzungsfragen

self-completion questionnaire (**market research**) a method of getting information in which the answers to a list of questions are filled in by the customer, member of the public etc. himself and not (as is usually the case) by an **interviewer**

◆ Fragebogen, der vom Befragten selbst auszufüllen ist

self-employed person a person who is working for himself and is not the employee of someone else. *In Britain, being a self-employed person means that you are taxed in a different way from those who work for someone else*

◆ selbständiger Erwerbstätiger

self-financing of a business, **operating** in such a way that the costs of buying new equipment, **shares** in other companies and similar **expenditure** are paid out of **revenue** (and not e.g. by borrowing)

◆ Eigenfinanzierung

self-liquidating (1) of a loan, being able to be paid back with **interest** from the profits of whatever business the money was borrowed for. *He had to borrow the money to buy his stock, but the loan was self-liquidating: in six months he had repaid it from his profits.* (2) of a **sales promotion,** where something is offered at a price which covers the cost of the promotion

◆ (1) sich selbst amortisierend (2) kostendeckend

self-service store a type of shop where the customer picks up his/her own choice of goods from the shelves, and pays for the goods when leaving. *See also* **supermarket, superstore, hypermarket**

◆ Selbstbedienungsladen

sell *verb* (1) to give (something) to someone else for money. *He's sold his house for £50,000.* (2) to be bought. *These goods are selling well,* i.e. many people want to buy them. (3) to deal or trade in. *Do you sell furniture in this store?* (4) to persuade people to accept. *He sold the government the idea of building a canal.* (5)

to be employed in the selling of. *He sells cars*

◆ (1) verkaufen (2) sich verkaufen (lassen) (3) führen (4), (5) verkaufen

sell *noun see* **hard sell, soft sell**

sell-by date the date by which a **product,** especially food, should be sold before it becomes unfit for use

◆ Haltbarkeitsdatum

seller's market a situation where there is a great demand for some **product,** giving an advantage to anyone selling it. *This is a good time to put your house up for sale: it's a seller's market*

◆ Verkäufermarkt

selling cost an amount of money which has to be paid out, e.g. for advertising, in order to sell a **product.** *See also* **distribution cost**

◆ Vertriebskosten

sell short to enter into an agreement to sell something now which one does not yet possess, because one expects to be able to buy it more cheaply than the agreed selling price. *I'm selling these shares short: the agreed price is £10 per share but I expect to be able to buy them at £9 before then*

◆ Leerverkauf vornehmen

seminar a meeting of an educational nature in which ideas are exchanged and discussed

◆ Seminar

semi-skilled worker a **manual worker** who has had a limited amount of training but not enough to qualify him as a craftsman

◆ angelernter Arbeiter

semi-variable cost a type of cost which increases only if the amount of goods produced or sold increases by a large amount, e.g. the cost of **supervising** groups of workers

◆ Sprungkosten

sentence completion (**market research**) a **technique** by which people being **interviewed** complete a sentence in any way they like, e.g. 'I like brand X because . . .', and which sometimes gives information which could not otherwise be predicted

◆ Satzergänzungstest

sequence *noun* (1) a number of things which follow one another: *a sequence of events.* (2) (**computers**) a set of items or instructions which have been put in a certain order

◆ (1) Folge (2) Sequenz

sequence *verb* to put (things) in a certain order, e.g. alphabetical order

◆ ordnen

sequential access storage (**computers**) a **system** of **storing** and retrieving **records** in a certain order (*or* **sequence**)

◆ sequentielle Speicherung

serial number a number given to one thing in a series

◆ Seriennummer

service *noun* (1) something done by one person for another: *to thank someone for his services.* (2) a department of government; people employed in a government department: *the civil service; the services* (i.e. Army, Navy and Air Force). (3) a supply of something (e.g. transport) for general use: *a good train service.* (4) *in plural* (**economics**) a class of things which can be bought and sold, but which are not manufactured goods, such as special knowledge, experience and skills. *Banking and medicine are services for the public.* (5) the way in which one's needs are attended to. *The service in this restaurant is terrible.* (6) the act of regularly checking up on a machine to make sure that it is working properly. *This car should have a service every 6000 miles.* (7) a set of dishes: *a tea service.* (8) the length of time someone has been employed. *My father was given a gold watch for* *his years of service in the company*

◆ (1) Dienste (2) Behörde (3) Versorgung (4) Dienstleistungen (5) Bedienung (6) Wartung (7) Service (8) Dienstzeit

service *verb* (1) to check up on (a machine) to make sure it is in proper working order. *You should get your dishwasher serviced at least every three years.* (2) to pay the **interest** on (a loan)

◆ (1) warten (2) Zinszahlungen leisten

service charge (1) an amount added to a bill in a hotel or restaurant (usually 10% to 15%) which is then shared among those who have given the customer **service,** so that a **gratuity** need not be given. (2) a bank charge. (3) an amount paid by those living in properties (e.g. in a block of flats) which share certain **services** (e.g. keeping a garden in order, cleaning etc.)

◆ (1) Trinkgeld (2) Bearbeitungsgebühr (3) Dienstleistungsgebühr

service department a part of a company which deals with the needs and complaints of customers to whom goods have been sold. *See also* **after-sales service**

◆ Kundendienstabteilung

service industries businesses which do not manufacture goods but which provide customers with **services** which they are willing to pay for, e.g. the hotel trade, the insurance industry

◆ Dienstleistungsgewerbe

set (1) a grouping together of things which have some feature(s) in common: *a set of even numbers.* (2) *(psychology)* a state of mind which will make it likely for a person to behave in a certain way: *a learning set.* (3) the scenery used in a film or play to show where the action takes place: *a film set*

◆ (1) Reihe (2) Disposition (3) Bühnenbild

set of bills an original **bill of exchange** and its copies: if any one is cashed, the others are automatically **cancelled**

◆ Wechselsatz

settle (1) to pay (a debt). (2) to give legally by means of a will or **contract.** *He settled all his property on his wife.* (3) to go to live somewhere; to cause (others) to do so. *They settled in Australia.* (4) to decide (something) by agreement: *to settle an argument; to settle out of court,* i.e. to solve a legal quarrel before it is decided by a judge

◆ (1) begleichen (2) vermachen (3) sich niederlassen (4) sich einigen

settlement (1) the act of settling. (2) a collection of houses, especially where people have not lived before. (3) a legal agreement by which money or property is given to a person: *a marriage settlement.* (4) an agreement which ends a legal quarrel: *an amicable* (i.e. friendly) *settlement*

◆ (1) Ansiedlung (2) Siedlung (3) Güterrechtsvertrag (4) Vergleich

settlement discount *see* **cash discount**

set-up cost an amount of money which has to be paid in making changes in machinery, when one type of **product** is stopped and another one has to be manufactured. *We don't switch products very often, so set-up costs are not significant*

◆ Umstellungskosten

severance pay money paid to a worker by his employer when the worker is dismissed from his job through no fault of his own. *See also* **golden handshake**

◆ Entlassungsabfindung

shake-out (*or* **shake-up**) (1) the **process** of lowering costs by lowering the number of people employed by a company. (2) the **process** of completely changing the way a company is run, which usually includes changing the top management of the company

◆ (1) Personalabbau (2) Umstrukturierung der Verwaltung

share one of the equal parts into which the money (**capital**) needed for starting or running a company is divided. For example, if a company needs £100,000 for its development, it can offer 100,000 £1 **shares** for sale, but the actual price of the shares will go up or down according to how well or badly the company is doing. *See also* **ordinary share, preference share**

◆ Aktie

share capital an amount of money which a company needs for carrying on its business, and which is related to the **shares** it offers for sale to the public. *See also* **issued capital, nominal capital, paid-up capital**

◆ Aktienkapital

share certificate (*US* **stock certificate**) a **document** given by a company to a person who buys one or more **shares** in the company as proof that he/she is the legal owner of the shares

◆ Aktienzertifikat

shareholder (*also, especially US,* **stockholder**) a person who owns **shares** or **stocks** in a company. *The shareholders will be invited to a meeting next month to meet the new members of the board*

◆ Aktieninhaber

share index a type of **index number** which takes the average rise or fall in the price of certain selected **shares** to show whether the price of shares in general (or a certain type of share) is rising or falling. *See also* **Dow Jones index, Financial Times industrial share index**

◆ Aktienindex

share issue the act of making **shares** available for buying

◆ Aktienemission

shelf life the length of time that a **product,** especially food, can stay on the shelf of a shop, store etc. before it becomes unfit for sale. *These tins of soup have a shelf life of three months*

◆ Haltbarkeit

shell company a type of company that exists in name only and does not do any actual business, useful, e.g. to a person who wants to start a business but wants to save himself the expense of setting up a company from the beginning

◆ Mantelfirma

shift *noun* (1) a movement; a change. *There has been a slight shift upwards in share prices.* (2) one of the periods of time (usually lasting about 8 hours) that the working day of a factory or other business is divided into, each period having a different group of workers. *In this factory, people work three shifts: 8 a.m. to 4 p.m., 4 p.m. to midnight, and midnight to 8 a.m. See also* **shift working.** (3) a group of workers who work during a certain **shift** (meaning 2). *The next shift will be starting in about an hour. See also* **night shift.** (4) (**computers**) an instruction which **shifts** (meaning 3)

◆ (1) Verschiebung (2), (3) Schicht (4) shift

shift *verb* (1) to move. *Could you shift these cases to the other end of the store, please?* (2) to pass on (the cost of a tax) to someone else. *The shopkeepers will shift this tax on to their customers.* (3) (**computers**) to move **bits, characters** etc. a certain number of places to the left or right

◆ (1) schieben (2) abwälzen (3) shiften

shift in demand a change in the kind of thing that customers want, or the amount of what they want. *We do our best to anticipate shifts in demand*

◆ Nachfrageverschiebung

shift key a key on a typewriter or **computer keyboard** which changes the position of the keys, e.g. to type capital letters

◆ Umschalttaste

shift working a method of organising work so that it is done by different groups of workers at different periods of the day. *The factory will be in use 24 hours a day from now on, so we shall have to start shift working. See also* **shift, night shift**

◆ Schichtarbeit

ship *noun* a larger type of boat

◆ Schiff

ship *verb* (1) to transport (something) by ship. *We'll ship the supplies you need immediately.* (2) *(especially US)* to transport by other means. *We can ship your goods either by road or rail*

◆ (1) verschiffen (2) versenden

ship broker a person who acts for a shipowner, by getting **cargo** and passengers for his ships, and also handling **insurance** and other matters

◆ Schiffsmakler

ship chandler a person or company that provides the things that are necessary for a ship

◆ Lieferant von Schiffsbedarf

shipment (1) the act of shipping goods. (2) a quantity of goods shipped

◆ (1) Verschiffung (2) Warensendung

shipper a person or company whose business it is to send goods abroad by ship

◆ Spediteur

shipping note (1) a note which gives the official in charge of the docks that a ship is leaving from, details of the goods which are to be shipped. (2) *see* **mate's receipt**

◆ (1) Schiffszettel

ship's articles a type of **contract** by which sailors agree to the conditions, payment etc. for the ship they are going to work on

◆ Heuervertrag

ship's certificate of registry a **document** which contains all the necessary details of a ship: its name, owner, weight (**tonnage**), and the country where it is **registered**

◆ Schiffsregisterbrief

ship's manifest a detailed description of a ship's **cargo,** to be sent to the agents abroad who will receive the cargo, and also given to the customs at the port that the ship leaves from

◆ Ladeverzeichnis

ship's report information which must be given about a ship to the customs officials of the port it has arrived at, giving details about the **cargo,** passengers, crew and any other matter that information is asked on

◆ Schiffsmeldung

ship's stores goods (such as food and drink) which will be needed by a ship's crew and passengers while at sea, but which are not part of the **cargo.** Such goods are noted by customs while the ship is in a foreign port and are put **under seal**

◆ Bordvorräte

shop *noun* (1) a place where goods are sold, usually **retail:** *a butcher's shop; a bookshop.* (2) a place where a certain kind of work is done: *a workshop. See also* **talk shop**

◆ (1) Geschäft (2) Werkstatt

shop *verb* (1) *often* **shop for** to go to one or more shops with the aim of buying something. *My wife is shopping for things for our new house.* (2) **shop around** to go to various shops or other businesses to buy something at the best value. *If you're* *buying a new car, it pays to shop around*

◆ (1) einkaufen gehen (2) sich umsehen

shop assistant a person who serves customers in a shop

◆ Verkäufer(in)

shop audit *see* **retail audit**

shop floor (1) the part of a factory etc. where the machines and the workers who run them are. (2) ordinary workers, especially when organised into a **trade union**

◆ (1) Produktionsstätte (2) Arbeiterschaft

shopper a person who is buying goods, or about to buy goods, from a shop. *The town was crowded with Saturday morning shoppers*

◆ Käufer

shopping (1) goods that have been bought from a shop or various shops: *the week's shopping.* (2) the act of buying goods from a shop or shops

◆ (1) Einkäufe (2) Einkaufen

shopping centre an area where there are a number of shops together. *They are building a large shopping centre near these new houses*

◆ Einkaufszentrum

shopping goods a type of goods (usually more expensive) which are bought after the customer has given some thought to the matter, e.g. after comparing prices

◆ Waren, die erst nach Preisvergleich gekauft werden

shop steward a person **elected** by the workers in a factory, shop etc. to put their complaints to their **trade union** and the management

◆ gewerkschaftliche Vertrauensperson

shop window (1) the window of a shop where goods are on show. (2) = **showcase** (2)

◆ (1) Schaufenster

short *see* **sell short**

short bill a **bill of exchange** which is payable at **sight,** on **demand,** or within less than ten days

◆ Wechsel mit kurzer Fälligkeit

short-dated securities (*or* **shorts**) certain types of **securities** which are repayable in less than five years

◆ Wertpapiere mit kurzfristiger Laufzeit

shorthand a method of writing things down quickly. *He took notes in shorthand and typed them later*

◆ Stenographie

short-term (1) lasting for a short time. *This investment has some short-term benefits but will not pay you much in the long run.* (2) having a **maturity date** that will come soon (e.g. in less than a year): *short-term credit; short-term debt*

◆ (1), (2) kurzfristig

short-term planning the act of making plans for things which will happen soon (e.g. within about a year). *Compare with* **long-term plan**

◆ kurzfristige Planung

short-time working a situation where an employer lowers the number of hours in the week that his employees can work (perhaps because of lack of orders, or because certain necessary supplies are not available)

◆ Kurzarbeit

showcard a card put near a **product** in a shop etc., giving information to help to **promote** it

◆ Reklameplakat

showcase (1) a container, usually of clear plastic or glass, which allows goods to be seen by possible customers, but keeps them safe from being damaged or stolen. *We have a showcase displaying our range of scarves in the main reception area of the hotel.* (2) any situation which allows a company's goods or **services** to be shown in a way which should make them attractive to possible customers. *The international meeting will be a showcase for the town's hotel facilities*

◆ (1) Ausstellungsvitrine (2) gute Werbung

shrinkage the amount by which anything becomes smaller. *If you buy this cloth, remember to allow for some shrinkage when it is washed*

◆ Einlaufen

shrink-wrap to cover goods (e.g. food etc.) with a thin clear plastic covering (**shrink-wrapping**) which is then **sealed** tightly round the goods by the use of heat

◆ in Schrumpffolie verpacken und einschweißen

shut-down the closing of a factory etc. for a certain length of time

◆ vorübergehende Stillegung

sickness benefit (*or* **sick pay**) *(UK)* money paid by the government (under the **National Insurance scheme**) to a worker who is too ill to work

◆ Krankengeld

sight: at sight of a **bill of exchange,** payable at once on presentation

◆ bei Sicht

significant (1) important; worth noting: *a significant drop in profits.* (2) (**statistics**) not to be explained by chance. *The difference between the results of the experiment and what was predicted is statistically significant*

◆ (1) bedeutsam (2) signifikant

sign on (1) to begin work etc., especially by signing one's name. (2) to register one's name in order to claim unemployment benefit

◆ (1) Arbeitsvertrag abschließen (2) sich arbeitslos melden

silent partner (*or* **sleeping partner**) a **partner** in a business who does not take an active part in running the business, but shares the profits, usually because he or she has **invested** money in it

◆ stiller Teilhaber

silicon chip *see* **chip**

simple interest: interest which is paid on the **principal** (amount of money borrowed) alone. *See also* **compound interest**

◆ Zinsen (ohne Zinseszins)

simulate (1) to pretend. (2) to imitate (a **process,** situation etc.) so as to find out more about it. *This wind-tunnel simulates the conditions that the aircraft will be flying in*

◆ (1) vortäuschen (2) simulieren

simulation (1) the act of pretending or imitating. (2) imitation of a **process,** situation etc. (usually involving mathematical calculations) so as to find out more about it. *In our business school, we do simulations of various business situations, using a computer to check on the results of our decisions*

◆ (1) Vortäuschung (2) Simulation

sine die *(Latin, meaning* without a day) without a date being fixed (for another meeting, for something to be done etc.). *The judge adjourned the case sine die*

◆ auf unbestimmte Zeit

single-entry book-keeping a very simple method of recording **accounts,** now seldom used, by which each business **transaction** is recorded only once

◆ einfache Buchführung

sinking fund an amount of money built up out of profits (or, in the case of a government, out of taxes) to meet some payment which has been foreseen, e.g. renewing a **lease** on some property

◆ Tilgungsfonds

sit-down strike a kind of **strike** in which workers refuse to leave the place where they work until their demands are met. *See also* **sit-in**

◆ Sitzstreik

sit-in a form of protest in which the people who are protesting occupy some place, e.g. an office, and refuse to leave it. *The students are staging a sit-in in the library. Also used as a verb:* **sit in.** *See also* **work-in**

◆ Sit-in

situation report an account of how things are, e.g. in any part of a business. *The sales manager will be giving a situation report with respect to the new sales drive at today's meeting*

◆ Lagebericht

skill ability to do something as a result of training or practice. *These young people are being trained in the skills of management*

◆ Fertigkeit

skilled worker a type of **manual worker** who, as a result of training, can do certain jobs which need a certain amount of skill and judgment; a craftsman

◆ Facharbeiter

skills analysis a method of examining in detail the different **processes** involved in performing some task for which training is needed, so that the training can be more effective

◆ Ausbildungsoptimierungsanalyse

skimming price a price of goods fixed at a level which will probably be attractive only to customers with high **incomes.** *See also* **penetration pricing**

◆ überzogener Preis

sleeper (1) a manager who is not active in doing business and looking for new business. *See also* **thruster.** (2) an address which is used to check that **direct mail shots** are reaching their **targets.** (3) a part of a train which is used for sleeping in during the journey; a train which has such compartments

◆ (1) träge Führungskraft (2) Wurfsendungskontrolladresse (3) Schlafwagen

sleeping partner *see* **silent partner**

sliding scale a method of deciding the amount of tax, **duty** or other payment to be made on something, by which the amount of tax etc. varies according to the value of the thing on which the tax is due. *See also* **pro rata**

◆ Staffeltarif

slogan a word, phrase or sentence which is related through advertising to a particular **product.** *In this competition, you get a prize if you can think of a good slogan for this new product*

◆ Slogan

slot machine a machine with a special hole (or **slot**) for coins from which one can buy, e.g. cigarettes, sweets, a spell at a game (operated by the machine)

◆ (Verkaufs-) Automat

slump *noun* (1) part of a **trade cycle** when unemployment is greatest and opportunities for business are at their lowest. (2) a sudden lowering, e.g. in prices, sales, production etc. *There has been a slump in the sales figures over the last few months*

◆ (1) Tiefstand (2) plötzliches Fallen

slump *verb* of prices, profits, employment etc., to become suddenly much lower or smaller. *Our profits have slumped considerably since last year*

◆ plötzlich fallen

slush fund an amount of money

which has been set aside for paying **bribes** and similar illegal or improper business or political activities. *He set up a slush fund for paying bribes to politicians*

◆ Schmiergeldfonds

snip *(informal)* something very cheap; bargain. *You should buy that car: it's a snip at £500*

◆ günstiger Kauf

social insurance a method of providing **insurance** which is organised by the government

◆ Sozialversicherung

socialism any of the various kinds of belief related to the ideas of property, factories, transport etc. being owned by the state for the benefit of everyone, not just by certain people for their own benefit, and equality in society rather than **competition** for wealth. *See also* **capitalism**

◆ Sozialismus

social responsibility a duty which a person or business owes to the society of which it is part: the person or business should not do anything which is harmful to society, and should even use some of its profits to improve society if it can

◆ soziale Verantwortung

social security a **system** by which the government pays money to certain groups of people who need it, e.g. the unemployed, the old

◆ Sozialhilfe

socio-economic grouping the division of society into social classes, e.g. from A (highest income, highest social position) through B, C1, C2, D to E (lowest income, lowest social position)

◆ sozialwirtschaftliche Gruppierung

sociology the scientific study of human society

◆ Soziologie

soft currency the money **system** of a country which is likely to fall in value usually because of an **adverse trade balance,** and is therefore not in demand by those who buy and sell currencies. *See also* **hard currency**

◆ weiche Währung

soft furnishings household goods made of cloth of any kind, e.g. curtains, cushions

◆ Vorhänge, Teppiche, Kissen usw.

soft goods cloth of any kind

◆ Textilien

soft sell a method of persuading people to buy goods without putting much direct pressure on them to do so. *See also* **hard sell**

◆ dezente Verkaufsmethode

software: programs that can be used in a **computer.** *See also* **hardware**

◆ Software

sole only; for or by oneself alone. *The agency has the sole right to sell the goods in France*

◆ alleinig

sole trader a person who runs his own business by himself, and not in **partnership** with anyone else

◆ Einzelkaufmann

solicitor (1) *(UK)* a lawyer who handles general legal matters, and who can also represent his clients in the lower courts. *See also* **barrister.** (2) *(US)* a lawyer who advises the officials of a town or city on legal matters. (3) *(US)* anyone who goes round looking for trade, business etc.

◆ (1) Rechtsanwalt (außergerichtlich und bei Gerichten unterer Instanzen) (2) Justizbeamter (3) Akquisiteur

solus position of an advertisement e.g. in a newspaper, in a separate position, away from other **competing** advertisements

◆ alleinstehend

solvency the state of being **solvent**

◆ Solvenz

solvent having enough money to pay one's debts

◆ solvent

source the person, thing or place from which something comes. *What is the source of your information?*

◆ Quelle

source language a **computer language** in which it is easier for the user to write **programs,** e.g. **BASIC, COBOL, FORTRAN,** but which has to be translated by the computer into **machine language** before the instructions to the computer can be put into effect. *See also* **machine language**

◆ Quellsprache

source program (**computers**) a **program** which has been written in a **source language** and not in **machine language**

◆ Quellenprogramm

sovereign *noun* (1) the king or queen of a country. (2) *(UK)* a coin formerly in use when it was worth one **pound sterling** but now no longer **legal tender,** although it is still **minted** and exported to certain countries, especially in the Middle East

◆ (1) Herrscher (2) 20-Schilling-Münze

sovereign *adjective* (1) having the greatest authority: *my sovereign lord.* (2) independent, not ruled by another country: *a sovereign state*

◆ (1) höchster (2) souverän

sovereignty (1) power. (2) independence. (3) the idea that the **consumer** has choice in the market and can reject goods or prices which are not found acceptable

◆ (1) Oberhoheit (2), (3) Souveränität

space in newspapers and magazines, the pages or parts of pages which can be used for advertising when everything else is printed

◆ Anzeigenraum

space bar the bar on the **keyboard** of a typewriter or **computer** which causes a move to the right

◆ Leertaste

space buyer *see* **media buyer**

span of control the range and number of **subordinates** that a manager at a certain level is directly in charge of. *According to our theory, the higher a manager's position, the wider his span of control should be*

◆ Kontrollbefugnis

spare part a part of a machine etc. which can be bought separately in case that part should fail

◆ Ersatzteil

special deposit *(UK)* an amount of money which a **clearing bank** has to leave with the Bank of England and which can be used by the government to lower the amount of money the clearing banks have available for lending, and therefore to lower **credit** generally

◆ vorgeschriebene Mindestreserven

special endorsement a statement on a **bill of exchange** which states to whom, or on whose order, the bill is payable

◆ Vollindossament

special feature a section in a magazine or newspaper, or in a special issue of a magazine or newspaper, which is concerned with a certain subject, often one which will attract advertising related to it

◆ Sonderbeitrag

speciality goods types of goods which are often sold, e.g. through advertisements and/or **door-to-door selling** rather than through shops or stores, e.g. double-glazing, encyclopedias

◆ Spezialartikel

speciality salesman a type of salesman who is concerned with the sale of **speciality goods**

◆ Verkäufer für Spezialartikel

specification a detailed description. *These tools that you have provided do not meet our specification*

◆ Spezifikation

speculate (1) to think about something without knowing all the facts; to guess. *We can only speculate about his early life, since he never discussed it with anyone.* (2) to be involved in some kind of risky business operation in the hope of making a large profit, e.g. by buying **property, shares** etc.

◆ (1) Vermutungen anstellen (2) spekulieren

speculation (1) the act of **speculating.** (2) a business operation which carries high risks but also hopes of great profits. (3) in the **stock exchange,** the act or an example of dealing in **futures** (where the dealer sells a **commodity** at a certain fixed price on a certain date, hoping that he will be able to buy it at a lower price before then)

◆ (1) Vermutung (2) gewagtes Unternehmen (3) Spekulation

speculative (1) of **speculation.** (2) related to any business operation where there is some degree of risk of failure. *Speculative builders often build houses in the hope that someone will want to buy them*

◆ (1) spekulativ (2) Spekulations-

splash story the main news story in a newspaper, usually appearing on the front page

◆ Titelgeschichte

split shift a type of **shift** (meaning 2) which is divided into two parts, so that workers are there when they are needed. For example, in a bus company, the drivers may work from 6 a.m.—10 a.m. and from 4 p.m.—8 p.m., if these are the busiest times

◆ Arbeit in wechselnder Schicht

split the difference *(informal)* to **strike a bargain** by choosing an amount exactly halfway between what each side has previously offered. *I'm asking £300 and you're offering £200: let's split the difference and agree on £250*

◆ sich auf halbem Wege einigen

sponsor *noun* (1) a person or group that supports some activity, e.g. a **competition,** performance, either for charity or as a form of advertisement. *The sponsor for this event is a local factory.* (2) *(especially US)* a business which pays for radio or television time to advertise its **product.** *We interrupt the programme for a message from our sponsor.* (3) *(US)* a **guarantor;** a person who **guarantees** a person or thing

◆ (1) Sponsor (2) Patronatsfirma (3) Bürge

sponsor *verb* to act as a **sponsor** to. *The company has sponsored various events, including a golf competition and an athletics meeting*

◆ fördern

spot a single period of time on television or radio used for advertising. *Our new product will be featured in two television spots every evening this week*

◆ Werbespot

spot price a price for goods, especially **commodities** that can be sold immediately

◆ Kassapreis

spot rate a type of **exchange rate** for currency that can be sold and delivered immediately

◆ Kassakurs

squeeze the controlling by a government of the amount of money used, e.g. to stop the rise of **inflation:** *credit squeeze*

◆ Restriktion

stabilisation the **process** by which a government stops sudden large-scale changes in the **economy,** e.g. by controlling **money supply** to prevent **inflation,** or by buying or selling currency to prevent large changes in the **exchange rate**

◆ Stabilisierung

stabilise to (cause to) become steadier; to stop changes in (something)

◆ stabilisieren

stabiliser any means which a government uses to **stabilise** the **economy,** e.g. control of the **money supply** to prevent **inflation,** or making new government jobs to lessen unemployment

◆ Stabilisator

stable market a type of market where the amount of goods sold is not usually seriously affected by price changes. *See also* **staple product**

◆ stabiler Markt

staff *noun* a group of people employed by an organisation. *Our staff are well paid and work hard. There is an annual football match between staff and students*

◆ Mitarbeiterstab

staff *verb* to hire employees for (an organisation): *to be fully staffed/ understaffed,* i.e. to have all the employees one needs/not enough employees

◆ mit Personal versorgen

staff association a group formed to represent the views of the employees of a particular company or organisation (usually **white-collar workers**); similar to a **trade union,** but not linked to any other group outside the company or organisation

◆ Personalvertretung

stag (**stock exchange**) a person who buys new **share issues** in the hope of selling them quickly for a profit

◆ Spekulant

staggered working hours an arrangement for working by which the employees arrive and leave at a time which is different from the other offices, factories, etc. in the area, usually to make travelling to work easier because fewer people will be using transport

◆ Staffelung der Arbeitszeit

stagnation the state of not growing or developing. *The economy has reached stagnation level*

◆ Stagnation

stale cheque a cheque which has been held for a long time without being handed over to a bank for payment; banks can refuse to cash cheques beyond a certain time, usually three months or six months

◆ verfallener Scheck

stamp duty the amount of money that must be paid to the government before certain **documents** are **valid** (recognised as legal), e.g. documents about the sale of **shares** and property

◆ Stempelgebühr

stand (1) something on which something else stands. (2) a place with shelves etc. where goods are shown, especially at an exhibition. *Come round to our stand and I'll show you our new products*

◆ (1) Ständer (2) Stand

standard costing a method of checking on the cost of producing something, by **estimating** how much it should cost (**standard cost**) and then comparing this to the actual cost; if there is a difference between the two figures, then the reason for this difference should be found out

◆ Normalkostenrechnung

standardisation the act of **standardising**

◆ Vereinheitlichung

standardise to cause to be made or done in the same way or according to some rule. *We are trying to standardise the design of all our goods*

◆ vereinheitlichen

standard of living the level at which a person, group of people, within a country can afford to live; one way of measuring this is by finding out how many hours a person has to work in order to buy a certain amount of certain goods. *Heavy increases in taxes are bound to affect everyone's standard of living*

◆ Lebensstandard

standard rate the basic rate of **income tax** which one pays on **income** after **allowances** have been taken off

◆ (Steuer-) Normalsatz

standard time the official local time for a country, or an area within a country. *Before you phone a foreign country, it is best to check what the standard time is there*

◆ Normalzeit

standby *adjective* ready to be used if needed: *standby arrangements*

◆ Standby

standby *adverb:* **go standby** to travel at the last minute on an aircraft at a lower fare, using a seat not already booked

◆ mit einem Standby-Ticket reisen

standby pay money given to workers who have to make themselves ready for work in case their **services** are needed

◆ Lohn für Bereitschaftsdienst

standing committee a group of people set up on a **permanent** basis to deal with a certain subject. *He is a member of the Standing Committee on Foreign Affairs*

◆ ständiger Ausschuß

standing order an instruction to a bank to pay out a certain amount of money at certain regular times (e.g. once a month). *I pay my rates by standing order. Compare with* **standing orders**

◆ Dauerauftrag

standing orders rules which have been drawn up for the proper running of the meetings of an organisation. *According to the standing orders, there must be at least one meeting of the executive committee each month. Compare with* **standing order**

◆ Geschäftsordnung

standstill agreement an agreement between two countries when one country cannot pay its debts to the other, that it will be given a certain fixed period of time to repay the debts

◆ Stillhalteabkommen

staple – **staple product**

staple product (1) a main **commodity** produced in a country or region. *The staple products of this region are wheat and dairy produce.* (2) essential goods, for which there will always be a demand, e.g. in UK, bread or milk. *See also* **stable market**

◆ (1) Haupterzeugnis (2) Grundnahrungsmittel

stapler a **device** for joining pieces of paper together by means of small pieces of metal

◆ Heftmaschine

statement (*or* **statement of accounts**) a **document** which is sent to a customer at a certain time, e.g. at the end of each month, to show him how much money he owes for goods or **services** received; it usually lists **invoice** numbers and amounts. *See also* **invoice**

◆ Rechnungsaufstellung

statistic *singular form of* **statistics** (meaning 1)

◆ Statistik

statistical of **statistics:** *a statistical report*

◆ statistisch

statistics (1) *(plural)* facts given in the form of numbers. *These statistics show that our share of the market is increasing.* (2) *(singular)* the science of collecting and understanding **statistics** (meaning 1). *Some knowledge of statistics is necessary for the study of market research*

◆ (1) Statistiken (2) Statistik

status inquiry the act of checking on an order or a possible customer, e.g. to see whether he will be able to pay his debts and whether he has failed to pay his debts in the past

◆ Untersuchung der Kreditwürdigkeit

status symbol something which is meant to show how important or wealthy its owner is and to make people think highly of him/her. *Some expensive cars are more than just a way of getting from A to B: they are status symbols*

◆ Statussymbol

statute a law passed by a law-making body

◆ Gesetz

statutory meeting a meeting that is required by law, e.g. of the **shareholders** of a new company

◆ Gründungsversammlung

sterling UK money: *one pound sterling; to have one's reserves in sterling*

◆ Sterling

stet an indication that something on a **document** (a word, phrase, number etc.) has been crossed out by mistake and should in fact remain as it was before

◆ stehenlassen

stevedore a person whose job it is to load or unload ships

◆ Stauer

steward (1) a person who runs a property for someone else. (2) a person who is in charge of the food and other things needed on a ship. (3) an official who helps with organising a crowd of people attending a meeting of any kind. (4) a person who acts as a waiter on an aeroplane or ship, and has certain other duties

◆ (1) Verwalter (2) Steward (3) Ordner (4) Steward

stewardess a female **steward** on a plane or ship

◆ Stewardeß

sticker a piece of paper which can be stuck onto some surface, e.g. window, envelope etc. for advertising purposes

◆ Aufkleber

stimulate (1) to excite; to make (a person) become interested. *We are trying to stimulate public interest in our new product.* (2) to make more active. *News of the recent oil discoveries has stimulated the stock market*

◆ (1), (2) anregen

stimulation the act of **stimulating**

◆ Anregung

stipend a salary, especially of a priest or minister

◆ Gehalt

stock *noun* (1) the amount of goods in a **store** or ship that have not yet been sold. *I don't know if we have any of these goods left: I'll check my stock.* (2) the amount of **raw materials** which are available for use. *The country has built up large stocks of coal.* (3) *in plural* **stocks = shares.** (4) **loan stock, securities** issued to raise loans for the government at a fixed **rate** of **interest** and which may or may not be **redeemable.** *See also* **gilt-edged securities.** (5) film material that has not yet been exposed: *film stock*

◆ (1) Lagerbestand (2) Vorrat (3)

Aktie (4) Staatsanleihen (5) unbelichtetes Filmmaterial

stock *verb* (1) to keep (goods) for sale. *We stock all kinds of wood.* (2) **stock up** *or* **up on** to get supplies of (something): *to stock up on food for the winter*

◆ (1) führen (2) Vorrat auffüllen

stockbroker a person who is an agent in the selling of **stocks** and **shares** to the public for a **commission.** *See also* **jobber**

◆ Börsenmakler

stock certificate *(US) see* **share certificate**

stock control the practice of keeping enough **stocks** (meanings 1 and 2) of goods or materials to meet the possible demands, but at the smallest cost in terms of **storage, bulk-buying,** etc. *See also* **buffer stock, economic order quantity**

◆ Bestandsüberwachung

stock cover the time that **stocks** (meanings 1 and 2) will last if sales and/or use of goods and materials continue at the usual rate

◆ Vorhalten des Vorrats

stock exchange (*or* **stock market**) a place where **stocks, shares** and government **securities** are bought and sold. *See also* **bourse**

◆ Börse

stockholder *(especially US) see* **shareholder**

stockholding cost money that has to be spent to keep a **stock** (meanings 1 and 2) or supply of goods or materials, e.g. by paying rent on **storage** space. *The problem about keeping large stocks is that it increases the stockholdings costs*

◆ Lagerhaltungskosten

stock-in-trade (1) goods or materials which a business has for sale; **stock** (meaning 1). (2) anything which a person or company normally does as part of their business. *As a successful hairdresser, being charming with women is part of his stock-in-trade*

◆ (1) Warenbestand (2) zum Geschäft gehörend

stockist *(UK)* a dealer

◆ Fachhändler

stock jobber *see* **jobber**

stock level the amount of goods or materials being held for sale. *See also* **stock** (meanings 1 and 2)

◆ Warenbestandsmenge

stock market *see* **stock exchange**

stockout the condition of having no supplies of a particular kind of goods or materials

◆ nicht vorrätig haben

stockpile *verb* to gather **stockpiles** of (goods or materials). *The nations of the world are stockpiling weapons at an alarming rate*

◆ Vorräte anlegen

stockpile *noun* a large amount of a certain kind of goods or materials that is kept together for possible future use

◆ Vorrat

stocks *see* **stock** *(noun)*

stocktaking the act or **process** of checking the actual amount of goods which one is holding for sale. *We have a stocktaking every year. See also* **inventory**

◆ Inventur

stock-turn (*or* **stock turnover**) (1) the total value of goods sold during a certain period, e.g. a year, divided by the average value of goods held during the year. For example, if the total cost of goods sold in a year came to £40,000 and the average value of goods being held unsold was £10,000, then the stock turnover would be 4:1. (2) (*also* **stock-turn**

rate) the total amount of a certain type of goods or materials available for sale over a period of time divided by the average amount available for sale at any one time. Thus if a business had 100,000 units available for sale over the year but only an average of 1000 units on any one day, then the stock turnover would be 100:1

◆ (1) Lagerumsatz (2) Umschlagsrate

stop to give written instructions to one's bank that (a cheque which one has signed) should not in fact be paid

◆ sperren

stoppage (1) a situation where work has stopped because of **strike** action. *But relations between management and workers have caused frequent stoppages.* (2) the act of keeping back some money from a worker's pay, e.g. because he owes money which has been given to him in advance of his wages. (3) the amount of money kept back in this way: *£10* in stoppages

◆ (1) Einstellen der Arbeit (2), (3) Lohnabzug

storage (1) the act of **storing** goods or materials; the space for storing them. *They put their furniture in storage while they were away last summer.* (2) the amount of money paid for goods or materials to be stored. *One of our biggest expenses last year was storage for goods that we could not sell*

◆ (1) Lagerung; Lagerraum (2) Lagergeld

storage device a part of a **computer** (often a **disk** or tape) on which information can be put in, kept and taken out again when it is needed

◆ Speichergerät

store *noun* (1) a place where goods and materials can be kept. *Get some more paint from the store.* (2) a shop: *grocery store.* (3) a shop where many kinds of goods are sold. *There is a very large store in the main street where you can buy almost anything. See also* **department store.** (4) a supply of goods or materials that has been built up for future use. *We've built up a nice store of vegetables from our garden that will keep us supplied for most of the winter.* (5) the state of being kept for future use. *We have plenty of materials in store.* (6) (**computers**) **— storage device**

◆ (1) Lager (2) Geschäft (3) Warenhaus (4) Vorrat (5) auf Lager

store *verb* (1) to keep for future use: *to store materials; to store information.* (2) to put in a **store** (meaning 1). *It will cost quite a lot to store all these materials.* (3) (**computers**) to put (information) into a **storage device.** *Store these data immediately*

◆ (1) lagern (2) auf Lager nehmen (3) speichern

stores requisition a written request for goods held in a **store** (meaning 1)

◆ Lageranforderung

storyboard a series of drawings which show the different parts of a film or television advertisement in the order in which they will appear

◆ Entwurfskizze einer Werbesendung

straight-line method of depreciation (**accounting**) a method of allowing for the **depreciation** cost of a **fixed asset** which is worth less as it gets older, by which the worth of the asset is lowered by the same fixed amount each year; the amount is arrived at by dividing the cost of the asset by the **estimated** number of years that it will be able to be used

◆ lineare Abschreibung

strategic planning *see* **corporate planning**

strategy a plan for reaching certain **targets** over a period of time. *See also* **tactics**

◆ Strategie

stratification (**market research**) a method used to make sure that the various groups making up the **target** group are properly represented in every **sample**

◆ Schichtung

stratified sampling: random sampling from a **population** (**target** group) that has been divided into various groups (e.g. according to age, sex, **income**). Each group is then properly represented in each **sample.** *See also* **quota sampling**

◆ nach Schichten gegliederte Stichprobenuntersuchung

stream: on stream especially of large units such as factories, large **computers** etc., in operation, in production. *Our new North Sea oil wells will be coming on stream later this year*

◆ in Betrieb nehmen

stress interview a type of **interview** where the people being interviewed for selection are questioned in an unfriendly way, so as to find out how well they can deal with this kind of difficult situation

◆ Streß-Interview

strike *noun* (1) the act of **striking** (meaning 1). *We have had several strikes in the factory this year.* (2) a situation where employees have refused to work: *to be on strike.* (3) the act of finding coal, oil, or similar **minerals.** *We have been prospecting in this area for months, and we expect to make a strike soon*

◆ (1) Streik (2) Ausstand (3) Fund

strike *verb* (1) to refuse to do one's work, usually because one feels that one is not being paid enough or because of one's working conditions. *The workers want a pay rise, and are threatening to strike.* (2) to find supplies of (a **mineral,** e.g. coal or oil) underground. *They claim to have struck oil*

◆ (1) streiken (2) fündig werden

strike a bargain to agree on a price that suits the buyer and seller; to come to an agreement that suits both sides. *Let's strike a bargain: we'll display your goods, if you display ours*

◆ Geschäft abschließen

strikebreaker a person who continues to work when others are on **strike** or in some other way causes the strike to have less effect

◆ Streikbrecher

striker a person who is on **strike**

◆ Streikender

structural unemployment lack of jobs because of large-scale changes in the way that society or the **economy** is organised. *There is a great deal of structural unemployment today because more and more manual and clerical jobs can be done by machines*

◆ strukturelle Arbeitslosigkeit

subassembly a number of pieces of machinery which are joined together to form a part of a larger machine

◆ Teilmontage

subcontract *verb* to make an agreement with someone else that they will do part of some job that one has agreed to do. For example, a builder may subcontract some of his work to another craftsman, such as an electrician

◆ an einen Subunternehmer vergeben

subcontract *noun* an agreement to **subcontract**

◆ Subunternehmervertrag

subcontractor a person who agrees to do parts of jobs that someone else has got a **contract** for. *Plumbers and electricians are very often subcontractors for builders*

◆ Subunternehmer

subject to contract words included in a written agreement which mean that the agreement will not be binding on either **party** until a proper legal **contract** has been signed

◆ unter Vorbehalt des Vertragsabschlusses

sub judice (*Latin, meaning* under a judge) being considered by a judge or court. *This case is still sub judice, so the newspapers are not being allowed to comment on it*

◆ rechtshängig

sub-lease to **lease** (property) from a person who has already leased it from someone else

◆ in Untermiete; Unterpacht haben

sublet to rent out to a person (a property or part of a property which one is already renting from someone else). *I am renting that house from Mr Smith, but I am not staying there myself as I have sublet it to Mr Jones*

◆ untervermieten

subliminal advertising a type of advertising where a message is put over to the audience in a way that they are not consciously aware of, e.g. by flashing up the message very quickly on a cinema screen. *Subliminal advertising is illegal in many countries*

◆ unterschwellige Werbung

submit (1) to give in (to someone or something more powerful). (2) to give (something) to a person, e.g. for a decision: *to submit a claim; to submit a plan to the authorities*

◆ (1) nachgeben (2) einreichen

subordinate *adjective* lower; less important: *a subordinate position*

◆ untergeordnet

subordinate *noun* a person who is in a lower position in an organisation. *A manager should always treat his subordinates with respect*

◆ Untergebener

subpoena *noun* a **document** put out by a court which orders a person to appear before that court (perhaps to be a witness or to answer charges etc.)

◆ gerichtliche Vorladung

subpoena *verb* to give a **subpoena** to (a person)

◆ vorladen

subrogation a **process** by which an **insurance company** that has paid a **claim** to an insured person can make its losses smaller by taking over the insured's rights, against a **third party** who is responsible for the damage (i.e. people who might have been to blame for the accident etc. having happened in the first place)

◆ Rechtsübertragung

subroutine a part of a **computer program** which carries out a specific repetitive task. When this has been carried out by the **computer** it automatically returns to the next instruction on the main **program**

◆ Subroutine

subscribe (1) **subscribe to** to promise to pay money to some organisation, usually regularly, very often used for a newspaper or magazine. *Do you subscribe to that journal?* (2) to sign one's name at the end of (a legal **document,** e.g. a **contract,** a will). (3) to sign the **memorandum** of a **proposed** new **registered company.** (4) **subscribe for** to ask for **shares** in a new company: *to subscribe for 500 shares. See also* **subscription**

◆ (1) abonnieren (2) unterzeichnen (3) Aktien unmittelbar bei der Gesellschaft beziehen (4) Aktie zeichnen

subscribed capital an amount of **authorised capital** in a new company that has been issued and paid for in cash

◆ gezeichnetes Kapital

subscriber a person who **subscribes** to something

◆ Abonnent

subscription (1) the amount that one pays for something over a certain period: *a subscription to a newspaper/a club/a private charity. The annual subscription to my golf club has been doubled.* (2) the act of signing a legal **document.** (3) a request to buy **shares** in a new company. *See also* **subscribe**

◆ (1) Beitrag (2) Unterzeichnung (3) Zeichnung

subsidiary (*or* **subsidiary company**) a type of company where more than half the **shares** are owned by another company or where another company can control who will be on the **board of directors;** the controlling company is called the **holding company** or the **parent company**

◆ Tochtergesellschaft

subsidise to help by giving a **subsidy** to

◆ subventionieren

subsidy (1) money given by the government to keep the price of some goods lower than it would otherwise be. *In some countries, there are government subsidies for rice, bread and other basic foods.* (2) money given by the government to businesses, e.g. to keep down unemployment, or to help the business over a difficult time in its affairs. *Sometimes the government gives subsidies to key industries.* (3) any kind of **financial** help

◆ (1), (2) Subvention (3) finanzielle Unterstützung

subsist to manage to stay alive. *The people in this area subsist on a diet of rice and fish*

◆ leben von

subsistence (1) the way in which one manages to stay alive: *to live at subsistence level,* i.e. to have only enough to live on, and no more. (2) (*also* **subsistence allowance**) the amount of money a person is paid to cover certain basic needs while he is away from home on business, e.g. food and the cost of a place to stay. *The company will pay you £20 a day subsistence*

◆ (1) Existenzminimum (2) Unterhaltszuschuß

substantial fairly large in size, value or importance. *There has been a substantial increase in our sales*

◆ erheblich

substitute *verb* to put (a thing or person) in place of another

◆ ersetzen

substitute *noun* a thing or person **substituted**

◆ Ersatzmittel; Ersatzmann

successor a person who, or thing which, follows another, especially a person in an organisation. *I'd like you to meet my successor as marketing manager*

◆ Nachfolger(in)

sue to bring a **claim** against (a person) in a court of law. *He was sued for not paying his debts. See also* **damages**

◆ verklagen

suggestion scheme a **process** by which any employee in an organisation with ideas for making it more efficient or profitable can make his or her ideas known to the management, usually in return for a reward of some kind

◆ Vorschlagswettbewerb für Mitarbeiter

sum insured the greatest amount that an **insurance company** will have to pay to a person who is insured with the company for any particular **claim.** *The sum insured for your house is £70,000: you can claim up to that amount but not any more than that*

◆ Versicherungssumme

summary a short account of something, giving only the most important points: *a summary of the report*

◆ Zusammenfassung

Summer Time the practice in some countries of putting clocks forward one hour in the summer months

◆ Sommerzeit

summons an official **document** which orders a person to appear before a court, either for trial or to give evidence

◆ gerichtliche Vorladung

sundries various, usually small things taken together. *The estimate should leave an allowance for sundries*

◆ Diverses

sunk cost (1) *(US)* an amount of money already spent on a business **project,** which cannot easily be recovered if the project is **cancelled.** (2) an amount of money spent on buying a **fixed asset**

◆ (1) Risikoinvestition (2) einmalige Produktionskosten

superannuate (1) to give (a person) a **pension** because he will no longer be able to work (usually because of age or ill health). (2) to get rid of (a person or thing) because he/it is out-of-date or no longer necessary

◆ (1) pensionieren (2) ausrangieren

superannuation (1) a **pension** that is paid to a person who is no longer able to work (usually because of age or ill health). (2) an amount of money that may be taken away each month from a worker's salary to pay for the pension he will get when he is no longer able to work. (3) the act of **superannuating;** a situation where a person or thing has been **superannuated**

◆ (1) Rente (2) Beitrag zur Altersversicherung (3) Überalterung

superintend to be in charge of; to see that (something) is done properly. *I superintend all the work that is done in this section*

◆ beaufsichtigen

superintendent (1) a person who is in charge of something, who sees that something is done properly. (2) in UK police, a person in the rank above inspector. (3) in US police, a person who is in charge of a police station

◆ (1) Aufsichtsperson (2) Kommissar (3) Reviervorsteher

superior *adjective* (1) better (than someone or something else); of higher quality. *Our tests show that this product is superior to all the others.* (2) of very high quality: *a superior brand of whisky*

◆ (1) besser (2) bester

superior *noun* a person who is in a higher position in an organisation. *It's not a good idea to annoy your superiors*

◆ Vorgesetzte(r)

supermarket a large **self-service store** which sells a wide variety of goods, but especially those in constant demand, e.g. food, drink, and household goods. *See also* **hypermarket, superstore**

◆ Supermarkt

superstore a very large store, selling food and other goods, between a **supermarket** and a **hypermarket** in size

◆ großes Warenhaus

supervise to watch to make sure that (something) is done properly or that nothing wrong or bad happens. *Would you supervise the work on the new project?; to supervise an examination; to supervise children at play*

◆ überwachen

supervision the act of **supervising.** *In that factory they are very worried about security; you will be under supervision the whole time,* i.e. you will be watched

◆ Überwachung

supervisor (1) a person who **supervises,** e.g. one in charge of a group of workers etc. (2) in a university, a lecturer who checks on a student's work

◆ (1) Aufseher(in) (2) Tutor; Doktorvater

supplement *noun* (1) something which is added to complete something else or to give more information about it. *A supplement which brings this report up-to-date will be appearing next week.* (2) a separate section of a newspaper or magazine. *This journal has a business supplement that now appears with every issue.* (3) **— supplementary payment**

◆ (1) Ergänzung (2) Beilage

supplement *verb* to provide something extra that is needed. *The workforce will be supplemented with extra men until the job is finished*

◆ ergänzen

supplementary extra; provided to complete something or make up for something that is missing: **supplementary payment,** i.e. extra payment

◆ Ergänzungs-

supplementary benefit *(UK)* an amount of money paid weekly by the government to various groups of people whose **income** is below a certain minimum level

◆ Sozialhilfe

supply *noun* (1) the act of giving something that is needed or asked for. (2) (**economics**) the availability of goods or materials. *The world supply of oil is a matter of great concern to world leaders.* (3) *in plural* **supplies** food and/or **equipment** needed for a certain purpose. *Charity organisations are sending food supplies to the famine area.* (4) *in plural* **supplies** goods needed by a company to run its business but not part of what it sells or produces: *office supplies,* i.e. paper, pens, notebooks etc.

◆ (1) Versorgung (2) Vorrat (3) Vorräte (4) Bedarf

supply *verb* to give (something that is needed or asked for). *Will you be able to supply spare parts for this machine?*

◆ liefern

supply curve a type of **graph** which shows in diagram form the information given in a **supply schedule.** *See also* **demand curve**

◆ Angebotskurve

supply schedule a list showing how much of its **product** a company is willing to sell at various prices; usually the higher the price, the greater the number of items supplied

◆ Angebotstabelle

support buying a situation where a government buys its own currency on the **foreign exchange market** in order to keep the value of the currency from falling

◆ Stützungskäufe

surcharge *noun* (1) an extra payment or tax that has to be paid. *We normally deliver goods in 48 hours, but you can have them delivered more quickly on payment of a surcharge.* (2) an extra amount that can be printed on a postage stamp to make it worth more

◆ (1) Zuschlag (2) Überdruck

surcharge *verb* (1) to make (a person) pay something extra. *You will be surcharged for any luggage above the allowed limit.* (2) to increase the value of (a postage stamp) by printing a new value across it

◆ (1) Zuschlag erheben (2) überdrucken

surety (1) *see* **guarantor.** (2) money or something of value given as a **guarantee** that something will not be lost or damaged, or that a person will act as he has promised to do

◆ (2) Sicherheit

surplus a quantity or amount of something that is more than is needed. *The EEC always has a surplus of food*

◆ Überschuß

surrender value (*also* **cash surrender value**) the amount of money which an **insurance company** is willing to give a person if he wants to give up his **life assurance policy;** usually the amount increases as the policy gets closer to its **maturity date**

◆ Rückkaufswert (einer Police)

survey *noun* (1) a general description of a subject. *A survey of economic trends in the last ten years has just been published.* (2) a measurement of an area of land. *They have just completed a survey of the northern section of the county.* (3) *(UK)* an examination of a house to see if there is anything wrong with it: *to pay for a survey to be done.* (4) an organisation which is concerned with **surveying** (meaning 3) an area or a country: *the Ordnance Survey.* (5) a study of what people want or think which uses **sampling** methods. (6) a careful examination of something in order to be able to make a report on it: *a survey of working conditions in factories*

◆ (1) Überblick (2) Vermessung (3) Begutachtung (4) ≃ Landesvermessungsamt (5) Umfrage (6) Untersuchung

survey *verb* (1) to look over (something); to examine. *From this hill, you can survey the whole city.* (2) to deal with (a subject) generally. *In his talk, the chairman surveyed the company's performance in the past year.* (3) to measure (an area) carefully paying special attention to heights and distances, so that a map or plan can be made of it. (4) to examine (something) carefully so as to be able to report on its condition: *to survey a ship; to survey something to see the extent of damage incurred. You should always have a house surveyed before you buy it*

◆ (1) überblicken (2) Überblick geben (3) vermessen (4) untersuchen

surveyor a person whose job it is to **survey** land, buildings etc.

◆ Landvermesser; Bauinspektor

suspend (1) to stop for a time. *Police have suspended their inquiries until they have more evidence to go on.* (2) to stop (a person) from doing his job for a time. *He has been accused of stealing company funds, and has been suspended from his duties until after his trial. See also* **suspension**

◆ (1) einstellen (2) suspendieren

suspend payment to stop paying out any more money, as when certain businesses discover that they are in danger of going **bank-rupt,** and so do not pay any of their debts until they are sure that they can pay all of them. *See also* **suspension**

◆ Zahlungen einstellen

suspend trading to stop carrying out one's business for a time or for good, depending on whether business problems can be solved. *See also* **suspension**

◆ Geschäft (vorübergehend) aufgeben

suspense account a type of **account** for things which cannot be put into the proper account for various reasons, e.g. not enough details are known about the **transaction,** as the transaction is not complete

◆ Interimskonto

suspension (1) the state of being stopped for a time, or until certain decisions are taken: *suspension of payments; suspension of trading.* (2) the act of stopping a person from doing his job; the condition of being stopped from doing one's job. *His suspension lasted three weeks, and during that time the police examined* *the charges against him. See also* **suspend**

◆ (1) Einstellung (2) Suspendierung

sweated labour work done for very low pay. *These goods are cheap because they have been produced by sweated labour*

◆ unterbezahlte Arbeit

switchboard a board where telephone lines can be connected, e.g. in a telephone exchange, office or hotel; the people who operate a switchboard

◆ Vermittlung

switch selling a method of selling goods, now illegal in UK, by which possible customers' attention is attracted by an offer of goods at an attractive price: but the salesman's aim is actually to persuade them to buy something else which is not nearly such good value

◆ Switch-Geschäft

SWOT analysis a method of judging how well a business or organisation is doing by examining its strengths (S), weaknesses (W), the business opportunities (O) it has, and any threats (T) or dangers that there might be to its success

◆ SWOT-Analyse

sympathetic strike a **strike** by a group of employees, not against their own employers, but because they want to show their support for another group of workers who are having a **dispute** with their employers; the two groups of workers may be in different factories etc., or perhaps even in different industries. *They say that the miners are going to have a sympathetic strike in support of the nurses' pay claim*

◆ Sympathiestreik

syndicate *verb* (1) to publish in several newspapers or magazines on a regular basis. *His articles on business trends are syndicated in newspapers all over the world.* (2) to form a **syndicate;** to manage something by means of a **syndicate**

◆ (1) in mehreren Zeitungen veröffentlichen (2) ein Konsortium bilden

syndicate *noun* (1) a group of businessmen who are working together for one **project** or to reach a certain business aim, with each member of the group working for his own profit, although he needs the help of the other members of the group to get it. For example, a group of **underwriters** who come together to **insure** a large risk, or a group of companies which come together to work on a large government **project.** (2) → **cartel**

◆ (1) Konsortium

syndicated market research a situation where the cost of carrying out **market research** is shared by a number of companies, which also, of course, share the results of the research, e.g. **consumer panel** and **retail audit** studies

◆ gemeinschaftliche Marktforschung

synergy a **process** by which taking two or more related actions achieves results which are greater than what might be expected from the effects of each separate action on its own, e.g. two companies deciding to use the same sales representatives; often described as 2 + 2 = 5

◆ Ergebnispotenzierung

system (1) a number of different things making one complete whole: *a computer system; the economic system.* (2) the way things have been or can be arranged to work; a method. *He is proposing a new system of transport for the city. We shall have to change our present system of working — it's useless*

◆ (1) System (2) Methode

systematic following a **system** (meaning 2); well-organised. *The plan was easy to understand because* *everything was laid out in a very systematic way*

◆ systematisch

systems analysis an area of knowledge concerned mainly with the way in which the advantages of a **computer** can be used by an organisation in the most effective way taking into account the needs of the organisation, the weak points of the present method of working etc.

◆ Systemanalyse

systems analyst a person whose job it is to deal with **systems analysis**

◆ Systemanalytiker

systems selling a **process** by which a number of different **products** which can be made to work together are sold together, and not separately, e.g. a video camera, videotape recorder and television set could be sold as one video unit

◆ Verkauf von kompletten Systemen

T

tab (*short for* **tabulator**) a key on a typewriter or **computer keyboard** which allows **columns** to be spaced automatically

◆ Tabulator

table *verb* to bring (something) before a meeting for discussion or for a decision. *I intend to table a motion tonight concerning the need to increase our membership fees*

◆ einbringen

tabloid a type of newspaper with a small page size (i.e. about 30 × 40 cm (12 × 16 inches)), and usually presenting news in a sensational way so as to attract the largest possible readership

◆ Boulevardblatt

tabulate to set out (information) in the form of a table. *Details of our current trading position are tabulated at the end of the report*

◆ tabellarisieren

tabulator *see* **tab**

tachograph an instrument which records the speed and distance travelled by a **vehicle**

◆ Fahrtenschreiber

tactics detailed ideas for reaching certain limited aims, which may be part of a larger **strategy.** *We should discuss now what our tactics are going to be at tonight's board meeting*

◆ Taktik

takeaway of food, which can be taken away and eaten elsewhere; of a shop etc., selling such food

◆ Speisen zum Mitnehmen

take-home pay the amount of money which is actually paid to an employee after the money he owes for **income tax, superannuation** etc. has been taken away. *I earn £1000 a month, but my take-home pay is only £750 a month*

◆ Nettolohn

take over *verb* (1) to gain control over. *His business is expanding fast: he took over three other companies last year.* (2) **take over from** to be responsible for duties previously done by someone else. *Watch what I do carefully: you'll be taking over from me soon*

◆ (1) übernehmen (2) ablösen

takeover *noun* the act of taking control of an organisation. *The bakery's sales have been better since the takeover by a grocery chain*

◆ Übernahme

takeover bid an attempt by a company to get control of another by offering to buy **shares** of the other company at a price that might be attractive to its present **shareholders**

◆ Übernahmeangebot

take stock (1) of a shop, store etc. to check all the goods on the shelves and make sure nothing has been lost or stolen. *We take stock on Sundays, when the shop is closed.* *See also* **stocktaking.** (2) to examine or think about (something) carefully so that a decision can be made. *We're taking stock of the situation: it may be we'll have to close down the business*

◆ (1) Inventur machen (2) Bilanz ziehen

takings the amount of money that has been taken in exchange for goods or **services.** *Every night the shopkeeper would carefully count the day's takings*

◆ Einnahmen

talk shop to talk about business matters with other people in the same business, especially in the situation where such matters might not normally be discussed. *This is supposed to be a party—you shouldn't be talking shop!*

◆ fachsimpeln

tally *verb* of figures etc., to be the same, to correspond. *My totals don't tally with yours*

◆ übereinstimmen

tally *noun* a record of something; something on which this is kept. *It is always better to keep a tally of your expenses*

◆ Aufzeichnung

tangible asset a physical thing of value belonging to a person or company, e.g. a house, furniture, machinery etc. *See also* **intangible asset**

◆ Sachanlagen

tape recorder a machine which can record and play back sounds, e.g. music, speech etc.

◆ Tonbandgerät

tare (*or* **tare weight**) (1) the weight of a box, wrapping or similar container (taken away from the total weight of goods sent). (2) the weight of a vehicle when it is empty of goods and passengers

◆ (1) Tara (2) Leergewicht

target (1) something aimed at; something one wants to reach. *Our target is to sell twice as much of our product as last year. We just failed to achieve our target.* (2) a person or thing that is the object of the bad remarks or feelings of others. *Because of the company's poor performance, the chairman has been the target of much angry criticism*

◆ (1) Ziel (2) Zielscheibe

target audience a group of people that advertising material is specially aimed at. *If you want to reach your target audience, you have to find out what newspapers and magazines they read*

◆ Zielgruppe

target market the market to which a company plans to sell, e.g. the student market, the overseas market

◆ Zielmarkt

tariff (1) a **levy** or tax that has to be paid on goods **imported** into a country. (2) a scale of prices charged for **services,** e.g. in a hotel. *If you look at the tariff, you'll be able to check the cost.* (3) *(UK)* the rate of payment for certain services. *The electricity board has a special tariff for customers using large amounts of electricity*

◆ (1) Zoll (2) Preisliste (3) Gebührentarif

tariff barrier the point at which a tax has to be paid when **importing** or **exporting** goods

◆ Zollschranke

task a particular piece of work to be done. *I've made a list of the various tasks you'll have to perform in the course of your duties*

◆ Aufgabe

task force a small group of workers and/or managers who have been brought together to deal with a certain problem or to reach a certain aim

◆ Arbeitsstab

task method of budgeting *(especially* **advertising)** a method of working out how much a **process** is going to cost by **analysing** in detail how it is to be done

◆ aufgabenbezogene Budgetierung

tax *noun* an amount of money which people or organisations have to pay to the government to pay for its expenses, e.g. raised on what people earn, what they buy or what they own

◆ Steuer

tax *verb* (1) to make (people or organisations) pay money to the government: *to tax earnings/profits etc.* (2) to make heavy demands on. *Finding the money for these new developments is going to tax all our resources*

◆ (1) besteuern (2) angreifen

taxable on which tax must be paid: *taxable income,* i.e. the part of what a person earns that he has to pay tax on

◆ steuerpflichtig

tax allowance an amount of **tax relief.** *You can claim a tax allowance on certain kinds of business expense*

◆ Steuerfreibetrag

taxation (1) the act of **taxing** (meaning 1). (2) the amount of money paid in taxation. *A large proportion of my income goes in taxation*

◆ (1) Besteuerung (2) Steuern

tax avoidance legal methods used in order not to pay more tax than one has to. *See also* **tax evasion**

◆ Steuerumgehung

tax credit an amount of tax on the **dividend** of a **share** already paid by the company and therefore not paid by the **shareholder.** *See also* **tax voucher**

◆ Steuergutschrift

tax evasion illegal methods used in order not to pay tax one really ought to pay. *See also* **tax avoidance**

◆ Steuerhinterziehung

tax exemption a situation where taxes do not have to be paid by an organisation because of the special kind of work that organisation does. *Churches and charitable organisations are usually given tax exemption*

◆ Steuerbefreiung

tax haven (*or* **tax shelter**) a country which encourages companies to have their **headquarters** in it, and rich people to come and live in it, by having very low taxes and perhaps other benefits

◆ Steuerparadies

tax rebate an amount of money which one gets back after having paid one's taxes, e.g. because one's **income** has dropped, or because one was charged too much tax in the first place

◆ Steuerrückvergütung

tax relief the amount of money that can be taken away from the total of **taxable income,** because it has been spent in a special way, e.g. in UK there is tax relief on **mortgages** (house loans) and certain kinds of personal **insurance**

◆ Steuervergünstigung

tax shelter *see* **tax haven**

tax voucher a **document** sent by a company to a **shareholder** showing how much has been held back by the company for the payment of taxes on **dividends:** the document should be kept by the shareholder as proof that the necessary tax has been paid. *See also* **dividend warrant, tax credit**

◆ Steuerbeleg

tax year a period of twelve months over which **income** is worked out for tax purposes. *See also* **fiscal year**

◆ Steuerjahr

technical (1) connected with a special area of knowledge, especially practical subjects, such as engineering. *He has great technical knowledge of car engines.* (2) difficult because of needing special knowledge. *I can't understand this book on motor mechanics: it is too technical for me*

◆ (1) technisch (2) fachspezifisch

technician a person who has a practical skill and knowledge, especially in connection with machines and machinery. *The factory employs several technicians to service the machinery. He works as a technician in the hospital laboratory*

◆ Techniker

technique (1) a special way of doing something which needs practical skill and knowledge. *We shall train you in the business techniques you will need for this job.* (2) a special ability. *He has this technique of persuading customers that his advice is the best available*

◆ (1) Methode (2) Technik

technological of **technology.** *Children will have to be educated so that they can deal with the technological change that is bound to come*

◆ technologisch

technology the area of knowledge that deals with applying the discoveries and inventions of science to industry and commerce. *It is technology that turns scientific inventions into profit!*

◆ Technologie

telephone answering service a method by which messages sent by telephone can be recorded when no one is there to answer them; they can thus be answered later

◆ Anrufbeantworter

telephone selling a method of selling goods in which contact with possible customers is by telephone only

◆ Verkauf per Telefon

teletext general name for information etc. displayed on a television screen under such **viewdata systems** as **Ceefax, Oracle, Prestel**

◆ Teletext

telex *noun* a machine which works like a telephone except that the messages sent or received are printed out. This means that the person who is to get the message does not have to be there at the time the message is sent, but can pick it up from the telex machine at any time: *to send a message by telex*

◆ Fernschreiber

telex *verb* to send (a message) by **telex**

◆ fernschriftlich mitteilen

teller (*also* **cashier**) a person who works in a bank and whose main job is to pay out and receive money

◆ Kassierer(in)

temp a person employed to work in an office on a **temporary** basis, usually doing typing and secretarial work. *See also* **temporary staff service**

◆ Aushilfskraft

temporary lasting for only a short time. *He has a temporary post as a telephone engineer. Compare with* **permanent**

◆ vorübergehend

temporary staff service an organisation that supplies **temporary** staff (especially for office duties), usually to cover holiday periods, illness etc., in return for a **fee.** *See also* **temp**

◆ Zeitpersonalvermittlung

tenant person who has the use of property that belongs to someone else in return for paying a certain amount of money (**rent**), usually every week or every month. *See also* **lease**

◆ Mieter

tender *noun* (1) an offer to supply goods or **services** for a certain amount of money. *The city council are inviting tenders for the building of the new school.* (2) something that can be used in exchange when buying and selling; currency. *See also* **legal tender**

◆ (1) Angebot (2) Zahlungsmittel

tender *verb* (1) *(formal)* to give; to offer. *If the company ignores my advice, I shall tender my resignation.* (2) **tender for** to offer to supply goods or **services** for a particular amount of money. *We are going to tender for the contract to build the new hospital*

◆ (1) einreichen (2) sich bewerben um

tenure (1) being in possession of property. *The property is yours if you agree to three conditions of tenure.* (2) being in possession of a particular job. *Tenure of this post is for four years.* (3) a situation where one is secure in one's job, after a period where one's **contract** has to be renewed from time to time. *Jack has finally got tenure in his job at the University. See also* **security of tenure**

◆ (1) Pacht (2) Amtszeit (3) Anstellung auf Lebenszeit

term (1) a word or phrase used to name something: *technical terms.* (2) a certain period of time, e.g. that during which a **lease** continues, during which an **insurance** lasts, for which a **bill of exchange** is drawn. *The term of this bill is one month from today.* (3) *in plural* **terms** the conditions, e.g. of an agreement. *If you want to buy our goods you will have to accept our terms*

◆ (1) Begriff (2) Laufzeit (3) Bedingung

term days *see* **quarter days**

terminal (1) (a building in) an airport; a large bus or railway station: *an airport terminal. See also* **air terminal.** (2) any **device** by which **data** may be put into or got from a **computer.** *There are several terminals linked to this computer, and there is at least one on each floor of the building*

◆ (1), (2) Terminal

term insurance a type of **insurance** by which money will be paid out if the insured person dies within a certain period of time. *He took out term insurance for 25 years*

◆ zeitlich begrenzter Versicherungsvertrag

term loan *(especially US)* a situation where money is lent to a person by a bank for a certain period of time, and has to be repaid to the bank by **instalments** over that period: *a ten-year term loan of $40,000*

◆ mittelfristiger Kredit

terms of trade the way of working out how well a country is doing in its trade with other countries by which a certain range of **import** prices is divided by another range of **export** prices, and the result multiplied by 100. If the figure is more than 100%, then the terms of trade are good (favourable) since import prices are lower than export prices; if less than 100%, the terms of trade are thought to be bad (unfavourable). *See also* **balance of trade**

◆ Verhältnis von Ausfuhr- zu Einfuhrpreisen

territorial waters the amount of the sea around a country over which the country **claims** a certain kind of legal control. *No foreign ships will be allowed to fish within our territorial waters*

◆ Hoheitsgewässer

testimonial (1) a statement as to the good qualities of a person or **product.** *He showed us several testimonials to his hard work and good character. They published many testimonials from satisfied customers.* (2) a public occasion when a person is honoured for what he has done

◆ (1) Referenz (2) Ehrung

test marketing a less expensive

method of finding out how attractive to customers a new **product** is likely to be, by which the product is **launched** only in one carefully chosen area, and this **sample** is taken to show how popular it will be all over the country

◆ Erprobung eines Produkts auf dem Markt

theory (1) a way of thinking about something, a number of ideas which make up a plan or **system.** (2) the ideas behind something (rather than its being put into practice). *That's all right in theory but can it really be done?*

◆ (1), (2) Theorie

theory X (**management training**) the idea that human beings are naturally lazy and that a manager's job is to order or force people to work

◆ Theorie X

theory Y (**management training**) the idea that human beings are naturally active and that a manager's job is to take advantage of this by showing members that it is in their own interests to help to reach the aims of the organisation

◆ Theorie Y

think tank a group of experts who are paid by a company or government to try to solve a certain problem, or a certain kind of problem

◆ Planungsstab

third-party insurance a kind of **insurance** which covers not the insured person himself but anyone who may be affected by his actions under certain conditions. A common example is with car insurance, where the driver is forced by law to insure for anyone who may suffer injury or damage because of his actions as a driver

◆ Haftpflichtversicherung

Third World the **less-developed countries** of the world, especially those of Africa, Asia and Latin America

◆ Dritte Welt

three-shift system a method of keeping a factory, shop etc. continuously working, by getting workers to work in one of three **shifts** of 8 hours each, so covering the 24 hours of the day

◆ Dreischichtensystem

threshold agreement a method of making sure that employees' wages keep up with the **cost of living.** The employer agrees that if prices go up by more than a certain amount (as measured by the **retail price index**), then he will increase his workers' wages by a certain amount

◆ Lohnschwellenvereinbarung

through bill of lading a type of **bill of lading** used when the **cargo** has to be handed on from one **carrier** to another

◆ Transitkonnossement

throughput the amount that can be produced or handled. *This machine has a throughput of 500 items per hour. Our computer can handle a throughput of 100 enquiries every 10 minutes*

◆ Durchsatz

thruster a manager who is very active in doing business and in looking for new business. *See also* **sleeper** (meaning 1)

◆ aktive Führungskraft

till (1) a container used in a shop in which money is put in and taken out as **purchases** are paid for. (2) (*also* **cash register**) a container as in meaning 1, which also adds up and usually **records** how much is put into it each time it is used

◆ (1) Kasse (2) Registrierkasse

time and motion study a form of **work study** in which a worker's movements are carefully watched to see if they can be done more quickly or efficiently

◆ Zeit- und Bewegungsstudie

time bill a type of **bill of exchange** which is to be paid on a certain date

◆ Nachsichtwechsel

time card a card which records the exact time that an employee starts and finishes work when he/she puts it into a **time clock**

◆ Stechkarte

time clock a machine into which an employee can put his **time card**

◆ Stechuhr

time deposit *(US) see* **deposit account**

time rate a method of paying workers by the amount of time they have worked, rather than by how much they have produced (usually so much per hour, or per day). *See also* **piece rate, time work**

◆ Zeitlohnsatz

time scale the amount of time that a certain piece of work will take. *The time scale for this project will be in the order of five or six years*

◆ Zeitvorgabe

time-sharing (computers) a **system** by which users at different **terminals** can use a computer at the same time

◆ Time-sharing

time sheet a piece of paper on which a worker records the hours he/she works

◆ Stundenzettel

time work work for which payment is made by the amount of time that is taken to do it. *See also* **piece work, time rate**

◆ Zeitlohn

time zone an area of the world in which the same time is used. *The earth is divided into 24 time zones*

◆ Zeitzone

tip *see* **gratuity**

TIR carnet *see* **Transport International Routier**

title (1) a name of a book, article, film etc. *He has written some excellent books on marketing: I'll just give you a note of the titles.* (2) a legal right of ownership. *As soon as the contract is signed, the title to the land passes to you*

◆ (1) Titel (2) Rechtstitel

title deeds a **document** which shows that a person is the owner of a property. *Before you buy any property from him, insist on seeing the title deeds*

◆ Besitzurkunde

token (1) a small piece of plastic etc. used instead of a coin in certain circumstances, e.g. in certain machines. (2) a piece of paper which can be exchanged for goods, e.g. in a shop: a book token. See also **gift voucher.** (3) a sign or symbol. *Please accept this small gift as a token of our gratitude*

◆ (1) Marke (2) Gutschein (3) Zeichen

token strike a very short **strike** (which may be followed by a longer one) to show how strong feeling is on some question

◆ Warnstreik

toll an amount of money that has to be paid for the use of certain roads and bridges etc. *The Forth Road Bridge is a toll bridge*

◆ Maut

ton a measure of weight equal to 2240 pounds (**long ton,** *UK*) or 2000 pounds (**short ton,** *US*). *See also* **metric ton(ne)**

◆ Tonne

tonnage (1) the measure of the amount of **cargo** that can be carried by a ship. (2) the measure of the weight of the cargo of a ship

◆ (1) Ladefähigkeit (2) Ladegewicht

tonne *see* **metric tonne**

total loss something that is **insured** which has been completely destroyed or so badly damaged that it cannot be repaired. *After the accident, my car was written off as a total loss*

◆ Totalschaden

tout *verb* (1) to try to sell (e.g. tickets) at a higher price than they are really worth. (2) to try to get business in a pushing way. (3) to try to get information about racehorses for betting purposes

◆ (1) schwarz verkaufen (2) aufdringlich Reklame machen (3) herumschnüffeln

tout *noun* a person who **touts**

◆ Schwarzhändler; Kundenfänger; Schnüffler

track record the past successes and failures of a person or an organisation. *Before you hire him, check to see what his track record is like*

◆ das, was man vorzuweisen hat

trade *noun* (1) the business of buying and selling goods and **services.** *Trade between Europe and the Third World is increasing. He is in the book trade,* i.e. the business of buying and selling books. (2) an occupation; a kind of work (especially skilled work). *You should learn a trade: it might make it easier to get a job later*

◆ (1) Handel (2) Handwerk

trade *verb* to buy and sell goods and **services.** *We are not allowed to trade on Sundays. See also* **trade-in, trade-off**

◆ Handel treiben

trade association an organisation set up by businesses within a certain trade to protect and develop it in various ways. *Compare with* **employers' association**

◆ Fachverband

trade barrier any kind of **tax** or **duty** which makes the buying and selling of goods and **services** between countries more difficult

◆ Handelsschranke

trade counter a counter in a **warehouse** etc. where goods are sold to **retailers**

◆ Ladentisch

trade cycle (*or* **business cycle**) a period of time during which business moves from a time of good profits and high employment (**boom**) to a time of low profits and high unemployment (**slump**), and then back to boom conditions again. *See also* **boom, depression, recession, slump**

◆ Konjunkturzyklus

trade deficit *see* **trade gap**

Trade Descriptions Act *(UK)* an Act of Parliament which makes it illegal to describe goods in any way which is false or could be misleading to the public

◆ Gesetz über die korrekte Bezeichnung von Waren

trade discount a lowering of the amount charged for goods by a manufacturer or **wholesaler** to one of his customers (who is also in business)

◆ Wiederverkäuferrabatt

trade fair (*or* **trade exhibition**) an exhibition where manufacturers and others who are in the same area of business come together to display their goods and to see what others have to offer

◆ Messe

trade gap (*or* **trade deficit**) the amount by which a country's **visible imports** are more than its **visible exports** leading to an unfavourable **balance of trade**

◆ Außenhandelsdefizit

trade-in *noun* the act of **trading in.** *If you decide to buy this refrigerator we will accept your old one as a trade-in*

◆ in Zahlung gegebene Ware

trade in *verb* to offer (something one has, e.g. a car, television set) as part payment for something else of the same kind. *I am trading in my old car for a new one*

◆ in Zahlung geben

trademark (*also* **trade name**) the name or special design put on goods made by a particular manufacturer to show that they have been made by that manufacturer, and not by someone else. This name or design can be protected by law and may not then be copied by others. *If you want to check whether the goods are genuine you should look carefully at the trademark. See also* **brand**

◆ Warenzeichen

trade mission a group of businessmen who make a short visit to another country to try and develop **trade** (meaning 1) between the two countries

◆ Handelsdelegation

trade name (1) the name under which a company does business. (2) = **trademark**

◆ (1) Handelsname

trade-off an exchange of one thing for another, especially as part of a deal. *Also used as a verb* **trade off**

◆ Tauschgeschäft

trade press magazines and newspapers which are aimed at those who are in a certain area of business, keeping them informed of new developments in that area

◆ Fachpresse

trade price the amount of money paid by a **retailer** to a **wholesaler** or manufacturer for goods which he is going to sell to the public

◆ Großhandelspreis

trade promotion the act or **process** of persuading **wholesalers** and/or **retailers** to keep a certain kind of goods in **stock**

◆ Handelswerbung

trade reference a **document** needed by a person who is asked to supply goods and **services** on **credit** to a business for the first time, which will show that the business has paid its debts to another **supplier** and is therefore a good **risk**

◆ Kreditauskunft

trade secret a particular part of the **process** of making a **product** which is known only to the manufacturers and to no one else

◆ Geschäftsgeheimnis

trade union (*or* **trades union**) a group of workers who have formed themselves into an organisation which can **negotiate** with employers about wages and conditions of service

◆ Gewerkschaft

trade union dues (*also* **trade union contributions**) the amount of money which a person who belongs to a **trade union** has to pay to the union

◆ Gewerkschaftsbeiträge

trade unionist a person who belongs to a **trade union**

◆ Gewerkschafter

trade union recognition an agreement by the management of a company to **negotiate** with a certain **trade union** or group of trade unions

◆ Anerkennung der Gewerkschaft

trading account a **document** giving the main facts relating to the **gross profit** (or loss) of a company; the amount of profit or loss is carried over to the **profit and loss account**

◆ Betriebskonto

trading certificate a **document** given out by the **Registrar of Com-**

panies which allows a company legally to start doing business

◆ Gewerbegenehmigung

trading down a **process** by which a business tries to attract customers by selling cheaper goods, hoping to increase profits or sales by selling more goods. *See also* **trading up**

◆ Handel mit Billigerzeugnissen zwecks Umsatzsteigerung

trading estate an area where there are a number of factories, usually built at government expense. They may be offered at lower than usual rents for a time in order to attract business to that area. *See also* **industrial estate**

◆ Industriegelände

trading stamps special stamps which are given away with certain goods, or by a certain **retailer:** the stamps can be saved and later exchanged for cash or a range of goods

◆ Rabattmarken

trading up the **process** by which a business tries to increase profits by selling a more expensive kind of goods. *See also* **trading down**

◆ Handel mit Waren höherer Preislage und größeren Gewinnspannen

train to prepare (a person) to be able to do something (or to do something better) by teaching, and giving useful experience; to prepare oneself to do something by learning and experience. *All our personnel are trained for two years before they take up their duties*

◆ ausbilden

trainee *noun, adjective* (a person who is) being trained in some skill: *a trainee manager. Our factory takes on trainees directly from school*

◆ Auszubildende(r); Ausbildungs-

training the **process** of being taught to do something, or of improving one's skills in something: *management training*

◆ Ausbildung

training manual a book or **document** which describes how people should be taught if they are to learn certain skills

◆ Ausbildungshandbuch

training programme a list of things which have to be done, and how they have to be done, when a particular group of students have to be taught certain skills

◆ Ausbildungsprogramm

transact to do, carry out (a piece of business)

◆ abwickeln

transaction (1) a piece of business that has been done. *Over a thousand transactions were recorded on the Stock Exchange today,* i.e. over a thousand deals where shares were bought or sold. (2) *in plural* **transactions** published records of a society, meeting etc.

◆ (1) Transaktion (2) Sitzungsbericht

transaction costs legal and other **fees** which have to be paid when a business deal is done. *The transaction costs incurred in buying or selling property can be quite high*

◆ Abwicklungskosten

transfer *noun* (1) act or **process** of **transferring** or being transferred: *the transfer of money/passengers etc.* (2) a person or thing transferred, e.g. a design, a football player. *The Rovers new transfer is playing for them today*

◆ (1) Überweisung; Umsteigen (2) Neuerwerbung

transfer *verb* (1) to move from one place to another. *He has been transferred from Glasgow to the main office in London. At Rome, you will have to transfer to another plane. I'd like to transfer some money from my* *deposit account to my current account, please.* (2) to change the legal ownership of (something). *I have transferred these shares to my son.* (3) to copy (a design, photograph etc.) from one surface to another

◆ (1) überweisen; umsteigen; versetzt werden (2) übertragen (3) nachzeichnen

transfer pricing a **process** in a company by which goods and services **transferred** from one section or division of the company to another are charged against the receiving section etc. for **cost control** within the company

◆ Übernahmekursfestsetzung

tranship (*or* **transship**) to load (goods) from one ship etc. onto another. *This cargo will have to be transhipped at New York*

◆ umladen

transhipment (*or* **transshipment**) (1) the act or **process** of **transhipping.** (2) **cargo** that has been transhipped

◆ (1) Umladung (2) Ladung

transmission (1) the act of **transmitting.** (2) something that is transmitted: *a radio transmission.* (3) part of a motor car which carries power from the engine to the wheels

◆ (1) Übertragung (2) Sendung (3) Getriebe

transmit (1) to send or pass on from one person or place to another. *Doctors are investigating how the disease was transmitted.* (2) to send by radio; to broadcast. *We are able to transmit messages to our ships at any time*

◆ (1) übertragen (2) senden

transnational of more than one country; having branches or interests in more than one country: *a transnational business group. See also* **multinational**

◆ übernational

Transport International Routier (carnet) (*or* **TIR carnet**) a **document** which allows a **sealed** container to be transported by road through different countries with very little or no payment of **customs duty** until the country where the container's contents have to be unloaded

◆ Carnet

traveller's cheque a special type of cheque which is easily changed for cash in foreign banks (often also in hotels and shops); the person using it will also be **compensated** for their value if they are lost or stolen

◆ Reisescheck

treasurer a person who looks after the money belonging to a club, society etc.: *honorary treasurer,* i.e. one who is not paid for his services

◆ Kassenwart

treasury (1) a place where large amounts of money and other valuables are kept. (2) (*often* **the Treasury**) a government department which is in charge of the **finances** of a country

◆ (1) Tresor (2) ≃ Finanzministerium

treasury bill *(UK)* a type of **bill of exchange** which is offered by the government at a **discount** (i.e. for less than the value of the bill), does not give any **interest,** and is repaid within a short time (usually three months); these bills are **tendered** for by **discount houses**

◆ kurzfristiger Schatzwechsel

treaty (1) a formal agreement between two countries: *a peace treaty.* (2) any kind of formal agreement: *for sale by private treaty,* i.e. privately between the buyer and seller not by **auction**

◆ (1) Vertrag (2) Übereinkunft

trend *noun* a tendency to go or develop in a certain way or direction. *The trend in retailing these days is awa* *from small shops and more towards supermarkets*

◆ Trend

trend *verb* to go or develop in a certain way or direction. *House prices are trending upwards again*

◆ tendieren

trial balance a method of checking the correctness of **accounts,** by listing all the **debit balances** in one **column** and all the **credit balances** in another, and adding them up to see if they agree: this will show up some kinds of mistake (e.g. adding incorrectly) but not others (e.g. some **transactions** completely missed out)

◆ Probebilanz

trial order the act of asking for a small amount of some goods to check, e.g. on their quality, or on how they will sell, before ordering the full amount. *I'll make a trial order of 500 units, and we'll see how they go*

◆ Probeauftrag

tricks of the trade *(informal)* things one learns to do as part of one's job. *As an assistant manager, I learnt most of the tricks of the trade by watching my boss*

◆ Branchenkenntnisse

trust *noun* (1) belief in the good qualities of a person or thing; confidence. *Don't put your trust in him: he's very unreliable.* (2) a situation where others have belief in one's good qualities, or that one will do things properly: *a position of trust.* (3) property or money which is managed by others for someone or something. *He set up a trust for the education of poor children.* (4) *(US)* a group of companies which have combined to have an unfair position of strength in a certain area of business; a **monopoly.** *See also* **investment trust**

◆ (1) Vertrauen (2) Vertrauensstellung (3) Treuhand (4) Trust

trust *verb* to have confidence or belief in (e.g. a person's good qualities or abilities). *You can trust him to do an excellent job*

◆ vertrauen

trustee a person who has the responsibility of managing money or property on behalf of others

◆ Treuhänder

trustee savings bank *(UK)* originally a form of **savings bank guaranteed** by the government, now a **commercial bank**

◆ Sparkasse

turnkey contract a type of agreement in which a person pays someone else to look after the setting up of a large **project;** when the project is set up, the person paying expects to be able simply to 'turn the key' to get everything working smoothly

◆ schlüsselfertiger Vertrag

turnover (1) the total amount of goods or **services** sold over a certain time, usually expressed either in terms of value or sometimes of units sold. *This company has a turnover of £300,000 a year.* (2) the rate at which new goods have to be bought in to replace those that have been sold. *Turnover of sports equipment goods always increases sharply in the summer as you would expect.* (3) the rate at which workers leave an organisation and are replaced by others. *Since unemployment has increased, the turnover of staff has got less*

◆ (1) Umsatz (2) Umschlag (3) Personalwechsel

turnover tax a type of tax which is charged on **products** at each stage of the **process** from manufacture to **retailer;** no stage is excused from paying the tax. *See also* **value added tax**

◆ Umsatzsteuer

two-bin system a method of **stock control** by which the goods in **stock** are kept in two separate containers;

when one container is empty, it means that it is time for fresh supplies to be ordered

◆ 2-Behälter-System

typing pool a group of typists who do typing for a number of people in a company

◆ Schreibzentrale

U

uberrimae fidei (*Latin, meaning* of the greatest good faith) of a **contract,** for it to be **valid,** all the facts related to it must be given

◆ höchste Gutgläubigkeit und Redlichkeit

ultimate consumer the person who actually uses or has the benefit of goods that are bought, e.g. a wife may buy things in a shop, not for her own use, but for her husband or children, who become the ultimate consumers

◆ Endverbraucher

ultimo (*or* **ult**) *(Latin)* last month, sometimes used in correspondence

◆ letzten Monats

ultra vires (*Latin, meaning* beyond one's powers) *(law)* beyond what a person or company is lawfully allowed to do. *As far as this committee is concerned, that matter is ultra vires, and will have to be dealt with by someone else*

◆ in Überschreitung der satzungsgemäßen Befugnisse

umpire a person who is called in to give a decision on a **dispute** when the **arbitrators** who have been appointed cannot agree

◆ Schiedsrichter

UN *see* **United Nations**

unanimous in complete agreement, with everyone agreeing: *a unanimous decision*

◆ einstimmig

uncalled capital an amount of money which a company has been allowed to raise as part of its **authorised capital,** which has been issued but not yet fully paid. *See also* **paid-up capital, unissued capital**

◆ noch nicht eingezahltes Kapital

UNCDF *see* **United Nations Capital Development Fund**

unconstitutional not allowed by the laws or **regulations** of an organisation or a country. *It is unconstitutional for the President to interfere with judges' verdicts in court*

◆ verfassungswidrig

unconstitutional strike a situation where workers refuse to work because of a **dispute** with the management in a way which goes against some agreement or **agreed procedure** (e.g. a no-strike **policy**). It may or may not be an **official strike.** *See also* **unofficial strike**

◆ Streik aufgrund von Verstößen der Betriebsleitung gegen Betriebsvereinbarungen

uncontrollable cost a cost which has to be met by a company but which is outside its control, e.g. one caused by changes in government **policy,** changes in the **exchange rate** etc.

◆ nicht beeinflußbare Kosten

uncontrollable factors the **environment** in which a company operates over which it has little or no control, e.g. political or social changes

◆ nicht beeinflußbare äußere Gegebenheiten

UNCTAD *see* **United Nations Conference on Trade and Development**

undercapitalised of a company, not having enough **capital** to support the kinds of things that have to be done

◆ unterkapitalisiert

underdeveloped country *see* **developing country, Third World**

underemployment (1) a situation where a person does not have enough work to do, e.g. if the work is too easy for him, or if there is not enough work available. (2) a situation of less than **full employment**

◆ (1), (2) Unterbeschäftigung

undermanning a situation where there are not enough workers to do a job that has to be done, or not enough to do it properly. *See also* **overmanning**

◆ Personalmangel

undermentioned mentioned later (in a letter etc.). *We shall be glad to discuss the undermentioned factors with you if necessary*

◆ untengenannt

undersell to sell goods more cheaply than others. *He stayed in business only by underselling his competitors*

◆ Konkurrenz unterbieten

understaffed *see* **staff** (*verb*)

undertake to agree to do (something)

◆ sich verpflichten

undertaking something **undertaken.** *This undertaking may prove to be too much for our resources*

◆ Unternehmen

underwrite (1) to agree to buy any **shares** that are left unsold when there is a new **share issue.** (2) (**insurance**) to agree to meet the costs of (all or part of a risk). (3) to **guarantee** to cover (the costs of a **project**) if it should fail

◆ (1) eine Wertpapieremission garantieren (2) Versicherungsschutz gewähren (3) Haftung übernehmen

underwriter (1) a person working for an **insurance company** who advises on what risks to accept and what **premiums** to charge. (2) a member of an **insurance** group (e.g. **Lloyds**) who agrees to meet the costs of all or part of a risk. (3) a person who, for a **commission,** agrees to buy up any **shares** left unsold from a new **share issue**

◆ (1) Assekurant (2) Versicherer (3) Garant einer Wertpapieremission

underwriting manager (1) — **underwriter** (meaning 1). (2) a person who arranges **insurance** on behalf of an **underwriter** (meaning 2)

◆ (2) Versicherungsagent

undischarged bankrupt a person who has been unable to pay his/her business **creditors** and who has not been legally released from the results of his/her **bankruptcy**

◆ nicht entlasteter Gemeinschuldner

undistributed profits *see* **retained earnings**

UNDP *see* **United Nations Development Programme**

undue influence a legal reason for a person not being bound by a **contract** he has signed: he can claim that he was persuaded to sign it under the strong influence of someone else, e.g. a parent

◆ unzulässige Beeinflussung

unearned income money which is not got from one's employment but from other **sources,** such as **investment;** sometimes this kind of **income** is more highly taxed

◆ Einkünfte aus Kapitalvermögen

uneconomic not profitable; costing too much to be worthwhile. *Some railway routes have been closed down because they are uneconomic to run*

◆ unwirtschaftlich

unemployed not having work, not able to find work

◆ arbeitslos

unemployment (1) the state of not

having employment. *Unemployment has been shown to have bad psychological effects.* (2) the number of people who cannot find work: *an area of high unemployment*

◆ (1), (2) Arbeitslosigkeit

unemployment benefit money that a person is paid by the government while he/she is **unemployed**

◆ ≃ Arbeitslosenunterstützung

unfair dismissal (*or* **wrongful dismissal**) the act of taking a person away from his or her job or being taken away from one's job for a bad or unimportant reason. *The female broadcaster is suing her employers for unfair dismissal: they said she was not attractive enough*

◆ ungerechtfertigte Entlassung

unfavourable balance of trade *see* **balance of trade**

unilateral on the part of one person, group or organisation only (where more than one are involved). *The union made a unilateral decision to break off the negotiations*

◆ einseitig

union *see* **trade union**

union shop a place of work where all the workers must belong to a **trade union;** new workers who are not union members may be taken on but they must join a union when they start work

◆ gewerkschaftlicher Betrieb

unique selling proposition (*or* **USP**) some attractive quality in a **product** which is not shared by any other competing product

◆ einzigartiges Verkaufsargument

unissued capital part of the **authorised capital** of a company which has not yet been given out in the form of **shares** to the **shareholders**

◆ noch nicht ausgegebenes Aktienkapital

unit cost (**accounting**) a cost used in the working out of the costs of goods; it is reached by dividing the total cost of the goods by the number of units of the goods in **stock.** *The company produced 500 articles. The total cost was £5000. Therefore the unit cost was 5000 ÷ 500 = £10*

◆ Stückkosten

United Nations (*or* **UN**) a union of independent states formed in 1945 for the development of friendly relations between states and for international cooperation. Membership: 157 countries. Headquarters: New York. Official languages: Arabic, Chinese, English, French, Russian, Spanish

◆ Vereinte Nationen (UN)

United Nations Capital Development Fund (*or* **UNCDF**) a **fund** formed by the **United Nations** in 1966 to help **developing countries** by means of **grants** and loans of money. Headquarters: New York

◆ Kapitalentwicklungsfonds der Vereinten Nationen

United Nations Conference on Trade and Development (*or* **UNCTAD**) a **United Nations** organisation formed in 1964 to help to speed up the **economic** growth of **less-developed countries** by helping their trade. Membership: 162 countries. Headquarters: Geneva. Official languages: as United Nations

◆ Handels- und Entwicklungskonferenz der Vereinten Nationen

United Nations Development Programme (*or* **UNDP**) a programme formed by the **United Nations** in 1965 to speed up the social and **economic** growth of **less-developed countries** by giving help on industrial matters. Headquarters: New York

◆ Entwicklungsprogramm der Vereinten Nationen

unit holder a person who has **invested** in a **unit trust**

◆ Anteilscheinbesitzer

unit price a statement of how much something costs according to each unit of measurement, e.g. so much per kilo, so much per ounce etc.; thus things can be more easily compared to find out whether they are good value

◆ Preis pro Maßeinheit

unit trust *(UK)* an organisation which gives people the opportunity to **invest** in **shares** in a way that is supposed to have less risk in that the investors (**unit holders**) buy units, and their money is then invested by the unit trust in a range of shares: the value of the units can rise or fall according to how the shares do

◆ Investmentgesellschaft

universe *see* **population** (meaning 2)

unlimited liability a situation where each member of a company is legally responsible for his share of the total debts of the company

◆ unbeschränkte Haftung

unlisted company (*or* **unquoted company**) a company the **shares** of which are not among those listed by the **stock exchange**

◆ amtlich nicht notierte Gesellschaft

unload (1) to take away a load or **cargo** from. *The ship's cargo will be unloaded before midnight.* (2) to get rid of. *When he realised what a bad state the company was in, he tried to unload as many of his shares as possible*

◆ (1) entladen (2) abstoßen

unofficial strike a **strike** when workers do not have the support of their own **trade union**

◆ wilder Streik

unquoted company *see* **unlisted company**

unsecured creditor a person who is owed money, but does not have as **security** something of value to the person who owes him money (the **debtor**); if the debtor goes **bankrupt** then he will be paid only after **secured creditors** etc. have received their share

◆ nicht abgesicherter Gläubiger

unskilled work work for which little training or skill is required

◆ Hilfsarbeit

unsocial hours time of working when most other people are able to relax, e.g. evening work, weekend work. *People in bars and restaurants often have to work unsocial hours*

◆ unsoziale Arbeitszeit

unsolicited goods goods which are sent to a possible customer who has not asked for them, in the hope that he/she will agree to buy them: in UK he/she is not legally required to return them

◆ unbestellte Warensendung

upgrade (1) to make (a job or the person doing it) more important or better rewarded, without changing the job itself much. *See also* **promote** (meaning 3), **downgrade.** (2) to improve (a **product**) without making basic changes in its **design.** *This model of car has now been upgraded in various ways: for example, a radio is now fitted as standard*

◆ (1) anheben (2) verbessern

upmarket of **products** which are expensive and more likely to be bought by better-off people. *This is a very upmarket perfume, and it's terribly expensive. See also* **down market**

◆ anspruchsvoll

upset price *(US and Scottish)* the lowest price that will be accepted by the seller at an **auction** or on the sale of property. *He has put his house on the market at an upset price of*

£50,000. See also **reserve price**

◆ Mindestgebot

USP *see* **unique selling proposition**

usury the act or **process** of lending money at an **interest rate** that is too high or illegally high. *The interest rates he charges amount to usury*

◆ Wucher

utility (1) usefulness. *This machine may not look all that good, but you cannot deny its utility.* (2) *see* **public utility**

◆ (1) Nützlichkeit

V

vacancy the state of being **vacant;** a post which is vacant. *There are vacancies for typists in our office*

◆ offene Stelle

vacant empty; of a job or building, not having anyone in it: *situations vacant:* i.e. advertisements in a newspaper etc. for jobs which are available

◆ offen; leer

vacation (1) *(UK)* the part of the year when the law courts or the universities are closed. (2) *(US)* a holiday

◆ (1) Gerichts-; Semesterferien (2) Ferien

valid (1) having some basis of truth; supported by evidence. *He made many valid points in his speech.* (2) following the necessary rules and laws, legally correct and acceptable: *a valid passport,* i.e. one which is not out-of-date etc.; *a valid contract*

◆ (1) stichhaltig (2) gültig

validate (1) to check and show that (something) is what it claims to be or is legally correct: *to validate a document.* (2) to make (something) legal or official

◆ (1) für gültig erklären (2) Rechtskraft verleihen

validity the state of being **valid.** *You had better check the validity of this document in overseas countries before you go abroad*

◆ Gültigkeit

valuation the act or **process** of **valuing** (meaning 1); the price arrived at in this way: *to get a valuation for one's house/a work of art etc.*

◆ Schätzung; Schätzwert

value *noun* (1) how much something is worth (which may be different from its price). *We decided to buy the car because it seemed such good value (for money),* i.e. it seemed to be worth as much as, or more than, its price. (2) how much something means to a person. *This brooch is of sentimental value only,* i.e. it is not worth much money, but it is valuable to me for other reasons

◆ (1), (2) Wert

value *verb* (1) to give an expert opinion on how much (something) is, or might be, worth. *That is a very fine painting: you should get it valued.* (2) to hold (something or someone) at a certain worth. *She is a very good secretary: I value her services highly*

◆ (1) schätzen (2) wertschätzen

value added the difference between what a business gets from selling its **products** and the amount paid for **supplies** and materials

◆ Mehrwert

value added tax (*or* **VAT**) a type of tax, commonly used in Europe, which is charged on the difference between what a person pays for goods or **services** and what he/she sells them for. For example, a **retailer** will pay VAT on goods that he buys (input tax) and charge his customers VAT on the goods when he/she sells them (output tax), and he/she will then pay to the government at certain fixed times the difference between all the input tax he/she has paid and all the output tax he/she has collected. *See also* **turnover tax, zero-rated**

◆ ≈ Mehrwertsteuer

value analysis a method of checking that the design, material and manufacture of a **product** are as **economic** as possible; each separate stage of the whole **process** is carefully examined to make sure that money is not being wasted

◆ Wirtschaftlichkeitsanalyse

valuer a person who **values** (meaning 1)

◆ Schätzer

value received words used on a **bill of exchange** to show that money or goods to the value of the bill have been received from the **drawer** of the bill

◆ Betrag erhalten

variable cost a situation where the amount it costs to produce something increases according to how much more is produced, and gets less according to how much less is produced. *See also* **fixed cost, semi-variable cost**

◆ variable Kosten

variance (1) the difference between what something actually costs and its **standard cost** (*see under* **standard costing**). (2) the state of one thing being different from another; disagreement: *to be at variance with,* i.e. not to agree with, or to be different from

◆ (1) Kostenabweichung (2) Unterschiedlichkeit; Meinungsverschiedenheit

variety reduction a method of lessening costs, e.g. of a **product,** by bringing about fewer differences in design, materials and manufacture. *See also* **standardisation**

◆ Produktrationalisierung

VAT *see* **value added tax**

VDU *see* **visual display unit**

vehicle something which can be used as a means of transport, especially one with wheels, e.g. a car, bus, lorry

◆ Fahrzeug

vending machine a machine which gives out e.g. drinks, sweets, cigarettes, stamps etc. when money is put into the machine

◆ Verkaufsautomat

vendor *(especially law)* a person who sells something

◆ Verkäufer

venture *noun* a business enterprise that carries a certain amount of risk. *I wonder if his new venture will succeed?*

◆ (gewagtes) Unternehmen

venture *verb* to do something which carries danger or risk; to risk (something). *He has ventured all his capital in the new business*

◆ wagen

venture capital *see* **risk capital**

verify to make sure that (something) is true or correct; to check

◆ überprüfen

vertical integration the joining of companies so that more of the various stages that a **product** goes through come under the same organisation, from the **raw materials** at one end to the **retailing** of the **product** at the other: if a cloth manufacturer bought a wool farm, or bought a chain of tailor's shops, both would be examples of vertical integration. *See also* **backward integration, forward integration, horizontal integration**

◆ vertikale Verflechtung

very important person *see* **VIP**

vested interest (1) a right to property which is legally **valid.** (2) a special interest in some matter, because it will cause personal loss or gain. *He should not judge this case, because he has a vested interest in it.* (3) a person or organisation, especially a powerful or wealthy one, which has such a personal interest in something. *There are many vested interests in* *this scandal which would like to prevent the truth becoming known*

◆ (1) Eigentumsrecht (2) persönliches Interesse (3) persönliche Interessen

vet to examine; to check up on. *This post involves security material: all candidates for it will be carefully vetted*

◆ überprüfen

video *adjective* connected with television; broadcast using television pictures; connected with **videotapes** or **video(tape) recorders**

◆ Video-

video *noun* (1) = **videotape** or **video(tape) recorder.** (2) a programme, advertisement or film which has been recorded on **videotape**

◆ (2) Videoaufnahme

videotape a tape which **records** a film and can be shown on a special television set

◆ Magnetband

video(tape) recorder (*or* **VTR**) a type of **tape recorder** for **videotapes;** it can also **record** and play back television programmes by means of **videotapes**

◆ Videorecorder

viewdata a **system** by which information can be called up and shown on one's television screen, using either television **transmissions** or the telephone line. In some cases goods and **services** displayed can be ordered by the user and paid for by **credit card:** in UK, a well known service along these lines is **Prestel,** run by British Telecom. *See also* **Ceefax, Oracle**

◆ Bildschirmtext

VIP (*or* **very important person**) *(informal)* a person who is important enough to have special arrangements made for him/her: *the VIP lounge in an airport; to give someone the VIP treatment,* i.e. to treat someone with great respect

◆ prominente Persönlichkeit

visa an official stamp which is put on a passport to allow its owner to enter or leave a country: *an entry visa*

◆ Visum

visible exports/imports goods and materials **exported** from or **imported** into a country as opposed to other **services** which can earn or cost foreign currency such as banking or **insurance.** *See also* **invisible exports/imports**

◆ sichtbare Ausfuhr/Einfuhr

visiting card *see* **business card**

visual *adjective* connected with seeing; able to be seen: *to use visual aids in teaching,* i.e. blackboard, photographs etc.

◆ visuell

visual *noun* a picture or drawing, which, e.g. a **representative** could use to give information about the **product** he is trying to sell

◆ Anschauungsmaterial

visual display unit (*or* **VDU**) a type of television screen on which information from a **computer** is shown

◆ Sichtgerät

vital statistics important information about the population of a country, e.g. how many are born and die each year, how many get married and divorced and so on

◆ Bevölkerungsstatistik

vocation one's chosen trade or profession; what one does, or would like to do, for a living

◆ Beruf

vocational guidance an area of knowledge which deals with advising people (especially young people) on the best kind of job for them to do, and the kind of training they will need to do that job. *See also* **occupational guidance**

◆ Berufsberatung

vocational training a kind of training that a person needs to do a certain job, especially a skilled or semi-skilled job

◆ Berufsausbildung

void (1) of a **contract, insurance policy** etc.; not having any legal force. *This contract has not been witnessed and it is therefore null and void.* (2) empty; not occupied by anyone. *No one has been appointed to his post meantime: it had been left void*

◆ (1) nichtig (2) leer

voidable contract a type of **contract** in which one of the people who have signed it can avoid meeting its terms because of a fault in the contract, e.g. an error, but the contract itself is still legal until the fault is declared

◆ anfechtbarer Vertrag

volume discount the amount by which the price of each unit of a **product** becomes less if a large enough number of the units is bought. *See also* **quantity discount**

◆ Mengenrabatt

volume of sales *see* **sales volume**

voluntary controls rules and **regulations** worked out by an organisation for its own members with the aim of making government action unnecessary: *voluntary controls in advertising*

◆ freiwillige Selbstkontrolle

voluntary group a group of **retailers** who sell the same kind of goods, who come together to buy these goods through one **wholesale** business (usually to cut costs)

◆ Einkaufsvereinigung

voluntary liquidation the **process** by which a company decides to stop operating; the directors would then have to make a **declaration of solvency**

◆ freiwillige Liquidation

voluntary redundancy the act of agreeing to lose one's job, in a situation where an organisation has too many workers; usually there is some kind of payment to persuade workers to agree to go

◆ freiwillige Aufgabe des Arbeitsplatzes

voting right the right of a **shareholder** to vote at the shareholders' meetings of a company, as stated in the **Articles of Association** of the company

◆ Stimmrecht

voucher (1) a **document** which shows that a certain amount of money was paid; a document which gives details of any financial **transaction.** (2) *(UK)* a document given out instead of money which may be used later to **claim** goods or **services.** *See also* **gift voucher, luncheon voucher**

◆ (1) Beleg (2) Gutschein

VTR *see* **videotape recorder**

W

wage (*often plural* **wages**) an amount that is paid to a person regularly (usually weekly) for work done. *He earns a wage of £150 a week. He collects his wages every Friday. See also* **salary**

◆ Lohn

wage differential the difference in the amount paid to workers at different levels within the same kind of work, or to different kinds of workers within the same organisation. *If we let wage differentials get too small, workers may lose their ambition to be promoted*

◆ Lohngefälle

wage freeze forbidding any increase in wages, usually as an attempt by the government to control **inflation**

◆ Lohnstopp

wage-price spiral a situation where an increase in wages causes an increase in prices, which in turn makes workers ask for higher wages, resulting in still higher prices and so on

◆ Lohn-Preis-Spirale

wage rate the amount of money that is paid to workers, expressed as so much per unit of time (hour, day etc.: **time rate**) or so much per unit of goods produced (**piece rate**). *His wage rate was fixed at £8 per hour*

◆ Tariflohn

wages *see* **wage**

wages policy (*or* **wage policy**) (1) the way in which an industry, company or factory acts in relation to wages, e.g. **systems** of payment, **wage differentials.** (2) the national **criteria** which affect the outcome of wages bargaining

◆ (1), (2) Lohnpolitik

wage worker a person who is paid weekly. *Compare with* **salaried**

◆ Lohnarbeiter

waiting time (1) the time when a worker is there and ready to work but cannot do so because of some reason beyond his control, e.g. if a machine has broken down. (2) the time that those providing certain **services** may charge for because their **clients** keep them waiting. *If you are not ready in time for a taxi, you may have to pay for his waiting time*

◆ (1) Verlustzeit (2) Wartezeit

Wall Street (1) a name often used to describe the New York Stock Exchange which is situated in Wall Street, New York. *Shares dropped on Wall Street.* (2) a collective name for US financial institutions. *Compare with* **The City**

◆ Wall Street

warehouse a large building for keeping goods in, e.g. for safekeeping, or until they can be moved into a shop for sale. *While we were abroad, we had our furniture stored in a warehouse. We need more supplies of tinned food from the warehouse*

◆ Lagerhaus

warehouse company (*or* **warehouseman**) a business that stores goods for others for a **fee**

◆ Lagerhausgesellschaft

warrant *noun* (1) a **document** that gives a person the legal right to something, or to do something: *a search warrant* (which gives the police the right to search someone's house); *a travel warrant* (which gives a person the right to travel at someone else's expense); *a share warrant* (which states that a person has the right to a certain number of **shares** in a company). (2) a **document** which states that a person is the legal owner of goods which have been left with a **warehouse;** ownership can be given to someone else by giving him/her the warrant

◆ (1) Ermächtigung (2) Warenschein

warrant *verb* (1) to give the right to do something; to give a good reason for. *I don't think the possible profits in that business warrant the amount of capital he has invested.* (2) to **guarantee.** *This company warrants all the cars that it sells*

◆ (1) ermächtigen; rechtfertigen (2) garantieren

warranty (1) a **guarantee** of goods bought, with arrangements to fix anything that goes wrong within a certain period of time. *All our used cars have a 12 month warranty.* (2) a promise made in a **contract** which is not, however, a main part of the contract: even if the promise is not kept, the contract is not held to be broken, but a **claim** for damages may be made against the person who has not kept his/her promise. (3) a statement made by a person that all the information he/she has given is correct, e.g. one who has taken out an **insurance policy;** a false statement means that the policy is **void**

◆ (1) Garantie (2) Zusicherung (3) Versicherung der Richtigkeit der Angaben

wastage *see* **natural wastage**

wasting asset a type of **fixed asset** which is gradually used up as the business goes on, e.g. in the coal-mining business the coal itself would be a wasting asset

◆ kurzlebiger Vermögenswert

waybill a **document** which is made out by the person responsible for moving goods from one place to another, giving details about the goods and the conditions under which they are being moved

◆ Frachtbrief

WDV *see* **written-down value**

wealth tax a type of tax which may be paid on property and other forms of wealth belonging to a person, when the total value of the wealth is greater than a certain amount

◆ Vermögenssteuer

wear and tear *see* **fair wear and tear**

welch (*or* **welsh**) to fail to pay a debt (especially a **gambling** debt); to fail to do something one has promised to do

◆ sich (vor Zahlungsverpflichtungen) drücken

welfare (1) of a person, being in a good state. *He is very anxious about their welfare.* (2) helping people in need, e.g. to see that they have enough food, clothes, medical care etc.

◆ (1) Wohlergehen (2) Wohlfahrt

welfare state a country which provides for the education and health of its citizens, and security against the effect of **unemployment,** sickness, old age etc.; a society which is organised along these lines. *Our population is getting older, so the expense of running the welfare state increases all the time*

◆ Wohlfahrtsstaat

wharf (*plural* **wharfs** *or* **wharves**) a platform built into the water where ships can load and unload

◆ Kai

wheeler-dealer *(informal)* a businessman who uses every chance to make bargains which will benefit himself personally. *Be careful if you have to do business with him: he is something of a wheeler-dealer, they say*

◆ gerissener Geschäftemacher

white-collar worker a person who does not work with his/her hands, especially someone who works in an office. *See also* **blue-collar worker**

◆ Angestellter

white goods (1) large machines used in the household (especially the kitchen) such as refrigerators, dishwashers and washing machines. (2) household linen such as sheets, tablecloths etc.

◆ (1) große Haushaltsgeräte (2) Weißwaren

whole-life insurance a type of **insurance** where the amount of money that a person is insured for is paid only on his death, and there is no other payment. *See also* **endowment**

◆ Lebensversicherung auf den Todesfall

wholesale *noun* the sale of goods in large quantities to shopkeepers and traders who then sell them to the public. *See also* **retail** *(noun)*

◆ Großhandel

wholesale *adjective* connected with **wholesale** *(noun). He started up with a wholesale business; later on he bought some shops. See also* **retail** *(adjective)*

◆ Großhandels-

wholesale *adverb* in quantity from or by a **wholesaler:** *to get goods wholesale. See also* **retail** *(adverb)*

◆ im Großhandel

wholesale *verb* to sell (goods) **wholesale.** *They wholesale fruit and vegetables. See also* **retail** *(verb)*

◆ einen Großhandel betreiben

wholesale-price index a method of showing how the prices of **wholesale** goods are going up or down by taking the average price of a range of the wholesale goods in one particular year (when the average will be said to equal 100), and then comparing that with prices in later years. Thus if the price of wholesale goods goes up, the **index** could become (for example) 108, 112 etc.

◆ Großhandelspreisindex

wholesaler a person who gets goods in large quantities from manufacturers etc., and sells them in quantity to shopkeepers and traders

◆ Großhändler

wildcat strike a type of **strike** which is started, often suddenly, by the workers without the approval of their **trade union** and without following **agreed procedures**

◆ wilder Streik

wind up (1) to close down (a company). *See also* **liquidation.** (2) to bring (a meeting etc.) to an end

◆ (1) eine Gesellschaft auflösen (2) schließen

winding-up *see* **liquidation**

window dressing (1) a **display** of goods in a window so as to attract the attention of possible customers. (2) trying to make something look better than it really is. *Don't be misled by their attractive offices: they are just window dressing for a very inefficient business*

◆ (1) Schaufensterdekoration (2) Mache

WIP *see* **work in progress**

withdraw (1) to take out or away (usually something which one has already put in): *to withdraw money from a bank. I am going to withdraw my name from the list of applicants for the job.* (2) to take back; to **cancel.** *I will withdraw the remarks I made about the chairman: they are not true*

◆ (1) abheben; zurückziehen (2) zurücknehmen

withdrawal the act of **withdrawing**

◆ Abhebung; Zurückziehung; Zurücknahme

without recourse (*or French,* **sans recours**) words written on **bills of exchange** etc., meaning that the person holding the bill etc. cannot come back to the person who has **endorsed** it for payment even if the bill is not **honoured**

◆ ohne Regreß

with-profits endowment assurance a type of **insurance** where the insured person gets a **guaranteed** amount of money after a certain period of time, and in addition a share of the profits which the **insurance company** has made over that period

◆ Versicherung auf den Erlebensfall mit Gewinnbeteiligung

word processor a machine with a **keyboard** and usually a **visual display unit** for printing, **storing** and retrieving text

◆ Textverarbeitungssystem

worker(s') director a person who represents the workers' interests on the **board of directors** of a company or similar organisation

◆ Arbeitsdirektor

workers' control a **system** of running an organisation by which all the important decisions are made by the workers themselves, or their **representatives**

◆ Arbeiterselbstkontrolle

work group a small number of people who work together, perhaps on a particular **project**

◆ Arbeitsgruppe

work-in a situation where workers stay in a factory etc. that is to be closed down and continue to work on as before. *The workers are furious about the closing down of the factory: they are going to stage a work-in. See also* **sit-down strike, sit-in**

◆ Fabrikbesetzung

working capital (*also* **circulating capital**) the difference between the **current assets** of a company and its **current liabilities;** this is the amount of money which the company can use to carry on with its business

◆ Umlaufkapital

working conditions the physical things which affect people as they are working, e.g. the amount of heat and light, how safe the machines they work with are

◆ Arbeitsbedingungen

working week the normal number of hours worked in a week; above this amount, **overtime** may have to be paid. *Our working week is 35 hours, from Monday to Friday*

◆ Arbeitswoche

work in progress (*or* **WIP**; *US* **work in process**) (1) **products** which are being manufactured but not yet completed. (2) the value of such incomplete products

◆ (1) halbfertige Erzeugnisse (2) Wert halbfertiger Erzeugnisse

work measurement the act of finding out how long it will take to do a certain piece of work. *See also* **work study**

◆ Arbeitszeitermittlung

workmen's compensation the amount of money which an employer has to pay to a worker who is injured in doing his/her duties, when it is not the worker's fault

◆ Unfallentschädigung

work permit a **document** given to a foreigner allowing him/her to work in a country for a certain time

◆ Arbeitserlaubnis

works council a type of committee within an organisation which has **representatives** of the management and other workers; it discusses matters affecting the organisation, especially as these relate to the interests of the workers

◆ Betriebsrat

work-sharing the act or **process** of making more employment available, e.g. by having less **overtime,** or by allowing two people to do a job as **part-time workers,** instead of having only one worker do it

◆ Arbeitsplatzteilung

work study (1) an area of knowledge which deals with the best and quickest ways of doing work, by carefully **analysing** how the work is done. (2) the act of **analysing** work in this way. *See also* **motion study, time and motion study**

◆ (1) ≈ REFA-Zeitstudie (2) Durchführung von Zeitstudien

work-to-rule *noun* a kind of action which workers can take against their employers if they do not want actually to **strike:** the workers obey every rule that exists affecting their work, which means that the work is done very slowly, and production suffers

◆ Arbeit nach Vorschrift

work to rule *verb* to carry out a work-to-rule

◆ nach Vorschrift arbeiten

World Bank *see* **International Bank for Reconstruction and Development**

wraps: under wraps *(informal)* hidden, out of sight. *We're keeping the* *new model of our car under wraps until the motor show*

◆ unter Verschluß

writ a **document** put out by a court which states that a person named on it must do something, or stop doing something, as decided by the court: *to issue a writ against someone*

◆ einstweilige Verfügung

write down (**accounting**) to record the value of (a **wasting asset**) at a certain lower level than the previous year

◆ Buchwert herabsetzen

write off *verb* (1) (**accounting**) to record (something) as having no **cash value,** e.g. a piece of machinery that cannot be repaired or a debt that cannot be paid back; the **book value** may be set off as a loss against any profits. (2) to lower gradually the book value of (a **wasting asset**) over a period of time. *This new machine will be written off over a period of ten years*

◆ (1) ausbuchen (2) abschreiben

write-off *noun* (1) something that has been **written-off.** (2) act of **writing off** something. (3) the **book value** of something that has been written off. (4) something so badly damaged that it cannot be repaired. *After the accident, my car was a write-off*

◆ (1) Abschreibungsgegenstand (2) Abschreibung (3) Buchwert (4) Totalverlust

write up (1) (**accounting**) to state that (some **asset**) is worth more than it actually is. (2) to write a description of (something) so as to bring it to public notice. *He has written up an account of the chairman's farewell party for the local press*

◆ (1) Buchwert heraufsetzen (2) ausführlich darstellen

writing-down allowance the amount of money that may be set against profits for tax purposes because of **depreciation** of **wasting assets**

◆ Abschreibungssatz

written-down value (*or* **WDV**) (**accounting**) the amount an **asset** is worth after **depreciation** has been allowed for

◆ Buchwert

wrongful dismissal *see* **unfair dismissal**

X

xerography a method of making copies of a **document,** chart etc. *See also* **photocopy**

◆ Xerographie

xerox *noun* (**trademark**) a method of **photocopying;** a copy made by this method

◆ Xeroxverfahren; Xerokopie

xerox *verb* (**trademark**) to make a copy by **xerox**

◆ xerokopieren

Y

year book a book which is published every year dealing with a certain area of knowledge, business etc., which gives up-to-date information on that area: *the Gardener's Year Book*

◆ Jahrbuch

year's purchase a method of stating how much a business or property is worth according to the number of years it will take for the buyer to get back the money he/she has paid. For example, if a property costs £70,000 and the profit from it comes to £10,000 per year, then the price is years' purchase of the profits

◆ Jahresertragswert

yield (1) the amount of money which a person receives from **stocks** and **shares,** either as a percentage of the original price paid, or as a percentage of their current value. (2) what is produced from something else, e.g.

land, a mine. *This land will give a good yield of crops*

◆ (1) Rendite (2) Ertrag

York-Antwerp rules (**marine insurance**) a set of rules to guide those concerned with **claims** arising from **financial** loss at sea

◆ York-Antwerpen-Bestimmungen

Z

z chart a **graph** which shows production or sales in 3 ways: (1) the totals for each week or month; (2) the total for the week or month added to the previous one; (3) the average totals

◆ Z-Diagramm

zero-rated with reference to **value added tax,** certain goods and **services** are within the **VAT system** but are rated at 0%

◆ befreit von Mehrwertsteuer

zipcode *US* – **postcode**

Deutsch-Englisches Register

Abbaurechte → MINERAL RIGHTS
abbröckeln → EASE
Abfindung → COMPENSATION FOR LOSS OF OFFICE
Abgabe → LEVY, RATE
abgesicherter Gläubiger → SECURED CREDITOR
abhaken → CHECK OFF
abheben → DRAW, WITHDRAW
Abhebung → WITHDRAWAL
ablösen → TAKE OVER
Abonnent → SUBSCRIBER
abonnieren → SUBSCRIBE
Abrechnungszeitraum → ACCOUNTING PERIOD
Abruf → CALL
Absatz → PARAGRAPH, SALE
Absatzdenken → MARKETING CONCEPT
Absatzförderung → SALES PROMOTION
Absatzgebiet → SALES TERRITORY
Absatzkontrolle → SALES CONTROL
Absatzplan → MARKETING PLAN, SALES BUDGET
Absatzplanung → MARKET PLANNING, SALES PLANNING
Absatzposten → SALES COSTS
Absatzprognose → SALES FORECAST
Absatzprüfung → SALES AUDIT
Absatzquote → SALES QUOTA
Absatzweg → CHANNEL OF DISTRIBUTION
Absatzziffern → SALES FIGURES
Abschlagszahlung → PAYMENT ON ACCOUNT
Abschlußbuchungen → CLOSING ENTRIES
Abschlußprüfer → ACCOUNTANT
abschreiben → WRITE OFF
Abschreibung → WRITE-OFF
Abschreibungsgegenstand → WRITE-OFF
Abschreibungssatz → WRITING-DOWN ALLOWANCE
abstoßen → UNLOAD
Abteilung → DEPARTMENT, DIVISION
Abteilungsleiter → BUYER
abwälzen → SHIFT
Abweichung → DEVIATION
Abwertung → DEVALUATION
abwickeln → TRANSACT
Abwicklungskosten → TRANSACTION COSTS
Adresse → ADDRESS
Adressiermaschine → ADDRESSING MACHINE
Agentur → AGENCY
Akkordarbeit → PIECEWORK
Akkordlohnsatz → PIECE RATE
Akkreditiv → LETTER OF CREDIT
Akquisiteur → SOLICITOR
Akte → FILE
Aktenmappe → FOLDER
Aktenordner → FILE
Aktenzeichen → REFERENCE
Aktie → SHARE, STOCK
Aktienbank → JOINT-STOCK BANK
Aktienemission → SHARE ISSUE
Aktiengesellschaft → JOINT-STOCK COMPANY, PUBLIC LIMITED COMPANY
Aktienindex → SHARE INDEX
Aktieninhaber → SHAREHOLDER
Aktieninvestition → CAPITAL INVESTMENT
Aktienkapital → SHARE CAPITAL
Aktienzertifikat → SHARE CERTIFICATE
Aktie zeichnen → SUBSCRIBE
Aktionsschwelle → ACTION LIMIT
Akzelerationsprinzip → ACCELERATOR
Akzept → ACCEPTANCE
Alkoholgehalt → PROOF
alleinig → SOLE
alleinstehend → SOLUS POSITION
Alleinvertretungsvertrag → EXCLUSIVE AGENCY AGREEMENT
alles in allem → ALL FOUND
allgemein → ACROSS-THE-BOARD
Alternativkosten → OPPORTUNITY COST
Altersversorgung → OCCUPATIONAL PENSION SCHEME
Altmaterial → SCRAP
Amortisation → AMORTIZATION
Amt → OFFICE
amtieren → OFFICIATE
amtlich → OFFICIAL
Amt niederlegen → RETIRE
Amtsträger → OFFICE-BEARER
Amtszeit → TENURE
Analogrechner → ANALOG COMPUTER
Analyse → ANALYSIS
analysieren → ANALYSE
anbieten → OFFER
Anbieter → OFFEROR
anfangen → LAUNCH
anfordern → REQUISITION
Anforderung → REQUISITION
Anforderungsschein → REQUISITION
Anfrage → ENQUIRY, SALES INQUIRY
Angebot → OFFER, TENDER
Angebotskurve → SUPPLY CURVE
Angebotspreis → OFFER PRICE
Angebotstabelle → SUPPLY SCHEDULE
Angeklagter → DEFENDANT
Angeld → EARNEST MONEY
angelernter Arbeiter → SEMI-SKILLED WORKER
Angestellter → WHITE-COLLAR WORKER
angreifen → TAX
Anhang → SCHEDULE
anheben → UPGRADE
Anklage → CHARGE
anklagen → CHARGE
Anlage → ENCLOSURE
Anlagekapital → FIXED CAPITAL
Anlagen → PLANT
Anlagenabschreibung → CAPITAL ALLOWANCE
Anlagen streuen → DIVERSIFY
Anlagevermögen → CAPITAL ASSETS, FIXED ASSETS

bewerben um → APPLY
Bewerber → APPLICANT
Bewerbung → APPLICATION
Bewerbungsausschuß → SELECTION BOARD
Bewerbungsformular → APPLICATION FORM
Bewertung → RATING
Bewertungsskala → RATING SCALE
Bewirtung → ENTERTAINMENT
Bewohnen → OCCUPANCY
bewohnen → OCCUPY
Bewohner → OCCUPANT, OCCUPIER
bezahlen → PAY, RENUMERATE
Bezahlung → PAYMENT, RENUMERATION
Bezogener → DRAWEE
Bezugsrechtemission → RIGHTS ISSUE
Bilanz → FINANCIAL STATEMENT
Bilanzaufstellung → BALANCE SHEET
Bilanzbuchhalter → ACCOUNTANT
Bilanzeinheit → PROFIT CENTRE
Bilanz ziehen → TAKE STOCK
bilateraler Handel → BILATERAL TRADE
bilaterales Abkommen → BILATERAL AGREEMENT
Bildentwurf → ARTWORK
Bildschirm → MONITOR
Bildschirmtext → VIEWDATA
billig → CHEAP
billige Handelsflagge → FLAG OF CONVENIENCE
billiges Geld → CHEAP MONEY, EASY MONEY
Billigladen → DISCOUNT STORE
binäres Zahlensystem → BINARY SYSTEM
Binnenmarkt → HOME MARKET
bis heute → DATE
Blankoindossament → BLANK ENDORSEMENT
Blankoscheck → BLANK CHEQUE
Blaupause → BLUEPRINT
Bodenschätze → NATURAL RESOURCES, RESOURCES
bohren → DRILL
Bohrer → DRILL
Bohrinsel → OIL RIG, RIG
Bohrloch → OIL WELL
Bohrmannschaft → DRILLING CREW
Bohrschiff → DRILL SHIP
Bonus → BONUS
Bordempfangsschein → MATE'S RECEIPT
Bordvorräte → SHIP'S STORES
Börse → BOURSE, EXCHANGE, STOCK EXCHANGE
Börsenhausse → BULL MARKET
Börsenmakler → STOCKBROKER
börsennotierte Firma → LISTED COMPANY
börsennotierte Wertpapiere → LISTED SECURITIES
Botschaft → EMBASSY
Boulevardblatt → TABLOID
Boycott → BOYCOTT
boykottieren → BOYCOTT
Branchenkenntnisse → TRICKS OF THE TRADE
Briefkopf → LETTERHEAD
Bruchschaden → BREAKAGE
Bruttoeinkommen → GROSS INCOME
Bruttoertrag → GROSS YIELD
Bruttogewicht → GROSS WEIGHT
Bruttogewinn → GROSS PROFIT
Bruttoinlandsprodukt → GROSS DOMESTIC PRODUCT
Bruttosozialprodukt → GROSS NATIONAL PRODUCT
Bruttoumsatz → GROSS SALES
Büchergutschein → BOOK TOKEN
Buchführung → ACCOUNTING, BOOKKEEPING
Buchführungswesen → ACCOUNTANCY
Buchungsmaschine → ACCOUNTING MACHINE
Buchwert → BOOK VALUE, WRITE-OFF, WRITTEN-DOWN VALUE
Buchwert herabsetzen → WRITE DOWN
Buchwert heraufsetzen → WRITE UP
Bühnenbild → SET
Bulletin → BULLETIN
Bummelstreik → GO SLOW
Bund → FEDERATION
Bürge → SPONSOR
Bürgschaft → GUARANTEE
Büro → OFFICE
Büro- → CLERICAL
Bürokratismus → RED TAPE

Carnet → TRANSPORT INTERNATIONAL ROUTIER
Charta → CHARTER
chartern → CHARTER
Chartervertrag → CONTRACT OF AFFREIGHTMENT
cif → CIF
Computersteuerung → NUMERICAL CONTROL
Container → CONTAINER
Containerisierung → CONTAINERIZATION
Containerschiff → CONTAINER SHIP

Darlehen → LOAN
Darlehenskonto → LOAN ACCOUNT
Darlehenssumme → PRINCIPAL
Datei → FILE
Daten → DATA
Datenbasis → DATA BASE
Datensichtstation → DISPLAY
Daten speichern → FILE
Datenverarbeitung → DATA-PROCESSING
Dauerauftrag → BANKER'S ORDER, STANDING ORDER
Debetsaldo → DEBIT BALANCE
Deckladung → DECK CARGO
Deckung → COVER
Deckungsbeitrag → CONTRIBUTION
Deckungsbetragsübersicht → PROFIT-VOLUME CHART

harte Währung → HARD CURRENCY
Häufigkeit → FREQUENCY
Hauptaktionär → MAJOR SHAREHOLDER
Hauptbuch → LEDGER
Haupterzeugnis → STAPLE PRODUCT
Hauptgeschäftsstelle → HEAD OFFICE
hauptsächlich → PRINCIPAL
Hauptsendezeit → PRIME TIME
Hauptversammlung → GENERAL MEETING
Haushalt → HOUSEHOLD
Haushaltsgeräte → WHITE GOODS
Haushaltskontrolle → BUDGETARY CONTROL
Haushaltsperiode → BUDGET PERIOD
Haushaltsplan → BUDGET
hausieren → PEDDLE
Hausierer → PEDLAR, PEDDLER
Hausmarke → OWN BRAND
Haussemarkt → BOOM MARKET
Haussier → BULL
haussierend → BULLISH
Haus-zu-Haus-Verkauf → DOOR-TO-DOOR SELLING
Heftklammer → CLIP
Heftmaschine → STAPLER
Hehler → RECEIVER
Heidengeld verdienen → MINT
heißes Geld → HOT MONEY
herabstufen → DOWNGRADE
Herausgeber → EDITOR
herstellen → MANUFACTURE, PRODUCE
Hersteller → MANUFACTURER, PRODUCER
Herstellung → PRODUCTION
herumschnüffeln → TOUT
Heuervertrag → SHIP'S ARTICLES
Hilfsarbeit → UNSKILLED WORK
Hinterleger → BAILOR
Hinterlegungsstelle → DEPOSITORY
Hochkonjunktur → BOOM
Hochschulbildung → HIGHER EDUCATION
Höchst- → MAXIMUM
Höchststand → PEAK
Hoheitsgewässer → TERRITORIAL WATERS
höhere Gewalt → ACT OF GOD
Holdinggesellschaft → HOLDING COMPANY
Honorar → FEE
Honorarvorschuß → RETAINER
Hörerforschung → AUDIENCE RESEARCH
horten → HOARD
Hypothek → MORTGAGE
Hypothekengläubiger → MORTGAGEE
Hypothekenschuldner → MORTGAGOR

im Auftrag → PER PROCURATIONEM
Immobilienmakler → ESTATE AGENT
Import → IMPORT
Importabgabe → IMPORT SURCHARGE
Importeur → IMPORTER
importieren → IMPORT
in Betrieb → OPERATION
Indexzahl → INDEX NUMBER
indirekte Steuer → INDIRECT TAX
Indossant → ENDORSER
Indossat → ENDORSEE
indossieren → ENDORSE
Industrie → INDUSTRY
Industriegebiet → INDUSTRIAL ESTATE
Industriegelände → ESTATE, TRADING ESTATE
Industrieller → INDUSTRIALIST
industrielle Revolution → INDUSTRIAL REVOLUTION
Industriezweig → INDUSTRY
Inflation → INFLATION
Informationsabruf → INFORMATION RETRIEVAL
Infrastruktur → INFRASTRUCTURE
Inhaberobligation → BEARER BONDS
Inhalt → EFFECT
Initialverkauf → PIONEER SELLING
Inkassomandatar → DEBT COLLECTOR
Inklusivpreis → ALL-IN-RATE
inoffiziell → RECORD
insolvent → BANKRUPT
Insolvent → BANKRUPT
Insolvenz → BANKRUPTCY
Instanzenweg → LINE OF COMMAND
instruieren → BRIEF
Instruktionen → BRIEF
inszenieren → PRODUCE
Inszenierung → PRODUCTION
integrieren → INTEGRATE
Intensivverkauf → INTENSIVE SELLING
Interaktion → INTERFACE
Interimskonto → SUSPENSE ACCOUNT
international → INTERNATIONAL
Interview → PERSONAL INTERVIEW
interviewen → INTERVIEW
intrinsischer Wert → INTRINSIC VALUE
Inventur → STOCKTAKING
Inventur machen → TAKE STOCK
investieren → INVEST
investiertes Kapital → CAPITAL EMPLOYED
Investition → INVESTMENT
Investitionsgüter → INDUSTRIAL GOODS
Investitionsgütermarkt → INDUSTRIAL MARKET
Investitionsplan → CAPITAL BUDGET
Investitionszuschuß → INVESTMENT GRANT
Investmentgesellschaft → UNIT TRUST
Investmenttrust → INVESTMENT TRUST
Irreführung → FRAUD

Jahrbuch → ANNUAL, YEAR BOOK
Jahresabschluß → QUALIFIED ACCOUNTS
Jahresabschlußprüfung → GENERAL AUDIT
Jahresbericht → ANNUAL REPORT
Jahresertragswert → YEAR'S PURCHASE
Jahreshauptversammlung → ANNUAL GENERAL MEETING
jährlich → ANNUAL
Joint-venture → JOINT VENTURE

Referenz → REFEREE, REFERENCE, TESTIMONIAL
Regalgroßhändler → RACK JOBBER
Regionalplanung → REGIONAL PLANNING
Register → INDEX, REGISTER
Registerführer → REGISTRAR
Registratur → REGISTRY
registrieren → FILE
Registrierkasse → TILL
Regreß → WITHOUT RECOURSE
Regreßanspruch → RECOURSE
Regressionsanalyse → REGRESSION ANALYSIS
regulieren → REGULATE
Regulierung → REGULATION
reif → MATURE
Reife → MATURITY
Reihe → SET
Reihenfolge → ORDER
reiner Wechsel → CLEAN BILL OF EXCHANGE
reines Konnossement → CLEAN BILL OF LADING
Reinvermögen → NET ASSETS
Reisescheck → TRAVELLER'S CHEQUE
Reklame → HANDOUT, TOUT
Reklameplakat → SHOWCARD
Reklamewand → BULLETIN BOARD
Reklamezettel → LEAFLET
Rekord → RECORD
Rekrut → RECRUIT
rekrutieren → RECRUIT
Rekrutierung → RECRUITMENT
Rekta-Indossament → RESTRICTIVE ENDORSEMENT
Rendite → NET YIELD, RATE OF RETURN, YIELD
Rentabilität → PROFITABILITY
Rente → SUPERANNUATION
Repräsentant → REPRESENTATIVE
repräsentativ → REPRESENTATIVE
reprivatisieren → DENATIONALISE
Reprivatisierung → DENATIONALISATION
Reserve- → BACK-UP
Reservewährung → RESERVE CURRENCY
Resolution → RESOLUTION
Resonanz → RESPOND
Respekttage → DAYS OF GRACE
Ressourcen → RESOURCES
Rest → BALANCE, RESIDUE
Restposten → BROKEN LOT, JOB LOT
Restriktion → SQUEEZE
Retouren → RETURN
Retourenquittung → GOODS RETURNED NOTE
retten → SALVAGE
Rettung → SALVAGE
Reviervorsteher → SUPERINTENDENT
Revision → AUDIT
Revisor → AUDITOR
Revolving-Kredit → REVOLVING CREDIT
Rezeption → RECEPTION
Rezession → RECESSION
Rikambiowechsel → REDRAFT
Ring → RING
Risiko → GAMBLE, HAZARD, RISK
Risikoanalyse → RISK ANALYSIS
Risikoinvestition → SUNK COST
Risikokapital → RISK CAPITAL
riskieren → RISK
Roboter → ROBOT
Robotertechnik → ROBOTICS
Rohstoffe → RAW MATERIALS
Rollenkonflikt → ROLE CONFLICT
Rollenspiel → ROLE-PLAY EXERCISE
rote Zahlen → RED
Rückantwortkarte → REPLY-PAID POSTCARD
rückdatieren → BACKDATE
rückgängig machen → CANCEL
Rückgreifen → RECOURSE
rückkaufbar → REDEEMABLE
Rückkaufswert → SURRENDER VALUE
Rücklage → PROVISION
Rücklagen → RESERVES
Rücktrittsklausel → ESCAPE CLAUSE
Rückvergütung → REBATE
Rückversicherung → RE-INSURANCE
Ruhestand → RETIRE, RETIREMENT
runde Zahlen → ROUND
Rundschreiben → CIRCULAR

Sachanlagen → TANGIBLE ASSET
Sachkonten → IMPERSONAL ACCOUNTS, NOMINAL ACCOUNTS
Sachleistung → BENEFIT-IN-KIND
Sack → SACK
Saisonabschlag → SEASONAL DISCOUNT
Saisonbedingtheit → SEASONALITY
Saisonberichtigung → SEASONAL ADJUSTMENT
saldieren → BALANCE
Saldo → ACCOUNT BALANCE, BALANCE
Saldoübertrag → BALANCE CARRIED FORWARD
Saldovortrag → BALANCE BROUGHT FORWARD
Sammelantrag → COMPOSITE MOTION
Sammelkonto → CONTROL ACCOUNT
Sammellieferung → GROUPAGE
Sample → SAMPLE
sanieren → REDEVELOP
Sanierung → REDEVELOPMENT
Sanktionen → SANCTION
Satz → RATE
Satzergänzungstest → SENTENCE COMPLETION
Satzung → ARTICLES OF ASSOCIATION, MEMORANDUM AND ARTICLES OF ASSOCIATION
Schadenersatz → DAMAGES
Schadensabschätzer → ASSESSOR
Schadensersatz → INDEMNITY
Schadensfreiheitsrabatt → NO-CLAIMS BONUS
Schadenssachverständiger → ADJUSTER

schaffen → MANAGE
Schallplatte → RECORD
Schalterbeamter → CASHIER
Schattenwirtschaft → BLACK ECONOMY
schätzen → ESTIMATE, VALUE
Schätzer → ESTIMATOR, VALUER
Schätzung → VALUATION
Schätzwert → VALUATION
Schaufenster → SHOP WINDOW
Schaufensterdekoration → WINDOW DRESSING
Schaufensterpuppe → DUMMY
Scheck → CHEQUE
Scheckheft → CHEQUE BOOK
Scheckkarte → CHEQUE BOOK
Scheinauktion → MOCK AUCTION
Schicht → SHIFT
Schichtarbeit → SHIFT WORKING
Schichtung → STRATIFICATION
schicken → MAIL
schieben → SHIFT
Schiebung → RACKET
Schiedsklausel → ARBITRATION CLAUSE
Schiedsmann → ARBITOR
Schiedsrichter → REFEREE, UMPIRE
schiedsrichtern → REFEREE
Schiedsspruch → AWARD
Schiedsverfahren → ARBITRATION
Schiff → SHIP
Schiffsbedarf → SHIP CHANDLER
Schiffskörper → HULL
Schiffsmakler → SHIP-BROKER
Schiffsmeldung → SHIP'S REPORT
Schiffsprüfung → MARINE SURVEY
Schiffsregister → REGISTRY
Schiffsregisterbrief → SHIP'S CERTIFICATE OF REGISTRY
Schiffszettel → SHIPPING NOTE
Schlafwagen → SLEEPER
Schleichwerbung → PLUG
Schleuderpreis → CUT PRICE
Schlichtung → CONCILIATION
schließen → WIND UP
Schlußkurs → CLOSING PRICES
Schmiergeld → KICKBACK
Schmiergeldfonds → SLUSH FUND
Schmuggelware → CONTRABAND
schneiden → EDIT
Schnittstelle → INTERFACE
Schnüffler → TOUT
Schreibarbeit → PAPERWORK
Schreibkraft → COPY TYPIST
Schreibzentrale → TYPING POOL
Schrift → SCRIPT
Schriftführer(in) → SECRETARY
Schuld → DEBT, LIABILITY
Schuldner → DEBTOR
Schuldposten → LIABILITY
Schuldschein → I.O.U., PROMISSORY NOTE
schwanken → FLUCTUATE
Schwankung → FLUCTUATION
schwarze Liste → BLACKLIST
schwarze Zahlen → BLACK
Schwarzhändler → TOUT
Schwarzmarkt → BLACK MARKET
schwarz verkaufen → TOUT
Schwerindustrie → HEAVY INDUSTRY
schwimmen → FLOAT
Schwindler → CON MAN, FRAUD
Seekaskoversicherung → HULL INSURANCE
Seeräuber → PIRATE
Seeräuberei → PIRACY
Seerecht → MARITIME LAW
Seeversicherung → MARINE INSURANCE
Seitentarif → PAGE RATE
Sekretär(in) → SECRETARY
Sektor → SECTOR
Sekundärdaten → SECONDARY DATA
selbständiger Erwerbstätiger → SELF-EMPLOYED PERSON
Selbstbedienungsladen → SELF-SERVICE STORE
Selbsteinschätzungsfragen → SELF-ASSESSMENT QUESTIONS
Seltenheitswert → SCARCITY VALUE
Semesterferien → VACATION
Seminar → SEMINAR
senden → TRANSMIT
Sendenetz → NETWORK
Sendung → TRANSMISSION
Senkrechtstarter → HIGH FLYER
Sequenz → SEQUENCE
Seriennummer → SERIAL NUMBER
Serienproduktion → BATCH PRODUCTION
shiften → SHIFT
Sicherheit → COLLATERAL, SECURITY, SURETY
Sicherheitsspanne → MARGIN OF SAFETY
Sicherheitsvorkehrungen → SECURITY
Sicherungsübereignungsurkunde → BILL OF SALE
Sichtgerät → VISUAL DISPLAY UNIT
Siedlung → SETTLEMENT
Siegel → SEAL
Simulation → SIMULATION
simulieren → SIMULATE
Sit-in → SIT-IN
Sitzstreik → SIT-DOWN STRIKE
Sitzungsbericht → TRANSACTION
Skonto → CASH DISCOUNT
Slogan → SLOGAN
Software → SOFTWARE
Soll → DEBIT
solvent → SOLVENT
Solvenz → SOLVENCY
Solvenzerklärung → DECLARATION OF SOLVENCY
Sommerzeit → SUMMER TIME
Sonderbeitrag → FEATURE, SPECIAL FEATURE
Sonderplazierung → PREFERRED POSITION
Sonderpreispackung → MONEY-OFF PACK
Sondervergünstigungen → PERQUISITES
Sortiment → RANGE
souverän → SOVEREIGN

Anhang

Gewinn- und Verlustrechnung

J Black & Company PLC

(Hersteller)
Gewinn- und Verlustrechnung
1.1. – 31.12.1984

	£	£
Umsatz		
Abzüglich:		3,206,900
Herstellungskosten:		
Materialkosten	1,260,000	
Fertigungslöhne	1,001,700	
Fertigungsgemeinkosten	258,300	
Gesamtherstellungskosten:		2,520,000
Bruttogewinn		686,900
Abzüglich Aufwendungen:		
Managementgehälter	20,000	
Vertreterfixum	13,500	
Vertreterprovisionen	5,010	
Marktforschung	10,000	
Agentenprovisionen	62,910	
Vertreterspesen	22,600	
Transport und Lagerung	100,080	
Werbung usw.	94,500	
Absatzförderung	12,000	
Allgemeine Verwaltungskosten	25,700	
Sonstige Aufwendungen	3,600	
Kapitalbeschaffung, Revisionsgebühren usw.	11,500	
Abschreibungen	22,000	
Gesamtaufwendungen		403,400
Gewinn vor Steuern		£283,500

Appendix 1 Profit and loss accounts

J Black & Company PLC
(Manufacturers)
Profit and Loss Account
for year ended 31 December 1984

	£	£
Sales		
Less:		3,206,900
Manufacturing Costs:		
Materials	1,260,000	
Direct labour	1,001,700	
Production overheads	258,300	
Total production costs:		2,520,000
Gross profit		686,900
Less expenses:		
Management salaries	20,000	
Sales salaries	13,500	
Salesmen's commission	5,010	
Market research	10,000	
Agents' commission	62,910	
Salesmen's expenses	22,600	
Transport and warehousing	100,080	
Advertising etc	94,500	
Sales promotion	12,000	
General administration	25,700	
Sundry items	3,600	
Financing, audit fee, etc	11,500	
Depreciation	22,000	
Total expense		403,400
Profit before tax		£283,500

Jones & Company Ltd

(Einzelhändler)
Gewinn- und Verlustrechnung
1.1 – 31.12.1984

	£	£	£
Bruttoumsatz			540,000
Abzüglich: Warenrücksendungen			40,000
Nettoumsatz			500,000
Kosten der gesamten Warenlieferung:			
Anfänglicher Lagerbestand		80,000	
Zuzüglich Aufstockung		290,000	
Kosten der zum Verkauf verfügbaren Waren		370,000	
Abzüglich: Abschließender Lagerbestand		70,000	
Kosten der verkauften Waren			300,000
Bruttospanne (Bruttogewinn)			200,000
Aufwendungen			
Vertriebskosten			
Vertreterfixum	60,000		
Werbekosten	20,000		
Lieferungskosten	20,000		
Gesamtvertriebskosten		100,000	
Verwaltungskosten			
Angestelltengehälter	30,000		
Bürobedarf	10,000		
Sonstige Aufwendungen	5,000		
Gesamtverwaltungskosten		45,000	
Allgemeine Aufwendungen			
Miete und Abgaben	15,000		
Allgemeine Aufwendungen insgesamt		15,000	
Gesamtaufwendungen			160,000
Gewinn vor Steuern			£40,000

Jones & Company Ltd
(Retailers)
Profit and Loss Account
for year ended 31 December 1984

	£	£	£
Gross sáles			540,000
Less: Returns			40,000
Net Sales			500,000
Cost of goods sold:			
Stock at beginning		80,000	
Plus Purchases		290,000	
Cost of goods available for sale		370,000	
Less: Stock at end		70,000	
Cost of goods sold			300,000
Gross margin (gross profit)			200,000
Expenses			
Selling expenses			
Sales salaries	60,000		
Advertising expense	20,000		
Delivery expense	20,000		
Total Selling Expense		100,000	
Administration Expense			
Office salaries	30,000		
Office supplies	10,000		
Miscellaneous expenses	5,000		
Total Administration Expense		45,000	
General expense			
Rent and rates	15,000		
Total General Expense		15,000	
Total expenses			160,000
Profit before tax			£40,000

Bilanzaufstellung

White and Company PLC

Bilanzaufstellung zum 31.12.1984

	£	£
Feste Anlagen		
Anfangskosten Grundstücke und Bauten	60,000	
Abzüglich: Abschreibungen	1,000	59,000
Anfangskosten Anlagen und Maschinen	40,000	
Abzüglich: Abschreibungen	4,000	36,000
Anfangskosten Fahrzeuge	5,000	
Abzüglich: Abschreibungen	1,250	3,750
Feste Anlagen insgesamt		£98,750
Umlaufvermögen		
Rohstoffe	25,000	
Halbfertige Erzeugnisse	12,500	
Fertigwaren	10,000	
Forderungen aus Lieferungen und Leistungen	50,000	
Barmittel	45,000	
Gesamtumlaufvermögen	142,500	
Abzüglich: **Kurzfristige Verbindlichkeiten**		
Verbindlichkeiten	45,000	
Fällige Kosten	2,500	
Steuerrückstellung	20,000	
Fällige Dividenden	3,000	
Kurzfristige Verbindlichkeiten insgesamt	70,500	
Betriebskapital		72,000
Nettobetriebskapital		170,750
Abzüglich: ANLEIHEKAPITAL (7% Anleihen auf feste Anlagen)		50,000
Eigenkapital der Firma		£120,750

Das obige **EIGENKAPITAL** wurde wie folgt finanziert:

	£	
Gezeichnetes Kapital		
100.000 Stammaktien zu je £1	100,000	
Rücklagen		
Allgemeine Rücklagen	20,000	
Gewinn- und Verlustrechnung	750	
Gesamte Aktienbeteiligung		£120,750

Appendix 2 Balance sheet

White and Company PLC

Balance Sheet as at 31 December 1984

	£	£
Fixed assets		
Land & Buildings at Cost	60,000	
Less: Depreciation	1,000	59,000
Plant & Machinery at Cost	40,000	
Less: Depreciation	4,000	36,000
Vehicles at Cost	5,000	
Less: Depreciation	1,250	3,750
Total fixed assets		£98,750
Current assets		
Raw Materials	25,000	
Work in Progress	12,500	
Finished Goods	10,000	
Debtors	50,000	
Cash	45,000	
Total current assets	142,500	
Less: **Current liabilities**		
Creditors	45,000	
Expenses due	2,500	
Taxation	20,000	
Dividends payable	3,000	
Total current liabilities	70,500	
Working capital		72,000
Net capital employed		170,750
Less: LOAN CAPITAL (7% Debentures secured on Fixed Assets)		50,000
Net worth of company		£120,750

The above **NET WORTH** has been financed as follows:

	£	
Subscribed Capital		
100,000 Ordinary Shares of £1 each	100,000	
Reserves		
General Reserve	20,000	
Profit and Loss Account	750	
Total shareholders' interest		£120,750

Appendix 3 Break-even chart

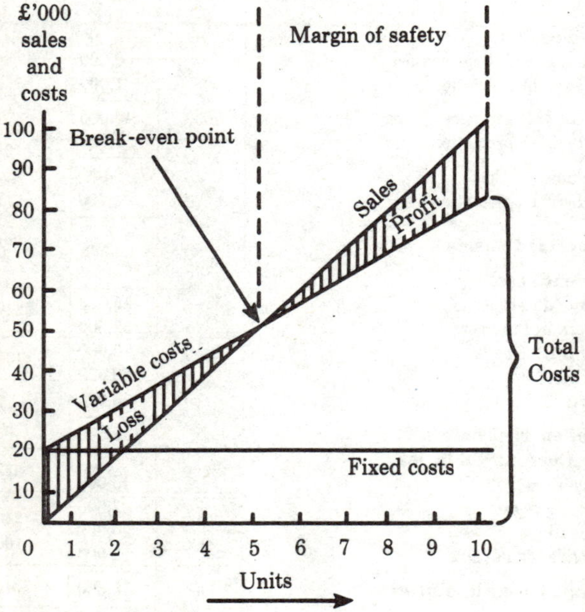

In this example:	
Selling Price of Machine:	£10,000 each
Planned Unit Sales:	10 machines
Planned Total Sales:	10 × £10,000 = £100,000
Variable Cost per Unit:	£6,000
Total Fixed Costs:	£20,000
Break-Even Point (Volume)	5 Units
Margin of Safety	5 to 10 Units

A *break-even chart* reveals the level of sales at which all costs are covered. Sales beyond the break-even point will result in a profit, while sales below it will result in a loss. The chart is commonly used in relation to a single project or product.

Appendix 4 Master budget

Computer manufacturers PLC

MASTER BUDGET
For the year ending 31 December 1984

		Computers		£'000
		Type A £	*Type B* £	*Total* £
1	**Sales** £'000	2000	1660	3660
	Manufacturing Costs:			
	Direct Labour	500	500	1000
	Direct Material	600	700	1300
	Factory Overheads	100	200	300
	Add Opening Stock / *Less* Closing Stock	30	30	60
2	**Cost of goods sold**	£1230	£1430	£2660
3	Gross Profit (1 less item 2)	770	230	1000
4	Selling and Distribution Costs	70	100	170
5	Administration Costs	400	100	500
6	Net Profit (3 less items 4 & 5)	£300	£30	£330
7	Fixed Assets	2200	200	2400
8	Net Current Assets	800	200	1000
9	**Capital employed**	£3000	£400	£3400
10	**Return on capital employed**	10%	7.5%	9.7%
11	**Liquidity ratio**	2:1	0.9:1	1:1

		£'000
12	**Profit appropriations**	
	Transfer to General Reserve	50
	Transfer to Asset Replacement Reserve	50
	Taxation	100
		200
13	**Estimated Dividend**	50
14	**Total appropriations**	250
15	**Profit and loss balance** (6 less item 14)	£80

Appendix 5 Circulating capital

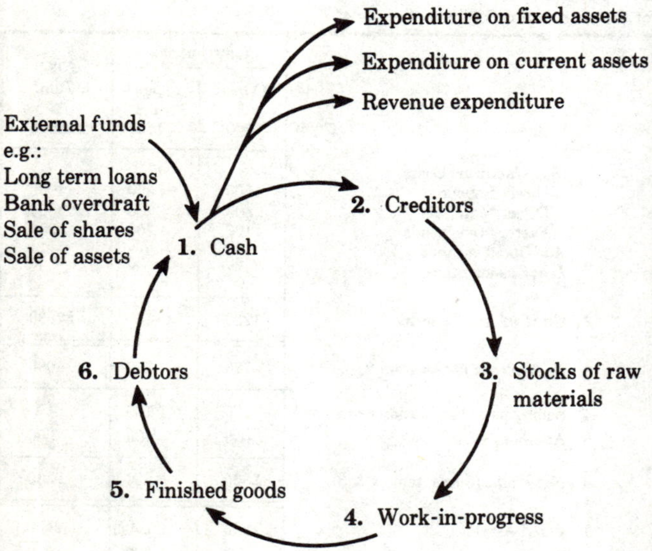

Appendix 6 Costs in a company

Reference to: total fixed costs, total variable costs, total costs, narginal cost, average fixed cost, average variable cost, average :ost per unit, direct materials, direct labour.

Fixed costs in a company are such costs as rent, rates, managers' salaries and any other item of expense which is not directly linked to he quantity of products produced.

Variable costs are costs which vary because they are directly linked o the number of products produced. These include costs such as lirect materials, direct labour, packaging etc.

The following table shows how total fixed costs, total variable costs, otal costs, marginal cost, average fixed cost, average variable cost nd average cost per unit can be worked out.

(1)	(2)	(3)	(4)	(5)	(6)	(7)	(8)
Quantity produced	Total fixed costs	Total variable costs	Total costs	Marginal cost	Average fixed cost	Average variable cost	Average cost per unit
			(2) + (3)		(2) ÷ (1)	(3) ÷ (1)	(4) ÷ (1)
0	£200	–	£200	–	–	–	–
1	£200	£60	£260	£60	£200	£60	£260
2	£200	£120	£320	£60	£100	£60	£160
3	£200	£180	£380	£60	£66.66	£60	£126.66
4	£200	£220	£420	£40	£50	*£55	£105

Note: Variable costs per unit may fall because of experience in the production of the oduct, resulting in less scrap, more efficient use of machines, men and materials etc.

Appendix 7 Channels of distribution

Example: The Grocery Trade

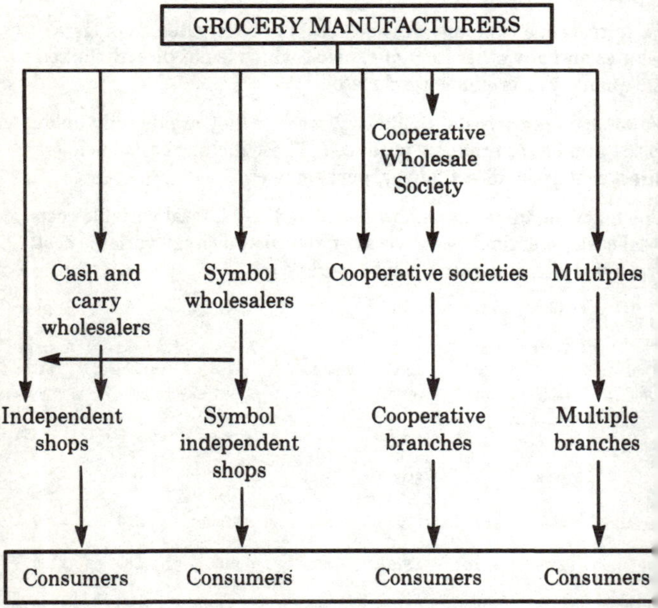

Appendix 8 Currencies of the world

Vote: Franc CFA — Franc de la Communauté Financière Africaine

;ountry	Unit of Currency
fghanistan	Afghani
Afghanistan	Afghani
lbania	Lek
Albanien	Lek
lgeria	Algerian dinar
Algerien	Algerischer Dinar
ngola	Kwanza
Angola	Kwanza
ntigua	East Caribbean dollar
Antigua	Ostkaribischer Dollar
rgentina	Austral
rgentinien	Austral
ustralia	Australian dollar
ustralien	Australischer Dollar
ustria	Schilling
)sterreich	Schilling
ahamas, The	Bahamas dollar
ahamas	Bahama-Dollar
ahrain	Bahrain dinar
ahrain	Bahrain-Dinar
angladesh	Taka
angladesch	Taka
arbados	Barbados dollar
arbados	Barbados-Dollar
elgium	Belgian franc
elgien	Belgischer Franc
elize	Belizean dollar
elize	Belize-Dollar
enin	Franc CFA
enin	CFA-Franc
ermuda	Bermudan dollar
ermuda	Bermuda-Dollar
livia	Bolivian peso
olivien	Peso Boliviano
tswana	Pula
otswana	Pula
azil	Cruzado
rasilien	Cruzado
unei	Brunei dollar
runei	Brunei-Dollar
lgaria	Lev
ulgarien	Lew
rma	Kyat
rma	Kyat
rundi	Burundi franc
urundi	Burundi-Franc
mbodia	Riel
ambodscha	Riel
meroon	Franc CFA
amerun	CFA-Franc

Country	Unit of Currency
Canada Kanada	Canadian dollar Kanadischer Dollar
Cape Verde Islands Kap Verde	Cape Verde Escudo Kap-Verde-Escudo
Cayman Islands Cayman Islands	Cayman Islands dollar Kaiman-Dollar
Central African Republic Zentralafrikanische Republik	Franc CFA CFA-Franc
Chad Tschad	Franc CFA CFA-Franc
Chile Chile	Chilean peso Chilenischer Peso
China, People's Republic of Volksrepublik China	Renminbi Yuan Renminbi Yuan
Colombia Kolumbien	Colombian peso Kolumbianischer Peso
Congo (Brazzaville) Kongo	Franc CFA CFA-Franc
Costa Rica Costa Rica	Colon Colon
Cuba Kuba	Cuban peso Kubanischer Peso
Cyprus Zypern	Cyprus pound Zypern-Pfund
Czechoslovakia Tschechoslowakei	Koruna Tschechoslowakische Krone
Denmark Dänemark	Danish krone Dänische Krone
Dominica Dominica	East Caribbean dollar Ostkaribischer Dollar
Dominican Republic Dominikanische Republik	Dominican peso Dominikanischer Peso
Ecuador Ecuador	Sucre Sucre
Egypt Ägypten	Egyptian pound Ägyptisches Pfund
El Salvador El Salvador	El Salvador colon El Salvador-Colon
Equatorial Guinea Äquatorialguinea	Ekuele Ekuele
Ethiopia Äthiopien	Ethiopian birr Äthiopischer Birr
Falkland Islands Falklandinseln	Falkland pound Falkland-Pfund
Faroe Islands Färöer Inseln	Krone Krone
Fiji Fidschi	Fijian dollar Fidschi-Dollar
Finland Finnland	Markka or Finnmark Finnmark
France Frankreich	French franc Französischer Franc

Country	Unit of Currency
Gabon Gabun	Franc CFA CFA-Franc
Gambia Gambia	Dalasi Dalasi
German Democratic Republic Deutsche Demokratische Republik	Ostmark or DDR-Mark DDR-Mark
Germany, Federal Republic Bundesrepublik Deutschland	Deutsche Mark Deutsche Mark
Ghana Ghana	Cedi Cedi
Gibraltar Gibraltar	Gibraltar pound Gibraltar-Pfund
Greece Griechenland	Drachma Drachme
Greenland Grönland	Danish Krone Dänische Krone
Grenada Grenada	East Caribbean dollar Ostkaribischer Dollar
Guadeloupe Guadeloupe	French franc Französischer Franc
Guatemala Guatemala	Quetzal Quetzal
Guinea Guinea	Franc Franc
Guyana Guyana	Guyanese dollar Guyana-Dollar
Haiti Haiti	Gourde Gourde
Honduras Honduras	Lempira Lempira
Hong Kong Hongkong	Hong Kong dollar Hongkong-Dollar
Hungary Ungarn	Forint Forint
Iceland Island	Icelandic krona Isländische Krone
India Indien	Indian rupee Indische Rupie
Indonesia Indonesien	Rupiah Rupiah
Iran Iran	Rial Rial
Iraq Irak	Iraqi dinar Irak-Dinar
Ireland Irland	Irish pound Irisches Pfund
Israel Israel	Shekel Schekel
Italy Italien	Italian lira Italienische Lira
Ivory Coast Elfenbeinküste	Franc CFA CFA-Franc
Jamaica Jamaika	Jamaican dollar Jamaika-Dollar

Country	Unit of Currency
Japan Japan	Yen Yen
Jordan Jordanien	Jordanian dinar Jordan-Dinar
Kenya Kenia	Kenya shilling Kenia-Schilling
Korea, Democratic People's Republic of North Korea Nord-Korea	Won Won
Korea, Republic of South Süd-Korea	Won Won
Kuwait Kuwait	Kuwaiti dinar Kuwait-Dinar
Laos Laos	Kip Kip
Lebanon Libanon	Lebanese pound Libanesisches Pfund
Lesotho Lesotho	Maloti Loti
Liberia Liberia	Liberian dollar (also US dollar) Liberianischer Dollar
Libya Libyen	Libyan dinar Libyscher Dinar
Liechtenstein Liechtenstein	Swiss franc Schweizer Franken
Luxembourg Luxemburg	Luxembourg franc Luxemburgischer Franc
Macau Macau	Pataca Pataca
Madeira Madeira	Portuguese escudo Portugiesischer Escudo
Malagasy Republic Malagasy	Franc Malgache MG-Franc
Malawi Malawi	Kwacha Kwacha
Malaysia Malaysia	Ringgit Malaysischer Ringgit
Maldive Islands Malediven	Rupee Rupie
Mali Mali	Mali franc Mali-Franc
Malta Malta	Maltese pound Malta-Lira
Mauritania Mauretanien	Ouguiya Ouguiya
Mauritius Mauritius	Mauritian rupee Mauritius-Rupie
Mexico Mexiko	Mexican peso Mexikanischer Peso
Monaco Monaco	French franc Französischer Franc
Mongolia Mongolische Volksrepublik	Tugrik Tugrug

Country	Unit of Currency
Montserrat	East Caribbean dollar
Montserrat	Ostkaribischer Dollar
Morocco	Dirham
Marokko	Dirham
Mozambique	Metical
Moçambique	Metical
Nepal	Nepalese rupee
Nepal	Nepalesische Rupie
Netherlands	Netherlands guilder
Niederlande	Holländischer Gulden
Netherlands Antilles	Antilles guilder
Niederländische Antillen	Antillen-Gulden
New Zealand	New Zealand dollar
Neuseeland	Neuseeland-Dollar
Nicaragua	Cordoba
Nicaragua	Cordoba
Niger	Franc CFA
Niger	CFA-Franc
Nigeria	Naira
Nigeria	Naira
Norway	Norwegian krone
Norwegen	Norwegische Krone
Oman	Omani riyal
Oman	Rial Omani
Pakistan	Pakistan rupee
Pakistan	Pakistanische Rupie
Panama	Balboa
Panama	Balboa
Papua New Guinea	Kina
Papua-Neuguinea	Kina
Paraguay	Guarani
Paraguay	Guarani
Peru	Inti
Peru	Inti
Philippines	Philippine peso
Philippinen	Philippinischer Peso
Poland	Zloty
Polen	Zloty
Portugal	Portuguese escudo
Portugal	Escudo
Puerto Rico	US dollar
Puerto Rico	US-Dollar
Qatar	Qatar riyal
Katar	Katar-Riyal
Reunion	Franc CFA
Reunion	CFA-Franc
Romania	Leu
Rumänien	Leu
Rwanda	Rwanda franc
Ruanda	Rwanda-Franc

Country	Unit of Currency
St Lucia Saint Lucia	East Caribbean dollar Ostkaribischer Dollar
St Vincent Saint Vincent	East Caribbean dollar Ostkaribischer Dollar
Saudi Arabia Saudi-Arabien	Saudi Arabian riyal Saudi-Riyal
Senegal Senegal	Franc CFA CFA-Franc
Seychelles Seychellen	Seychelles rupee Seychellen-Rupie
Sierra Leone Sierra Leone	Leone Leone
Singapore Singapur	Singapore dollar Singapur-Dollar
Somalia Somalia	Somali shilling Somalischer Schilling
South Africa, Republic of Republik Südafrika	South African rand Rand
South West Africa (Namibia) Südwestafrika	South African rand Rand
Spain Spanien	Spanish peseta Peseta
Sri Lanka Sri Lanka	Sri Lanka rupee Sri-Lanka-Rupie
Sudan Sudan	Sudanese pound Sudanesisches Pfund
Surinam Surinam	Surinam guilder Surinam-Gulden
Swaziland Swasiland	Lilangeni Lilangeni
Sweden Schweden	Swedish krona Schwedische Krone
Switzerland Schweiz	Swiss franc Schweizer Franken
Syria Syrien	Syrian pound Syrisches Pfund
Taiwan Taiwan	New Taiwan dollar Neuer Taiwan-Dollar
Tanzania Tansania	Tanzanian shilling Tansania-Schilling
Thailand Thailand	Baht Baht
Togo Togo	Franc CFA CFA-Franc
Tonga Tonga	Paanga Paanga
Trinidad and Tobago Trinidad und Tobago	Trinidad and Tobago dollar Trinidad-und-Tobago-Dollar
Tunisia Tunesien	Tunisian dinar Tunesischer Dinar
Turkey Türkei	Turkish lira Türkisches Pfund
Uganda Uganda	Ugandan shilling Uganda-Schilling

Country	Unit of Currency
United Arab Emirates Vereinigte Arabische Emirate	Dirham Dirham
United Kingdom (UK) Vereinigtes Königreich	Pound sterling Pfund Sterling
United States of America (USA) Vereinigte Staaten von Amerika	US dollar US-Dollar
Upper Volta Obervolta	Franc CFA CFA-Franc
Uruguay Uruguay	Uruguayan peso Uruguayischer Peso
USSR UdSSR	Rouble Rubel
Venezuela Venezuela	Bolivar Bolivar
Vietnam Vietnam	Dong Dong
Virgin Islands Jungferninseln	US dollar US-Dollar
Western Samoa Westsamoa	Tala Tala
Yemen Arab Republic Arabische Republik Jemen	Yemeni riyal Jemen-Riyal
Yemen, People's Democratic Republic of Demokratische Volksrepublik Jemen	Southern Yemen dinar Süd-Jemen-Dinar
Yugoslavia Jugoslawien	Yugoslav dinar Jugoslawischer Dinar
Zaire Zaire	Zaire Zaire
Zambia Zambia	Kwacha Kwacha
Zimbabwe Zimbabwe	Zimbabwe dollar Zimbabwe-Dollar